The Washington, D.C. of Fiction

A Research Guide

James A. Kaser

The Scarecrow Press, Inc.
Lanham, Maryland • Toronto • Oxford
2006

SCARECROW PRESS, INC.

Published in the United States of America
by Scarecrow Press, Inc.
A wholly owned subsidiary of
The Rowman & Littlefield Publishing Group, Inc.
4501 Forbes Boulevard, Suite 200, Lanham, Maryland 20706
www.scarecrowpress.com

PO Box 317
Oxford
OX2 9RU, UK

British Library Cataloguing in Publication Information Available

Library of Congress Cataloging-in-Publication Data
Kaser, James A., 1960-
   The Washington, D.C., of fiction : a research guide / James A. Kaser.
      p. cm.
   Includes bibliographical references and index.
   ISBN-13: 978-0-8108-5740-7 (pbk. : alk. paper)
   ISBN-10: 0-8108-5740-5 (pbk. : alk. paper)
   1. American fiction--19th century--Bibliography. 2. American fiction--20th
century--Bibliography. 3. Authors, American--19th century--Biography--
Dictionaries. 4. Authors, American--20th century--Biography--Dictionaries. 5.
Washington (D.C.)--In literature--Bibliography. I. Title.
   Z1231.F4K37 2006
   [PS658]
   016.813008'032753--dc22   2006001888

To Michael for his support during the writing of this book and, as always, to my family.

Contents

Preface

Prior to the 1980s, catalogers rarely gave subject designations for works of fiction. Increasing researcher interest did not lead to the issuance of official cataloging guidelines by the American Library Association until 2000. So, although very complete databases of bibliographic information are available to scholars, these tools are of little use in locating works of fiction set in Washington, D.C., published before the 1970s. This work guides scholars to these works and was created by consulting libraries with collections of Washington, D.C., fiction, as well as published bibliographies that offered a subject approach to fiction.

Acknowledgments

Research for this work was funded in part by grants from the Professional Staff Congress of the City University of New York. Further support was obtained from the College of Staten Island/CUNY in the form of reassignment leave used for extended periods of research.

I am also grateful for the encouragement and assistance I received from a number of people. The enthusiasm and advice of my department chair, Prof. Wilma Jones, Chief Librarian, College of Staten Island, kept me focused and productive over two years of research and writing. In addition, she proofread the manuscript, as did my colleague Prof. Linda Roccos and my friends Ted Cornwell and Sally Milner. For seeing all to which I was blinded by authorial propinquity, I am grateful. Finally, I thank the staff of the Interlibrary Loan Office at the Library of Staten Island; the staff of the Library of Congress; Michael North, Head of Rare Books and Manuscripts at the National Library of Medicine; and Lyle Slovick, Assistant Archivist in George Washington University's Archives and Special Collections, for aiding me in accessing information and many of the books annotated in this volume.

Introduction

This book includes works of fiction set in Washington, D.C., specifically novels and published collections of short stories for juveniles and adults (dramatic works are not included). Both works that deal with official Washington and center on office holders and are set in the offices and hearing rooms of Capitol Hill and those set in residential Washington are included. Annotations are provided for works dating from 1822 to 1976; bibliographic information for works dating after 1976 are included in an appendix. While attempting to be as inclusive as possible, some works have been excluded. Such books might have only a few pages, or even a chapter, or more, set in Washington, but few references to the city. A good example of this sort of book is any of the many works of international espionage that include brief sections in which the protagonist is given an assignment in a federal government agency, or reports to such an agency during an investigation. On the other hand works that are mostly or wholly set in the city, but have little overt Washington content are included. Furthermore, works that have as little as a chapter set in Washington were sometimes included if the use of the city was significant. In these works, Washington usually has a strong symbolic role throughout the book. For instance, through the majority of a book a man might be seeking a congressional office and dream of the federal city as a goal.

The decision not to annotate works published after 1976 responds to a publishing phenomenon. After the era of Vietnam protests and Watergate, everyone, the *Washington Post* noted, seemed to be writing a Washington novel. Often these are works of genre fiction in which Washington serves as a backdrop. Although this phenomenon is interesting to note, the researcher is not presented with the same challenges in accessing these books as they are with works published in earlier time periods. Librarians often began responding to the flood of Washington novels by including a note on the setting in their catalog records. This cataloging trend is one factor that led to the creation of an official geographic descriptor for fiction works in cataloging rules published in

2000. So, scholars can use standard bibliographic databases to find these books. Furthermore, because of their recent publication dates, copies of these post-1976 texts can also be easily located physically. The decision not to provide annotations for this material should not be read as a judgment on their quality, since many of them are insightful literary novels of a caliber rarely found in the earlier books.

Because of the obscurity of so many authors of pre-1976 books, biographical information is provided in a section that also serves as an author index. The reader who wishes to browse this section will discover the wide range of people who were motivated to write about the city, including journalists, politicians, society women, and freelance writers of genre fiction. As in any group of people randomly gathered, there are also some remarkable lives presented worthy of further exploration, including an early feminist who willed her brain for comparison with a famous scholar's, and a man who died heroically on the Titanic.

An appendix presents citations for the pre-1976 fiction in a chronological arrangement so that themes common to a specific era can be easily discovered. As a researcher, one of the most appealing aspects of the project was seeing the culture of the period in which a work was written reflected in the author's perspective on Washington.

From early novels, one can easily see the pride with which Americans regarded their new Federal City. Clearly, authors were responding to a public desire to read descriptions of the place and the way people lived there. Of course, none of these works was merely descriptive—they were always vehicles through which the author expressed a particular view of society. In the post-Civil War period this view became jaundiced, and social issues, such as civil-service reform, the plight of women in a sexist society, and the moral failings of politicians and society figures (often the newly wealthy) were analyzed. As the turn of the century approached, the history of the city was long enough that works of historical fiction were published, many dealing with the Civil War. After the turn of the century, mystery novels and works of political espionage appeared, genres that would come to dominate Washington fiction in the twentieth century. Often the setting in these works becomes a carpentered backdrop for the action. However, dramatic social changes brought about by the growth of the federal government during World Wars I and II, and the accompanying population increases that would eventually transform Washington into a city, also prompted realistic literary works.

Although, as a reader, I was fascinated by what the novels revealed about changing understandings of Washington and what the city symbolizes, my role in this book is merely to identify the books that future

researchers will use to construct artful essays analyzing the novels and their interrelationships.

Annotated Bibliography, 1822-1976

1. Aarons, Edward S. [Ronns, Edward, pseud.]. *State Department Murders*. New York: Fawcett, 1950. 171pp.

Barney Cornell, a security officer on a top secret atomic project, is called before a House committee and accused of passing secrets to the Russians. In fact, he merely sent toys to a boy whose father had helped him during World War II when he broke his leg landing in a parachute jump behind enemy lines. As Cornell tries to prove his innocence, he needs to elude the journalists and the security detail assigned to follow him as he tries to disappear into Washington's working class and disreputable neighborhoods. He also rendezvous with his lover, Mrs. Kari Stone, wife of a powerful politician. In the course of the novel, he discovers that Kari is bisexual and that her friend Paul Evarts, a colleague of Cornell's from the atomic project, is gay. Kari's husband, wealthy Pittsburgh industrialist Jason Stone, has directed the false accusations against Cornell because Cornell thwarted him on an atomic project policy matter. When Stone is murdered, Cornell is the main suspect, but he eludes the police long enough to find the real murderer and clear his name. Descriptions include traveling by trolley in rush hour, a restaurant patronized by gays and lesbians near Rock Creek Park, 1950s apartment buildings, and the Calvert Beach art community on the Patchacoulee River.

2. Adams, Charles [Templeton, Timothy, pseud.]. *The Adventures of My Cousin Smooth*. New York: Miller, Orton, and Mulligan, 1856. 236pp.

Set in the 1850s, this satire is presented mostly in epistolary form, through letters written by Solomon Smooth, whom the compiler describes with admiration as a member of the "Young America" party and, although "somewhat primitive" in appearance. According to the third-person introduction, Smooth would make a good representative of America to the world. An advocate of the most inclusive republicanism, Smooth's letters to Uncle Sam describe the specific corruption of the Pierce administration and of Washington political life and society.

The work includes descriptions of the National Hotel, African Americans, Irishmen, office seekers, and legislators representing various states. Through satire, Smooth attacks slavery and narrowly focused regionalism. Only about half of the work is set in Washington; Smooth travels around the globe making stops in London and Ostend. This political satire does more to evoke the political debates of the 1850s than to describe unofficial Washington. However, the work does help the reader understand Washington social life before the power of the federal government was strengthened by the Civil War. Here, representatives from very distinct regions of the United States, each with their own cultures and political convictions, are brought together in Washington hotels and boarding houses during legislative sessions without much feeling of unity.

3. Adams, Henry. *Democracy; an American Novel.* Leisure-Hour Series 112. New York: Henry Holt, 1880. 374pp.
    Mrs. Lightfoot Lee, a wealthy widow bored with New York City, hopes that she will be exhilarated by the power centered in Washington. Much of the plot revolves around her successful entrance into Washington society and the romantic and political rivalry that develops between two of her suitors: the corrupt, but powerful, Senator Ratcliffe and the genteel and impoverished lawyer, John Carrington. Mrs. Lee finally refuses Ratcliffe's marriage proposal but only after he confesses the degree to which he has built his fortune through selling his votes and influence to the highest bidder. With everyone gossiping over her refusal and a violent incident between Ratcliffe and another suitor, a titled ambassador, Mrs. Lee realizes she must leave Washington never to return. Adams uses Mrs. Lee's intelligent and socially agile progress through 1870s Washington society and the rivalry between her suitors to express his political views, particularly on civil service reform, and his disgust with the corrupt politics of the Grant administration. His characters were drawn from life and included a President mostly modeled on Grant with some elements of his successor Rutherford B. Hayes, upon whose wife the First Lady in the novel is based. Of the many politicians in the novel, the one satirized most unmercifully is Senator James G. Blaine in the guise of Senator Ratcliffe.
    Adams kept his authorship of the novel a secret throughout his life. As the ultimate Washington insider, observing the city from his residence on Lafayette Square and the grandson and great-grandson of Presidents, there is an effortless verisimilitude in his description of Washington types, social events, political debates, and even the clothing and residences of Washingtonians.

4. Adams, Samuel Hopkins. *The Gorgeous Hussy*. Boston: Houghton Mifflin, 1934. 549pp.

The author describes Peggy Eaton, his protagonist, as "the most colorful, glamorous woman in the annals of America." This treatment of her story was made into a movie of the same name starring Joan Crawford. The historical Peggy was born Margaret O'Neale (1796-1879), a Washington tavern keeper's daughter, whose first marriage to John Timberlake, purser of the *U.S.S. Constitution* when he had supposedly committed suicide in despair over her romantic affairs. Her relationship with John Eaton, Andrew Jackson's first secretary of war, was considered scandalous because it was said to have begun before Timberlake's death and she was accused of having a miscarried pregnancy prior to her second marriage. Although Jackson supported the couple, the social outcry mounted by the women of official Washington brought the downfall of Jackson's first cabinet.

5. Adams, Samuel Hopkins. *Plunder*. New York: Random House, 1948. 348pp.

Martin Strabo, a World War II profiteer, is in Washington in 1950 attempting to translate his wealth into political power. He establishes himself in an 1820s mansion on Scott Circle and doles out cash to public relations firms and advisors. The novel details the tax loopholes he manipulates. His schemes include presenting entertainments for legislators, owning sports teams, and fixing sporting competitions. He is handed an unexpected tool in Professor Tozer. Tozer, whose son was killed from radiation poisoning after atomic tests in the Bikini Islands, approaches Strabo with an invention, later named "tozerite," which will protect humans from the effect of radiation, and, most importantly, shield men from radiation-induced impotence. Strabo, considering the invention's effectiveness immaterial, buys Tozer's invention and sets him up in a laboratory. He quickly secures government contracts by promising key senators paid consultant jobs with his firm after they retire. Strabo's public relations firm mounts an effective news campaign about tozerite advancing Strabo's reputation enormously, assuring him of the ambassador post he desires. When reasonable voices question the effectiveness of tozerite, they are attacked as Communist sympathizers. Eventually, Strabo's firm begins marketing "protectorsex" garments, inducing the public to prevent race suicide by protecting American manhood. As an advertising ploy, his firm drops a fake bomb on Washington. The explosion produces only flyers telling people not to panic...this time. Hysteria disrupts the city. Later, when Strabo is nearly assassinated, his public relations firm seizes the moment to establish him as a national hero. However, the seemingly minor accusation that he fixed the Army-Navy game leads to a search warrant. Fearing release of the evidence of more serious wrongdoing contained in his safe, Strabo, and many other Washington powerbrokers, flee to countries where money buys anonymity and protection from extradition. Part of the story is narrated through the gossip of members of the press corps who are savvy to the way that money is used to manipulate information through public relations firms. The novel provides little physical description of Washington, but attempts to skewer the way its politicians and lobbyists work.

6. Adams, Samuel Hopkins. *Revelry*. New York: Boni & Liveright, 1926. 318pp.

The author's concern for the future of democracy in the United States prompted this caricature of American political institutions and the debauched and corrupt inhabitants of appointed and elected office. The main character, President Markham, is supposed to represent Warren G. Harding. The Washington of this novel is a nighttime place of poker, cigars, and buxom blondes. Political power is in the hands of newly moneyed men scheming to increase their fortunes.

7. Adler, Warren. *The Henderson Equation*. New York: G. P. Putnam's Sons, 1976. 382pp.

Convinced that the President was corrupt, the executive editor of the *Washington Chronicle*, Nick Gold, encouraged investigative journalist Harold Gunderstein to pursue the story, and the paper was, in the end, credited with toppling the administration. Now, the paper's editorial staff and publisher, tough-minded Myra Pell (clearly modeled on Katherine Graham), face a dilemma. They destroyed a corrupt presidency with the weapon of journalistic truth. Should they also destroy the political career of Senator Burton Henderson, a man they believe the country needs? Evidence suggests that Henderson, a liberal and front-runner for his party's presidential nomination, had been directly involved in Central Intelligence Agency plots to assassinate the leaders of foreign governments, and Gunderstein wants to pursue the story. As a secondary plot, the story of Charlie Pell, Myra's husband, who struggled with depression before committing suicide, is told through extended flashbacks and is used to speculate on the philosophy and practice of journalism. Throughout the novel key moments in Washington's political and social history are presented. There is description of social events, which contrast surprisingly with those in earlier novels for their informality, as does the social and political power of newspeople in post-Watergate Washington. One of the most important social events is viewing a Redskins football game from the owner's box. The Washingtonians in this novel are more likely to spend Saturday in their offices than riding in Rock Creek Park and even the most socially and politically powerful dine out in restaurants in casual clothing.

8. Adler, Warren. *Options*. Ardmore, Pa.: Whitmore, 1974. 289pp.
    Senator Donald Benjamin James is charismatic, attractive, and politically powerful. Everyone believes he will certainly become president. When his African American mistress accidentally drowns during a pre-season weekend at Rehoboth, his political career could be ruined. The story is told from the perspective of James, his wife, his staff and that of investigative reporter Ernie Rowell. The novel contains no physical description of Washington.

9. Alexander, Holmes. *West of Washington*. New York: Fleet, 1962. 254pp.
    A man's death in the early 1960s brings together his sons and relatives at an old family house just outside of Georgetown. During the course of the novel, the family's history—its tensions and darker moments—are revealed along with the lifestyle of a certain type of upper-class Washington family.

10. Altsheler, Joseph A. *A Herald of the West: An American Story of 1811-1815*. New York: D. Appleton, 1898. 359pp.
    Philip Ten Broeck is a Kentuckian whose father fought in the Continental Army during the Revolution and against the Indians in the Northwest Territory at the famous battles of Blue Licks and Fallen Timbers. Ten Broeck is in Washington working as a clerk for Albert Gallatin, secretary of the Treasury, and living in one of the Six Buildings in Georgetown. He is in love with Marian, daughter of Cyrus Pendleton, a major Kentucky landholder, whose ideas of American aristocracy prevent him from seeing Ten Broeck as an appropriate suitor. Philip's cousin, Gilbert Northcote, whose family remained loyal to Britain during the Revolution, is also in town. By contrasting the viewpoints of Philip with those of his cousin and acquaintances in Washington, Altsheler articulates many perspectives on the future direction of the United States. Philip sees himself and other Westerners as new beings with distinctive accents, manners, clothing, and physiques. A number of people in Washington still ape European fashions and customs, and, for some of these, like Northcote, the unfinished Federal City is clear evidence of why the United States should reunite

with Britain. To Philip, its incompleteness and discomforts are temporary inconveniences in a place that will soon be notable. After he turns
evidence over to Gallatin that his cousin Gilbert is a British spy,
Gallatin commissions him to travel to Philadelphia, Boston, and New
York to assess public opinion concerning the seemingly inevitable war
with Britain. This provides Altsheler with a chance to describe travel
and conditions in East Coast cities in 1811 and, through the adventures
of Philip, present examples of dueling, impressments, and the British
Blockade. When he returns to Washington, he fights in the Battle of
Bladensburg and witnesses the burning of the Capitol. Later, he fights
in the Battle of New Orleans.

11. Anderson, Patrick. *Actions and Passions: A Novel of the 1960s.*
Garden City, N.Y.: Doubleday, 1974. 371pp.
     Through the story of a young senator named Charles Pierce and his
wife, Carol, who struggles to be independent while preserving her marriage, Anderson presents many of the major social issues of the 1960s:
the idealism of the Great Society, the fervor of the anti-war movement,
and the challenges of women's liberation.

12. Anderson, Patrick. *The Approach to Kings.* Garden City, N.Y.:
Doubleday, 1970. 373pp.
     The novel's focus is on a Presidential speechwriter's personal life
and provides little insightful description of Washington. Instead, the
speechwriter's sex life and marital difficulties take precedence in this
work from the eve of the sexual revolution.

13. Anderson, Patrick. *The President's Mistress: A Novel.* New York:
Simon & Schuster, c. 1976. 319pp.
     When a beautiful young woman is found murdered in a George-
town mansion, her former lover tries to solve the crime. His search
leads him to the President, with whom the woman was having an affair.
Along the way, he learns about a number of sexual, financial, and political scandals connected to the White House. He also meets an as-
sortment of Washington characters, including a former CIA agent, who
will do anything for the President, and a sharp-tongued social columnist.

14. Andrews, Mary Raymond Shipman. *The Perfect Tribute.* New
York: C. Scribner's Sons, 1906. 47pp.
     In this fictionalized account of events surrounding Lincoln's

speech at Gettysburg, the President realizes the true importance of his address while he is at the bedside of a dying Confederate soldier.

15. Anonymous. *Brisée*. Philadelphia: J. B. Lippincott, 1862. 255pp.

Clare Hungerford, the offspring of an old family with an estate on the Hudson, is presented to Washington society shortly after her seventeenth birthday. Her parents have taken a suitable house for the social season and she and her older sister Marian meet lobbyists, congressmen, department clerks, navy and army officers, and gentlemen of independent means at a round of social events organized by their mother and the acquaintances the family makes. While meeting potential suitors, Clare struggles to discern the nature of true love. After meeting and falling in love with Walter Mordaunt, a man who feels he cannot marry Clare since he has no prospects, the season ends and Clare and her family return to New York. Upon her return to the Hudson, she meets and falls in love with Edward Lorimer, a young man with a considerable fortune, engaged in a military career, who had dueled with a man named Ferrer to defend his sister's honor. When the family returns to Washington for another season, Clare tries to remain faithful to Lorimer, in spite of her encounters with Mordaunt. Her second Washington season ends in her marriage to Edward Lorimer. However, while living with Lorimer in a fort in the West, her thoughts return to her Washington seasons and Mordaunt. Her longing ends when Lorimer is posted to Washington. They enter a social world that includes Mordaunt and Ferrer. The note Clare writes to Mordaunt telling him that she had loved him falls into Lorimer's hands through the actions of Ferrer. The novel ends soon after with a duel at Bladensburg orchestrated by Ferrer at which Lorimer is killed and the way seems cleared for Clare's marriage to Mordaunt.

16. Anonymous. *Scenes at Washington: A Story of the Last Generation; By a Citizen of Baltimore*. New York: Harper & Brothers, 1848. 197pp.

In addition to including descriptions of actual politicians and social figures, as well as social events in Washington and boarding house life, this novel deals with the role of religion in American society. The author also sets forth views of the appropriate role of women in society and what constitutes a suitable marriage.

Although the novel spans almost a decade, most of the action is set in Washington during the congressional session of 1807/1808. The widowed Mr. Sydenham, who fought in the Revolution and helped form the Maryland state government, has been elected to Congress.

Since his daughters, Clara and Agnes, are of marriageable age, he takes them with him for the season. Charles Leslie is already courting nineteen-year-old Clara. Although she realizes that Charles, also from an old Maryland family, is a perfectly appropriate suitor, she is concerned about his religious conversion. Thinking that his piety will make for a dull social life, she is eager to visit Washington. Charles fears the effect the city will have on Clara. He already considers her prideful and too worldly.

In the city, the Sydenhams live in a fashionable boarding house frequented by other members of their father's political party. The girls are chaperoned by a widow from Vermont, but are taken up by Mrs. Stanley, a Southern widow with a reputation for intelligent conversation, who enables their entrance into Washington society. Charles is suspicious of her and disapproves of the girls spending their time pleasure seeking and dancing, rather than in reading and acts of charity. Although he realizes he must give Clara the freedom to learn from making wrong decisions, he cannot resist censuring her for behaving unwisely, particularly when she accepts the company of suitors like Mr. Hollis, a humanist. Outraged by Charles' distrust, Clara refuses to see him. Although she meant the separation to be temporary, when he is sent to Paris and London with government dispatches events conspire to keep them apart for years. When Charles finally returns to the United States, he assumes that she has married and only much later finds out that she has been chastened by the death of her sister and brother and lives in retirement with her father. When they are reunited, she describes her religious conversion and they are wed.

17. Argenteuil, Paul d'. *The Trembling of Borealis.* New York: F. Tennyson Neely, 1899. 316pp.

This work satirizes elements of late nineteenth-century American culture through descriptions of an imaginary country in the year 5000 A.D. The focus is on the inappropriate power of corporations, the evil of hired journalism and its influence on elections, the injustice of the accumulation of great wealth by a few, and the corruption of the political process. Usually described as a utopian novel, most of the work actually details corruption, and the new social order created after an insurrection at the end of the work is incompletely articulated.

Steel magnate Pigaureus, whose business is headquartered in Pitts (i.e., Pittsburgh), wants to be the leader, or Plutissimo, of his country, named the Provinces of Borealis. He decides to buy a newspaper whose columns will promote him. When the wife of John Pennington, a man who has been reduced to penury by Pigaureus' unfair wages, appeals directly to him on behalf of her family, he hires their son Henry, a reporter, as the assistant editor of his newspaper. Pigaureus and his fellow plutocrats eventually organize a war against a South American country in order to advance their political ambitions. They fight the war themselves and are then forced to cover up its mismanagement. Disillusioned by his coverage of the war, Pennington finds outlets for alternative journalism that attacks monopolies and the plutocrats. He even publishes stories criticizing the "Peace Jubilee" held in Capitus, the country's capital, as a cover-up attempt. However, the plutocrats are able to accumulate huge campaign funds to guarantee their candidates are elected to office and acquire even more wealth by getting legislation passed favoring their businesses, decreasing wages, and stifling competition. Finally, the "microbes of Borealis" (the common citizenry) band together against the National Plutonican Party and take over the legislature through an armed insurrection. They present a list of demands that include nationalization of major transportation networks and utility companies, an end to taxation of food and clothing, a sales tax on luxury goods, and an income tax on the wealthy.

18. Arnold, Elliott. *Everybody Slept Here.* New York: Duell, Sloan & Pearce, 1948. 345pp.
  Set in World War II Washington, this novel focuses on residents of the Capitol House, a brand new apartment building in Northwest, D.C. Housing shortages in the city put all of the residents in the thrall of Mrs. Dwight, the building manager, whose demands and imperiousness they must suffer with resignation. Dwight reads their mail, listens into their telephone conversations from the switchboard when she is not reading from her vast pornography collection, and forces them to keep their windows closed even though the ineffective air-conditioning system has little impact on the summer's heat. Most of the characters in the novel are military officers and their wives who came from towns and cities around the country to work in the Pentagon. The fact that they receive federal salaries in addition to the peacetime income they continue to draw from their prospering businesses and investments means they are able to live in a fashion they had not known before. They all somewhat dread the end of their "good war," even though they expect to return home to greater wealth due to the connections they have made and their enhanced reputations. In addition to the good wars of the main characters, several vignettes are presented of overseas officer corps in conquered areas where military staff members have established themselves in castles and palaces with chefs and servants. Although the housing shortage means that Capitol House residents live

in modest apartments, they enjoy Washington's nightlife and eat and drink in a fashion that the rest of the food-rationed nation can only dream about. They also adopt a loosened sexual morality inspired by the war and separation from their hometowns. The novel is filled with descriptions of nightlife, mostly dining out, and entertaining in apartments. Many details are provided concerning menus, clothing, apartment furnishings, transportation within Washington, and venues (The Statler, Mayflower, Arbaugh's, Harvey's, and The Occidental). Diets in the novel mostly consist of bacon, butter, eggs, and steak, washed down with alcoholic drinks at every meal.

The author contrasts two couples in the novel. The Temples are from Riverside, California, and live in the Capitol House's finest apartment because of William Temple's connections through the Optimist's Club, which also got him his Pentagon job. William makes dresses for his wife, wears a corset to conceal his bloated figure, and spends a good deal of his time at the Pentagon lunching and making connections to obtain rationed food, which he turns into elaborate meals. In contrast, the Brents live in the worst apartment. John Brent is a morally upright young man and an aviation expert. Although the value of his analyses earns him promotions, he is considered too independent-minded to ever make it as a career officer. He always places pilot safety above "policy." Unlike other members of the Capitol House set he has had frontline experience in the war, and his clear-eyed perspective is not entirely welcome. However, a period of re-assessment is triggered for everyone in the social circle when William Temple's soldier son is killed. Attitudes and behavior are transformed: the floozy discovers true love, the disaffected wife realizes her love for her husband, and the calculating William realizes the seriousness of war.

19. Atherton, Gertrude. *Senator North.* New York: John Lane, 1900. 367pp.

When Washingtonian Betty Madison, a beautiful, wealthy, twenty-five-year-old "cave dweller," decides to become acquainted with politicians, her mother, who has always boasted that she has never permitted one in the house, is horrified. In this novel of social manners, Betty meets a number of men in public life and comes to regard several as potential suitors; however, her emotions are most deeply aroused by a married senator with an ill wife. When the wife dies at the end of the novel it seems inevitable that Betty, a Southern girl, will break off a previous engagement and marry Senator North. This novel is interesting for the attention it pays to questions of etiquette; descriptions of life at resorts in California, the Adirondacks, and Narragansett; and its summaries of political arguments concerning the Spanish-American crisis and the silver standard. Atherton lived in Washington while researching her novel and loosely based Senator North on Senator Eugene Hale of Maine.

20. Ayers, Daisy. *The Conquest.* New York: Neale, 1907. 344pp.
   Silas Ware is in Washington as a senator from Nevada. A "Midas of the Mines," he is newly wealthy. His wife, Cynthia, intimidated by the thought of D.C., stays in Nevada during his first session. She feels that she will hinder Ware's career since life there is so alien to the simple life filled with economic struggles to which she is accustomed. When Silas' letters home are filled with accounts of a widow named Mildred Levesque, Cynthia realizes she must learn how to be a society lady. Under an assumed name, she writes to Levesque to seek advice, and eventually pays for tutelage in how to dress and behave. Levesque sends her New York clothes and beauty and etiquette experts, and she joins women's clubs and civic societies in her hometown. Eventually, she arrives in Washington as "Mrs. Acton" to be tutored in person by Levesque and her friends. She quickly learns that Levesque has no interest or even respect for Ware and also realizes that her husband has been socially ineffectual, although he has had some political successes. She, by contrast, meets with great social success and is soon being pursued by an Italian count. During the whole time she is in Washington, she evades her husband but is the cause of scandal when she is seen leaving the sickroom where her husband lies unconscious. When Ware recovers, the count challenges him to a duel, although Cynthia persuades the count to withdraw the challenge. After she witnesses Levesque encouraging Ware to divorce and marry her, she returns home at the end of the season. When Ware follows, he finds her dressed and behaving like a "lady," and she extracts his plea for forgiveness.

21. Babcock, Bernie. *Lincoln's Mary and the Babies.* Philadelphia: J. B. Lippincott, 1929. 316pp.
   Babcock recounts Lincoln's biography from his days practicing law in Springfield, Illinois, through his assassination, but her focus throughout is on his domestic life. The narrative is filled with accounts of Mary Todd Lincoln, including her love of fine clothes and domestic furnishings and her domestic activities, including special meals and family celebrations. However Babcock's main focus is on Mary and Abe's love of their sons. Stories of the children's illnesses, adventures, pets, and clever sayings are recounted as well as the internal reflections

of Mary and Abe on their lives. Approximately the first half of the novel is set in Springfield; the town gossip and local characters make it seem like a quaint, small town. The second half of the novel, set in Washington, concerns adjustments to life in the White House, the boys' adventures as members of the First Family, Mary's domestic concerns, the tragic death of Willie Lincoln, and the mischief of Tad. Most of the account focuses closely on the White House, although some description is given of wartime Washington.

22. Babcock, Bernie. *The Soul of Abe Lincoln.* New York: Grosset & Dunlap, 1919. 328pp.
    Shortly before the Civil War, Ann Leuin Laury, the daughter of a wealthy Mississippi judge and plantation owner, becomes engaged to Del Norcross, a Virginian. Each of them has dramatic experiences during the conflict. Ann stays in the South and lives with her Confederate family; out of a strong commitment to the concept of federalism, Del enlists with the Union army. As the war comes to a close, each travels to Washington to search for the other, and they meet shortly after the Lincoln assassination. Only relatively brief sections of this novel are set in Washington. However there are descriptions of the Lincoln inauguration, wartime Washington, army hospitals visited by Clara Barton and Walt Whitman, the conspirators in the Lincoln assassination and the places they frequented, the White House, and Ford's Theater.

23. Badeau, Adam. *Conspiracy: A Cuban Romance.* New York: R. Worthington, 1885. 324pp.
    Several chapters of this novel are set in Washington; however, it is a Washington contained within the corridors of politics, and the plot focuses on diplomatic intrigue in Cuba.

24. Bailey, Temple. *Dim Lantern.* Illustrated by Coles Phillips. Philadelphia: Penn, 1923. 344pp.
    Twenty-year-old Jane Barnes lives in her childhood home with her brother Baldwin, Jr. (Baldy) in Sherwood Park, a once pretentious suburb twelve miles outside of Washington that has declined. Their father, a clerk in the Pension Office, bought the house on an installment plan, and by the time he died, exhausted by thirty years of his tedious job, it was still not paid off. Their mother has also died, and Jane has become accustomed to making the household run smoothly. She raises chickens to help out with expenses, while twenty-four-year-old Baldy, who had served in World War I, works in the Pension Office like his father in

the hope of finally paying off the house so that he will have enough freedom to pursue his real career interest—painting.

The Barneses live next door to Mrs. Follette and her son Evans. Holding onto a past which she has, perhaps, aggrandized, Mrs. Follette makes certain her farm is referred to as Castle Manor and, in spite of the fact that she must support herself with a dairy business, she dresses and carries herself in such a way that everyone in the area grudgingly acknowledges her claims to social superiority. Her son, who had begun a career as a lawyer before fighting as a soldier, has returned from the war an emotional invalid. Although he is in love with Jane, both of them know that the romance can never lead to marriage until he has recovered.

Driving to work one day, Baldy has a chance encounter with Edith Towne. He is immediately smitten, although she is from a very wealthy family. When Edith's uncle, Frederick Towne, meets Jane, he falls in love with her, partly because of her appearance, but also because of her practicality and forthright personality. As the plot unfolds, the author contrasts the new world of post-war Washington with a more idealistic, settled time. In addition, she compares the life of activity that eventually revitalizes Evans, with the passive existence of the idle rich (like the Townes). She also contrasts the romantic idealism grounded in the practicality of characters like Jane with the unrealistic emotionalism of the Townes.

25. Bailey, Temple. *Wallflowers*. Philadelphia: Penn, 1927. 350pp.

Madge Claybourne brings her daughters Sandra and Theodora from Windytop, their family home in Virginia, to live less expensively in Washington and find husbands. The young ladies, eighteen-year-old twins, are agreeable, but they do not finding acclimatizing themselves to 1920s Washington easy. The clothes, hairstyles, manners, and dances they know are out of date. However, Mrs. Claybourne has social connections and a confidence that respect is their due because of their distinguished ancestors.

She installs them in an apartment in the most fashionable neighborhood she can afford, even though the baronial furniture from their Virginia home will barely fit. She and her daughters are without pretension or greed, however, and suitors are evaluated for their natural gentility, stemming from generations of prominent ancestors, not their wealth. One suitor, Rufus Fiske, had a privileged upbringing, but the death of his mother was soon followed by the installment of a stepmother not much older than himself. Upon the sudden death of his father, he discovered he had been cut out of the will. Now a shell-shocked veteran, he wants to live in a simple cottage in the country and write. Theodora's suitor comes from a wealthy Georgetown family. However, upon his father's sudden death he discovered that the family wealth had been squandered in bad investments. He and his mother sustain themselves by selling family heirlooms and paintings from their house. Each relationship undergoes extreme trials, but in the end fortunes are restored and true love is victorious.

An antiques shop near Lafayette Square is at the center of the novel. The shop owner's ability to recognize the value of antique silver and ivory carvings earns him a handsome living and social status. He sees the true worth of the twins and helps others to recognize their value as well. Although the physical description of Washington is not extensive in the novel, apartment living is described, as well as some locales, and forms of socializing typical of the period.

26. Baldwin, Faith. *Washington, U.S.A.* New York: Farrar & Rinehart, 1942. 364pp.

This book of love stories captures World War II Washington as a city preoccupied by the grave threat faced by the nation during the war. The characters and most of the people they meet are newcomers. The romances are of interest for their evocations of the tension and hectic pace of the wartime city.

27. Banks, Stockton V. *Washington Adventure.* Illustrated by Henry C. Pitz. New York: Whittlesey House / McGraw-Hill, 1950. 191pp. young adult.

In 1800, Scottish immigrant David Cameron travels to the new Federal City to live with his brother Robert Cameron. He arrives to find his brother gone, probably on business, leaving most of his possessions at a hotel. When David goes to his brother's room, he witnesses a thief leaving. While he is waiting for Robert, he meets people from all stations in life and learns about the construction of the city. Eventually, he discovers the thief was Mr. Blaze, a land speculator. David pursues Blaze, suspecting he has locked up his brother to prevent him from buying land he was commissioned to purchase by a Philadelphia investor. In time, David comes to live with the MacDonald family, which owns a Georgetown warehouse, and employs him as a messenger. They treat him as a near relation and take him on a daytrip to Mount Vernon, which gets a detailed account. On an errand to Foxhall's Foundry, he discovers where Robert had been held and finds a message about his current location near Little Falls. With the help of the MacDonalds he frees Robert and captures Blaze. At the end of the novel, President Adams comes to town to open a session of Congress and the Cameron brothers decide to buy land in the District and settle down.

28. Barry, John D. *The Congressman's Wife: A Story of American Politics.* Illustrated by Rollin G. Kirby. New York: Smart Set, 1903. 359pp.

In the preface, Barry declares his intent to examine the "human and social complications" faced by a modern-day politician forced by the pressures of his office to compromise his principles. At the beginning of the novel, forty-two-year-old Congressman Douglas Briggs seems to have much in which to take pride. He is respected by senior politicians and is hosting a ball at his grand new Washington house. The most distinguished members of Washington society will be in attendance and his thirty-five year old wife, Helen, who is acknowledged to be one of the most beautiful women in the city, will preside. However, in the course of his triumphant evening a journalist's questions about his connections to the Transcontinental Railroad remind him of how he attained his affluence and position.

In his first year in office, he garnered attention from leaders of his political party who groomed him for a role in the party machine. Their patronage gave him political power, but Washington's social life brought heavy debt. Franklin West, the lawyer for the Transcontinental Railroad, paid off Briggs' debt in return for advancing the interests of the railroad in Congress. Briggs fended off qualms of conscience with the rationale that legislators are not paid enough to cope with the social demands of office.

At the ball, his wife learns of his work on behalf of the railroad from West who confesses his love for her and then demands her attention by informing her that his money paid for the lifestyle she enjoys. Too fearful to tell her husband of West's insulting behavior, she does confront him about his moral failure and declares her alienation from him. For Briggs, who believes that every man needs a good woman to be complete, life becomes anguished. He reconciles with his wife by separating himself from the railroad syndicate and party machine and is voted out of office. However, his wife realizes he will never be happy until he returns to politics and decides to support him, so long as he regains his moral integrity.

The novel contrasts Briggs with Congressman Burrell, a self-made man with little taste for the social game. Burrell's personal wealth gives him power and authority within his circle, even if it does not lead to social advancement. By the end of the novel his wealth supports Briggs' household when he hires Briggs to do legal work for him involving patents and pays him to let his daughters benefit from life in his Washington household under the tutelage of Mrs. Briggs.

The nature of political journalism is a major theme in the novel. Reform journalism is presented as a social good through the description of William Farley, a founding member of a club established to bring about political reform. In contrast, the various motivations of society reporters are discussed and illustrated in the course of the ball that opens the work.

29. Barton, George. *The Ambassador's Trunk*. Illustrated by Charles E. Meister. Boston: Page, 1919. 310pp.

Captain Vance Prescott, a soldier who had been seriously wounded in a World War I battle, wants to rejoin his regiment. However, while he is awaiting a decision from the Army, he works in Washington for the Intelligence Bureau of the War Department. He is in love with Hope Vernon, daughter of an assistant secretary of state. Prescott grew up in Washington and is still adjusting to all of the changes caused by the war. Invited for a weekend at the Vernon country house, Idlewild, Prescott is asked to carry secret documents to Vernon, including unexecuted contracts which will give the Allies a monopoly over Mexican oil fields. The house party includes Thomas Warner, a reporter for the *Washington Planet*, and the South American diplomat Count Castro. Bromley Barnes, a character from earlier Barton novels who is a retired U.S. Secret Service agent, soon arrives to protect the documents while they are at Idlewild. When the papers are stolen, Barnes must unravel the mystery with the help of Prescott. The solution centers on the trunk of a Russian diplomat. Although the papers are stolen at Idlewild, much of the remainder of the novel is set in a Washington filled with plotters against the government, Mexican spies, veterans, soldiers on leave, and Liberty Bond ralliers.

30. Barton, George. *Barry Wynn; or, The Adventures of a Page Boy in the United States Congress*. Illustrated by John Huybers. Boston: Small, Maynard, 1912. 348pp. young adult.

Congressman Carlton, a friend of the deceased father of fifteen-year-old Barry Wynn, aids Wynn with a page appointment. Traveling from his hometown of Cleverly, Wynn is inspired by his first sight of the Capitol and works hard to learn and conscientiously perform the duties of a page, which are described in some detail (filling inkwells, finding legislators during roll calls, assisting with correspondence, maintaining documents, and creating news clipping files). He also learns about the duties of a congressman and the many demands placed upon Carlton. The legislative process is made immediate for Wynn when Carlton tells him that before his death his father had begun work on a plan to have a naval repair station built at Cleverly. Wynn witnesses the political chicanery of Carlton's opponents and plays an important role in efforts to get the naval base for Cleverly. Through his work for Carlton, Wynn learns important values, such as frugality, truthfulness, humility, friendship, liberality to friends, and promptness in performing one's duties. He lives in a three-story boarding house near Foggy Bottom, and his experiences as a boarder give some insight into this way of living. Since his landlady and her dead husband were great friends of President Garfield, he hears a good deal about that man's virtues and reads a biography of Garfield that is summarized at length. In the end, the bill that will give Cleverly a naval base is passed, the President gives Wynn a signing pen, and he returns to his hometown to share in a triumphal celebration for Carlton.

31. Barton, George. *The Pembroke Mason Affair.* Illustrated by Charles E. Meister. Boston: L. C. Page, 1920. 331pp.
     Pembroke Mason, a corporate lawyer and resident of Washington, is about to retire after arguing a case before the U.S. Supreme Court. A widower, he lives with his niece, Marian Cooper, an orphan who will be his heir. The case he is to argue concerns whether railroads can mine ore on their lands. Before he can argue the case, Mason is found dead by his niece. Bromley Barnes, a character from earlier Barton novels who is a retired U.S. Secret Service agent, investigates and Mason's law partner, Floyd Graves, and a man impersonating multi-millionaire John Fairfield are suspects. Another suspect is Marian's suitor, Walter Miles, of whom Mason had disapproved. One important clue is a swastika symbol found near Mason's body. Barnes also learns that someone had threatened Mason a year before his death, indicating that he would die on the date he did, and labor union officials had bribed a fortuneteller to tell him that the threat was accurate. The novel contains little significant description of Washington, although Union Station and some government buildings and neighborhoods are mentioned.

32. Barton, George. *The Strange Adventures of Bromley Barnes.* Illustrated by Charles E. Meister. Boston: L. C. Page, 1918. 345pp.
     Bromley Barnes collects first editions and lives in the St. Regis, in a bachelor apartment overlooking the Capitol building. Employed as a U.S. Secret Service agent for thirty years, he finished his career as Chief of Special Affairs at the U.S. Treasury Department. Along with his assistant Cornelius Clancy, he continues to be called upon for espe-

cially sensitive investigations. Only five of the twelve stories in this volume are set in Washington; the rest are set in New York City.

One of the longer of the Washington stories is "The Thirteenth Treaty." The treaty is a draft of an agreement between the United States and Sweden for the purchase of the Pauline Islands. If a recently formed European Alliance hears of the treaty ahead of time, they may be able to take offensive action and the deal, important to the defense of the United States, will fall through. Barnes has only thirty-four hours to find the missing document. During the course of his search, he pursues known spies and representatives of foreign governments all around Washington and some indication is given of the lives of people from various social classes, including ambassadors living in Georgetown mansions and apartment dwellers.

Other stories focus on the mysterious death of an inventor working on a system to destroy submarines; the identification of a person leaking the President's decisions before they are announced so that someone can make a fortune on Wall Street; and the death of the commandant of the new National Arsenal and the bombing of the facility.

33. Barton, Wilfred M. *The Road to Washington.* Boston: Richard C. Badger / Gorham Press, 1919. 197pp.

As war breaks out in Europe in the summer of 1914, Bill and Jay travel to Washington with their Uncle Fred and learn about the invasion of Washington by the British one hundred years before. Historic images and contemporary photographs are included in this account, which is presented as a driving tour of the city.

34. Bayne, Jessica. *When Love Must Hide.* New York: Lancer Books, 1964. 142pp.

Twenty-two-year-old Lizbeth Moore had been working as a junior executive in the Commerce Department and living with Phyllis Chapman, her older lesbian lover, until her life fell apart. Their friend Doris had announced that she would soon marry and give up her lesbianism and her lover Fern had exacted revenge by meeting with Doris' fiancé, Leo Vincent. Vincent called off the marriage and Doris committed suicide, leaving a detailed note outing Fern and urging her congressman father to investigate lesbianism in the federal government. Before this can happen, Fern is approached by Vincent and learns that he is the agent of a powerful business lobby that had been trying to influence Doris' father. For pledging to work with the lobby by gathering incriminating evidence on her friends, Fern avoids investigation and receives a large cash payment. With compromising photographs of

Lizbeth and Phyllis in hand, Vincent approaches the couple, promising their secret will never be revealed if they seduce Harriet, a senator's daughter. Thinking they have no alternative, they meet with Harriet who actually seduces Lizbeth. Phyllis secretly photographs their encounter. After the lobby achieves its goals Phyllis and Lizbeth believe they have escaped. However, the senator calls for an investigation of the lobby and Lizbeth and Phyllis learn that Harriet has killed herself. Forced to testify, at first they plead the fifth, but when Lizbeth takes the stand she courageously reveals her lesbianism and confirms the senator's story and Phyllis confirms her testimony. At the end of the novel the two are planning to leave Washington for New York City where they can live and work in anonymity without the constant threat of dismissal that had characterized their civil service jobs.

35. Bell, Margaret. *Hubble-Bubble.* New York: Dodd, Mead, 1927. 337pp.
        Thirty-four-year-old Paul Wentworth, an Oklahoma oil millionaire, and his wife, Sylvia, arrive in Washington for Paul's first session in the House of Representatives. The society they enter is divided in loyalty between the national set, headed by Jane Hurlburt, and the foreign set, headed by Caroline Mojesco, a Kentuckian married to the Minister from Beretania. Sylvia and Paul each find confidantes and guides in their new city from entirely different sets.
        Madame Mojesco takes up Paul, giving him advice on making his mark in political circles. Sylvia is welcomed into the artistic set by Cyril Hargreave. Although Sylvia is an atheist, she embraces a higher code of morality than Paul, who is most interested in social and political advancement. A Bryn Mawr graduate, Sylvia is presented as an intellectual with titles in her personal library that include works by Jung, Bergson, Cather, and Spinoza. Both Sylvia and Paul are tempted to be unfaithful to each other, and this becomes the narrative drive of the novel.
        Although Sylvia understands passion, she believes the restraining influence of civilization is a good thing and spiritual union is to be preferred over physical union. She loves Paul as someone at a lower stage of evolutionary development whose primitivism must be understood and condoned. She embraces the idea that no matter how painful, the freedom of each individual to work out his or her destiny should be sacrosanct. Sylvia wants to transform society, removing social distinctions and building all human relationships on the foundation of ideas and "honest thinking" and supporting all efforts at self-realization. Her credo's emphasis on human complexity and perfectibility through ex-

perience leads her to think she can have a spiritual union with Cyril Hargreave, while being married to Paul. Paul is attracted to Madame Mojesco's social prominence and cunning; Sylvia is attracted to the free thinking of the aesthetes (who, when in the country, engage in a phallic festival). Eventually, Paul is duped into investing in an Ural oil field so that Madame Mojesco can get her husband appointed to the Court of St. James.

The novel has little physical description of Washington, although efforts to build Washington Cathedral play a role. The novelist is concerned, however, with presenting insights about the city's social life. The novel includes descriptions of purchasing bootleg alcohol, managing personal publicity, seasonal transformations of drawing rooms, entertainments, and charity events, and includes references to Freud, current fashions (bobbed hair and cosmetics), face lifts, spiritualism, and anarchism.

36. Benjamin, Lewis. *Why Was It?* Chicago: Belford, Clarke, 1888. 257pp.

This temperance novel, set in 1870s Washington, is narrated by a man with a beautiful younger sister named Clare. Clare marries Hugh, the narrator's best friend in college. Hugh and Clare begin their life in the city in a boarding house on K Street, NW, but, perhaps due to Hugh's position in an important law firm or Clare's beauty, they attend social functions along with diplomats and politicians. Clare attracts powerful men and the resentment of powerful women, and plots are laid to win her away from her husband and destroy her reputation. The Washington of this novel is focused on the areas around Franklin and Farragut Squares. The society depicted is one in which the trusting and innocent can come to great harm at the hands of the ambitious and manipulative. A weak spirit and drink bring the downfall of Hugh (and his eventual death). Clare and her brother must suffer through physical trials on the Western frontier before returning to Washington to begin redeemed lives. When they return, each of them finds a spouse with wealth and political power.

37. Benson, Mildred Wirt [Emerson, Alice B., pseud.]. *Betty Gordon in Washington, or Strange Adventures in a Great City.* New York: Cupples & Leon, 1920. 210pp. young adult.

The orphaned Betty Gordon's only relative, Uncle Richard Gordon, is a Washington, D.C.-based investor with interests in oil wells and mines. During summer holidays, Betty goes to seaside areas, Western ranches, or Northeastern farms and has adventures, described in a series of novels. Her school days are spent at Shadyside School in the D.C. suburbs. In this novel, a follow-up to *Betty Gordon at Bramble Farm*, Bob Henderson, the orphan boy who was taken in by a miserly farm owner, escapes to Washington to seek information about his origins, and Betty follows soon afterward to find him. However, through missed communications, her uncle has left town before she arrives, although through a fortunate coincidence she meets the Littell family of Fairfields, a country estate near Fort Myer. She and the Littell girls make sight-seeing trips to the Washington Monument, White House, Capitol, Octagon House, Bureau of Engraving and Printing, and Mount Vernon, as she continues to seek information about Bob. When the two are reunited, a series of adventures ensue, including getting trapped in an elevator after enjoying the view in Washington's tallest building and dealing with the miserly farmer who has come after Bob. Intended for a schoolgirl audience, the novel conveys an impression of upper-middle-class life in and around Washington through its descriptions of entertainments, meals, and clothing.

38. Benson, Mildred Wirt [Emerson, Alice B., pseud.]. *Betty Gordon on the Campus; or The Secret of the Trunk Room.* New York: Cupples & Leon, 1928. 208pp. young adult.

Despite the setting in a girl's school near Washington, the novel has few descriptions of the city, with the exception of Union Station and the shopping district along F Street, NW. The plot centers upon school rivalries, sporting competitions (rowing, tennis, basketball), and a mysterious man, first spotted on a train, later on the streets of Washington, and finally on the grounds of the school itself. When the mystery is solved, everyone with a good character is rewarded by the course of events.

39. Benton, John. *Faith, Hope and a Horse.* New York: D. Appleton-Century, 1940. 249pp.

Edward Wilson, who lives on racetrack winnings and the assistance of his friend Jimmy Chase, meets Lila Allen at the Hagerstown Fair. She is an itinerant missionary from Oklahoma who travels pulling a "gospel trailer" with her car. Believing that she can do more good in Eastern cities than anywhere else, she has come to deliver her message of love, hope, and salvation. She immediately wins over Wilson, although she suggests a number of practices he should give up, including drinking and gambling. For Wilson, her appeal is more romantic than spiritual and he signs on as her assistant. When the two reach Washington, they meet "Major" Layton, head of the D.C. branch of the

United Rescue Mission, and Lila starts preaching for him while finding
a place to live and a job for Wilson at the Mission. Wilson quickly discovers that Layton and his organization are crooked. Layton uses a call
list to solicit donations to pay for milk and bread for the poor that other
donors have provided free. The telephone solicitation is done by hard-
boiled characters who use their commissions from each donation for
alcohol. Layton's racket is a franchise of a national organization and he
pays a percentage of the take to a "general" in Philadelphia. Because of
Wilson's description of Franklin Square in Philadelphia as the locale
filled with the most hardcore of sinners, Allen establishes a personal
goal to set up a mission there. So, Allen and Wilson travel to the Philadelphia branch of the Mission to consider an offer to take it over. They
are told that the present "colonel" is moving, and for $1,000 (to reim-
burse his costs) they will be able to take over his establishment. Wilson
develops a successful plan for getting Allen her mission in Philadelphia
and throwing over the crooks who operate the United Rescue Mission.
The novel includes some cursory descriptions of places where men
from all social settings, including senators, go to bet on horses. In general, the novel presents D.C. as a place where vice is rampant.

40. Bergengren, Anna Faquhar. *Her Washington Experiences: As Related by a Cabinet Minister's Wife in a Series of Letters to Her Sister.*
Illustrated by T. de Thulstrup. Boston: L. C. Page, 1902. 222pp.
    This epistolary novel consists of letters written by a cabinet minis-
ter's wife, Amelia T. Cummings, to her sister Lydia from October to
the end of May in the 1890s. The chapters originally appeared as in-
stallments in *The Lady's Home Journal.* Amelia and her wealthy, self-
made husband live in an elegantly furnished rented house and employ a
butler, cook, housemaid, and coachman. She grew up in Ohio and
worked as a schoolteacher before marrying and can hardly believe that
she is now intimate with the President and socializing with the politically powerful and internationally notable. Amelia details her interactions with servants, journalists, tradesmen, and members of various
social sets (literary, political, "Georgetown people," and "trades-peo-
ple" who have made their money in commerce). She provides information about her social responsibilities as a cabinet minister's wife and
the forms of protocol, etiquette, and attire and their importance. She
describes social events, including receptions and teas, the social workings of the White House, the challenges and costs of organizing a major
social function, D.C. landmarks, women society reporters, Washington
hostesses ambitious to be courted by powerful men, the plight of widowed and unmarried women working as civil service employees, the

marriage prospects for young women (dismal), affluent "coloured people" [*sic*], and visits by distant relatives of modest social attainments. A romance that ends in a wedding between two of Cummings' friends provides the overarching plot of the novel.

41. Black, Alexander. *A Capital Courtship*. New York: Scribner's Sons, 1897. 104pp.

This is the book version of a story originally prepared as one of Black's innovative photoplays—a series of still photographs projected to give a sense of movement, accompanied by dialogue. Black was able to coax important political and social figures, such as President Cleveland and Sir Julian Paunceforte, to cooperate in his project. The book is illustrated with a few of the 250 photographs used in the photoplay and, as its title implies, is a romance set in the nation's capital.

42. Blair, Anne Denton. *Arthur, the White House Mouse*. Illustrated by Lily Spandorf. Washington, D.C.: Media / America, 1975. 25pp. juvenile.

Arthur descends from a long line of mice that lived in the White House. Lonely because "the Family" is away at Christmas, he is admiring the Christmas tree, when he notices a number of young mice come through the window and begin eating decorations. They make such a commotion that the White House housekeeper notices them. After chasing them away, she announces she will set traps. Arthur decides the mice must be offspring of cousins and travels to St. John's Church where these relations live. He is pleasantly reacquainted with his family who appreciate his warning against future raids of the White House and returns to his home with a sense of satisfaction and young relative in tow whom he entices to come live with him as a White House mouse.

43. Blair, Clay. *The Board Room: A Novel*. New York: Dutton, 1969. 352pp.

Leland Warwick Crawford, Jr., has been a Washington reporter for thirteen years. He has just been named editor in chief of *The Weekly Tribune,* a once influential mass-circulation magazine. Russell Pratt, head of a wealthy non-profit family foundation, purchased the publishing company that owns the *Tribune* and hired Crawford to revitalize the publication, which is headquartered in a thirteen-story building on Lafayette Park across from the White House. The building's interior is museum-like and tenanted by staff who are remnants of a less advanced era of publishing. Crawford must overthrow a large bureaucracy and introduce new approaches to journalism and office management. Only the first chapter of the novel is set in Washington, after that Crawford is moved into other components of the Marshall Publishing Company which owns the *Tribune*.

44. Blair, Clay. *Pentagon Country.* New York: McGraw-Hill, 1971. 318pp.

During a three-day period, U.S. Navy submarine Captain William Montgomery King faces a number of crises. Despite his hope to attain flag rank, his wife begs him to retire. His son has turned into a hippie pacifist and is campaigning for the dismantlement of the Navy in very public ways that could disgrace King. Finally, the Defense Department is planning to end funding for the new missile system on which he has spent years of his Pentagon career working. The setting is primarily in the Pentagon but portrays the military bureaucracy of which a significant percentage of Washingtonians are members.

45. Blatty, William Peter. *The Exorcist.* New York: Harper & Row, 1971. 340pp.

In this novel on which the successful movie was based, actress Chris MacNeill rents a brick colonial house neighboring Georgetown University and situated on an embankment above M Street, NW. MacNeill's social life burgeons with astronauts, high-level civil servants, senators, and prominent clerics. However, her daughter, Regan, soon dominates her life with mysterious behavior that is eventually identified as evidence of demon possession.

46. Blythe, Samuel G. *The Fakers.* New York: George H. Doran, 1914. 388pp.

Although Senator Paxton hates "demagogism," he takes pleasure in demagogues. Regarding the general population with contempt, he believes they get the politicians they deserve. Describing his high political position and wealth, he says that the people allowed him to swindle them, and he utilized every opportunity they gave him. One of the young men in his office, Tommie Hicks, delights Paxton as a demagogue in the making. Hicks' skills as a "faker" have a long history. Even as a boy he always claimed the position of hero and leader, whether he deserved it or not. Much of his skill is based on a talent for self-promotion and the manipulation of publicity. After campaigning locally for William McKinley in 1896, he wheedles his way to Washington by pretending an acquaintanceship with Mark Hanna, giving up the study of law to work in the office of Senator Paxton from his home district. The novel traces the ways in which Hicks promotes himself and builds his career with the help of Paxton, who treats him as an experiment—eager to see how far he will go. In addition to cataloging Hicks' political chicanery, the novel includes descriptions of the ways he manipulates social events and connections in his favor. The novel provides many details about the clothing, home furnishings, food, and social functions of members of various social classes. In addition to the calculating politicians he meets, Hicks interacts with a number of social fakers, people educated above their class and refined beyond the status their birth would dictate. Although they have barely enough money on which to live, they manipulate appearances by wearing the right clothes and speaking of summers in Newport. Hicks ends up marrying one of these social fakers who views Washington as the ideal place to live comfortably and fashionably through the aid of friends, visiting in their houses and spending as little of her own money as she can. Hicks is eventually elected to the Senate. However, when his hypocrisy and corruption are exposed, he is forced out of office, resigning himself to exile in Paris and living on the leftover prestige of his former office.

47. Blythe, Samuel G. *The Price of Place.* New York: George H. Doran, c. 1913. 359pp.
   Newly elected Congressman John Marsh arrives in Washington to begin his term and must deal with a socially ambitious wife, party politics, and the political boss who got him elected. When he realizes the expenses of establishing a position for himself and his wife, he learns to play the game of politics to the financial advantage of himself and his backer. In the end, a crisis of conscience prevents him from becoming President. The title of the book is not only metaphorical; the novel is filled with details about the cost of dresses, suits, entertainments, and housing. Since Marsh is on the District of Columbia committee, there are descriptions of the degree to which real estate is the major business in the city and how those involved in the real estate business develop political influence.

48. Blythe, Samuel G. *A Western Warwick.* New York: George H. Doran, 1916. 345pp.
   Cynical after having been voted out of power, William Henry Paxton, who was instrumental in the election of President James Jason Rogers, gives a detailed account of his own political machinations. Essentially, Paxton and the alliance he formed are fierce protectionists who got corporations to put up large sums of money to convince the public that protective tariffs are in the interest of all Americans. Paxton

establishes an office in Washington to distribute money and promises in exchange for allegiance to the Rogers campaign whose slogan is "Rogers and Prosperity." When Rogers is elected, economic life is soon dominated by the formation of large corporations valued at two or three times their real asset value. Inflation follows, leading to an economic downturn, and Rogers is voted out of office, although the fortunes he and his cronies amassed remain intact. When the novel focuses on Washington, it looks at official Washington and presents opportunists, career political appointees, high-level civil servants, career politicians, office seekers, and lobbyists.

49. Bogy, Lewis Vital. *In Office: A Story of Washington Life and Society*. Chicago: F. J. Schulte, c. 1891. 202pp.

Tula is forced to obtain a job to support her invalid mother when her father's death reveals that he had lost his money in the fever of stock speculation. Luckily she lands a civil service position in Washington, far from the disgrace her father had brought upon the family. She suffers many trials, including sexual harassment by her supervisor and the slanderous destruction of her reputation. The story is meant to prove the author's assertion that so long as political influence is weighed above all else there will be appalling abuses of power in government offices

50. Bowles, John. *The Masked Prophet; a Psychological Romance*. New York: Alliance, 1900. 190pp.

Washington lawyer Reginald Irving enjoys rural walks and frequents a particular grove that is dominated by an ancient tree. In the center of a clearing is a pyramid of rose bushes. One day, when he cuts his hand on a rose thorn, he has a series of visions that show him the interconnectedness of life from the microscopic organisms in his blood drop to the workings of the cosmos. He is guided in his vision by a male being, Alta, the father of a female spirit, Aleita. Irving is both enamored of Aleita and transformed by his visionary experience. Although he would like to live within his visions, Alta reminds him that he still lives in the world and that he cannot live an entirely spiritual existence. Instead, he should practice altruism to develop spiritually. He describes his experiences to his friends, Richard and Amy Stoddard. Richard is skeptical, but Amy is intrigued. Reginald decides to use his wealth to improve the lot of the people who live in London's East End. Soon after he leaves Washington, Amy realizes she is pregnant. When she gives birth to a daughter, strange lights appear in the sky above Washington, and a halo forms over the Stoddard house. An Eastern mystic named Dr. Moombjay is attracted by the light and becomes a friend of the Stoddards, who name their daughter Aleita. He explains theosophy to them as the religion of everyday life that is suited to everyone and is based on the scientific fact of electromagnetism. In the meantime, Reginald has been applying business theory to solving the problems of poverty in London. After nineteen years pass, he feels that he has established a sound enough institution to serve the needs of East Londoners and returns to Washington. He describes the beauties of the city with rapture, commenting on the greater number of parks and the dreamlike white Capitol dome. When he meets Aleita he believes that she is the spirit that he had met many years before. Alta returns to confirm that Aleita decided to enter enmattered existence out of love for him, and the rest of the novel concerns the beauty and tragedy of that choice.

51. Brossard, Chandler. *The Bold Saboteurs.* New York: Farrar, Straus & Young, 1953. 303pp.

Through the character of Jimmy (nicknamed Yogi), the son of a violent alcoholic, Brossard presents Washington and the social settings of the marginalized from the perspective of someone alienated from society. Yogi's brother Roland is a skilled thief who teaches him how to steal from stores. His mother forces him to work a paper route so that he can steal milk and food from doorsteps in the early morning. For a time his aunt, vaguely connected to the Bureau of Home Economics, tries to affect his growth by feeding him the latest bizarre health concoctions. As a way of developing Yogi's skills to protect himself from his father, Roland tries to build his endurance by depriving him of sleep and forcing him to exercise and run for miles. After permanently driving off his father, Roland begins to focus on romancing girls and starts to influence Yogi in more subtle ways, encouraging him to read the classics of Western literature and train his mind. At about the same time, Yogi's aunt moves to South America. For the first time in his adolescence he is on his own.

Yogi haunts Monroe Park and becomes the only friend of a muscular Irishman nicknamed Bobo, whom everyone fears. When his brother secures a government clerk job in the Department of Agriculture, Yogi begins work as a Western Union messenger and later as a caretaker for a paralyzed man. Eventually, he joins a gang that steals cars, mugs homosexuals in Lafayette Park, and steals from country club locker rooms. Yogi describes cruising in Lafayette Park, gay bars, black neighborhoods, prizefighters at Miller's Gym, and hustling tennis players in Rock Creek Park. He finds a mentor in Perez, an artist who lives in a loft over a downtown garage that he must beat off rats to enter. Perez finds Yogi a job as an art school model, and he meets another model who hustles and performs in homosexual clubs. The two form an intimate friendship that ends tragically. Throughout the novel Yogi falls into dissociative states and recounts dream-like encounters.

52. Brown, George Rothwell. *My Country: A Story of Today.* Illustrated by Chase Emerson. Boston: Small, Maynard, 1917. 359pp.
  The family of the widowed Mrs. Sigbert, consisting of four girls, is joined by her half brother and his twin sons, Wilhelm and Karl Hartmann. Although Sigbert has longed to return to her native Germany, the Hartmanns are eager to establish themselves in America. After the death of Mr. Hartmann, the youngest Sigbert girl, Elfrieda, sings before the famous German opera star Madame Ruhlman, who offers to coach her for the stage at no expense, and the Sigberts and Karl Hartmann return to Germany. Wilhelm, however, has been offered an appointment at the U.S. Naval Academy through Congressman Marshfield, an acquaintance of family friend Adolph Burch. Years later, when his twin brother, a captain in the German Navy, appears mysteriously in Washington, Germany and the United States are on the verge of war. Through his brother, Wilhelm discovers that his academy appointment and rapid advance in the Navy was part of a German espionage plan created by the powerful Burch. Most of the complicated plot, involving a submarine, seaside mansion, and beautiful women, is set outside Washington. However, Hartmann discovers the espionage while living in Washington, and there is some description of the city and an apartment building there called The Summit, as well as several illustrations of Washington scenes.

53. Brown, Zenith Jones [Ford, Leslie, pseud.]. *All for the Love of a Lady.* New York: Charles Scribner, 1944. 261pp.
  Widowed Grace Latham observes World War II Georgetown from the perspective of a native, a distinction she and everyone in her acquaintance take very seriously. In this murder mystery, Grace's acquaintance Courtney had been expected to marry Cass Crane but instead wed rich newcomer D. J. Durbin, and Crane married Molly, who had been courted by Randy Fleming. Courtney still loves Crane and offends Molly at a dinner party by telling her that she has heard that Crane is coming home from the war. Molly is so upset that she had not heard from her husband about his plans that she abandons her house to stay with Grace Latham. The first night Molly stays in Latham's house, Durbin's chauffeur is found murdered on Crane's doorstep. Suddenly

all of the misaligned lovers are implicated in various ways, although Latham believes that the solution to the murder has some connection to gun-bearing foreigners or an Indian holy man. Wartime references include victory gardens, international cartels involved in war profiteering, blackouts, and ration books. Georgetown is being transformed by the wartime housing shortage, and very affluent people are suddenly living in renovated houses located beside abandoned mansions or the dwellings of their servants. The city that had formerly slept all summer has become a year-round city, and the war has given it a new, central place in the world.

54. Brown, Zenith Jones [Ford, Leslie, pseud.]. *False to Any Man.* New York: Scribner, 1939. 254pp.

The widower Grace Latham, who lives on P Street, NW, in Georgetown, is drawn into a mystery surrounding the death of Karen Lunt, whose parents were killed in a car accident years before. Judge Candler, who may soon be appointed to the Supreme Court, has served as Karen's guardian. Philander Doyle, one of Candler's former law partners, had prospered while Candler suffered an illness that was expected to claim his life. When Candler was forced to sell his ancestral home, Doyle bought it. Candler's daughter Jeremy has been in love with Doyle's son Roger for years. Although Roger has pledged his love in return, he is now being forced to marry Karen, and Jeremy is being forced to sign over her stocks to Karen. Both young people are being threatened with the disclosure of damaging information that would prevent Candler's Supreme Court appointment. Suddenly Karen is found dead. The mystery is solved in a setting of rich social details about life in Alexandria and Georgetown with a focus on furniture, clothing, conversation, food, and drinks.

55. Brown, Zenith Jones [Ford, Leslie, pseud.]. *Washington Whispers Murder.* New York: Charles Scribner, 1953. 194pp.

Mrs. Sybil Thorn, a Washington socialite with an elegant house on Woodley Road, is grooming Congressman Hamilton Vair for the Senate. After his election, but not before, she will marry him. Vair requires much grooming, due to his crude, man-of-the-people manners. In part, his rise to national prominence stems from destroying the reputation of Rufus Brent, a man selected to head the Industrial Techniques Commission. Vair has a personal and unreasonable animosity for Brent. The battle is waged through distorted newspaper stories fed to reporters by Vair. However, Washington powerbrokers are more influenced by social exchanges at dinners and parties, and Vair's manners contrast poorly with Brent's. When Vair has the gall to appear at a garden party in Brent's honor and is shat upon by a large bird at the moment he is about to shake Brent's hand, all of Washington society is abuzz with delight, and his downfall is imminent. Then, a murder occurs that upsets the reader's expectations. The novel includes descriptions of Georgetown locales, houses, and furnishings. To contrast the manners of outsiders and insiders, many revealing exchanges are included to construct a social portrait, although one assumes a strong element of satire.

56. Bugbee, Emma. *Peggy Covers Washington.* New York: Dodd, Mead, 1937. 297pp.

Peggy Foster, reporter for *The New York Star*, travels to Washington for the first time to cover the international "Women of Tomorrow" conference. As a newcomer, Foster learns about the operations of the White House Press Office, security procedures, and the regulars of the White House press corps. She also visits the Washington bureau of her own newspaper and learns how that office works. She attends a White House tea party hosted by the First Lady and hears about the objects and rooms in the mansion. Through other women reporters, she learns about the changing roles of female journalists. Foster decides to try for a position in the Washington bureau and soon achieves her goal. Her treatment as a woman, her news assignments, the social status of reporters, and how she balances her job with a New York City boyfriend (who is an aviator) are all themes. Peggy befriends another woman reporter who has covered Washington for years and lives in Georgetown. Through her, she learns more about the trials of the correspondent's life, particularly as a single woman. When the President travels to Virginia and Tennessee to support hydroelectric power, Foster is part of the press corps and has the new experience of traveling on a junket. The novel ends with the annual dance hosted by the White House for the press corps. Although Foster has been offered a permanent job as a Washington reporter, it seems fairly clear that she will accept her boyfriend's marriage proposal and return to New York.

57. Burnett, Frances Hodgson. *Through One Administration.* Boston: J. R. Osgood, 1883. 564pp.

Although she is best known for her children's writing, Burnett wrote several works for adults, including this one. The novel's protagonist, Bertha Amory, is a talented woman who, having only limited opportunities as a female, lives a life of outward gaiety but inner sadness. Reflecting Burnett's experience in Washington, the author dramatizes social and political intrigue.

58. Camera, Cara, [pseud.]. *Society Rapids: High Life in Washington, Saratoga and Bar Harbor; by "One in the Swim."* Philadelphia: T. B. Peterson, 1888. 250pp.

Twenty-year-old Eveline Mason has become anxious that she is still not married. She has been assured of her physical attractiveness, and, although her father died when she was three and her remarried mother is a missionary in a remote area, she has lived with the Eurlburts, her eminently respectable aunt and uncle (a retired brigadier general). While at Saratoga for the season she observes the other women and decides that, although she finds their flirtatious behavior shocking and their innuendos insufferable, she must give up dignified and ladylike ways and emulate them. When the Eurlburts and Eveline travel to their house in Washington for the season, everyone is talking about Victor Van Vroom, a wealthy Hudson River Valley aristocrat who has just returned from a European tour to set up elegant bachelor's quarters in Washington. Because of Van Vroom's reputation as a dandy and ladies' man, Eveline decides to flirt with him to attract attention and create the social stir that will garner notice from more suitable men. In some ways, her plot does not go as she expected. She does become a social success when Van Vroom pays attention to her. However, he falls in love with her and proposes. When she rejects him because she does not love him, he leaves on his yacht, and resentful society women are left to gossip that Eveline's pursuit had driven him away. Fortunately, the attention of Congressman Harmon Livingstone, a young friend of Mrs. Eurlburt whose political future seems assured, turns romantic after Van Vroom's departure. The two marry and pledge never to practice the faithless, unloving marriage style of the society people around them. Although the author's concern with social exchanges and the unseemly behavior of society women dominates, the novel includes descriptions of clothing, social events, and activities like carriage drives through the grounds of the Smithsonian and the Soldiers' Home.

59. Carter, John Franklin. *Corpse on the White House Lawn.* New York: Covici-Friede, 1932. 274pp.

Dennis Tyler, Chief of the Bureau of Current Political Intelligence, quietly solves problems from within the State Department. In this novel, he is on the scene when Mexican double agent Ramon Sanchez is found dead on the lawn of the White House. Fearing publicity from a police investigation, the President's secretary Grosvenor Suckling accepts Tyler's offer of a secret investigation. Although there are references to locales, clubs, and businesses in D.C., the city does not play a prominent role in this murder mystery. Bootlegging and the politics of illegal alcohol is referenced, as is the White House Christmas tree lighting, the secretary of state's annual New Year's breakfast at the Pan-American Union, the Mayflower Hotel, and the Binnacle Apartments, a nautical-themed building on Connecticut Avenue, NW, above Dupont Circle.

60. Carter, John Franklin. *Murder in the Embassy*. New York: Jonathan Cape & Harrison Smith, 1930. 250pp.

Prince Hojo, cousin of the Emperor of Japan, has secretly traveled to Washington to sign a treaty. However, he is found murdered in the Japanese embassy library near the unconscious body of Lord Robert Murray, a British diplomat, who is reeking of gin and with a poker in his hand. The case is turned over to Dennis Tyler, Chief of the Bureau of Current Political Intelligence. Since the murder occurred on Japanese territory, the police are excluded, and Tyler tries to solve the crime on his own. Eventually, the girlfriend of the accused, the secretary of state, a local bootlegger, and a journalist are all sequestered in the embassy, which becomes the primary setting, although there are references to Washington locations, clubs, and businesses.

61. Carter, John Franklin. *Murder in the State Department*. New York: Jonathan Cape & Harrison Smith, 1930. 253pp.

When the Under Secretary of State Harrison Howard is found dead in his office with a filing spike through his heart, the status of Anglo-American relations is so delicate that solving the mystery is entrusted to the Chief of the Department's Bureau of Current Political Intelligence, Dennis Tyler. The novel presents an insider's view of Washington diplomatic circles, but does little to illuminate residential Washington. Interestingly, from the standpoint of social history, the villain turns out to be a prominent pacifist.

62. Cater, Douglass. *Dana, The Irrelevant Man*. New York: McGraw-Hill, [1970]. 275pp.

Before the start of the novel, a top Presidential advisor suffered a crisis that led to the President's resignation. When David Bohn, a sensitive young scholar, is commissioned by the advisor's wife to write his biography, he cannot resist delving into the secrets that ended the

Presidency. Washington outsider Bohn comments on all aspects of life in the city.

63. Chambrun, Mme. De. *Pieces of the Game.* New York: G. P. Putnam's Sons, 1915. 259pp.

When Frenchman Christian de Troyes marries Oriel Arden (from an old, respected, but impoverished, Virginia family) without properly informing his uncle and patron, Antoine, Duc de Troyes, estrangement results. Christian must begin living on a diplomatic post's modest salary, previously negotiated for him by his uncle. Despite their small income, the couple's social connections provide entrée to full participation in a social world peopled by other members of the diplomatic corps, politicians, and Americans of independent means. Oriel's Southern ways (such as her familiarity with her African American houseman) and her modern, independent thinking and behavior are the source of tensions within their set. Oriel, who is highly principled, is troubled by the loose talk of the women in her circle, their calculating behavior, and her second-hand impressions of French cynicism and loose sexual mores. Although socially popular, a generalized anti-foreign sentiment attaches to de Troyes, and when a woman associated with a scandal from his past appears, whispering begins, filling Oriel with anxiety. Circumstantial evidence seems to confirm her worst fears and leads her to a rash action with a tragic ending. The novel includes accounts of at-homes, bridge parties, White House musicales, dinners, the St. Gaudens "Grief" monument, and loving descriptions of Washington scenes. The admired figures in the narrative are noted for their intelligence, cultural knowledge, and personal achievements, instead of their wealth or inherited social position.

64. Chatfield-Taylor, Hobart C. *The Vice of Fools.* Illustrated by Raymond M. Crosby. Chicago: Herbert S. Stone, 1897. 310pp.

Through this narrative, Chatfield-Tayler sets out to prove his book's epigraph, written by Alexander Pope, that claims that pride is "the never failing vice of fools." In his account, bureaucrats and elected officials find opportunities in Washington to enter a social arena dominated by international culture represented by members of the diplomatic corps and forever unobtainable to them had they remained in their provincial hometowns. Even though the novel's message is that true gentility is based in intellect (the novel overflows with witty dialogue focused on cutting parvenus down to size), all the characters would agree that money to expend on lavish entertainments is also necessary to establish oneself socially.

The plot centers on a beautiful young woman's behavior as she chooses an appropriate husband. She marries out of pride, selecting a man she knows will bring her political power and wealth. However, she later realizes the true nature of love, and she and her husband give up political and social life to devote themselves to philanthropy. The novel includes descriptions of clothing, social activities (cotillions, balls, golf parties, diplomatic receptions), and Washington types. Although the characters talk a great deal about the role of women in society, an enlarged role for them is never advocated.

65. Chatterton, Ruth. *The Betrayers.* Boston: Houghton Mifflin / Riverside Press, 1953. 310pp.
    Celia Mills, a lawyer, lives in post-World War II Washington and is the wife of Senator William Taylor Mills and the daughter of a former attorney general, Judge Worthington Gregg. William is appointed to a subcommittee investigating possible disloyalty by Atomic Energy Commission physicists. The Mills' social set is eroded by the appointment and other government loyalty investigations. Celia is outraged by the "witch hunts," and her relationship with her husband is endangered, particularly when she begins to take an active role as a defense attorney. The novel captures the dinner conversations, gossip, and political opinions common in the early Cold War period.

66. Chidsey, Alan Lake. *Heintz.* Illustrated by F. Moylan Fitts. Kingsport, Tenn.: Southern Publishers, 1945. 155pp.
    Heintz of Bundy Centre, Iowa, was denied a commission in the Quartermaster Corps. As a German-American, he has known prejudice, and a mob killed his father in Hoboken, New Jersey, during World War I. He decides to go to Washington and make a direct appeal to his senator. During his stay, he is introduced to the wartime city and is surprised by the crowded transportation and rudeness of the inhabitants. Government bureaucracy is fully described, particularly once Heintz is appointed to a civil service position in the Pentagon. Illustrations provide humorous portrayals of the bespectacled Heintz in various settings.

67. Childs, Marquis W. *Washington Calling!* New York: William Morrow, 1937. 280pp.
    Senator Charley Squires is disturbed by the influx of government workers and journalists changing Washington from a town to a city. He lives on Belmont Road, and his great personal sorrow is the death years before of his wife in childbirth to a stillborn son. His current challenge,

the alcoholism of his sister, though troubling, cannot compare. His only consolation is his daughter Darnell and the financial security he has built through his years in office. Squires has had little concern with legislation, focusing his energies on serving the needs of corporate America. He is invigorated when he is contacted by the Esterbrooks, brothers seeking sixty-four million dollars in federal monies to bulk up their once lucrative railroad. Twenty-seven-year-old Darnell, asked along on a trip by private railroad car to meet with the brothers, is introduced to Bob Esterbrook, the heir to the Esterbrook fortune. The senator has little difficulty securing the passage of the legislation favoring the Esterbrooks, even though a new President has taken office after a fiscal crisis and Washington is filled with talk of the "New Age" and Securities and Exchange committee investigations. By the end of the novel prosperity seems to be returning to the country as Squires and his daughter sail for Europe. Observations of the city mostly focus on social events that occur inside houses and clubs, and much is made of the contrast between old Washingtonians and the newcomers attracted by President Winthrop's administration (presumably based on Franklin Roosevelt's New Deal team).

68. Clarke, Arthur C. *Imperial Earth.* New York: Harcourt Brace Jovanovich, 1976. 303pp.

Set in the year 2276, Duncan Makenzie has been sent as an emissary from Titan to Terra (Earth) on the quincentennial of the creation of the United States. He visits a perfected Washington. The perfections reveal the main problems the city faced from the perspective of the 1970s and focus on racial and gender equality and sensitivity to the natural environment.

69. Clemens, Samuel L., and Charles Dudley Warner. *The Gilded Age: A Tale of Today.* Hartford, Conn.: American Publishing, 1874. 574pp.

This collaborative novel has been written about frequently and analyzed extensively. From original manuscripts we know that Clemens wrote the first eleven chapters of the book and created many of the key characters. Although parts of the story are set in Tennessee and Missouri, eventually all the main characters end up in Washington. Colonel Sellers has a scheme to secure congressional appropriations for the Columbus River Slackwater Navigation Company and the Salt Lick Extension of the Pacific Railroad. These projects would enrich him by creating a transportation hub in the remote, unsettled area where he lives and owns land. The Hawkins family is trying to promote the selection of their Tennessee land for the site of Knobs Industrial University, a school that will supposedly benefit freedmen but will actually give the "Christian Statesmen" who sponsor the bill an opportunity to surreptitiously enrich themselves from the natural resources under the land.

Clemens' portraits of senators are often closely based on actual people, and the legislation and court trials in the novel parallel real bills and cases. In addition to giving a name to the great age of speculation after the Civil War (the "Gilded Age"), Clemens' characterization of Washington society as divided between the "Antiques" (he also sometimes refers to them as the "real inhabitants," or the "exclusives") and the "Parvenus" (whom he also labels the "barbarians," and the "mob") has endured. His satires of corrupt politicians, railroad lawyers, rapacious private companies profiting from publicly funded projects, and women lobbyists would be followed by several generations of similar literary attacks.

70. Cleveland, Cynthia Eloise. *His Honor; or, Fate's Mysteries: A Thrilling Realistic Story of the United States Army.* New York: American News, 1889. 258pp.

The novel's convoluted plot generally deals with the redemption of the wrongly besmirched honors of several of the protagonists. Much of the action is set in a past related through jarring flashbacks and centered in the Bad Lands and the Montana Territory. However, the present of the 1880s is primarily set in Washington, D.C. The city is the home base for soldiers who are on leave, retired, or occupying elected office. Several of the female characters have professions, one as a doctor and another as a lawyer. Evocative descriptions of Washington include street sweepers, African American servants on their early morning way to work, huge flocks of birds, milk wagons, Roman Catholic immigrants on their way to early mass, and a child sickened nearly to death by sewer gas in a boarding house.

71. Cleveland, Cynthia Eloise. *See-Saw; or, Civil Service in the Departments by One Of'm.* Detroit, Mich.: F. B. Dickerson, 1887. 226pp.

Much of this novel is told as an extended flashback. Colonel Ralph Winston had courted Margaret Wayland. When Winston suddenly marries another woman, Wayland and her friends decide he is a scoundrel. A lengthy flashback details Margaret's background, including an earlier romantic disappointment and her work for the Woman's Christian Temperance Union, Presbyterian colleges, and the Democratic Party. When her indictments of the Republicans for giving public lands to the railroads are published widely, she becomes a popular speaker and meets Colonel Winston after one of her speeches. When Democrat Grover Cleveland takes office in 1885, Margaret expects a political appointment; instead, she must take the civil service examination. Although she eventually receives an appointment in the Treasury Department, it is only as a substitute at half pay. Despite her own disappointments, when Winston is proposed for an appointment, she offers to use her connections to have him confirmed, although he rejects her offer. During this time period, Margaret and Winston have many lengthy political conversations dealing with civil service reform and the role of women in society. When the novel's action returns to the present, and Margaret discovers that Winston was forced to marry in order to guarantee an appointment in a Western territory, she forgives him. After his bride is killed in a steamboat boiler explosion, Winston returns to Margaret, who finally has a full-time civil service appointment.

72. Colby, Merle. *The Big Secret.* New York: Viking Press, 1949. 373pp.

Daniel Upstead, a young, naive physicist from Berwick College, Maine, travels to Washington, D.C., for a conference at which his former professor and mentor, world-famous physicist Dr. Christopher Trebst, is to speak. When Trebst announces that "the Washington authorities" rescinded their approval, and an agent from the Military Security Commission oversaw the destruction of his paper, Upstead and his colleagues are outraged. These physicists who had grown up between the two world wars believe that there should be no secrets in basic scientific research. Because Upstead needs to use a computer at the Bureau of Industrial Research to perform some calculations, he remains in Washington and tries to see the President to plead the cause of reason. He discovers that a group named the Senate Temporary Committee on Subversive Action and Disloyal Thoughts has been influenced by the powerful Whigs Resurgent for Independent Action to squelch the sharing of scientific research as too dangerous in the atomic age. During his stay in Washington, Upstead talks with politicians, lobbyists, statisticians, and federal scientists and hears all sides of the issue of the free sharing of scientific information. Using the earnest Upstead as a foil, insightful satires of federal agencies, bureaucracy, and the politically powerful people who shape policy are presented. The novel includes descriptions of Washington hotels (including the Shoreham and the Hotel Lee, where Upstead stays and finds a rope-pull elevator), the bohemian artist district in the shadow of St. Matthew's Church, horseback riding in Rock Creek Park, Potomac houseboat life and canoeing, the Cosmos Club, and the National Press Club. Unlike other novels of this and earlier time periods, African Americans are treated with equality and respect by the protagonist.

73. Cole, Cyrenus. *From Four Corners to Washington: A Little Story of Home, Love, War, and Politics.* Cedar Rapids, Iowa: Torch Press, 1920. 80pp.

A farm couple, Mark and Elizabeth Miller, travel from Buena Vista, Iowa, to Washington, D.C., to visit their son Mark Miller, Jr. Mark had been the first in his county to enlist to serve in World War I. In doing so, he followed a long tradition, for a Miller had served in every U.S. war since the Revolution. Mark was among the first American soldiers to arrive in France and fought in the Battle of the Marne and Meuse-Argonne. Even though the war is over, he is still in a hospital with a slow-healing hip wound. When the Millers arrive in Washington, they are pleasantly surprised to find Mark able to walk with the aid of a cane. They are also pleased by the surprise announcement that he has fallen in love and is engaged to marry one of his nurses, who is also from Iowa. When they meet the nurse, they wholly approve, in part because of her no-nonsense dedication to her work. They also meet one of Mark's friends, the recently discharged Sergeant Clarence Watson, who works as a reporter. Most of the novella consists of conversations with Watson in which he expatiates at length on the mismanagement of the war on the home front. Supplying names and figures he presents a nauseated indictment of waste and profiteering. The Millers' Washington sightseeing mostly consists of seeing the War Risk Insurance Building so that Watson can talk about the scandal of how it got built and contrast it with the unfinished Lincoln Memorial. Washington is viewed as a place where even good men lose their way, falling into the temptation of political corruption, and where the rest of the country seems far away. There is also a trip through the Maryland countryside to Camp Holabird, where thousands of never used trucks, automobiles, and motorcycles purchased for the war effort have been left to decay. As an example of Republican campaign literature, official or not, the work's focus on women (who would be voting for the first time in 1920) is of interest.

74. Colver, Anne [Graff, Polly Anne, pseud.]. *Mr. Lincoln's Wife.* New York: Farrar & Rinehart, 1943. 406pp.

The novel covers Mary Todd Lincoln's life from 1837 until 1881. The focus throughout is on Mrs. Lincoln's personality as revealed through her interactions with others. The portions set in Washington are mostly focused on the White House, the "summer White House" at the Soldier's Home, and on specific historic events. Mary Todd's attempt to win the acceptance of Washington society and end its domination by Southerners is recounted, and, later, debates are rehearsed over the form official socializing should have in time of war. Changing attitudes toward the war and the social status of African Americans in the city are also discussed.

75. Copley, Frank Barkley. *The Impeachment of President Israels.* New York: Macmillan, 1913. 124pp.

This extended first person narrative by "Mr. McIntosh," the personal secretary of David Israels, recounts Israels' rise to political prominence and the reasons for his impeachment. As a Jew and millionaire, whose fortune, in good part, came from inherited wealth, Israels was an unlikely candidate for public office and was reluctantly called to service. Previously, he was primarily interested in philanthropies of his own creation. A firm believer in democracy, he treats the members of the public as equals and wins their respect and votes by appealing to their higher nature. This is in contrast to other politicians who appeal to their prejudices and appetitive natures. When Germany begins arming and kills some American sailors, President Israels believes he can prevent war by addressing the higher nature of German politicians. Furthermore, he does not begin arming the United States, since to do so would lead directly to armed conflict. In public addresses he espouses the belief that human evolution is a sign of divine providence, claiming that war between nations of similar stages of advancement can be prevented. Public outcry against the "white-livered Jew" is unrelenting, engendering impeachment proceedings when Israels orders the Navy to sail to Turkey to take part in ceremonies to which they had been committed long before. This action leaves the United States defenseless against naval attack. When Israels appears before the U.S. Senate his address reverberates around the world. He claims it was his duty to prevent the American people from following their basest instincts in clamoring for vengeance and to trust that the German government would make appropriate reparation for the death of the American sailors. He also points out that sending the U.S. Navy on a peaceful mission demonstrates the trust he has in German civilization, a civilization that he analyzes and praises extensively. Although he quells the impeachment and forces Germany to make appropriate reparation, the strain of resisting the masses and making his final extemporaneous speech expends all of his strength. He collapses and dies after reasserting that evolution is now taking place on the mental, rather than the physical, plain.

76. Crane, Laura Dent. *The Automobile Girls at Washington; or, Checkmating the Plots of Foreign Spies.* Philadelphia: Henry Altemus, 1913. 253pp. young adult.

High school senior Barbara Thurston and her younger sister Mollie are traveling once again with their friends Grace Carter and wealthy Ruth Stuart in Ruth's automobile. Their past adventures, in which they foiled criminals and solved mysteries, have earned them newspaper coverage and the sobriquet, the "Automobile Girls." In this adventure, they visit Ruth's cousin, Harriet Hamlin, in Washington, D.C. Harriet is the daughter of Assistant Secretary of State William Hamlin. The girls are thrilled to sightsee in the capital and receive invitations to official functions, such as receptions, dinner at the Chinese Embassy, and lunch with the President. Barbara, however, must thwart spies who want to steal documents from Hamlin's office in order to redeem her reputation for honesty, which the spies have besmirched through false accusations. She is aided by a young woman who must earn her living as a newspaper reporter by covering social events and society figures. Although specific places in Washington are not described in much detail, many aspects of upper-middle-class life are presented.

77. Crawford, Theron Clark. *A Man and His Soul.* New York: Charles B. Reed, 1894. 255pp.

An investigative reporter meets and befriends a retired U.S. Navy officer, Captain Harcourt, who has experienced a deep spiritual enlightenment that he shares and uses to transform Washington society. After defusing several political conflicts, Harcourt has an opportunity to influence the President and commence building an improved society. Harcourt resides at the Arlington Hotel, and scenes of hotel life, including comments on the African American staff and the politicians in residence, figure prominently. Theosophical discourses, including occult experiments, form a backdrop for discussions of true honor, gentility, and morality against which the behavior of ignoble politicians are measured. Descriptions of receptions, balls, official and unofficial dinners, the gallery of the U.S. Senate, horseback riding, and carriage driving are included, and a panoply of Washington characters, particularly socially powerful women and politically powerful men, are introduced. The novel implicitly criticizes the way politicians make political appointments and concern themselves with social precedence. The work's reform message includes an extended description of the ideal nation the

United States could become if each individual cultivated his soul through practicing love, charity, kindness, and aesthetic appreciation. In this novel, cultivation of one's soul involves developing an ability to literally see one's inward essence.

78. Crissey, Forrest. *Tattlings of a Retired Politician.* Illustrated by John T. McCutcheon. Chicago: Clarkson & Cooper, 1904. 487pp.

In the guise of a seasoned politician writing to a younger colleague, the author relates fictionalized accounts of political campaigns, legislative battles, party politics, and power brokering. The general setting for this material is Capitol Hill.

79. Cruger, Mrs. Julie Grinnell [Gordon, Julien, pseud.]. *The Wage of Character.* New York: D. Appleton, 1901. 272pp.

The novel contrasts representatives of Hudson River aristocracy, in the person of Hazard Thorne, with rich Westerners, in the personae of Hamilton Darrell and his sister Coralie. Thorne, physically attractive, full of vitality, and with cultured tastes but no significant income, is compared with Darrell, who is timid, self-effacing, plain, and extremely wealthy. When the two meet at Harvard, Darrell devotes himself to Thorne and eventually hints that if Thorne could meet his sister he would find her an appropriate bride. Furthermore, should the two marry, Darrell would settle half his wealth on the couple. They do meet, and their intense attraction for each other quickly leads to marriage. Settling in New York, the direct, vital Coralie has difficulty making her way socially, despite the tutelage of an effeminate bachelor. However, when Thorne is elected to Congress, Coralie has a chance to enter a social milieu that rewards energy and intelligence. She is extravagantly happy in Washington, until, despairing over Thorne's character flaws, she separates from him, eventually moving to Rome and becoming the most respectable and fulfilled of "matrons" in the Classical sense of that word. The novel's view of the newly rich as admirable and of Washington as a social environment where strength of character can bring social advancement is in marked contrast to other novels written at the time.

80. Cunningham, Chet [Derrick, Lionel, pseud.]. *Capitol Hell.* Los Angeles: Pinnacle Books, 1974. 188pp.

Mark Hardin exposed a military insider ring that diverted supplies to the black market that were intended for U.S. troops. The illicit gain enriched corrupt U.S. officers, as well as South Vietnamese officials. Instead of being celebrated Hardin was reviled for his disloyalty and imprisoned. After his release, he focused his civilian life on destroying the Mafia, a role he performed so successfully that he has earned the nickname "The Penetrator." When Fred Walters, a friend of Hardin's who has recently been appointed a White House secretary, is shot on the grounds of the White House, Hardin rushes to Washington to investigate. He eventually realizes that members of an exclusive club, the Société Internationale d'Élite, are responsible. Among the members are important businessmen, politicians, embassy staff, and Mafia members. They have gained influence over the Vice President and are plotting to assassinate the President. Hardin thwarts their scheme, but not before a great deal of bloodshed. Except for mentions of the Washington Hotel, the Tidal Basin, Arlington, and George Washington University Hospital, little of the content is specific to Washington, D.C.

81. Curtis, Isabel Gordon. *The Congresswoman*. Chicago: Browne & Howell, 1914. 505pp.

At the end of an unhappy marriage, a woman is left widowed on the Oklahoma frontier with her difficult, grown children. Initially, she fears poverty; however she discovers that her husband owned ten miles of supposedly worthless land on which oil has been found. Released from her burdensome marriage and financial worries, she is receptive to the appeals of local suffragettes to run for Congress. However, her Washington experiences transform her perspective, and she culminates her successful political life with a speech in which she claims that universal woman's suffrage is just as wrong as universal suffrage. She announces the formation of a commission to prevent the "immigrant rabble" from having the right to cast ballots. She later resigns her position to marry and return to the domestic life that she decides is more suitable for women than politics.

82. Curtis, Isabel Gordon. *The Woman from Wolverton: A Story of Washington Life*. New York: Century, 1912. 342pp.

Pauline's husband, Lemuel Shipe, is elected to Congress after a long career as a lawyer in the small Western town of Wolverton. The senator who shepherded his nomination through the Republican political machine makes it clear to Pauline that she will be crucial to Lemuel's political success. Because of the couple's early financial struggles, Pauline has great sympathy for workers and people of modest means. When the couple arrives in Washington, the city is seen from her perspective, that of a down-to-earth housekeeper, so there is a great deal of description of clothing and domestic arrangements. In addition to employing her intuition and common sense to advance his career, Lemuel assigns Pauline the duty of "breaking into Society." She is daunted by the task, which seems overwhelming. However, she quickly discovers that if one serves good food, people will come to one's house and issue reciprocal invitations. Pauline's skills as housekeeper and hostess are accompanied by a strong moral sense that helps her serve as Lemuel's conscience. As a member of the District Committee, he is poised to accept a land deal that is clearly a bribe by real estate developers. Pauline asks enough questions so that Lemuel turns down the deal, avoiding the scandal that envelops other politicians. However, she is involved in a minor scandal after a journalist tricks her into sharing her anti-suffragette views. The book includes the text of the lengthy speech she makes before a woman's group to successfully defend her position. Although Lemuel is cheated out of office when a corporation backs the opposing party candidate, he returns to Wolverton with his integrity intact. The couple realizes that they met many cunning, self-serving people in Washington, but they also discovered people of true worth and maintained their own sense of honor and patriotism. Pauline is happy to return to her modest house in Wolverton, but their senator friend believes Lemuel will one day be a senator and hopes Pauline will continue to support him in getting to know the common, rural people and their needs and ways of looking at life.

83. Dahlgren, Madeleine Vinton. *Chim: His Washington Winter.* New York: C. L. Webster, 1892. 334pp.

Dahlgren presents Washington society through the experiences of Chim, a Skye terrier, and his mistress Alma, "a brave, talented, handsome, musical, beautiful," but genteelly impoverished, young lady. Chim arrives in the city before his mistress, taken there by gypsies who have stolen him. The good manners Alma taught him quickly earn him a place in the house of a society woman. She is interested in spiritualism and believes Chim to be a reincarnated Anglican cleric. The proof lies in the way he drinks tea by raising the cup to his muzzle with his paws. Chim is reunited with Alma when she arrives with a letter of introduction to his interim protector. Dog and owner travel in high society circles heavily populated with spiritualists. Through a series of coincidences, Chim reveals a secret that enables Alma to inherit the fortune that should have been hers all along.

84. Dahlgren, Madeleine Vinton. *A Washington Winter.* Boston: James R. Osgood, 1883. 247pp.

In her preface, Dahlgren declares her intention to present certain "Washington types," interspersed with descriptions of actual "public men" to add historical interest. The novel is framed by the beginning and end of the social season: New Year's Day and Ash Wednesday. Although presented in the form of a novel, the main plot, which revolves around romance and marriage for the debutantes, is subsidiary to details about social life in Washington that could be used as a guidebook for the uninitiated. Everything from the days on which the wives of political officials receive guests, to the hours for various meals, to the proper etiquette for card leaving is covered. Often information is provided by counter-example, especially when Mrs. Wilton and her friends describe the faux pas of the newly wealthy and the high-ranked politicians of lowly origins.

One politician, Silvester [*sic*] Spangler, is described at great length. The only son of a poor widow, Spangler began as an agent in the Indian Territory, where his fraudulent activities brought suffering to the Indians and wealth to himself. When he had accumulated enough capital, he moved to the city, bought a mansion, devoted himself to entertaining the powerful to gain publicity, and was soon elected to political office.

Dahlgren also portrays Mme. Beaulieu, a Southern plantation owner's daughter who has returned to the United States to present a claim against the government based on wartime "use" of her family's lands. In doing so Dahlgren depicts the claims system with its lobbyists and politicians ready to sell their influence. Generals Grant, Sherman, and Garfield all appear, as do former carpet baggers who are now wealthy politicians.

As the social season progresses, teas, lunches, and balls are described, and gentlemen and gentlewomen are contrasted with "vulgarians," most of whom, including Spangler, receive their comeuppance by the novel's conclusion. Throughout the work Dahlgren's criticism of inappropriate behavior by the nouveaux riches (not providing chaperones for young women, not making introductions, ostentation, constructing houses for their size instead of as architectural statements) has a pedagogical intent. The dominant message is that true social status cannot be purchased but must derive from "merit, or inherited respectability."

85. Dahlgren, Madeleine Vinton. *The Woodley Lane Ghost.* Philadelphia: D. Biddle, 1899. 474pp.

This book of short stories includes tales set in the Blue Ridge Mountains, New Orleans, New York City, Paris, western Pennsylvania, and Washington, D.C. In some way all of the stories involve Eastern religions and the supernatural. In the title story, Dr. Rawle, a physician, and his new wife, Cynthia, are driving their carriage on Woodley Lane in Washington when they see a bicyclist have an accident. They drive the injured man to his substantial house on Tenleytown Road. He is a scientist and refuses treatment since he knows it will be useless, asking instead that Dr. Rawle fetch his lawyer. The cyclist turns out to be Java Aleim, a respected Brahmin, and immediately after willing his house and possessions to the physician and his wife, he dies. The two are happy and rich until supernatural events plague them and the wife becomes ill and dies.

Four other stories in the volume have Washington settings. In "The Amulet Ring" a dying clairvoyant confesses to her daughter Alida that they are not actually related and that she had kidnapped Alida as an infant many years before. Her real father is a U.S. Army general living in Washington, where Alida is reunited with him. An incipient opera prima donna finds success in "Earth Bound" after she moves to D.C., where talent and intelligence are rewarded with social acclaim. Her story turns tragic when the wicked tenor who has manipulated her into marrying him dies and begins haunting her Washington mansion. In "Trouble of a Double," newly elected Congressman Frank Heminway travels to Washington without his wife. Unbeknownst to him, a man who is his double is also in D.C. pursuing a young woman. When an acquaintance sees this couple and mistakes the man for Frank, she causes trouble by reporting back to Mrs. Heminway. The protagonist of "Poor Author," a young girl with literary talent and ambition, moves to D.C. because she believes it to be a literary center where she will receive the recognition she deserves. After a period of poverty, she ends up in a lunatic asylum.

86. Dall, Caroline. *Patty Gray's Journey: From Baltimore to Washington.* Boston: Lee & Shepherd, 1870. 283pp. young adult.
     This novel is part of a series entitled *Patty Gray's Journey to the Cotton Islands* intended to inspire children to think about the causes of the Civil War and the needs of freedmen. Patty Gray, a Bostonian, wanted to see slavery first hand and traveled to Washington in the 1850s. In 1868, she revisits the South to observe the conditions of freedmen. Patty and her parents stay in a scientist's household in Washington and through him meet artists and anthropologists who talk about the American Indians in the West and Egypt. They are also served food and drink from other countries that Patty finds exotic. While in D.C., the family spends a good deal of time visiting "colored schools" and Howard University. However, they also visit more common tourist sites and get very thorough tours of the Capitol and White House.

87. Darling, Mrs. Flora Adams. *A Social Diplomat.* New York: National Book, 1889. 186pp.
No additional information available.

88. Darling, Flora Adams. *A Winning, Wayward Woman: Chapters in the Heart-History of Amélie Warden.* Judge's Novels 4. New York: Judge, 1889. 158pp.
No additional information available.

89. Davidov, Len, and Bob Mooney as told to Lou Marco. *The Zinger.* New York: Zebra Books / Kensington, 1976. 238pp.
When new typewriters valued at seventy-five thousand dollars are stolen from the Department of the Interior, the D.C. police commissioner orders a raid on the largest fencing operation in the city. The typewriters are recovered and the fencing operation closed down, but none of the criminals are convicted. This experience, and many others like it, inspire the police to set up their own fencing operation so that they can scrupulously gather evidence to convict every criminal who comes through the doors (the criminals need to provide two forms of identification and are secretly photographed). The detailed characterizations of the criminals and the police present a range of Washington types (recent Polish, Irish, Italian, and Puerto Rican immigrants; the beautiful, wealthy, kleptomaniac wife of a highly placed State Department officer; and African American police officers and criminals) and convey a sense of social tensions along the divides of class and race. Specific types of crimes against the government are detailed, and Northeast D.C., the 14th Street, NW, corridor, and the Embassy District are all used as settings. Several characters relate information about the sociological determinants of crime and the problems of incarceration and recidivism. The novel ends with a grand party in honor of a New York "Godfather." The "Don" is, of course, a policeman, and his colleagues arrest 185 of the fencers.

90. Davies, Acton, and Charles Nirdlinger. *The First Lady in the Land; or, When Dolly Todd Took Boarders.* Illustrated by Howard Giles. New York: H. K. Fly, 1912. 309pp.
The first two-thirds of this book are set in Philadelphia where Dolly Todd, a young widow, operates a boarding house patronized by politicians during the legislative session of the U.S. government. Both Thomas Jefferson, a friend of hers from childhood, and Aaron Burr, who is infatuated with Dolly, stay with her. Other boarders are an English ambassador and his wife, and other persons of influence. Historical

figures like George and Martha Washington and Madam Jumel play important roles in the novel, which is mostly a tale of romance. Dolly's most ardent suitor, Aaron Burr, introduces her to James Madison, who is immediately attracted to her. The story of Dolly's romantic life is told against the historical background of Jefferson's election to the Presidency, the conflict between Burr and Hamilton, and their duel. Burr's role in the duel proves decisive in Dolly's consideration of whom she will marry; she chooses Madison. The two travel to the Federal City, where Madison takes up his responsibilities as secretary of state, and Dolly sets up a domestic establishment for the unmarried Jefferson in the White House and serves as official hostess. Although many politicians and diplomats are disdainful of the new city, Dolly is not concerned about the rough conditions. She comments on the pleasant, rural setting and appreciates the equality that the uncomfortable conditions impose on everyone, from the President to the stable hand. Throughout the novel, much is made of Jefferson's disdain for social pretense, and his disregard for ceremony receives a good deal of comment in the Washington section of the novel.

91. Davis, Harriet Riddle. *In Sight of the Goddess: A Tale of Washington Life.* Philadelphia: J. B. Lippincott, 1896. 228pp.
     After difficulty finding work (despite his college education and law degree), Stephen Barradale, a native-born Washingtonian with social connections, enters the civil service. He is subsequently appointed personal assistant to Secretary of State Horatio Childs, an affluent man from the West who had been appointed because of his wealth. To Barradale's surprise his job mostly consists of teaching the cabinet member and his family the skills necessary to advance in society. Much of Barradale's time is spent keeping Mrs. Childs' visiting book, making out her visiting list, and arranging the social functions she hosts. His major consolation is the beauty of the Childs' daughter, Constance. Constance also develops an interest in him, and the novel is written in their alternating voices

92. Davis, Mary Lee. *Polly and the President.* Illustrated by Jan Jackson. Minneapolis, Minn.: Lerner, 1967. 32pp. juvenile.
     Polly, a little girl interested in television news programs and newspaper accounts of the President, travels with her parents to Washington. The first night in town she is delighted to eat at a Chinese restaurant and to read her fortune from a cookie. The next morning she wakes early, sneaks out of the hotel, and goes back to Chinatown to buy a bag of fortune cookies. Carrying out the rest of her plan, she goes to the

White House and, spotting the President walking across the lawn to a press conference, hurries after him. Eluding the guards and overcoming her fear at being challenged by the Secret Service officers, she gives the president her "advice." The press enthusiastically captures the event, and Polly gets to spend the day at the White House. By the next day, her story is on television and in newspapers across the country.

93. De Forest, John William. *Honest John Vane.* New Haven, Conn.: Richmond & Patten, 1875. 259pp.

John Vane, an icebox manufacturer from Slowburgh, is a simple businessman at the beginning of this novel. His sincerity and irreproachable background make him an ideal candidate for a congressional election in which the last holder of the office was forced to resign bemired in scandal. When Vane publicly denounces an attempted bribe, he wins the title "Honest John Vane." His ambitious wife, who rejected his first marriage proposal but, after his election, enthusiastically accepted his second, forces him to spend more money than he earns so that she can establish herself in Washington society. The prospect of deepening debt and the observation that every other lawmaker supports "special legislation" eventually leads Vane into complicity with the "Great Subfluvial" scheme to build a roadway underneath the Mississippi River (a satire of the Credit Mobilier whose agents, in the guise of railroad builders, corrupted Congress and looted the U.S. Treasury). Although a scandal ensues, the newly wily Vane escapes with his honor intact. The novel decries the tax system and the use of federal funds to aid private corporations, but few insights are provided into the city outside the halls of Congress.

94. De Forest, John William. *Justine's Lovers.* Library of American Fiction 2. New York: Harper's & Brothers, 1878. 135pp.

Bostonians Justine Vane and her widowed mother are very wealthy women, and Justine has received a marriage proposal from a young, New York lawyer with many prospects and from a good family. However, the Vanes' world crumbles when bonds signed by the deceased Mr. Vane come due and the other bond holders, former business partners, abscond, leaving the creditors to pursue the Vanes for the full amount. They lose everything, and Justine's fiancé forces her to withdraw from their engagement. Nearly destitute, Justine moves to Washington to live with family friends near Howard University (in a house that is said to look like an upended brick) and seek a civil service appointment. Her efforts and the efforts of her acquaintances to lend support meet with dismal results, and she is forced to open a kindergarten.

Eventually, she accepts the marriage proposal of a wealthy, older suitor, whom she decides she must marry out of respect and need, rather than out of love. However, the suitor dies on a trip to San Francisco throwing everyone into despair until his will is discovered and Justine is named his primary beneficiary. The novel addresses the role of women, racial prejudice, and civil service corruption. Unlike many Washington novels of this period, descriptions here are of lower-middle-class Washington social life.

95. De Forest, John William. *Playing the Mischief.* Illustrated by John Hyde. New York: Harper, 1875. 185pp.

This satirical tale, set during the Grant administration, focuses on the claims system, and the female lobbyists use wiles to sway legislators. Although Grant receives no direct criticism, the thinly disguised Benjamin Franklin Butler (appearing as General Bangs) is heaped with scorn. In addition, the character Jessie Cohen, a painter who lives on government commissions achieved through political machinations, bears some resemblance to sculptress Vinnie Ream. Subsidiary topics include currency reform, the journalistic distortion of Civil War battles that advanced the political careers of some veterans, Darwinian theory, and women's suffrage.

The narrative centers on Josephine Murray who travels to Washington to pursue a claim for a barn destroyed during the War of 1812 (a short time before De Forest's work was published, Congress had passed legislation funding pensions for veterans and widows of the war that had been fought more than sixty years before). Murray is coached by other female lobbyists in how to pursue claims and build alliances with politicians through playing upon personal allure.

Although a political satire, De Forest presents a great deal of information about the physical realities of life in Washington before Alexander Shepherd's public engineering projects were completed. He also provides insights into the establishment of social class through what was later described as conspicuous consumption. One of his catalogs of domestic and sartorial luxuries occupies several pages and concludes with one of the female lobbyists literally smacking her lips at the ostentation. The contrast of such luxury with the sparsely furnished rooms in which the claims seekers are forced to entertain is sharply drawn.

96. Deiss, Joseph Jay. *A Washington Story.* New York: Duell, Sloan & Pearce, 1950. 313pp.

Faith Vance lives with her husband in Georgetown. The couple have two young children and an African American maid, but Faith is the sole support of the family. Her husband, Thatcher, is a veteran who has been an alcoholic since his discharge from the U.S. Navy. Faith works as executive assistant to Duval Cunningham, a man who had come to Washington as a New Dealer and has an important position in the State Department. When Faith receives a subpoena to appear before the House Committee on Un-American Activities, her world begins to fall apart. By the end of the novel, her patriotism has been questioned, her reputation ruined, and her marriage destroyed. In addition to capturing what it was like to be attacked as a Communist, the novel describes 1950s Washington.

97. Denison, Mary Andrews. *That Husband of Mine.* Library of Popular Fiction 36. New York: American News, 1905. 227pp.

Unlike many other works published around the same time, this book does not focus on society figures, but on middle-class domestic life. The main characters are Washingtonians with respectable white-collar jobs and enough money to live in a row house, but not enough to have servants or a carriage. Although there is a good deal of joking about these privations, on the whole the characters are satisfied with their lot and their domestic arrangements.

Protagonists Charlie and Elsa live on G Street, NW. When Elsa's sister Lina visits, she meets Jack Inglehart, a great friend of Charlie's who lives in a boarding house nearby, and the two fall in love. However, Mr. St. Olave, an older bank manager in Lina's hometown of Scranton, New York, was already courting her. St. Olave, unlike Jack, can provide handsomely for Lina's material comfort. After much soul searching, Lina is persuaded that it is all right to choose a love match over a more calculated match, and she and Jack marry and buy a house only a few doors away from Charlie and Elsa. Interestingly, although Lina chooses love over wealth, St. Olave dies a few years later and bequeaths Lina a significant amount of money so that she has both love and wealth. The novel details domestic arrangements, relations between men and women, and interactions among neighborhood residents.

98. Derville, Leslie. *The Other Side of the Story: A Novel.* New York: G. W. Dillingham, 1904. 318pp.

When pretty and innocent Gertrude Downing of Corinth, Tennessee, travels to Washington to begin a job as a government clerk with the U.S. Census Bureau, she is filled with hope for her future. As her co-workers initiate her to life in a government office, disillusionment sets in; despair soon follows, which leads her to suicide. The novel is filled with details that seem to be drawn from first-hand observation. Convincing descriptions are given of boarding house life, the working life of female government employees and their interactions with each other and their superiors, the relations between men and women, and the nature of official receptions. Although love affairs and personal tragedy fill the plot, the main purpose of the novel is to condemn the corruption of the civil service system.

99. DeVries, Julian. *The Campfire Girls at the White House.* Cleveland, Ohio: World Syndicate, 1935. 250pp. young adult.

Five members of Oakdale's Wa-Wan-Da den of the Campfire Girls have been selected by the group's national commander, the First Lady, to go to Washington, D.C., and help organize an effort to enlist Campfire Girls all over the country to improve living conditions for underprivileged girls. The Oakdale girls travel by airplane to the capital and stay at the White House. The girls are quickly utilized in a public relations effort to support the passage of the Coe Bill to raise the standard of living of the poor. The bill is opposed by a "Western syndicate" of wealthy men. The girls use Campfire Girl dens to persuade people to write letters in support of the Coe Bill to legislators. As part of their responsibilities, the girls learn about the workings of the legislative process. They also find time to enjoy typical Washington sites and activities and are invited to the teas and receptions of official Washington society. Because of their success, in the second half of the novel the girls are recruited for a top-secret mission.

100. Dillon, Mary C. *The Patience of John Morland.* Illustrated by C. M. Relyea. New York: Doubleday, Page, 1909. 406pp.

This work retells the story of Margaret "Peggy" O'Neale Eaton (1796-1879). In her preface, the author notes that she has changed names in order to give herself some latitude in creating a work of fiction. However, most historic characters keep their names or are easily identifiable. Peggy, "Kitty McCabe" here, is portrayed as a "natural" figure, unspoiled by the airs of civilization, who also happens to be more beautiful than other women. After an early infatuation almost ends in elopement at the age of fifteen, she is sent to boarding school, first in New York City, then at Miss English's school in Georgetown. Her later social difficulties are ascribed to the revenge taken on her by a snubbed lover and the laziness of an African American servant woman assigned to chaperone her. The novel is filled with details of federal period social life (dress, etiquette, food, and the elements of social status and reputation), as well as dramatizations of famous politicians

and historical events. After the suicide of her first husband and her re-
marriage to an early true love, Eaton still faces unfair gossip, but by the
end of the book she escapes by accompanying her husband on his posting as ambassador to Spain.

101. Dos Passos, John. *District of Columbia.* Boston: Houghton Mifflin, 1952. 446pp.
    This volume brings together the trilogy *Adventures of a Young
Man* (1939), *Number One* (1943), and *The Grand Design* (1949). The
first of these is not set in Washington. The other two novels are listed
here and discussed separately in the year of their publications.

102. Dos Passos, John. *The Grand Design.* Boston: Houghton Mifflin,
1949. 440pp.
    This is the third in Dos Passos' *District of Columbia* trilogy. He
uses two characters to tell his story of New Deal Washington—Millard
Carroll and Paul Graves. Carroll is a successful businessman and has
accepted an appointment as the head of a New Deal agency. Graves is a
subordinate official in Carroll's agency. Through Carroll, who has a job
just under cabinet rank, Dos Passos explores the viewpoint of high-
level government officials, and through Graves he presents the impact
of the New Deal on the lives of Americans outside Washington. Carroll
arrives in Washington filled with idealism but is soon disillusioned by
the power that has accumulated in the hands of non-elected officials in
government agencies and the way their decision making has more to do
with advancing their own power than serving the American people.
Carroll struggles against the bureaucracy that is destroying the ideals he
embraced. Through his character, the reader comes to understand the
degree to which parties and other Washington social events are used to
perpetuate and increase political power. Graves, a foot soldier in the
New Deal, must rely upon Carroll as he constantly struggles with department officials and, when Carroll is forced to resign, has no options
but to also leave office.

103. Dos Passos, John. *Number One.* Boston: Houghton Mifflin, 1943.
303pp.
    This is the second book in Dos Passos' *District of Columbia* tril-
ogy. Homer T. "Chuck" Crawford is a demagogue from the fictional
town of Texarkola. Knowing nothing of Crawford's actual practices,
Tyler Spotswood, looking for leadership, is inspired by the ideals that
Crawford preaches and his man of the people background and mode of
address. Spotswood is employed as Crawford's private secretary, de-

voting himself to getting Congressman Crawford elected to the Senate. Ostensibly Crawford's campaign manager, Spotswood does not realize that Crawford wins the election through secret deals and manipulation. However, Spotswood begins to realize Crawford's wickedness when he befriends Sue Ann Crawford, the senator's wife, and must lie to her about Crawford's drinking and parties with dancing girls. Soon after Crawford's election, he secretly organizes a corporation to take advantage of oil leases on public lands in his state, making Spotswood a dummy officer. He also uses the corporation to fund his Every Man a Millionaire Corporation and a radio station that he uses to promote himself. He collects high salaries from both these endeavors. When Crawford begins attacking the administration of President Franklin D. Roosevelt, an investigation of the oil company begins and Spotswood is called upon to testify. Totally disillusioned and fully understanding Crawford's malevolence, Spotswood still refuses to turn state's evidence. He does not want to hurt Sue Ann and believes that nothing can really hurt Crawford. He decides that remaining loyal to his ideal is more important than saving himself from jail.

104. Douglas, Amanda Minnie. *Honor Sherburne.* New York: Dodd, Mead, 1904. 340pp.
    Honor begins her life in Washington as a newlywed. Her husband, Edward Sherburne, is a widely respected lawyer and associate of an important firm. Husband and wife each come from long-settled, cultivated, upper-middle-class families with ancestors who were professionals engaged in public service, including national politics. With only a slight plot to intrude, the author details the material culture, social engagements, and foodways of upper-middle-class Washingtonians around the turn of the twentieth century. Honor often engages in dialogues about the role of women (she is a college graduate), marrying for love versus other reasons, and the true marks of gentility (which are never to be confused with wealth, even though in rare instances the wealthy can be cultured). Decades after the post-Civil War expansion of the federal government, the Washington of this novel is filled not just with politicians but with skilled men, including economists, scientists, and scholars. Furthermore, for many of the people in the novel, the Washington season is just one of several seasons that are just as likely to include Paris or Rome, as well as New York.

105. Douglas, Amanda Minnie. *A Little Girl in Old Washington.* New York: Dodd, Mead, 1900. 319pp.
    Through the eyes of the extended Mason family (Patricia, Jacque-

line, and Randolph) and Annis Bouvier, Douglas tells the story of historical events at the time of the Madison administration, including the construction of the Federal City and the War of 1812.

106. Drake, Alice. *Miss Hutchinson Steps Out.* New York: House of Field / Doubleday, 1946. 77pp. juvenile.

The doll, Miss Hutchinson, is a Washingtonian, but in the course of the novel spends very little time in that city. She travels to Vermont, Seattle, and Ohio. She is named for Anne Hutchinson. The book's author seems to have been the wife or daughter of a politician and, in a preface, she notes that she tried to capture the relationship between her own daughter and the doll Miss Hutchinson. One of the most vivid descriptions of Washington focuses on a women's reception hosted by Eleanor Roosevelt. Speakers include Senator Carraway, Alice Rodgers Hager (one of the novelists included here), Fannie Hurst, and Representative Edith Rogers. Miss Hutchinson spends a good deal of time traveling, and the passenger train experience of the time is described. During one of the trips Orson Welles' "War of the Worlds" broadcast is on air, and there are comments about the reactions of other passengers.

107. Drury, Allen. *Advise and Consent.* Garden City, N.Y.: Doubleday, 1959. 616pp.

When the President nominates Bob Leffingwell to be secretary of state, Robert Durham Munson, majority leader of the U.S. Senate, knows he will face a major struggle in seeing Leffingwell confirmed. During thirteen years in public service, Leffingwell has been able to convince a significant majority of journalists to write about him favorably and support him on issues. Legislators, however, have found him arrogant and resent the fact that he can take matters directly to the people and significantly shape public opinion. Those most opposed to his appointment scorn him as a compromiser, never taking a strongly held position, but always equivocating, trying to find some gray area between conflicting principles. The senators consider his appointment to be of great consequence because of the Communist threat, the fact that the President does not seem well, and because Vice President Harley Hudson is a weak man. Everyone knows Leffingwell would wield the real power if the President were to die.

Drury tells his story from the perspectives of four senators, although he includes depictions of many other senators, giving the background of these men and the allegiances and animosities that exist between them. He also presents other powerbrokers in Washington who do not hold office, including members of the diplomatic corps and

Washington's powerful hostesses. One of these is Dolly Harrison, who came to Washington hoping correctly that she could buy her way to influence. Everyone of importance attends parties at her mansion, Vagaries, and the events often receive national attention. She has pledged her support to Munson and frequently uses her social events to assist him.

By the end of the novel, Leffingwell's nomination has been defeated, the President has died, and the Soviets have made a successful manned landing on the moon. Although the plot of the novel focuses on political matters, Drury describes the important role played by the legislators' personal lives and their interactions off Capitol Hill.

108. Drury, Allen. *Come Nineveh, Come Tyre: The Presidency of Edward M. Jason.* Garden City, N.Y.: Doubleday, 1973. 492pp.

The novel begins with an account of what happened at the Washington Monument in *Preserve and Protect*, answering, as that novel does not, the question of who was killed: Orrin Knox and Governor Jason's wife. This book tells the story of Jason's presidency. By the end of the novel he has made accommodations to the Soviets on all fronts and is about to sign a treaty that would provide for the withdrawal of U.S. forces around the world and cede the leadership role in peace keeping and foreign policy to the Soviets.

109. Drury, Allen. *Preserve and Protect.* Garden City, N.Y.: Doubleday, 1968. 405pp.

In an election year, U.S. involvement in the African country of Gorotoland to combat Communist insurgency is on the rise, and an anti-American plot is about to explode in Panama. When President Hudson is killed in the crash of Air Force One, the country is thrown into disarray, and the recently ended struggles of his party's nominating convention reopen. After a long conflict and despite Orrin Knox's opposition to everything Governor Edward Jason stands for, Knox finally concludes it is best for the country to choose Jason as his Vice Presidential running mate. However, on the day the two are to publicly announce their campaign on the grounds of the Washington Monument, one of them is killed, although the novel ends without telling us which.

110. Drury, Allen. *The Promise of Joy.* Garden City, N.Y.: Doubleday, 1975. 445pp.

Like *Come Nineveh, Come Tyre*, the novel begins with an account of what happened at the Washington Monument in *Preserve and Protect*, but provides a different answer to who was killed: Governor Jason and Orrin Knox's wife. This book tells the story of Orrin Knox's presidency. By the end of the novel, the war that has begun between Russia and China has escalated to include nuclear weapons, and Knox has made a decision, left unanswered in the novel, about which side to support.

111. Eaton, Paul Webster. *The Treasure.* New York: R. F. Fenno, 1909. 410pp.

This swashbuckling, action-filled tale is set during the War of 1812, and its action ranges up and down the East Coast and as far away as the Goodwin Sands off the coast of England. Young John Webster discovers the location of Captain Kidd's treasure, hidden about 125 years before, on Jewell Island near his home off Falmouth. Before Webster can recover the treasure, however, a modern-day British privateer and spy, Roland Courtenay, becomes his rival for the booty, as well as for the hand of the woman he wishes to marry. With the treasure in his possession, Courtenay and his ship become involved in the action of the War of 1812. Eventually, he and Webster are both in Washington. Courtenay is there as a spy and Webster, through a letter of introduction from cousin Daniel Webster, as a guest at the White House. John Webster participates in the battle that leads to the capture of Washington and helps Dolly Madison escape. When he goes back to recover the inadvertently abandoned Declaration of Independence, he witnesses an accident that engulfs the White House in flames. Many dramatic scenes later, after a sea chase over the ocean, he observes the drowning of his rival and the sinking of the treasure within a short distance of the English coast. The author relied on numerous historical resources to construct his narrative, duly footnoting certain passages, although he provides no separate bibliography. The novel describes Washington in 1814 in detail and at some length, as well as the city's surroundings, historic personages, sea battles, and capture by the British.

112. Eberhart, Mignon Good. *The Man Next Door.* New York: Random House, 1943. 281pp.

This novel of political suspense is set in a World War II Washington filled with spies and newly arrived government workers, many of them women. The protagonist is Maida Lovell, secretary to Steve Blake, a man with an important position in a government agency that patriotism motivated him to accept. As she tries to solve a murder and avoid a blackmailer who demands state secrets, she moves through a backdrop of offices, carbon paper, filing cabinets, mimeographs, and typewriters. She and other new residents of the city live in modest apartments and work long hours.

113. Edwards, James A. *In the Court Circle: A Tale of Washington Life.* Washington, D.C.: Columbian, 1895. 167pp.

This novel's wide cast of characters includes Senator Moneybags and his niece; crude but endearing Indianan Senator Bolinbroke; long-suffering Bertha Raymond; and hardworking Tom Rumley. The heroes in this book are people with genteel origins living in reduced circumstances, and the work's humor skewers upper-class life. The novel includes detailed descriptions of various Washington settings common at the time. Boarding house life, with its conflicts among guests, management, and servants (mostly African American) is a major focus. Civil service office life is also described. In fact, the machinations and rivalries of office holders provide the backdrop for a tale that ends happily for the worthy, who enter married bliss with good prospects ahead of them.

114. Ehrlichman, John Daniel. *The Company.* New York: Simon & Schuster, 1976. 313pp.

Published two years after Watergate conspirator and Nixon domestic policy advisor Ehrlichman was released from prison, this fictionalized account of the Nixon administration and the events surrounding the Watergate scandal was praised by many for its credibility.

115. Eiker, Mathilde. *Key Next Door.* Garden City, N.Y.: Doubleday, 1937. 354pp.

Holden and Claire Satterfield, the parents of two children, often spend weekends looking at houses for sale as a free activity, not because they are really interested in buying. Claire, in particular, loves acting the part of a homebuyer. After viewing a house they happen upon adjacent to Rock Creek Park while looking for shelter during a storm, Claire decides she must have the property. The house appeals to her, not because it is substantial and beautifully maintained, but because she believes it will provide entrée to the lives of the former owners, a wealthy family, and to the stylish and attractive next-door neighbor Agnes Thomason, a writer of highly regarded short stories. Claire's husband also desires the house because he immediately desires Agnes Thomason. The novel has few details specific to Washington, except for an episode involving one of the characters, somewhat tertiary to the plot, who becomes enmeshed in a political scandal. One of the major themes is the way property (letters, silver, books, gardens, houses) is expressive of and connected to individuals.

116. Eiker, Mathilde. *The Lady of Stainless Raiment.* Garden City, N.Y.: Doubleday, Doran, 1928. 340pp.

Julian Haldane moves to Washington to take over the house he inherited from his Aunt Henrietta. Henrietta had lived in the seclusion of social disgrace after returning from France, where she had cohabited with a Frenchman for whom she had left her husband. Julian is taken up by Mrs. Chapelle, the widow of a general living in reduced circumstances but continued social prominence, across the square from Haldane's residence. Trained as a lawyer, Julian aspires to be a portrait painter, and Mrs. Chapelle introduces him to potential patrons, including senators and other socially prominent Washingtonians. However, her goal is for Julian to wed her granddaughter, Claudia Lanson. In a short time, Mrs. Chapelle succeeds, and Julian's fortune is utilized to enhance the social prestige of Mrs. Chapelle and her family. Soon the house Julian inherited is exchanged for a more impressive one in a more prestigious area of the city. Claudia makes the most of the opportunities Julian's money affords to add to the prestige her beauty wins her. Washington has little significance in the novel except as a backdrop where the women can meet and entertain senators who can aid them in their schemes. Primarily, the novel is about the roles of men and women in society and what it means for women to be worshipped as if they are on pedestals. As supplicants, the men in the novel give up their true vocations to be controlled by the women they love. Extended sections of the novel take place in France, Virginia, and North Carolina.

117. Eiker, Mathilde. *Mrs. Mason's Daughters.* New York: Macmillan, 1925. 367pp.

Three middle-class sisters take emotional control of their lives after the death of their strict mother. Pauline becomes a nun, Bette obtains a divorce, and Fernanda quits her job as a high school teacher and lives as an unwed mother and restaurateur. In addition to interesting physical descriptions of Washington, the novel includes information about apartment life in the city during the 1920s.

118. Eiker, Mathilde. *The Senator's Lady: A Novel.* Garden City, N.Y.: Doubleday, Doran, 1932. 306pp.

In Eiker's novel personal relationships are threatened, and often warped, by family ties. The family in question is the Carrolls, members of which from the perspective of conservative family members have recently made bad marriages. For example, one eighteen-year-old girl, Cicely Prescott, has married the wrong kind of Jewish man—poor and undistinguished. Furthermore, Cicely's uncle, Carroll Beattie, a respected engineer, has married the divorced Marylily Sutcliffe, whose husband received a decree against her based on proof of her affair with Carroll. Horace Prescott, connected to the Carrolls through his wife Leona, fears these scandals will damage his political career. However, to his relief, his wealth and political connections get him elected to the U.S. Congress anyway.

Surprisingly, Marylily, who had fallen out of love with Carroll even before they were married, becomes Horace's biggest supporter, and Horace, gratified by her attentions, decides he would rather give up politics than Marylily. However, Marylily is more attracted to Horace's career than to him and is pleased to quietly divorce Carroll and live in Washington as a congressman's mistress. Engaging in a scandalous marriage with Horace would mean she would probably end up living with an anonymous, although wealthy, husband. After her divorce, Marylily takes up residence on a quiet street in Georgetown, which is becoming newly fashionable.

Eiker portrays Washington as the ultimate small town where everyone from everywhere eventually meets up. Horace's extended family is no exception. His son Paul arrives to lead the life of an eligible young bachelor with the approval of Leona, who hopes he will find an heiress. With Horace footing the bill, Cicely's husband finishes medical school and moves to Washington as an intern. Another family member, Leona's sister, comes to town for a long visit. Through an accidental meeting, she discovers Horace's affair and reports her news to Leona, who, by sheer accident, is given the opportunity to run down Marylily. The hit and run leads to a major scandal. To protect his U.S. Senate race, Horace must stand beside Leona, but his double life comes out, and he eventually resigns his office. In doing so, however, he takes satisfaction from having freed himself from worrying over public opinion. When Leona divorces him, he is also freed from the Carroll family. The novel ends in Paris.

119. Erskine, John. *The Start of the Road.* New York: Frederick A. Stokes, 1938. 344pp.

This novelization of Walt Whitman's life, drawing on his poetry and Horace Traubel's writings, begins in 1848 with the trip he took with his brother Jefferson to New Orleans. As presented, the trip inspired Whitman's sensitivity to issues of racial politics and included an important romance with Annette Clovis, an octoroon, which Erskine maintains shaped the rest of Whitman's life. Many details are given about New Orleans and the way in which Walt covered the news for the local newspaper. Whitman returns to his life in Brooklyn and develops a friendship with Ralph Waldo Emerson, traveling between New York and Boston. Only the last third of the novel deals with Whitman's time in Civil War Washington, but many physical details are presented. Erskine also captures the social intimacy of Washington during this time period and the operations of the government offices with which Whitman came into contact in his efforts to aid wounded soldiers.

120. Eustis, Edith. *Marion Manning*. New York and London: Harper & Brothers, 1902. 338pp.

Marion is the daughter of a former colonel in the Confederate Army, who had a plantation and long ancestry in Virginia. He had been impoverished by the war but chanced to meet a Northern heiress and fell in love. She died when her daughter was only eight years old and her wealth transferred to Marion who grew up in the Southern society of her father, mostly centered on Richmond and Georgetown. Marion meets John Manning from New Hampshire, a man who had grown up impoverished, but went to Harvard on a scholarship and has begun a rapid climb in the world of politics. They marry after a brief courtship, and Marion is quickly introduced to the Northern society that dominates Washington. She observes the contrast between the cold and reserved politicians' wives she meets and the open and generous women of her youth. She is also soon forced to unwelcome realizations about her husband, John. A congressman, he is involved in personal and political intrigues. For many years he has been having affairs. He has also been unfaithful to the electorate. A party politician, he has devoted himself to taking advantage of the political spoils system and is currently supporting a subsidy bill exclusively because of the fortune he hopes to make when it passes. Even their marriage, Marion discovers, was a form of intrigue designed to get control of her money. She leaves him. Years later, he dies, and the disillusioned Marion comes to believe that she will live the rest of her life as a widow. To her surprise, she befriends another politician, George Hood. Through his actions and convictions, he convinces her that politicians can be just as devoted to ideals as she is, and she eventually marries him. The novel is filled with descriptions of Washington and observations about political life and society.

121. Fairbank, Janet Ayer. *The Lion's Den.* Indianapolis: Bobbs-Merrill, 1930. 374pp.

Dan Carson, a farmer and Progressive Republican from Phillipsburg, Wisconsin, is elected to serve out the term of a deceased congressman. Appointed to the Committee on the Disposition of Useless Executive Papers and cautioned by experienced politicians that he should not speak in the House before serving a few terms, Daniel resigns himself to unimportance and lives modestly, saving most of his salary to pay off the mortgaged farm he inherited from his father. Washington, particularly the official Washington of committee meetings, congressional dinners, and political maneuvering, is presented through Carson's naïve eyes. Prohibition is in force, and some attention is given to bootleg liquor. Other cultural references include contract bridge, art deco interiors, eating artichokes, playing backgammon, and listening to Gershwin. Through the patronage of a senator's wife his lifestyle changes, and he is invited to dinner parties, changes his lodgings to an apartment hotel, buys evening clothes, and is selected by his party to speak on the floor. He also begins investing in stock on margin to finance his new mode of life. When the senator gets him appointed to the World War Veteran's Legislation Committee, he is approached by veterans and their families seeking appropriate compensation, as well as landowners whose properties may be purchased for veterans' hospitals. He opposes the plan to buy an island in his own district for a great deal of money that is owned by wealthy Hi Hyland. Letters and telegrams from party supporters and constituents orchestrated by Hyland begin to flow into his office. He is about to give up his opposition when Irma Schmultz, his campaign manager and the girl to whom he confessed his love before leaving for Congress, appears in Washington and confirms his opinion of Hyland's land. A break with the senator's wife occurs when she sees him with Irma. He explains Irma away, and she takes him back, but when Carson proposes marriage, she throws him out as a fool. Various direct pressures are applied to influence Carson to vote in favor of buying Hyland's land. Despite a stock market crash in which he loses everything, he continues to resist the land deal, and, to his surprise, everything turns out all right when the building on Hyland's land burns to the ground (Hyland had claimed it was fire-proof). Suddenly he seems to be at the beginning of a significant political career. The end of the novel finds him traveling at great expense by mail plane to find Irma and propose marriage.

122. Farrar, Larston D. *Conflict of Interest: A Novel.* New York: Bartholomew House, 1970. 275pp.

The President is about to appoint a new justice to the U.S. Supreme Court, and Steve Levitt is the frontrunner. However, politically powerful Grover Cleveland Curtis finds his candidacy objectionable. In addition to Levitt's political incorruptibility, he had a relationship with Curtis' daughter. Curtis begins an attack utilizing every contact and tactic in his power. He mounts a smear campaign and hires thugs, while doing everything in his power to make certain to secure the appointment of his own favorite, who will secure him significant financial advantages, is appointed.

In this novel of political intrigue, the concern is with official Washington, and the city primarily serves as a backdrop. However, there are insightful descriptions of Southwest D.C., the downtown area, and restaurants and hotels where powerbrokers meet, as well as social conditions such as violence, crime, and illiteracy. Curtis is portrayed as a Washington type—a man who has grown wealthy from a local social phenomenon. He has benefited from the large numbers of people who pass through the city, living in hotels and then apartments. This is a political environment in which corporations like Curtis' are essentially monopolies. These corporations become increasingly wealthy and develop ever-stronger political power in the process. For a price, the Curtises of the city provide the transient population with the basic needs of housing, food, pharmaceuticals, and sundries.

123. Farrar, Larston D. *The Sins of Sandra Shaw.* New York: New American Library, 1958. 126pp.

As Rex Barker, a television political correspondent, boards the Pennsylvania Railroad's "Congressional" for first-class express train service from New York City to Washington, a beautiful young woman literally runs into him. Sandra Shaw, a graduate of Smith College who had been working for two years as a model in New York City, quickly entrances Rex because of her beauty (which he describes in breathless detail, including her measurements), her intelligence, her knowledge of how to please and interest men, and her interest in the inner workings of Washington politics. Before the two arrive at Union Station, Rex has offered Sandra the second bedroom in his lavish apartment on Massachusetts Avenue. After the two have such intense sex that evening that that Barker describes Sandra as a woman who "might as well have been from a different planet," he discovers that Sandra is not just looking for a job in Washington: she is on a mission. A bank owned by her hometown's powerful and wealthy Senator John Stone ruined her father, and she has pledged vengeance. Touched by her story, Barker uses his connections to get her a job with an important, elderly senator and takes her to social events where she meets Washington's political and socially powerful. Barker's narrative recounts how Sandra quickly establishes herself as the most sought after woman in the city and wins over Stone, despite his marriage to an invalid. When Stone's wife dies, Sandra makes an unexpected move, prompting a crisis for both her and Stone. The novel includes mentions of the most popular restaurants, hotels, and nightspots in 1950s Washington. In between descriptions of Sandra's wardrobe, power over men, and physical attributes, our narrator Barker provides a jaundiced view of politicians who secretly accept the kickbacks of lobbyists and vote for legislation that will benefit their own investments. Author Farrar uses his insider knowledge in presenting social life that includes weekends at hunt country retreats in Virginia and mountain lodges in West Virginia reached by helicopter.

124. Fergusson, Harvey. *Capitol Hill: A Novel of Washington Life.* New York: Alfred A. Knopf, 1923. 309pp.

Ralph Dolan, a native of Muncie, Indiana, where his family had lived for several generations, was on his way to New York City in the autumn of 1912 to take up a job in a brokerage house. On the strength of three hundred dollars of gambling proceeds, he had quit his previous work traveling selling fraternity jewelry to college men. However, after one night in Washington, spent with a woman who turns out to be a thief, he is left with ten dollars. Self-confident, a compelling storyteller, and good at games of chance, Dolan is accustomed to living by his wits and sets out to replenish his bank account. Washington is described in great detail through his eyes. He is distressed by the lack of industry and realizes that wealthy men constructed the beautiful mansions in Northwest D.C. merely to establish residency and obtain a lower tax rate. Although the beauty, historical sites, and monuments of the city hold no appeal for Dolan, the affluence of civil servants and legislative appointees do, as do the many single, young women. His social class places him on the margins of respectable society, and he begins working at a lunch counter on the margins of racially divided Washington. He also spends his time in "Hooker's Division" (the city's red-light district) and areas dominated by bars and poolrooms. On his way up the social ladder, he holds progressively more respectable jobs, including bill collector for the gas company, folder of speeches in the House Office Building where legislators' mailings are prepared, congressional secretary, and journalist. The comfort in which he lives also progresses from rooming houses, the YMCA, and an apartment in a house, to an apartment in an apartment building. Throughout the novel, Dolan has conversations with people from all social stations, and the reader learns of the plight of women who work as escorts, male clerks, impoverished congressmen and their families, housewives, female secretaries, and self-made politicians. Through his newspaper job, he becomes acquainted with a wide-range of politicians and lobbyists, including woman suffragists, and eventually meets a wealthy bachelor who is at the center of Washington society. The bachelor introduces him to people and gives him inside information. As war approaches, Dolan's connections pay off, and a lobbying firm, the National Commercial Association, hires him. The Washington branch of the association is primarily concerned with entertaining and rewarding congressmen and feeding stories to the press; other branches are concerned with strikebreaking. When war breaks out, Dolan quickly finds a way to serve without enlisting and at the same time financially profit as the private secretary of a wealthy man who has been appointed to head the Red Cross. After the war, Dolan marries a wealthy debutante and subsequently becomes the president of the National Commercial Association, an organization that is rapidly growing in influence, for everyone believes the war was won through propaganda. Although the novel includes physical descriptions of Washington, its usefulness lies in the many characters that illustrate the reasons people come to Washington and the lives they lead upon arriving in the city.

125. Fitzgerald, Robert. *The Statesmen Snowbound.* Illustrated by Wad-el-Ward. Washington, D.C.: Neale, 1909. 217pp.
    A group of legislators representing all regions of the country accompany the body of a deceased senator to his Kentucky home for burial. The material comforts of the senator's house and the well-appointed special train that carries the legislators turn the trip into a junket. To everyone's satisfaction, the return trip is prolonged when a snowstorm traps the train in the mountains. The legislators enjoy the abundant food and attentive service of "President Madison," the African American steward who is prompt to fill drink orders. To pass the time the legislators each tell a story. Several of the tales have D.C. settings or include comments about the nature of life in Washington. The high costs of hotel and boarding house life on a congressman's salary is decried, as is the presumption of African Americans who consider themselves the equals of whites. In addition, one story describes Chinatown and the behavior and vices of its corrupt inhabitants. Another story incorporates an extended description of the mood on the streets during the excitement leading to the Spanish-American War. Indicative, perhaps, of a

common anxiety of the time, several tales involve the swindling of their narrators by beautiful young women aided by "foreigners," and one of these is set in a disreputable part of Washington.

126. Fleming, Thomas. *Around the Capital with Uncle Hank.* New York: Nutshell, 1902. 346pp.
This patriotic celebration of the nation's capital includes line drawings of Washington's politicians and prominent social figures, as well as illustrations of the major buildings and monuments. The Uncle Hank of the title is Henry Slocum, a Yankee, visiting the capital for the first time. He is patriotic and respectful, but does not resist lampooning self-serving politicians, following up on hints of corruption, and political stances which he opposes. As he makes his way through the city, Hank gathers current political and social gossip. He spends a great deal of time at the newly finished Library of Congress, but in addition to visiting sights, explores the industrial areas of the city and the fashionable shopping and residential streets.

127. Fradin, Morris. *Hey-Ey-Ey, Lock!* Cabin John, Md.: See-and-Know, 1974. 112pp. juvenile.
In the summer of 1908, Captain Tom Clark, his wife, daughter Abigail, and English nephew Michael Walsh travel from Lock 3 in Georgetown to Cumberland, Maryland, on the C & O Canal. This fictional account for children provides information about canal operations, indicates what the canal and the towns along it were like during this time period, and presents the history of the canal, as well as landmarks along its route.

128. Frank, Pat. *An Affair of State.* Philadelphia: Lippincott, 1948. 256pp.
Nicholas Baker is employed in the U.S. State Department as a clerk. He is very conscious of his low social status, and when his son Jeff is born in 1919 can think of nothing better for him than becoming a career diplomat—a status he will never be able to achieve. The author provides details about clothing, food, and housing that characterizes Baker's social status. Throughout the novel, actual historical details are also provided. For instance, Baker is devoted to Wilson's League of Nations. When Wilson has a stroke, Baker senses that all is lost for the nation but names his son Jefferson Wilson Baker in honor of his heroes.
Jeff grows up and serves in World War II. His father dies while Jeff is abroad, and in settling his estate Jeff realizes the extent to which

his father's life had been bound by the financial confines of his clerk-ship. Jeff sells his father's double-mortgaged Georgetown house and moves in with a friend in Riggs Court Apartments near Dupont Circle. Jeff's friends and acquaintances work in the National Archives and office of the secretary of state, and he eventually finds a job with the State Department. The conversations included in the novel capture the gossip and concerns of post-war Washington, and the descriptions of Jeff's new employee orientation and work in the State Department seem to demonstrate knowledge of the inner workings of the Depart-ment.

Jeff is assigned to Budapest in an atmosphere in which war with Russia seems inevitable, and in preparation he works on the Atlantis Project to establish an organized spy network that would continue to function after a Russian takeover. Jeff's activities are misrepresented, and he is forced to resign from his post and return to Washington. However, in the end he is vindicated and returns to his job overseas.

129. Futrelle, Jacques. *Elusive Isabel.* Illustrated by Alonzo Kimball. New York: A. L. Burt, 1909. 273pp.

In this tale of international espionage, the U.S. Secret Service learns of a clandestine agreement to be signed in Washington, D.C., by representatives of the "Latin" countries: France, Italy, Spain, and two unnamed South American republics. In addition to these countries, oth-ers have been invited to join in banding together against the United States and Great Britain, including Germany, Japan, Portugal, and Rus-sia. Mr. Grimm (his first name is never given) is assigned to investi-gate. The most promising source of information is a woman named Isabel Thorne who arrived in Washington a few days before and whose beauty has drawn great attention at diplomatic functions. Subsequently, she appears to be connected with the shooting of a Mexican diplomat, the theft of a large sum of gold from the Venezuelan legation, and the disappearance of the French Ambassador. Grimm soon discovers that she is an Italian secret agent using an assumed name. He eventually solves all of the mysteries in the case and prevents the signing of the Latin compact. He also foils a plan to undermine British and American harbor defenses with a radio-activated detonation device Britain and the United States are in the process of purchasing for use on their underwa-ter mines. The plot includes devices such as the tapping of Morse code with an ivory fan at a party, invisible ink, and the drugging and kidnap-ping of Grimm. Although references are made to areas of Washington, Alexandria, and Baltimore, these are fairly shallow backdrops.

130. Gallagher, Phyllis Moore. *All Is Not Quiet on the Potomac*. Baltimore: Reid, Alton, 1962. 374pp.

Ralph Varner is a handsome bachelor with a drinking problem. He comes to Washington experienced in espionage through his Far East service in World War II. This confidence man has formed an alliance with Senator Herman Bates in order to destroy Senator Caleb Stockton's nomination for President. In return, Varner will receive a large financial settlement, but also get a political appointment when Bates is elected President. Varner has gathered evidence that the married Stockton is having an affair with famous society hostess Mona Darton, widow of the very wealthy Cyrus Darton. On the night that Varner is to blackmail Stockton into giving up his nomination and pledging all of the money he had raised to Bates, he experiences a crisis of conscience. The suicide of a woman he cared about causes him to see himself in a new light, and he forces Bates to resign, instead of Stockton. The novel is filled with details about upper-middle-class life.

131. Galsworthy, John. *Two Forsyte Interludes: A Silent Wooing, Passers By*. New York: Charles Scribner's Sons, 1928. 60pp.

In "Passers By," Englishman Soames Forsyte reflects on sites in Washington and finds in them inspiration for his own life. He visits Mount Vernon and St. Gaudens' "Grief," which he considers the finest human achievement in the United States. He stays at the Hotel Potomac, and the Corcoran and Freer galleries are mentioned. The latter inspires him to reflect on leaving his own paintings to the English people so that his name will live on after his death.

132. Gardener, Helen Hamilton. *An Unofficial Patriot*. New York. R. F. Fenno, 1898. 351pp.

The novel uses the life of Griffith Davenport to illustrate major political and social issues of the period from 1825 through the 1860s. Davenport is born to a wealthy Virginia family. He converts to Methodism, abandoning the Episcopalian faith of his family and ancestors, and becomes a circuit rider. Although he resists owning slaves, his wife brings them as dowry, and he is bequeathed many more by his father. Out of moral conviction, he plans to relocate to Indiana and set free his slaves in Washington, D.C., taking only those with whom he was closest to work as employees in his new home. To his distress, he soon realizes that many free blacks in Washington have a hard life. He also learns that even though Indiana is a free state, it has passed a law barring free blacks from entering the state to work for whites. In the end, he and his family leave Washington secretly, abandoning all the former slaves to fend for themselves. When war breaks out, all three of Davenport's sons join Union regiments, and Davenport is called into service as a guide for Union troops in the South after a personal meeting with Lincoln in Washington. He is forced to make a poignant return to the Southern countryside and the people there he still loves. Soon after returning to Indiana at the end of his service, he dies of a heart attack, and his wife is left to bemoan the choices he made. The novel's scenes of wartime Washington are not extensive and deal, primarily, with the situation of free African Americans in the city from the viewpoint of an author with a clear political agenda.

133. Gardenhire, S. M. *The Long Arm.* New York: Harper & Brothers, 1906. 345pp.

The short stories in this book record the successful detective work of LeDroit Conners, an artist who solves mysteries through deduction and calmly deals with any physical danger he meets. Only one of the tales, "The Case of the Ambassador," takes place in Washington. In the story, an expensive, fraudulent invitation to an exclusive diplomatic event that solicits a cash donation for a memorial has been mailed to thirty thousand households in the name of an ambassador's wife. Conners has been called in to solve the case and redeem the honor of the woman. As Conners tries to find the criminals and prevent a public scandal, his exploration takes him into the residences of the ambassador and of a nouveau riche Washingtonian.

134. Gardenhire, S. M. *Purple and Homespun.* New York: Harper & Brothers, 1908. 371pp.

Senator John Marshall Treemon started life as the son of a well-to-do farmer whose land was near Monmouth, Illinois. Working his way through college and law school, he finished a degree at the University of Michigan (Ann Arbor). Soon after passing his bar exam, he was elected to the state legislature and then served several terms in the U.S. Congress. In addition to the successful legal practice to which he devoted himself between terms, he made investments in Western mines and before long was a millionaire. The fact that he was honest, well spoken, and attractive made him popular with his constituency and with the society people he meets from around the country and around the world in Washington. One of these is Victoria Wemyss, daughter of Lord Francis Wemyss, British Ambassador and heir to one of the noblest names and estates in Britain. Although he is very much in love with Victoria, he resists pressing his suit because he has learned he was adopted. With some effort, he discovers that he is the son of an alcoholic Irish immigrant who lives on the lower East Side of New York City. When Treemon confesses his humble origins to Victoria, she assures him that his own achievements are more important to her than her family, and the two become engaged. The novel is set in Washington for only eight out of thirty-five chapters. The city is treated as the place that brings people from many different social settings together for a few months out of the year, but this milieu is very significant in their lives year round.

135. Gardiner, Ruth Kimball. *The World and the Woman.* New York: A. S. Barnes, 1907. 292pp.

Marian Macross, the daughter of noted statesman Franklyn Lindsley, spent her youth in Washington and cherishes the memory and heirlooms of her father, although he has been long dead and generally forgotten. She lives as a single mother in the rural town of Gordonsville; her husband, Robert Macross, disappeared years before. When Macross reappears unexpectedly, Marian rejects him because he betrayed her with another woman and refuses to reveal his true identity to their daughter Lindsley. However, his reappearance forces her into action, for his government pension had been one of her few means of support. She closes up her house, sells off her father's library, and goes to Washington to present Lindsley in society and find her a husband. Renting the house she had lived in with her father, she renews her friendship with socialite Mrs. Beauchamp who instructs her in the ways of "new" Washington and catches her up on society gossip. Marian effortlessly makes her return, and her daughter is immediately popular for her natural grace, forthright manner, and beauty. To stretch her money Marian helps an old friend by contributing items to a society newspaper and learns from him to make stock investments with insider information. All goes well for Marian, even when Robert appears in Washington seeking reappointment to his government position. Her friends protect Lindsley from seeing him, and Robert himself decides to embrace anonymity rather than spoil Lindsley's debut year. Marian's luck changes, however, when a stock transaction fails, and she is forced to tell Lindsley of her financial ruin. Lindsley's marriage to a rich, elderly senator who had been kind seems like the only solution. When the engagement is announced all of Washington is abuzz over the fact that Marian is selling off her daughter. Henry, Mrs. Beauchamp's son, steps in, however, and Lindsley elopes with him. Most of the description in the novel focuses on social matters, and a wealth of detail is presented in the form of information conveyed to Marian about the new Washington.

136. Garland, Hamlin. *A Spoil of Office: A Story of the Modern West.* Boston: Arena, 1892. 385pp.

At the beginning of the novel, Bradley Talcott is a hired hand living near Rock River, Iowa, and enamored of a girl from a higher social class. He decides to make himself worthy of his intended by going to high school and college. He realizes that the socialization he receives in college is just as important to him as classroom studies. By joining a fraternity, he learns the importance of dressing well and the thrill of oratory and political debate. The focus of his ambitions changes from a woman to Washington. He dreams of the city as place where he can escape his background and become an important man. Judge Brown, struck by his gifts as an orator, encourages him to become a lawyer and takes him into his household. He also lends him money to study law in Iowa City and, when he returns to his hometown, aids his election to the Iowa state legislature. Talcott runs as an Independent, building a coalition of Democrats and Republican farmers frustrated by the Republican Party machine that favors the interests of businesses and townspeople. Talcott's opposition to railroads, nepotism, and lobbies (the school book lobby, the university lobby, and the Armour Foods Company lobby) draws attention, and he is soon elected to the U.S. Congress. His perspective on Washington is fully recorded through lengthy physical descriptions of the city, boarding house life, and his excitement over opportunities to view art and discuss literature. He regards other aspects of the city with distaste, including machine politics and the way wealthy legislators live. When he is defeated in his bid for re-election, he cannot resign himself to living as a small town lawyer after the excitement of his life in Washington. His marriage to farm girl Ida Russell revitalizes his commitment to the rural community, and, with his wife's skills at organizing farmers, it seems likely that he will be re-elected.

137. Garland, Rufus Cummins. *Zaléa: A Psychological Episode and Tale of Love.* Washington, D.C.: Neale, 1900. 146pp.

M. Paul Dumons, a society figure who winters in Washington, is murdered at D.C.'s fashionable Hotel Montrose, and Chief of Police Major Byrne and Detective Edward Sanford are called in to investigate. They interview hotel staff members, including an African American porter and chambermaid, each of whom provides lengthy monologues intended to be humorous for their content and dialect. The scene of the murder investigation quickly shifts to New York City, where Detective Sanford is assisted by members of the Study for the Advancement of Psychology, particularly spiritualist Mrs. Smythe, who conducts a séance and determines that the murderer was a jealous Spanish woman, Zaléa Gonzales. Gonzales, the opera star, used a stiletto Dumons had given her in a love pact years before with the agreement that she was to use it to kill him if he engaged in treachery, just as he was to use a stiletto on her if she cheated on him. The novel includes lengthy flashbacks in which Zaléa presents the story of her life and her reasons for killing Dumons and the woman with whom he cheated. The victim of a weak heart, she dies at the conclusion of her confession and is subsequently buried in a beautiful gravesite with a marker that provides assurance of the immortality of her soul.

138. Garth, David. *Gray Canaan.* New York: G. P. Putnam's Sons, 1947. 280pp.

A secret Confederate plan, code named "Canaan," may or may not have been stolen by a female Union spy. However, a Confederate Army captain must take extraordinary measures to make certain the plan does not reach Union officials. This novel of espionage and counter-espionage has short passages set in wartime Washington; it is primarily set in Richmond, the countryside of Maryland, and the area around Manassas.

139. Gerould, Gordon Hall. *A Midsummer Mystery.* New York: D. Appleton, 1925. 256pp.

Ben Wells had been sent by his widowed sister Mildred to find a suitable furnished house to rent in Washington. Mildred is accustomed to the best, and the first house Wells is shown located on Connecticut Avenue, NW, seems perfect. However, on a tour with real estate agent Wilbur Edge, a corpse is discovered laid out for burial on the dining room table. The man turns out to be the owner of the house, Senator West, whose daughter Wells had known years before in New York before she married Dr. Rabinoff. At the inquest, Wells meets Rabinoff, whom he describes as "black-browned" with an "Oriental" beard, and immediately dislikes him. Wells and Edge take it upon themselves to solve the crime, and most of the novel's action unfolds through automobile travels around the capital. Places that are mentioned and/or described include Rock Creek Park, The Somerset (on F Street, NW), the Federal Club on Lafayette Square, The Hotel Jefferson, the District Club, the National Zoo, the downtown shopping district, and the Maryland countryside, with its dirt roads, that lies just beyond the district. In the end, the villains are Rabinoff, a Russian, an Italian, and a "paranoiac."

140. Gerry, Margarita Spalding. *The Toy Shop: A Romantic Story of Lincoln the Man.* New York: Harper & Brothers, 1908. 50pp.

In this brief book, the author imagines and describes the emotional importance that his visits to the Schotz toy shop in Washington had for President Lincoln.

141. Glenn, Isa. *The Little Candle's Beam.* Garden City, N.Y.: Doubleday, Doran, 1935. 307pp.

Cecilia Tabor Masefield married a Foreign Service officer eighteen years her senior. Her family, "cave dwellers," objected, describing him as part of "that set" who fix up and move into Georgetown houses and wear white spats. Widowed early, she is left to support herself and her son, Thomas Quarles Masefield. Her father had died, leaving everything to his wife for her lifetime, in trust for the children. Cecilia and her sister Phoebe find their mother parsimonious, and she frowns upon any contact with newcomers. In casting about for suitable occupations, Cecilia's friends rehearse a list of undertakings that others of her class forced to earn a living had followed. These include teaching horsemanship, running a bookshop, operating a cafeteria, and entering the civil service. She rejects each of these to become a society reporter for the radio and meets a suitor, Alfred Orme. When her son rejects Orme with great animosity, Cecilia gives up hopes of marriage and becomes Orme's mistress, feeling that by doing so she will not betray her son. Most of the novel takes place in a social world focused on Dupont Circle, Lafayette Square, and Sheridan Circle. While Cecilia tries to live independently, challenges keep arising. Acknowledging the primacy of family, she decides to move back in with her mother, with the implication that she will be under her thrall for the rest of her days. Although part of the novel takes place during the financial crisis of the 1930s, there are few changes in Cecilia's world, for even the government clerks are paid in a timely fashion. Only the appearance of the Bonus Marchers brings to the capital some of the problems facing the rest of the country. The novel also mentions several inaugurations and the end of Prohibition. Since Cecilia's job requires her to mingle with people from several Washington social circles (e.g., "cave dwellers," newcomers, and retired military officers), the author is able to provide social details for many types of Washingtonians, relate a wide range of overheard anecdotes and gossip, and describe the city in depth.

142. Godfrey, Hollis. *The Man Who Ended War.* Boston: Little, Brown, 1908. 301pp.

James Orrington, a Columbia College (New York City) graduate,

is working as a reporter in Washington when he attends a press conference by the secretary of war and hears about a letter sent to the most
powerful countries in the world warning them to disarm or suffer the
destruction of their weapons, armies, and fortifications. Although the
government laughs off the warning, Orrington investigates with the
help of some of his Columbia classmates working in Washington. Two
of these, Dorothy Haldane, with whom Orrington immediately falls in
love, and her brother Tom, are wealthy and use their scientific education to pursue research projects in their private laboratory. They play a
crucial role in Orrington's investigation due to their scientific knowledge and the chauffeured cars and private yachts they can put at his
command as the trio pursues clues in New York City, London, and
Amsterdam. Battleships start to disappear, and the Haldanes supply
Orrington with a theory about how electrons could be broken down to
cause mass destruction. Their connection with another scientist who
had been working on the practical implications of radioactive forces
help them fully understand the device causing the destruction. Only
after the governments of the world disarm do they discover the identity
of the "man who ended war" just as he destroys his infernal machine
and himself.

143. Goldsmith, John Francis. *President Randolph as I Knew Him: An
Account of the Historic Events of the 1950s and 1960s Written from the
Personal Experiences of the President.* Philadelphia: Dorrance, 1935.
448pp.
    This utopian, futurist novel follows the career of Daniel Randolph,
a "typical American" with a mixed ancestry of Dutch, English, French,
and German. He is an average student but an independent thinker and
popular with his fellow students. He enters politics as an ambitious
lawyer climbing from state Assembly to Congress and the Senate. As
the result of a political deal, he serves a term as secretary of state and is
then elected President. Out of a concern that Western civilization will
destroy itself with new means of mass destruction, Randolph successfully advocates for a world-wide government and is elected its first
President. The novelist presents an impressive amount of material to
tell his story, including campaign speeches presenting differing viewpoints, court case briefs, newspaper stories written from various political perspectives, political debates, Supreme Court decisions, and the
new world government's lengthy constitution.

144. Gould, Elizabeth Lincoln. *Polly Prentiss Goes A-Visiting*. Philadelphia: Penn, 1913. 200pp. young adult.

Polly Prentiss of Pomeroy Oaks journeys from her Quaker school near Philadelphia to act as a bridesmaid for a friend whose uncle is a senator. She travels with school friends by train and, when they arrive in the city, rides in an automobile for the first time. Through Polly's eyes, the reader gets detailed accounts of the senator's house and furnishings, the clothing and rituals connected with the wedding, and the major Washington tourist sites, including the White House, Washington Monument, and Mount Vernon. The descriptions of social events capture the city at the height of the social season and sometimes provide a foil for explanations of the Quaker religion.

145. Grant, A. F. *The War Detective; or, The Plotters at Washington, a Tale of Booth's Conspiracy*. New York: War Library / Novelist Publishing, 1883. 96pp.

In this novel, Union secret service agents have uncovered the Booth plot and are actively trying to thwart it. Leon Lennox has been working as a Union spy behind enemy lines in Richmond, using several aliases. He gains the confidence of Jefferson Davis and Colonel Opal. His young assistant, Paul Phillips, is entrusted to carry news of Booth's plot to Colonel Baker in Washington. When Lennox arrives in the federal city, having escaped the Confederates who learned his true identity, he finds that Phillips never arrived and successfully goes back to rescue him. A former girlfriend of Phillips, Pauline Dupont, is also a Union spy, and when the Confederates capture her, Lennox tries to save her and is duped into a trap that prevents him from saving Lincoln. However, he plays an important role in the capture of all the conspirators.

146. Grant, Robert. *Unleavened Bread*. New York: Charles Scribner's Sons, 1900. 431pp.

This extended parable holds that political power combined with social status in Washington is the ultimate goal of the social striver. The central character, Selma White, gives up small-town teaching to become the wife of Lewis Babcock and move to a rapidly growing midwestern city. In addition to the moral calling of marrying and raising a family, middle-class comfort and social status appeal to her. When her baby dies and Babcock has an affair, she finds the example attractive of a socially connected acquaintance who lives the life of an intellectual, independent woman, and she divorces Babcock. However, she remarries again when an architect from New York City of unimpeachable cultivation, if simple tastes and means, seems to hold out greater social recognition. Living in New York City, she is soon disappointed by her new husband's lack of ambition. By comparison, a neighbor, a stock speculator, is soon affluent enough to move to a better neighborhood and garner society page mentions. Her shrill criticisms make her husband increasingly unhappy. When he becomes ill and dies, she returns to the midwestern city where she formerly lived, but this time as a private secretary to a wealthy gentleman. She finds ways of establishing herself as a social power in the city by convincing him to endow a hospital of which she becomes president of the board of trustees. She then pursues and wins a marriage proposal from a lawyer who has become wealthy through covert investments in corporations while portraying himself as a great populist opposed to corporate theft. Selma wagers her future on the belief that he will be elected to Congress and she will then be at the pinnacle of social power. Disillusioned by her first visit to Washington as the wife of her newly elected husband, she vows never to return until she can come back as a senator's wife and hold social sway. By the end of the novel her husband has his senatorial seat and she looks forward to true social prominence in Washington. Although only a small percentage of this novel is set in D.C., the book is of interest for the role it ascribes to social life in the city as the object of the socially ambitious.

147. Green, Anna Katherine. *The Filigree Ball: Being a Full and True Account of the Solution of the Mystery Concerning the Jeffrey-Moore Affair.* Illustrated by C. M. Relyea. Indianapolis: Bobbs-Merrill, 1903. 418pp.

This murder mystery is told through the narration of a Washington police detective. The plot is advanced through his review of notes, interrogations, courtroom accounts, and newspaper stories. Much of the mystery centers on events at an eighteenth-century house in downtown Washington. Other locations include the commercial district on N Street, NW; the Cosmos Club; and Rock Creek Cemetery. Although the plot centers on characters who are part of Washington society, no insights are afforded about that society. The plot involves elements of contemporary topical interest, including typhoid fever, the Spanish American War, and the Klondike gold rush.

148. Greene, Talbot. *American Nights' Entertainments; Compiled from Pencilings of a United States Senator; Entitled a Winter in the Federal City.* Jonesborough, Tenn.: William A. Sparks, 1860. 266pp.

The author sets his work in antebellum America, a sort of golden age when the President and the country's citizens were carefree and prosperous. Inspired by the presence of Sulciman Effendim, Turkish diplomat and first cousin of the author of *The Turkish Nights Entertainments,* legislators and other Washington figures gather at the White House to entertain each other with stories of romance and adventure. Although a few tales have European settings (mostly Spain), the rest take place in the United States. Some are set in New York City, but most in the South: Richmond; New Orleans; Jonesborough, Tennessee; New York City; Norfolk; New Bern, Asheville, and Hamburg, North Carolina; and Savannah. The story tellers include Martin Van Buren (who talks about courting and marrying Alice Smith), R. M. T. Hunter (Virginia), Zebulon Vance (North Carolina), William Aiken (South Carolina), Aaron V. Brown (Tennessee), General Whitfield, Senator Hayne (South Carolina), Colonel Landon Haynes (Tennessee), General Sam Houston (Texas), Alexander Boteler (Virginia), Hon. T. A. R. Nelson (Tennessee), Hon. John Bell (Tennessee), [Judah] Benjamin (Louisiana), James Buchanan (Pennsylvania), Andrew Johnson (Tennessee), Parson Brownlow (Tennessee), T. B. Graham, and Col. Horace Maynard (Tennessee). The themes of the stories include gentility versus the crude manners of country folk and frontiersmen, interactions with Native Americans, horse trading, courting and romance, descriptions of food, reversals of fortune, the discovery of hidden treasure, contests of strength, stories of the supernatural (mostly involving Satan), ethnic types (Dutchmen and Mexicans), the evils of drink, the nature of social order, the importance of stewardship, paeans to manifest destiny, storms at sea and shipwreck, adventures on the road, brigandage, travel by stage coach, epidemics of yellow fever and cholera, house fires, and dueling. Although there is no physical description of Washington, the book presents an aspect of the city's social life. Legislators came together from all regions, and it would be very natural for them to tell stories to each other about their own adventures, particularly ones that emphasized regional differences.

149. Griffith, Patricia Browning. *The Future Is Not What It Used to Be.* New York: Simon & Schuster, 1970. 224pp.
     Sunny Tidwell, the twenty-six-year-old daughter of a Texas politician, refuses to pursue the life her father wants for her. Instead, unemployed, she lives in an impoverished, frightening neighborhood and dates a young man interested in political struggle. The novel's descriptions of people, street life, and the riots following the assassination of the Rev. Martin Luther King, Jr., capture the character of 1960s Washington.

150. Gunter, Archibald Clavering. *Her Senator; A Novel.* New York: Hurst, 1896. 261 pages.

When Arthur Ellison, a Wall Street broker who had made a fortune and moved to Paris, dies in a shipwreck, his broker and executor, Over-hand Guernsey, assumes guardianship of his daughters. Guernsey, who had squandered his own assets in unwise speculation, takes Ellison's assets as his own and assigns the daughters to an orphanage operated for profit by a fake minister. Guernsey rebuilds his fortune and acquires large tracts of land in a Western territory. Smitten by his conscience he returns with his son, a Yale-educated physician, to find Ellison's children. The oldest, Evelyn, has run away from the home, pledging to find a means of rescuing her sister, Mathilde. The men look for Evelyn but eventually return to the West with only Mathilde. Evelyn becomes an artist's model and singer in bohemian New York. Her constant motivation is to get revenge by marrying a fortune and punishing Guernsey. When she discovers that Guernsey has died, her focus shifts to his son, James, now a senator. She accumulates money for her campaign with the assistance of a successful investor who sees an opportunity to ad-vance his financial interests by using Evelyn to persuade Senator Guernsey to pass certain legislation. Meeting Guernsey "by accident" at Saratoga, Evelyn quickly has the senator intrigued, and he follows her to Narragansett. By the time she arrives in Washington for the sea-son, establishing herself on Connecticut Avenue not far from Dupont Circle, Evelyn knows she can spring her trap. However, her conviction that James Guernsey is as evil as Overland Guernsey falters, then fails, as evidence accumulates that he is that rare thing, an honorable politi-cian and man of wealth, and a love match develops. Although only one-third of the novel is set in Washington, a great deal of attention is paid throughout the book to discussing the corruption of politics by mon-eyed interests and introducing Washington types.

151. Hackett, Francis. *The Senator's Last Night.* Garden City, N.Y.: Doubleday, Doran, 1943. 272pp.

Senator John Copley is presented as an isolationist in time of war, morally duplicitous, mean to everyone around him, and fueled by a sense of his own power. He is friends with only one man, Senator Jas-per Sargent. Disappointed in his life and his wife, Senator Copley thinks of giving everything up and pursuing a romance with Mary In-nis. The novel is mostly occupied with contemporary debates over ways of living, the nature of the social order, ethics, and social life in Washington. Physical descriptions of the city are slight, however some effort is given to present its symbolic power. Portions of the novel consist of exchanges among Senator Copley's servants who are Scottish, Irish, and Swedish that further articulate issues of social class and identity politics. Through the eyes of visitors to the city, Washington is presented in dramatic contrast to the rest of the country and the world. Here luxury and beauty can still be found everywhere, and the city is untouched by wartime privations. Dinner party talk also elucidates social attitudes and opinions on world events. Critiques are made of the narrowness of senators, many of whom grew up in small towns, have little experience of the world, and have mostly been drawn from the legal profession. Anyone wishing to read the opinions characteristic of this time period may find this book a useful social document.

152. Hager, Alice. *Cathy Whitney, President's Daughter*. New York: Julian Messner, 1966. 192pp. young adult.

Cathy's family lives in San Francisco and enjoys an affluence stemming from her great-great-grandfather's discovery of a gold mine and the family's subsequent real estate investments. Her father, Mark Whitney, is a veteran fighter pilot, who worked in the space program as an aeronautical engineer, was twice mayor of San Francisco, and is president of the State University. His party has just chosen him as a presidential candidate. Unlike the rest of the family, including college senior Lars and college junior Anne, who are excited, Cathy is fearful. She realizes that the breakup of her family life will accelerate if her father is elected, and, besides, she will have to live in Washington, far away from her horse. Her father counsels her that every American should accept the call to give up personal comfort for the good of the country and respond to the challenges life presents. Even before her father is elected, Cathy learns to sacrifice her privacy as reporters barrage the family. When the family moves into the White House she is forced to make a number of personal sacrifices, including rarely getting to see her parents and being separated from Lars when he enters the U.S. Air Force. In this Vietnam War era novel, patriotism is foremost as all of the characters struggle to accept the responsibilities that come with personal freedom. Cathy's Washington is a city that few ever experience and mostly centers on the White House, although her rides in Rock Creek Park and dates that include performances at the National Theater and dancing at the Shoreham Hotel are described. In prefatory matter, Hager, a Washington journalist, assures the reader of the accuracy of her accounts of everything from Air Force One to the family quarters at the White House.

153. Hager, Alice. *Janice, Air Line Hostess*. New York: Julian Messner, 1948. 190pp. young adult.

Janice Hartley, who had worked as an airline hostess before World War II and served in a flight evacuation unit during the war, returns to civilian life and takes a position with Wide World Airlines, which has just gotten approval for flight routes that will take passengers around the globe. Janice is responsible for training new hostesses and setting up housing arrangements for flight crews along Wide World's routes. Therefore, this novel for young adults is set in far-flung locations. However, several chapters take place in Washington when Janice and some of her friends participate in a fashion show for airline hostesses at the Congressional Country Club. They stay at the Mayflower Hotel, do some touring, and have dinner at the National Press Club. As the high point of her visit, Janice receives the Legion of Merit from the President for her work during the war.

154. Hager, Alice Rogers. *Washington Secretary*. New York: Julian Messner, 1958. 192 pp. young adult.

Carolyn Markham travels with her college junior class from Brooks University on her first trip to Washington. An American history and political science major, she is intensely excited. The Easter holiday is in full swing, and high school and college classes from around the country are in the city. Her friend Jim Nolan is the great-grandson of a senator and wants to enter the U.S. Foreign Service. Carolyn wants to be an elected official, too, and is offended when she is told that such work is not for women. When she meets with Congresswoman Sloan from her home district, a woman who first entered office by serving out her deceased husband's unfinished term, Sloan offers Carolyn the chance to become a junior secretary. Although Carolyn bridles at starting at the bottom, she discovers the importance of secretaries to the operations of the government. In college, Carolyn was surrounded by young people who took politics very seriously in light of the recent war and the sacrifice of so many for freedom. However, in Washington she meets even more intensely patriotic politicians and civil servants. In addition to finding out about the workings of political offices, she learns about political journalism and social life in the city. She works in Washington for almost two years before becoming engaged to a congressman and during that time is exposed to the political issues of immigration, refugees, the space race, and unrest in Southeast Asia.

155. Hall, A. Oakey. *The Congressman's Christmas Dream; and the Lobby Member's Happy New Year.* New York: Scribner, Welford, 1870. 64pp.

The actors Mr. and Mrs. Darby Dilks visit Washington to attend the inauguration of General Jackson. Standing too close to a cannon, Darby loses an eye. No longer able to act, he is given a patronage position as Deputy Sergeant of Arms in the U.S. Congress, and Mrs. Dilks opens a boarding house to which the couple's political friends send a steady flow of clerks. One of their boarders is Captain Sherburne, a ninety-year-old Revolutionary War veteran, who has for decades been pursuing legislation to obtain pensions for veterans of the Revolution. Now Martin Van Buren is in office, Sherburne's bill is before Congress, and Lysander Lillington is a newly elected congressman. His adopted son, Edmund Burke Lillington, the child of his deceased sister, has met Agnes Sherburne after hearing her beautiful voice in church and has secretly been courting her. When Captain Sherburne meets the congressman, he innocently reveals that Edmund has been visiting the Sherburnes at their boarding house. Although Lillington is opposed to a match between Edmund and an impoverished girl, when he meets Agnes he is struck by her beauty and deportment, as well as her resemblance to someone from his past. His first love appears to him in a dream, and he subsequently confirms that Agnes is the daughter of this woman. Out of obedience to his love, Lillington gets the pension bill passed and ends his opposition to Edmund's marriage to Agnes.

156. Hansbrough, H. C. *The Second Amendment.* Minneapolis: Hudson, 1911. 359pp.

The novel is set in the near future of the time of writing. Skyscrapers have risen more than sixty stories, a subway has been constructed in Minneapolis, "autochines" are common, airships have become commonplace, "lower Alaska" has become a state, and Canada is about to become one as well. In addition to the technical innovations, and the expansion of U.S. territory, a major change in politics has occurred. The Altocrat party, whose goal is altruistic and puts individuals before big business, has become so popular that an Altocrat is in the White House. However, opposition by Conservatives, millionaire manufacturers, and their lobbyists and lawyers is strong. Although these groups do not have the people behind them, their power can still shape legislation, particularly through illicit means that their money can buy and cover up afterward. At the beginning of the novel a "Purchase Bill" is before the Senate. Although it is not described in any detail, the legislation seems to be aimed at breaking monopolies through government purchase. A "second amendment" has been proposed, again not very well described, that would, instead, allow employees to purchase monopolies. Later in the novel, we find that corporations have lined up employees so that if the second amendment is passed monopolists will still be in control, even if, on paper, someone else owns their corporations. When an unexpected roll call vote is announced, Senator Cornelius Twain is absent. His vote is needed to defeat the amendment. So the Altocrats find a means of tabling the amendment until he can be found. Months intervene, for the senator has disappeared. The plot alternates between the investigation and following the kidnappers and their bosses. Although some of the novel is set in Washington, with a great focus on the homes lining Rock Creek Park, the characters also travel by yacht, private train (with remarkable technological features), and airship to a Blue Ridge mountain summer resort, Chicago, Mexico, New York, St. Louis, and a generic Western state. Interactions between characters are often dominated by political discussions, and the novel is more concerned with illustrating political and business types than the setting of Washington. After hundreds of pages, the senator is retrieved, and he makes a dramatic speech on the floor of the Senate in which he presents a proposed substitute for the Purchase Bill. His proposal is simply an elaboration of a section of the Sherman Law and would effectively break monopolies through direct takeover by the federal government in a condemnation process.

157. Harrison, Mrs. Burton. *The Count and the Congressman*. Illustrated by Alex O. Levy. New York: Cupples & Leon, 1908. 300pp.

A wealthy young congressman from the "middle West" maintains a lavish Connecticut Avenue residence which he fills with European art treasures. He has chosen for his bride Margot Methuen, the beautiful daughter of an impoverished Virginia gentleman with long and respectable antecedents, but Margot rejects his suit. The rest of her family, so painfully embarrassed to be trying to live on the father's income as a government clerk, cannot understand the rebuff. The congressman, however, continues to pursue the young lady through indirect means, in ways like buying the old family homestead and restoring it. Margot, who resents being asked to enter into anything other than a love match, finds her true love while traveling in Italy with her wealthy aunt. However, the Italian count, who is equally smitten by her, is impoverished, and, for the good of the family, Margot finally decides she must return to America and marry the congressman; but information she hears from her father on his deathbed prevents her from this fate. The congressman had cheated her father out of a share in the silver mine from which his current wealth stems. In the end, Margot restores the family's fortunes through legal remedies and marries the count. She departs to live in Italy, leaving Washington to be presided over by people like the congressman. Many of the Washington scenes of this novel are set during the summer with discussion about the nature of the city in that season when the legislature is not in session and everyone has gone to resorts.

158. Hart, Frances Noyes. *The Crooked Lane Mystery*. Garden City, N.Y.: Doubleday, Doran, 1934. 310pp.

Karl Sheridan, son of an assistant secretary of state and grandson of the Austrian ambassador, returns toWashington, where he had lived in his youth, to start a lab for the "Division of Investigation." In Vienna, he was trained as a criminologist and achieved distinction. At the dinner party hosted by his godmother to welcome him, he meets Tess Stuart, daughter of a senator, and realizes that she had been his playmate when the two of them were young enough to have snowball fights on Lafayette Square. When Stuart returns to her Massachusetts Avenue mansion to find her beautiful, younger sister Fay dead, she immediately contacts Sheridan to investigate the murder disguised as a suicide. During the course of Sheridan's investigation, he learns that Fay was a sometime alcoholic and drug addict who fed news items to a society scandal columnist; he seeks her murderer in the Washington society circles she frequented. Due, perhaps, to the post-Crash period in which the novel was written, food, drinks, clothing, and interiors are described in great detail.

159. Hay, James Jr. *The Melwood Mystery*. New York: Dodd, Mead, 1920. 323pp.

Jefferson Hastings of the U.S. Department of Justice investigates how the President's plans for post-war economic development were stolen. Zimony Newman, a female German spy and popular Washington figure, had been seeking the plans but has been killed. On the night of her death at the Melwood Apartments on 18th Street, NW, she had a number of visitors. Larry Thayer, Senator John Thayer's brother, had been dating her and left her after getting her some post-coital ice cream. His brother had also been at the apartment building, summoned by a note from Newman, but claims he did not actually go up to her apartment. If his visit is made public his reputation will be destroyed. Felix Conrad, a wealthy society figure who had made his money from soap production and distribution, is also concerned about his reputation. He lives across the street from the Melwood and is a friend of artist, Frederick Marcello, who has been charged with the crime. Despite false leads, like the interrogation of Prof. Knowles, the inventor of torpedo-proof vessels who believed that Newman had stolen papers from him, Hastings discovers the truth with the aid of David Gower, Conrad's secretary. Although Gower's testimony is compromised by the fact that he is a "dope fiend," Hastings discovers physical evidence that confirms Gower's claim that Felix Conrad was the spy responsible for the misappropriation of all the missing documents, as well as the death of Newman.

160. Hay, James Jr. *The Unlighted House.* New York: Dodd, Mead, 1921. 281pp.

This mystery focuses on missing government documents that had last been in the hands of Senator Bruckner. However, during his search for the documents, George Darden of the U.S. Justice Department uncovers other secrets and must find a murderer. As the story develops, it seems that Edward Revis offered to procure the documents for a Latin-American agent. Revis is connected to Mary Haskell, who is secretly engaged to the senator and lives with her friend Addie Colvin. Tom Malloy is also a suitor of Haskell's and does not know that she has accepted the senator's proposal. On the night that Revis is murdered in the mansion he has rented on 33rd Street, NW, in Georgetown, Darden discovers Malloy and Haskell at the scene. He also determines that an unidentified woman was present. Despite false leads exhaustively pursued, Darden finally discovers that the murderer is a jealous woman with whom Revis had had a dalliance in Washington. When Darden also discovers that Bruckner sold the missing documents to a foreign power, Haskell is disgusted, and Malloy wins her hand.

161. Hay, James Jr. *That Washington Affair.* New York: Dodd, Mead, 1926. 254pp.

Carston J. Vail has tired of a Washington social life dominated by false aristocracy and cocktail party wit and is looking for excitement. He would also welcome an opportunity to relieve his poverty and become the man of wealth he appears to be. His opportunity comes through Alberto Barrone, a South American living in an elegant mansion on Q Street, near Dupont Circle. Barrone informs him of a planned coup in Saragonda, a Central American republic rich in natural resources. The plot involves some native Saragondans committed to replacing the corrupt regime with an honorable one and Americans looking to make large amounts of money by taking advantage of the rich natural resources of Saragonda. The Americans, New York bankers, are providing the money to arm the insurgents and do whatever else is necessary. They want to hire Vail to influence his friend, Assistant Secretary of State Barfield, to guarantee that the insurgent leader will gain official recognition after the coup. Vail's task seems easy, backed as he is by influential men. However, when a beautiful woman is murdered and an all too intelligent detective is put on the case, everything changes in this novel that is partly murder mystery, partly a novel of international intrigue, and partly a romance. Settings include the Wareham Hotel on F Street; Chevy Chase Country Club; the Spectators Club on 15th Street, NW, between I and K; an apartment house on B Street, SW; an exclusive H Street, NW, club; and social events hosted by the Washington diplomatic community.

162. Hayworth, A. D. *Uncle Hank and Aunt Nancy in Washington.* Washington, D.C.: Hayworth, 1897. 165pp.

After a lifetime in Indiana, Hank and Nancy Hopkins decide to fulfill their long-held dream to visit the nation's capital. When they announce their plans, their neighbors are critical and point out that their money could be better spent on more useful purchases than a sightseeing tour. Hank and Nancy attribute these comments to jealousy, and, when they do board their train, the whole township turns out to see them go. During the trip, Hank discusses politics with new acquaintances (primarily talking about Prohibition) and has some difficulties navigating the train system. When they arrive in Washington, the reader gets a chance to see the city through the eyes of these naïve country people who comment as much on political corruption, social customs, and prices as on the tourist sites. They visit a friend from their hometown who has a government job and lives in a house near 19th and N Streets, NW. His struggle for and ultimate success in obtaining a patent is recounted. In addition to tourist sites, Hank makes sure his friend takes him to a "hell" so he can be prepared to lecture the people back home on the immorality of the opium "dens" in Chinatown.

163. Higgins, George V. *A City on a Hill.* New York: Alfred A. Knopf, 1975. 256pp.

Since this entire novel consists of dialogue, without the narrative voice typical of most works of fiction, there is no significant physical description of settings and little of people. The main character, Hank Cavanaugh, works on the staff of Congressman Sam Barry. His big assignment is to garner support years in advance for a presidential bid by Barry's ally, Senator Paul Travis, a task he finds very difficult. Most of the sections of the novel set in Washington take place in Capitol Hill offices or in restaurants, like The Jockey Club. Other settings include restaurants, houses, and airport lounges in Boston, Detroit, Nantucket, and New York City. Cavanaugh and Barry were Kennedy supporters, and there is some reminiscing about the past, as well as discussion of the current political climate in which the Watergate scandal is being played out. The novel reveals the motivations and frustrations of working in a congressional office. Through extended exchanges Cavanaugh has with his wife and his mistress, the impact of politics on personal lives is also explored.

164. Hill, Grace Livingston. *Marigold.* New York: Grosset & Dunlap, 1938. 299pp. young adult.

Marigold Brooke works as a schoolteacher and lives with her widowed mother, Mary, a librarian. Her father had been a minister. Laurence Trescott, the son of a wealthy family, is courting Marigold, but both Marigold and Trescott's mothers consider the match inappropriate because of the difference in social status between the two. Marigold herself becomes concerned after she buys an expensive dress to attend a Trescott party. Thinking remorsefully that her mother cannot afford to travel to Washington to help her sister celebrate her birthday, she decides to return the dress and use the money for the trip. When they arrive in the capital, Marigold finds that her Aunt Marian has arranged for young Ethan Bevan to meet them, and the next day he takes her on a tour of the city. As she comes to know Ethan, she realizes what Laurence had been lacking: spiritual maturity. Ethan shows her museums and art galleries and takes her to a symphony concert, not things that would interest Laurence; but he also witnesses to her about his Christianity, and her own spirituality is reawakened. When she reads an account of the Trescott party that she missed, she has difficulty seeing how she could fit into such worldly entertainments. Returning to her hometown before her mother, Marigold is shocked to find that Laurence has started drinking. She is eventually rescued by Ethan, who takes her back to Washington about which she rhapsodizes as the capital of a Christian country.

165. Holden, E. Goodman. *A Famous Victory.* Chicago: Jansen, McClurg, 1880. 368pp.

Brewster, a millionaire textile mill owner from Roxbury, Connecticut, is campaigning to be President. Just before his party's nominating convention, his strongest rival is found dead. Many such "coincidences" favor Brewster through a campaign orchestrated by a party machine that he funds. Despite the machine's alternate use of blackmail and the promise of rewards, Brewster loses the popular vote.

The Electoral College is more easily manipulated, and he triumphs. The Washington section of the novel primarily deals with how Brewster and his cronies divide up the spoils and prevent the revelation of the ways he manipulated the Electoral College vote and practiced political corruption. The spoils system of civil service appointments and currency policy are the major political issues discussed. Through minor characters, the suffering of the general population brought about by inflation, the corrupt party system, and the overreaching greed of capitalists is illustrated. In the end, Brewster is punished when workers burn his mill and a mob breaks into his house in Roxbury. Although his daughter is not killed, her true love is murdered before her eyes, and her grief, along with the newfound knowledge of how much the workers hate her father, send her into a coma from which she may not recover. Brewster, himself, is later discovered dead in his library, just as his political rival had been found at the beginning of the story.

166. Holmes, John. *Magdalen: A Novel of the Social Crusade.* Washington, D.C.: Columbia, 1897. 128pp.

Maggie O'Connor attempts a personal transformation. Giving up her life of prostitution, she is assisted by Mother Mudd, director of a mission for the reform of fallen women. Hailed as a saved woman, Maggie finds a waitressing job and begins her new life. However, unable to cope with the way people continue to identify her with her past life, she returns to her brothel. Mother Mudd's son, eighteen-year-old Tommy, who had wanted to marry Maggie, seeks her out. She ignores the purity of his motivations, simply waiving her usual fee for the sensual pleasures to which she introduces him. At the end of the novel, Mother Mudd sends Tommy to boarding school, and Maggie disappears forever into Washington's notorious red-light district.

167. Holmes, Marjorie. *Cherry Blossom Princess.* Philadelphia: Westminster Press, 1960. 188pp. young adult.

Recent high school graduate Martha McCarron travels from a small Iowa town to Washington to visit her Aunt Kitty and Uncle Grant Griffith, who is assistant secretary of state in charge of Public Affairs. Martha's relatives live in a Georgian-style house in the Virginia countryside near Washington. Soon after her arrival, her uncle arranges for her to meet with a senator from her home state so that she can be considered for Cherry Blossom princess. She lunches in the Senate Restaurant and is chosen for the honor. The book details all of her activities as a princess, including buying clothes and having her hair styled in Georgetown, attending receptions at the Statler-Hilton and the Mayflower, participating in the ceremony near the Tidal Basin, and making official tours of Washington sights. Her social world broadens during her stay when she meets the twin sons of her uncle's neighbors who are members of the local hunt club and take her horseback riding. She also spends time with an air force officer who is her official escort. From her uncle and aunt she discovers the financial difficulties of working for the State Department since government expense accounts never cover the costs of all the entertaining and gift-giving expected of a diplomat. However, they willingly make the sacrifice because of their allegiance to the United States as a country that provides freedom and the highest standard of living in the world. The festival gives Martha access to gowns, furs, jewelry, limousines, and sports cars, and even when it is over she feels that she is in a new world of personal freedom and material comfort.

168. Holmes, Marjorie. *Follow Your Dream*. Philadelphia: Westminster, 1961. 188pp. young adult.

High school student Tracey Temple lives with her grandmother and widowed mother near Silver Spring, Maryland. Though she has been told repeatedly that veterinary medicine is not a profession for girls, she can think of nothing else and idolizes Dr. Jane Baldwin, the president of the District of Columbia Veterinarians' Association. She finds a job in Baldwin's office, and the novel details all of her work there and her romance with Baldwin's attractive young assistant, Whit. Baldwin's office is in Georgetown, and Tracey exercises animals in Rock Creek Park. Tracey and her family eventually move to a house owned by her great aunt Azalea that is located in Georgetown overlooking Oak Hill Cemetery. Her romance with Whit finally ends maturely when Whit leaves to finish veterinary school in Ontario and he assures Tracey that she can achieve her dream of becoming a veterinarian.

169. Holmes, Marjorie. *Senior Trip*. Philadelphia: Westminster, 1962. 191pp. young adult.

Fran Mathusek is a high school junior in a small town on the bluffs of the Wapsipinicon River in Iowa. Even though her father is the most important man in town, the family does not have much money—no one does—and the opportunities for young people are very limited. Fran's class decides to go to Washington for their senior class trip, instead of Davenport, Iowa, where senior classes typically go. Fran is particularly eager to visit the National Gallery since she paints murals influenced by Iowa artist Grant Wood and has never seen the work of other artists.

However, their school principal objects to the trip to Washington, and Fran's class members must begin a struggle that they equate with a political campaign for independence. They must also earn travel money. Despite the difficulties, one of their fathers reminds them that anything is possible in the United States. The class holds fish fries, operates a hot dog stand at the State Fair, has clothing drives, and does odd jobs, and soon the whole town is supporting them as they slowly raise the money for the trip. They finally set off across country in a chartered bus. They see every conceivable site in Washington and sail the Potomac to Mount Vernon. The novel includes emotional descriptions of the city. Throughout the novel, they learn of opportunities beyond their hometown, but are reminded that the Midwest also has a great deal to offer.

170. Hope, Laura Lee, [pseud.]. *The Bobbsey Twins in Washington.* New York: Grosset & Dunlap, 1919. 250pp. juvenile.

Mr. and Mrs. Bobbsey and their two sets of twins (Bert and Nan and Flossie and Freddie) leave the Eastern city of Lakeport in which they live to visit a business acquaintance of Mr. Bobbsey who also has two sets of twins. Electric lights are just being installed in Washington, and although the President has two automobiles, he still rides through the city in a carriage. They visit one of the city's markets and remark on the "Negro" women selling odd barks, herbs, and roots. They also take a tour on a large sightseeing auto that often needs its radiator refilled with water. The rest of their trip includes the more familiar sights of the East Room of the White House, the Washington Monument, the Library of Congress, and Mount Vernon (to which they travel by steamboat). When they go to the theater they are delighted to see the family of the Chinese minister dressed in their traditional clothing. Many people in the audience, including the Bobbseys, are more interested in the "Oriental" children than in the play. Before the end of their trip they enjoy the excitement of snow in Washington.

171. Hopkins, Pauline Bradford Mackie. *The Washingtonians.* Boston: L. C. Page, 1902. 357pp.

Portia Matthews, the self-confident daughter of a Cabinet secretary (the fictionalized Salmon P. Chase), is married to General Tom Matthews. To be near Washington during the Civil War, she and her husband live at her father's house in the countryside outside the city. Fiercely devoted to her father, she builds alliances with a senator and a newspaperman (a fictionalized Horace Greeley) to win the presidential nomination for her father. By the end of the novel, she has come to realize that her political involvement was unwomanly. The war is re-mote, evidenced only by wounded veterans, displaced blacks, and gos-sip about and discontent with President Lincoln. Descriptions of Washington emphasize the mud and dust and include accounts of La-fayette Square, Central Market, Ford's Theatre, Willard's Hotel, and the soldier-filled streets. There are also extensive descriptions of the affluent country house setting outside Washington financed by the wealth of Chase's son-in-law. The dramatic climax of the plot centers on the secretary's position on "Negro suffrage." A sub-plot concerns Mr. La Cerf, a former ward of General Matthews. He is an Episcopa-lian and Harvard graduate, but Portia distrusts him, in part because he is an American Indian.

172. Hopkins, William B. *Milliner to a Mouse: A Capital Chat*. New York: Knickerbocker, 1903. 119pp.

In this brief novel, an American girl is wooed and won by a wealthy Englishman. Her uncle, a man of respectable but modest line-age, attains a fortune and the rank of Russian nobility through his in-tellectual and diplomatic accomplishments. The story illustrates the idea that nobility of spirit is respected and rewarded. As sub-themes, the author satirizes American snobbery and the crudeness of regional politicians who, ill prepared for national office, cannot bring them-selves to understand the importance of creating a national capital to exceed European capitals. Instead, they are content that the city be the "garden spot of the world for politicians and niggers." From a twenty-first-century perspective the author's attitude toward the social status of African Americans, although a minor theme, will seem quite troubling. Descriptions are given of social life at the New Willard Hotel, recep-tions, and a public restaurant that serves pasta to the delight of people who have traveled in Europe.

173. Howard, Milford Wrarison. *If Christ Came to Congress*. Wash-ington, D.C.: Author, 1894. 364pp.

Through the story of Jennie Harmon, Howard demonstrates that Washington is filled with vice and corruption which originates with the politicians in control of the government and warps the social fabric of the city that exists to serve them. Eighteen-year-old Jennie arrives hop-ing to support her family with a government job. Congressman Snolly-goster, whose assistance she solicits, helps her take the civil service examination, but when she spurns his lustful advances, he thwarts her efforts to get a job. Near starvation, she finally succumbs to the con-gressman in return for a position. Later, when she angers Snollygoster, she loses her job, turns in desperation to prostitution, and eventually commits suicide.

174. Howard, Milford Wrarison. *What Christ Saw: Sequel to "If Christ Came to Congress."* Washington, D.C.: The Author, 1897. 96pp.

The dedication of this volume reveals its intent to condemn the presidency of Grover Cleveland and the corruption of Washington politicians. The inequalities of wealth that allow the few to indulge in ostentatious display while the majority go hungry is the evil that motivates the writer to condemn social events that most other Washington writers of the period celebrated. In addition to accounts of specific extravagances, including the salary of the President, Howard condemns drinking, gambling, and prostitution. He includes a map of houses of ill repute with a list of their proprietors that one assumes was not intended to serve as a tourist guide.

175. Hubbard, Freeman. *Vinnie Ream and Mr. Lincoln.* New York: Whittlesey House, 1949. 271pp.

A work of historical fiction, this book tells the story of the seventeen-year-old young woman who sculpted Lincoln from life and later was commissioned to produce a statue of the slain president. The book also includes the story behind her statue of Admiral Farragut located in Farragut Square.

176. Hughes, Robert. *The Cup of Fury: A Novel of Cities and Shipyards.* Illustrated by Henry Raleigh. New York: Harper & Brothers, 1919. 350pp.

On the day of the Lusitania's sinking, a dinner party gathers in London at the house of wealthy Sir Joseph Webling, a German who has become a naturalized British citizen. Among the Americans present is Mary Louise the adopted daughter of Webling. She grew up in a midwestern town, which she escaped to join a vaudeville troop. Lady and Sir Joseph Webling were moved to tears when they saw her perform in Berlin because of her resemblance to their deceased daughter. Intensely loyal to her adopted parents, when they ask her to carry letters to mysterious people in out of the way places, she squelches her misgivings. Unfortunately her concerns were well founded, and one evening she returns home to discover secret agents have the Weblings in custody. Only the suicide of the Weblings, her convincing denials, and her American citizenship prevent her prosecution. She returns to wartime Washington to begin a patriotic life engaged in the shipyards as a secretary to a man who eventually becomes her fiancé and, in the fullness of time, her husband. Not, however, before German spies appear and she is falsely implicated in espionage of which she is eventually proved to be innocent. The novel includes extended descriptions of Washington during World War I, presenting observations on the patriotism that attracted everyone to the city during this period, making it a truly national capital. The narrative includes general accounts of springtime in the city, Rock Creek Park, Massachusetts Avenue, wartime privations, and the influenza epidemic. Through the dialogues of characters and narration the rights of women and workers and the role of wealth in a democratic society are debated.

177. Hulbert, James. *Noon on the Third Day.* New York: Holt, Rinehart & Winston, 1962. 366pp.

Senator John Burnett of Missouri has been in office since the New Deal. One of Roosevelt's team, he is proud of his role in some of the important legislation of that era. His reputation as a liberal on social policy issues means that his fellow politicians, the press, and his constituents all believe he will vote against a union-breaking bill before Congress. By showing the reader Burnett's home life in Georgetown, his pragmatic campaign considerations that lead him to court wealthy men for whom he has no respect, and his distaste for the current leader of the most powerful labor union, Hulbert surfaces all the complex factors that go into Burnett's decision making. When the son of his black maid is arrested for a vicious crime that Burnett knows the youth committed, he sympathizes with his maid and hires a first-class lawyer to defend the youth, leading to attacks by other politicians and the press. As campaign season is about to begin he surprises everyone by voting for the labor bill, even after his attempts to amend it fail, because he believes that although it may hurt union management, it is in the interest of laborers. The vote is used as evidence that he has abandoned his principles for an under-the-table deal. During the campaign he is also attacked for the vaguely Communist ties in his speechwriter's distant past. The young businessman who mounts an insincere and manipulative campaign against him wins the election, bringing at noon on the third day of January an end to his thirty-five years in office.

178. Hunt, E. Howard. *The Berlin Ending: A Novel of Discovery.* New York: G. P. Putnam's Sons, 1973. 310pp

Neal Thorpe, a Vietnam veteran, is an architect and a partner in Dawes-Thorpe Associates, a Georgetown firm with offices at Canal Square. Returning from the airport one evening, Thorpe gives Annalise Bauer a lift into the city because a taxi strike is in progress. A few days later he sees an advertisement seeking information about a woman who matches her description. Thorpe is quickly enmeshed in a mystery that turns into political espionage, and he begins working again for the CIA and falls in love with Bauer, as he lends her his help. Although much of the novel is set in European capitals, the sections set in Washington include detailed and convincing descriptions. At this point, Georgetown, where Thorpe lives as well as works, was a destination for people involved in the various youth and protest movements. Details concerning local restaurants and their menus, and the kinds of possessions typical of a well-traveled Georgetowner, provide useful social information. In search of anonymity, Bauer submerses herself in the environs and accoutrements of the alternative youth culture, and clothing and housing details are provided.

179. Hunt, E. Howard [Dietrich, Robert, pseud.]. *The House on Q Street*. New York: Dell, 1959. 160pp.

When Harris Gurney, a lawyer and yachting friend of accountant Steve Bentley, contacts him about a potential job, Bentley thinks Gurney has merely steered an important new client, Major General Walter Ferrand Ballou, his way. Due to his respect for Ballou, a military hero in the Korean War, in which Bentley also fought, and his infatuation with Ballou's daughter, Francie, Bentley soon finds himself investigating a murder that he fears one of them committed. He successfully protects the Ballous, even though the general is guilty, and, in doing so, he must cooperate with a Maryland gangster and participate in the death of one of the mobster's hoodlums, so that the dead man can take the blame. In the course of the novel, Hunt describes a Georgetown dominated by designers and homosexuals, Q Street, NW, mansions and their affluent inhabitants, sidestreets in Kalorama with mansions cut up into shabby apartments, and a French Chateau-style country house that has been turned into a nightclub for a very affluent clientele.

180. Hunt, E. Howard [Dietrich, Robert, pseud.]. *Murder on the Rocks*. New York: Dell, 1957. 192pp.

Steve Bentley is a veteran of both the Korean War, where he did counter-intelligence work, and the U.S. Treasury Department, where he gathered evidence in major tax cases. He now has his own tax law practice and lives a comfortable life centered on a Massachusetts Avenue, NW, apartment and a ketch moored at the Yacht Club, where he is an active member. One oppressively hot summer day, his plans to sail down the Potomac for the weekend are disrupted by a visit from a beautiful woman, Iris (Calvo) Sewell. Mostly against his will, Iris and her even more beautiful sister Sara involve him in solving a mystery involving two murders and a famous emerald missing from their South American diplomat father's safe, and he tries to protect them from damaged reputations and sinister men. Bentley brings the criminals to justice and saves the diplomat from dire consequences, but not before narrowly surviving a murderous attack. The evil men in this novel tend to be smugglers of drugs from South America and their foot soldiers. The most successful smuggler, Vance Bodine, has accumulated enough wealth to buy respectability along with a huge Virginia estate where he can expect to attract all of Washington society when he hosts a party. Through Bentley's jaundiced eyes, Hunt describes the horsey set of Warrenton, Virginia, and the various social circles of Georgetown. Many snipes are made at the increasingly visible gay and lesbian community in Washington. Physical descriptions include interiors of Georgetown houses expensively renovated into apartments, a fleabag hotel in Chinatown, a fashionable nightclub called The Bagatelle near the Mayflower Hotel, and modest, seedy businesses on the side streets of Georgetown.

181. Hunt, E. Howard [Davis, Gordon, pseud.]. *House Dick*. Greenwich, Conn.: Fawcett, 1961. 144pp. Later published as, *Washington Pay-Off* (New York: Pinnacle, 1975).

Pete Novak is employed as a house detective by the Hotel Tilden on K Street, NW, near 17th. One evening, Novak is called to the room of Mrs. Julia Boyd of Winnetka, Illinois, whose husband, Chalmers, is in town for a convention. Several aspects of the interview with Mrs. Boyd puzzle him. She is perfectly calm in reporting the theft of expensive jewels, refuses to call the police, and says she does not want to tell her husband. A Dr. Edward Bickel is accompanying the Boyds, and Novak quickly decides he is not a real physician (he turns out to be an herbalist whose primary medicine is laced with mescaline). On his way back to his office Novak investigates suspicious sounds from a room near the Boyds and finds the beautiful, scantily clad Paula Norton, who has clearly been beaten by the man in her room, Ben Berada. When he knocks Berada out, Norton draws a gun on him and Novak leaves with the explanation that Berada is Norton's ex-husband. The mystery deepens when Chalmers Boyd barges into his office to claim that his wife suffers from delusions and that no jewelry was stolen. Then, Norton telephones in hysterics, and when Novak arrives in her room he finds the body of Chalmers shot to death on her bed. Since she claims she did not shoot him, Novak protects her by moving the corpse to the Boyds room. He then tries to stay one step ahead of the police as he investigates who really committed the murder, since Norton could be considered a prime suspect, given the fact that she had been having an affair with Chalmers and that she had been given the jewelry that Mrs. Boyd had reported stolen. Subplots include insurance fraud, drug addiction, and a powerful mobster pursuing Berada, who owes him a huge gambling debt. Unlike other novels by Hunt, the characters in this novel have bleak existences and no social refinement. Washington is portrayed as a city of strangers, besieged by a steady influx of tourists and conventioneers, and the action mostly takes place in seedy areas. Novak lives in a boarding house near 17th and N Streets, NW, and describes other once fashionable Northwest and Southwest neighborhoods now filled with impoverished transients.

182. Hunt, Una. *Young in the "Nineties."* New York: Charles Scribner's Sons, 1927. 313pp.

This slightly fictionalized autobiographical account describes Washington from the vantage point of a Northern girl living in the city with her family. The father is a scientist with the U.S. Geological Survey, and an uncle is an explorer with the survey, traveling most frequently to Alaska. Although the family is described as poor, living on the salary of a federal worker, they are, of course, poor only by comparison with "the snobby girls on Dupont Circle" and others who summer in Europe. This family summers in New England and has "Negroes" to help out around the house, rather than liveried servants. The father seems mostly engaged in research on atomic weights and in building the mineral collection at the National Museum. They live on Riggs Place, NW, a street where houses are brand new when they move in. Their neighbors include a highly placed diplomat involved in negotiations over Hawaii, an Alaskan explorer and uncle of the author, a Supreme Court Justice, and the minister of the newly constructed Swendenborgian church on the corner. However, their circle is mostly composed of families of scientists with the Coast and Geological Surveys. The author's milieu brings her into contact with notables including Dr. Mary Walker, Alexander Graham Bell (the author's uncle is a lawyer for the Bell Company), the king and queen of Hawaii (whom her family accompanies along with a presidential delegation to Mount Vernon), Major Powell (head of the Geological Survey), and Arctic explorer Adolphus W. Greeley. The author only has one brush with society through her friendship with "Mrs. Evelyn" (presumably Evalyn Walsh McLean), whose grand house is filled with furniture and rugs and governed by rules of etiquette that trip the author, literally and figuratively. Declining an invitation to summer in Bar Harbor to meet young men and launch a social career, instead the author continues to dream of becoming an ethnologist among the American Indians like her family's friends, Mrs. Stevenson and Miss Fletcher. The account begins with the author's thirteenth birthday and ends when she is eighteen and has begun studying at the Museum School in Boston. In addition to the level-headed descriptions of a Washington that seems like a small-town but happens to be filled with the famous and accomplished, the work provides intimate details of household life in a middle-class family, including frank discussions of flirtation, courtship, and the rather scandalous decisions some women of the time made to seek a career in addition to a husband.

183. James, Leigh. *The Capitol Hill Affair.* New York: Weybright & Talley, 1968. 213pp.

CIA agent Ernie Sessena is assigned to investigate civilian Pentagon employee Bart Williams, who purchased a ten thousand dollar Italian sports car in Italy, which he paid for with money he had received in Zurich by converting Vietnamese currency. Sessena is warned not to let anyone in the FBI know about the investigation. He begins by recruiting informants. Since Williams frequents 14th Street, NW, burlesque houses, his first recruit is Rosie Dawn, who is won over when he falsely claims to have served with her dead husband in Vietnam. He also recruits the fifteen-year-old-son of a friend who happens to be in the boy scout troop Williams leads, a "Negro" postman who delivers mail to Williams' Dupont Circle apartment, and the publisher of a Washington scandal sheet. Sessena's search for information takes him to many locales in Washington, including affluent suburbs off Rock Creek, the "mews" apartment of a Georgetown swinger, the National Press Club, trendy Georgetown restaurants, the City Club, a mansion on Foxhall Road, and an alternative bar named Jackson's Hole that is described as "hip, homosexual, and interracial," where Sessena is physically attacked as a "whitey." He eventually learns that secrets have been passed to the enemy concerning bacteriological warfare and that the information was sent by photographed "microdots."

184. Janeway, Elizabeth (Hall). *The Question of Gregory.* Garden City, N.Y.: Doubleday, 1949. 309pp.

John Gregory is the Undersecretary of the Department of Public Information, and he has just learned that his son, Tim Gregory, was killed in November 1944 near Aachen. The secretary who gives him the telegram is shocked that he does not weep. When she hears the news, his wife accuses him of never trying to obtain a deferment for their son because he was afraid it would hurt his career. She also claims that President Roosevelt and Washington have dehumanized him, destroying his honesty and decency. Grieving over his son's death and regretful for the way he has spent his life, Gregory empties his bank account and goes on a journey of self-discovery. His first stop is Key West, but, when his money is stolen, he travels to Vermont where he works in a factory. Only after several years is he able to return to Washington and try to figure out what had happened to him there. He knows he originally left his university job and went to Washington out of devotion to Roosevelt and a desire for greater contact with the real world. He is not able to accept all the subsequent decisions he made, however, and leaves Washington again to work in a Detroit factory. When he tries to reunite with his wife, she has become mentally unbalanced, and he has reached a point of detachment so deep that he can no longer care about anything or anyone.

185. Johnson, William Franklin. *Poco a Poco*. Illustrated by W. H. Fry. Akron, Ohio: Saalfield, 1902. 307pp.

This convoluted story is loosely knitted together by the idea of founding a national university in Washington that some of the characters heartily embrace and pursue, others modestly assist, and still others vehemently oppose. The two main protagonists are John Hume (most recently from the West and a promoter of an electric company) and Margaret Wistar, the cultivated daughter of a wealthy and powerful senator. The plot is set in motion when an anonymously received proposal for a national university is published in a Washington newspaper. The proposal, copied by other news outlets, attracts Hume to come East and assist in promoting the project. He is accompanied by the inventor whose work had inspired the establishment of the electric company Hume had been touting and who had seemed only a few steps away from the breakthrough that would make everyone involved in the venture wealthy. The proposal also inspires Margaret Wistar, who wants her father to perform an instrumental role in creating the university. A beautiful young actress, Mrs. la Rue, is also interested in the proposal because she thinks it was written by her missing husband, Robert Wistar, the estranged son of Senator Wistar.

When Hume arrives in Washington, he and the inventor end up living in the same boarding house as a mysterious, young, bearded cellist who plays a "Strad" and after many plot twists is revealed to be Robert Wistar. Hume eventually makes the breakthrough electrical discovery the inventor had failed to make. In doing so, he makes a fortune for himself and redeems his reputation, wins the hand of Margaret Wistar, and founds the national university along with the friends, like Robert Wistar, who had helped in his struggles. Everyone involved in the project earns "world-wide fame."

Although the novel does not have a great deal of physical description of Washington, a description of a séance that takes place on K Street, NW, the venue for a prize fight, the N Street, NW, boarding house where Hume and most of the other characters live, the F Street, NW, office of Senator Wistar, and his Dupont Circle mansion all seem to be based on direct observation.

186. Jones, John Beauchamp. *The Rival Belles; or, Life in Washington.* Peterson's Dollar Series. Philadelphia: T. B. Peterson Brothers, 1878. 270pp.

In this tale of the reversal of fortunes, the Spanglers are an old Philadelphia family who possess noble qualities of character but no money. The Tingles are pretentious nouveaux riches consumed with petty jealousies and ignoble emotions. Ironically, the first Tingle in the country had arrived as an Irish indentured servant, waited table in the Spangler household, and got a start in the grocery business with funds from the Spanglers. The Spanglers subsequently lost their money when some of their ships were seized by the British during the Revolution. The Tingles prospered to the point that their grocery origins were obscured, and their current sizeable income stems from passive investments. The Tingles embark for a season in Washington at the same time that the young male scion of the Spanglers leaves for California and the gold fields. Through image manipulation (the Tingles even employ a publicist) and ostentatious display, the Tingles soon attract a great deal of attention in Washington, but other skilled manipulators forward their own ends by publicizing the false rumor that Mr. Tingle will be appointed secretary of state. When he is not appointed, the family returns to Philadelphia chagrined, but no poorer. In fact, the experience has fueled hitherto non-existent ambitions in Tingle who invests heavily in cotton to increase his fortune. Harry Spangler, on the other hand, through the advice and assistance of men who recognize his superior qualities, attains prosperity through land investments, making a substantial amount from selling California land to the federal government. He returns home to establish an investment firm in Philadelphia and buy the Tingle mansion, which that family had to vacate after the crash of the cotton market. By the end of the novel, everyone has returned to their original place in society: the Spanglers to affluence and Mr. Tingle to the respectable life of a debt-free grocer. The novel includes extended descriptions of Washington social events, including a public reception at the White House.

187. Just, Ward S. *The Congressman Who Loved Flaubert, and Other Washington Stories.* Boston: Little, Brown, 1973. 178pp.

This book of short stories captures very different types of insider Washingtonians at revealing moments. In one story, a congressman must put aside the only worthwhile legislation of his career in order to help a friend with a resolution. He knows that the legislation will accomplish nothing, but it will be wildly publicized and help him with a Senate campaign. In other stories, a congressman deals with a divorce, a White House staffer leaves his job after sixteen years, and a state department man faces an international crisis.

188. Kane, Harnett T. *New Orleans Woman: A Biographical Novel of Myra Clark Gaines.* Garden City, N.Y.: Doubleday, 1946. 344pp.

Myra is the adopted daughter of military hero Colonel Samuel Davis and Marianne Rose Baron Boisfontaine, whom he rescued during a slave uprising in Santo Domingo and later married. Myra's real father was Daniel Clark, a wealthy Southern landowner, and soon after her 1832 marriage to Will Whitney, she discovers that property she should have received as a bequest from his estate was misappropriated. The novel recounts in lengthy detail Myra's struggle to gain her inheritance, and it is set in New Orleans as well as Washington.

After Will Whitney dies, Myra eventually marries the powerful General Edmund Gaines. Through his efforts, parts of her case are argued before the Supreme Court, requiring the couples' presence in Washington. In the 1840s Gaines takes command of the Army's Eastern Department, and the couple moves to Washington again. The novel includes physical descriptions of the city, analyses of its qualities, and accounts of social customs as Myra tries to befriend influential people who may help with her search for justice. After winning her court case to prove that Clark was her father and she his legal heir, further court cases loom, but the death of Gaines brings years of struggle. Myra returns to Washington in the 1850s and again in 1860, staying through 1861. Through her eyes the reader sees all the changes that have occurred. By the time the Supreme Court reaches a decision favorable to her, the Civil War has broken out. After the war land records in the South are in disarray. She continues her legal struggle and returns to Washington to live in a boarding house in 1873. However, by the time of her death in New Orleans in 1885 her legal case is still not settled. Only in 1896 is the suit resolved and Myra's heirs receive $923,788.

189. Karig, Walter. *Caroline Hicks*. New York: Rinehart, 1951. 438pp.

Caroline Hicks, having taken the Civil Service Examination in her hometown of Corinth, Pennsylvania, arrives in Washington during World War II to become a part of "Washington's cosmopolitan gynocracy." For her, and many of her friends, Washington is a symbol of personal independence, and the novel minutely details what it was like for a woman without much money to live in the city during the war. As a relative innocent, Caroline is taken in hand by her new acquaintances who spend a good deal of time explaining the city to her, defining slang terms, and instructing her on how to dress, behave at her office job, and interact with suitors. The novel exhaustively describes boarding house life (with its physical privations and lack of privacy), furnished apartment living, public transportation, cafeteria and restaurant food, clothing, drinking, nightlife, and the trials of menial office work. Typical conversations, gossip, and slang of the period are also recorded, and a major topic is wartime immorality, featuring greed (war profiteering) and lasciviousness (makeup, tattoos, and extramarital sex). Much of the plot focuses on heterosexual romance, although references are made to homosexuality. At the war's end, many of Caroline's acquaintances leave town to marry, but she rejects a proposal, deciding to continue a life in Washington that, although ordinary from many perspectives, has become too exciting to give up. She sees herself as living at the center of the world.

190. Karp, David. *The Brotherhood of Velvet*. New York: Banner, 1967. 159pp.

James Reed Watterson is a thirty-six-year-old undersecretary in a federal government agency and the son of a New York City civil contractor who built Manhattan subways and worked on highway projects. Watterson's wife, Vivian, heiress to an old Long Island fortune, brought true wealth and social prominence to their marriage. The couple maintains a Washington apartment and a Georgetown house and frequently appears in the society pages. Watterson is confident that much greater prominence will be his: he is a member of the Brotherhood of the Bell. Members are secretly chosen from among the students at the prestigious all-male preparatory school Watterson attended. Less than two hundred, life-long members of all ages hold some of the highest positions of political and corporate power in the country, and when young members begin their careers, they need only name the positions they want. After his life has gone so well for so long, Watterson is surprised when Chad Hammond, his main contact with the Brotherhood, gives him an assignment from the group. He must discredit his close friend Clark Sherrell to force Sherrell out of the job Watterson had gotten for him in his own agency—the Brotherhood wants to put someone else in the position. Although Watterson has permission to defend his friend in public, he must make certain that a false affidavit that Sherrell had a homosexual liaison with another boy when he was fifteen is used to force him from government service. Watterson's attempts backfire to persuade Sherrell to resign, and soon investigations are underway to weed homosexuals and other "deviates" out of federal jobs. Vivian divorces him, and he is fired. However, neither of these events is as disturbing as the Brotherhood's pledge to destroy him. He ends up impoverished and unable to get even the humblest of jobs. Although some physical descriptions of Washington are included in the novel, the book is more interesting for evoking a dark vision of the corruptibility of Washington politicians and career civil servants through the power of national corporate interests.

191. Keats, Charles B. *Petticoat War in the White House: A Novelized Biography of Peggy O'Neal.* Fort Lauderdale, Fla.: Heritage Hall, 1973. 323pp.

This account of the historical figure Margaret "Peggy" (O'Neal) Eaton begins in January 1815 and ends with her death in 1879. Keats does not list his sources for this novel that emphasizes O'Neal's rebellion against being trapped in any one social rank in a society that prides itself on being democratic. She is also portrayed as a political strategist on a par with famous elected officials and party leaders of her time.

192. Keenan, Henry Francis. *The Money-Makers.* Boston: D. Appleton, 1884. 337pp.

This response to James Hay's attack on labor unions, *The Breadwinners* (1883), is not physically set in Washington, although it is often referred to as a Washington novel, since corrupt national politics play such an important role in the story. Since the claim of the novel is that "wealth alone dominates in this country," it is not surprising that the novel is set in New York City, the country's financial center. The Washington types in the novel, lobbyists (some women), party leaders, and corrupt politicians, are displayed in the setting of New York society events and the social season at Saratoga Springs.

193. Kennelly, Ardyth. *The Spur.* New York: Julian Messner, 1951. 304pp.

This historical novel presents the life and motivations of John Wilkes Booth. A sense of Washington in the last year of the Civil War is conveyed, although all descriptions are focused on Booth and his activities.

194. Keyes, Frances Parkinson. *All That Glitters.* New York: Julian Messner, 1941. 820pp.

This very lengthy novel traces the story of Arkansas Senator Morton's family from their arrival in Washington in December 1927 until the beginning of World War II. Morton's wife is Helen, and they have a son, Robert, and a daughter, Helen. The newly arrived Mortons establish themselves in Washington through Mrs. Endicott, one of the wealthy widows in control of society. Their experiences are characterized by the title of the novel's first half, "The Fat Years." Money rules the city, which is awash in bootleg alcohol, and time is passed eating course after course of elaborate meals. Even lunches might include lobster Newburg and filet mignon, and, on a single day during the season, one might attend three or four dinners, but stay for only one course at each. Keyes provides as much social detail about these events as any society reporter of the time, including anecdotes, gossip, and descriptions of music, floral decorations, dress, food, and houses. Although most of the characters are members of Washington society, there are some outsiders. One is the reporter Zoe Wing, whose efforts to gather information for her column are detailed; another is Alfredo Terraza, a Mexican. In addition to breaking into society, Senator Morton learns the political ropes, Mrs. Morton throws herself into the poliltics of the Daughters of the American Revolution, and the younger Martins pursue matrimonial prospects. Their thinking alternates between choosing a socially prominent mate (Veronique Alfieri and Giles Arnold) or a mate who is merely socially active (Zoe Wing and Alfredo Terraza). After a great deal of debate and plot twists, the Morton children each reject their opportunities to marry up and choose Zoe and Alfredo. Soon afterward, the first half of the novel ends with the stock market crash of 1929, which brings dramatic changes for the Morton family and for Washington society.

In the second half of the novel, Washington is transformed as people lose their fortunes and mansions that had been the site of the most exclusive balls are turned into boarding houses. The social set of the 1920s disperses back to their still affluent surroundings in the country and the international set (particularly the British) and the politically able begin to dominate society. In this environment, Zoe's journalism brings her great success, and she becomes internationally known through her book *Capital Kaleidoscope* (a work by the same title was published by Keyes). Her husband, Robert, works the connections he

makes as his senator father's secretary, writing magazine articles about
the homes and gardens of the affluent and a screenplay fictionalizing
their lives. Eventually, he and Zoe establish their own news bureau. As
political upheavals around the world begin to dominate everyone's attention the characters are drawn away from Washington. Helen, who
had moved with Terraza to Mexico, is widowed during a political uprising. She eventually marries Guy Grenville, son of Lord and Lady
Grenville, and as war looms the focus returns to Washington as international diplomats host party after party to establish American support
for their countries. As a symbol of the international importance of
Washington, a new airport is under construction, and the capital's
streets are filled with traffic. In the novel's final scene a party on a
yacht is in progress in honor of Helen and Guy Grenville, and the news
comes of the fall of France to the Germans.

195. Keyes, Frances Parkinson. *Honor Bright.* New York: Julian Messner, 1936. 583pp.

Several chapters of this society novel are set in Washington. When
Honor Bright returns to the capital in the 1920s after working in New
York City and becoming a successful reporter, she takes a house on
Meridian Hill that is described in detail, as are the politicians and social
events that form her social life from 1922 through 1924. Other settings
include Boston and a Virginia plantation.

196. Keyes, Frances Parkinson. *Queen Anne's Lace.* New York: Horace
Liveright, 1930. 288pp.

This novel relates the story of fictional character Anne Chamber-
lain, who is born to a family of modest means in Wallacetown, Maryland, but becomes First Lady of the land. She marries Neal Conrad,
who is ambitious and sociable, over the objections of Conrad's status-
conscious mother. For their honeymoon Anne fulfills her wish to see
Washington and in doing so finds out that Neal has political ambitions
for national elected office. The two stay at the Hotel Hamilton, see the
tourist sites (including the newly completed Library of Congress), and
have a special meal at the Shoreham, where they meet Clarence
Hathaway, a classmate of Neal's, who is in the State Department.

Time passes as Neal steadily rises through the political ranks,
aided by Anne, who finds ways to economize and make his modest
earnings stretch. During World War I, he gets his first chance to travel
regularly to Washington as a state "Food Administrator." On one trip,
Hathaway inspires Neal to see that Anne needs the chance to fulfill her
destiny as a social hostess, rather than remaining a housewife. He in-

sists that the Conrads go to Paris for the summer to acquire social poise. During the trip, Neal learns of his senate appointment to fill out the term of a recently deceased member. When the couple arrives in Washington, Anne finds social life difficult until the Vice President's wife takes her up, and she quickly establishes herself as a hostess. The book details what Anne learns about social matters, such as the Senate Ladies' luncheon club, the rules of precedence, the Congressional Club, and "at homes." As with the rest of the novel rich descriptions are provided of clothing, furnishings, and food. Although Anne follows the dictates of custom, her intelligence and natural courtesy inform all of her actions, distinguishing her from many other successful hostesses. She is also savvy about financial matters. She quickly sees the good real-estate value of Georgetown, finds a Georgian-style mansion there, and oversees its renovation. This trend setting is also expressed through her taste in her clothing and her creation of a true European-style salon, turning her back on social events consisting of mere social chatter. By the end of the novel, her husband has earned the role of President through his statesmanship, and she has earned the role of First Lady through her social achievements. And so, the girl from Wallacetown, who could be satisfied with the wildflower "Queen Anne's lace," ends by wearing real lace fit for a queen.

197. Keyes, Frances Parkinson. *Senator Marlowe's Daughter.* New York: Julian Messner, 1933. 465pp.

Faith Marlowe's family, which has been involved in politics at the national level since the time of the Revolutionary War, settled in Washington while the Federal city was still under construction. Her connection with the city is broken in her youth when her senator father is voted out of office. Her mother Flossie refuses to return with him to their New England farm, insisting that she travel in Europe with Faith, where they live in Paris and Spain. Marlowe divorces Flossie for desertion, and she is later murdered. Faith is forced to marry a German nobleman, who is subsequently posted as a diplomat to Copenhagen and Granada. She returns to the United States a beautiful, sophisticated woman with a young son. When war breaks out between France and Germany, her true love, Sam, fights for France, and her husband for Germany. Faith becomes increasingly active in politics and accepts the position of national committeewoman for her political party. When a townsman is elected President, she mounts a successful campaign for the U.S. Senate, despite accusations of spying for her German husband's country and being a Catholic convert. Although less than thirty pages of the novel are physically set in Washington, Faith's goal to return to her hometown and recover her family's lost status is a central theme.

198. Knebel, Fletcher. *Dark Horse*. Garden City, N.Y.: Doubleday, 1972. 367pp.
When their presidential nominee dies only twenty-two days before the election, a political party must quickly find an effective replacement. The opposition candidate is Governor Hugh G. Pinholster, whose popular appeal stems from his connection to counter-culture intellectuals and his public image of radical trendiness. In a race in which the eighteen- to twenty-year-old vote counts heavily, Pinholster will win, unless the opposition can find a candidate to appeal to those who are tired of dissenters and want to return to a "work-and-prosper" ethic. They need someone who is white, suburban, and middle-class yet "ethnic." They find him in Eddie Quinn, a former truck driver who is a New Jersey highway commissioner and lives in a motel. Knebel outlines the selection process, campaign, and public relations ploys of the campaign managers and depicts the divided America of the time.

Although it had seemed that Quinn would make a docile party representative, he begins a campaign attack against the rich who control the political process, claiming they increase their own wealth and power by turning the citizenry into mere consumers. The party leaders turn against him, but the public is intrigued. Although Quinn does not win the election, he reawakens political discussion in the country. Through the voice of Quinn, the author lays out a vision of an improved United States.

Knebels' references to cultural figures and events from the time period seem comprehensive and touch on personalities ranging from Johnny Cash to Lieutenant Calley, and issues from busing to abortion. In this novel, Washington is viewed mostly from the windows of hotels like the Hay-Adams and Statler-Hilton, or the offices of politicians, where press conferences and campaign strategy sessions are held.

199. Knebel, Fletcher. *Seven Days in May*. New York: Harper & Row, 1962. 341pp.
President Jordan Lyman and representatives of the other nuclear powers have signed a self-policing treaty to bring an end to nuclear testing. The treaty is very unpopular in the United States, and Colonel Casey, a Pentagon officer, has been assigned to show the effectiveness of defensive measures in deterring a nuclear attack. While preparing for the drill, Casey discovers a plot by members of the military to stage a coup, usurping the power of the executive and derailing the nuclear

treaty. The coup is defeated, but only after an involved struggle. The Washington in which the novel is set is that of the offices and meeting rooms of highly placed Washington officials.

200. Knebel, Fletcher. *Vanished.* Garden City, N.Y.: Doubleday, 1968. 407pp.

Miguel Loomis spends the summer in Washington as a doctoral fellow at the Atomic Energy Commission. He settles easily into life in the city through his father's connections, primarily Stephen Greer, law firm principal and Presidential friend and advisor; and White House press secretary, Gene Culligan, from whose perspective the plot's action is recounted. The elder Loomis is an important political fundraiser and owner of Educational Micro, a Los Angeles company that supplies microfiche printing to schools and the government. Greer and Culligan introduce Loomis to their friends, and girls and take him to the Metropolitan Club, the Jockey Club, and to nightspots such as Bayou and Dialogue in Georgetown. When Loomis discovers a CIA effort to recruit young physicists to spy on their colleagues, he immediately asks Greer and Culligan to persuade the President to end the program, pointing out that President Johnson had officially ordered the CIA to end its involvement in student and education organizations. They discover the President has no knowledge of the CIA activity. Greer and Culligan investigate, and the stakes rise when Loomis disappears. Throughout the novel, the author provides rich social details about official Washington, the operations of the CIA and FBI, and the lives of Washington's political elite and of the counter-culture in Georgetown. The novel includes criticism of the CIA and FBI for trying to establish themselves as more powerful than the executive branch and of the executive branch itself for acting in secret without providing information to the American people and seeking a mandate. There is also discussion of the nuclear threat and the importance of international law and global disarmament.

201. Knowland, Helen. *Madame Baltimore: A Novel of Suspense.* New York: Dodd, Mead, 1949. 210pp.

Harriet Berkeley's affair with the married Foster Ford is grounded in the understanding that he will divorce his wife and marry her. To her dismay, she discovers Ford is having an affair with another woman named Madame Baltimore and confronts him with the evidence. Ford claims Harriet should have known all along that their relationship was just a dalliance and blackmails her into lending him four thousand dollars, threatening that he will tell her husband about their affair and the fifteen hundred dollars she had already lent him. Ford's wife, Drucie, also learns of Madame Baltimore and decides to stop footing the bills for Ford's lifestyle, immediately firing the butler and other household staff. When Ford is murdered, Drucie, Harriet, and her husband Bob Berkeley are all suspects. Though readers of the novel know immediately who killed Ford, some mysteries remain to be solved. The plot unfolds in settings such as the Sulgrave Club, the Jefferson and Mayflower hotels, and the Cleveland Park neighborhood.

202. Lasalle, Mrs. E. L. *Magdalen, the Enchantress: Founded on Fact.* Philadelphia: J. B. Lippincott, 1858. 302pp.

Social rivalries begin early for Magdalen Shelby, an heiress known from an early age for her beauty. To Magdalen's frustration, her schoolmate, Grace Richmond, known for her angelic personality and innocent looks, wins people over without any effort, including Neville Heath, who Magdalen had intended for herself. When Grace and Neville marry, Magdalen confesses her love to Neville and Grace fearfully claims that Magdalen is an enchantress who can win any man away from any woman. Even as Magdalen's mother takes her to Europe to find a nobleman for a husband, Magdalen pledges that she will be Neville's wife within five years. When her mother dies, she returns from Europe more sophisticated and with a sizable fortune. Her schemes to win Neville are recounted in detail and involve poisoning, gambling, alcoholism, dueling, a self-serving interest in Catholicism, and an ability to employ her wealth to control others. When her gambling depletes her fortune, she steals Charles Clinton away from his naïve fiancée to gain access to his wealth. Clinton's spurned fiancée falls ill and dies seven months after Magdalen and Charles marry, leaving Charles to blame himself and ruefully claim that he would still be happy had he never met Magdalen. Soon afterward, he, too, dies and Magdalen gives birth to his son several months later. Seemingly unfazed by her experiences, all Magdalen can think when Grace dies is that her long-held goal seems within her reach. However, Neville has been accused by Grace's brother of poisoning her and challenged to a duel. Neville successfully kills the brother and marries Magdalen, but the union is clouded by Neville's remorse, which he tries to assuage through excessive drinking. The unhappiness and eventual death of Neville inspires Magdalen to acknowledge the evilness of her behavior and to devote herself to a quiet family life. Disciplined by fate, she becomes humble, gentle, and charitable. The fact that the author considered Washington the most appropriate setting for such a tale is, perhaps, of more interest than the slight content specific to the Washington area, such as picnics at Great Falls, the White House New Year's reception, and locales in Alexandria.

203. Lasselle, Mrs. Nancy Polk. *Annie Grayson: or, Life in Washington.* Washington, D.C.: H. Laselle, 1853. 345pp.

Annie Grayson is bound by social constraints and controlled by her cold mother, who married not out of love, but to form an alliance with the most socially distinguished man she could find. Annie obeys her mother's injunction that she avoid "mere common people" and act like a "proper" society girl. Although she travels to the South and West to visit relatives and sees ways of living that differ from those to which she is accustomed, when she returns to Washington and all of her friends are marrying, she marries as well. Although she is not in love with Congressman Edwin Stanmore, the brother of her best friend, she marries him for his social standing rather than waiting for a love match. Her mother approves the respectability of the marriage, and the novel ends by celebrating Annie's faithfulness to her mother's lessons.

204. Lasselle, Mrs. Nancy Polk. *Hope Marshall; or, Government and Its Offices.* Washington, D.C.: H. Laselle. 1859. 396pp.

The patriarch of the Kentucky-based Marshall family has served as a judge and ambassador to Spain. His tireless efforts on behalf of his party, including a loan of his own money, result in assurances that he will be appointed secretary of state when a new administration takes office. He rents out his Louisville, Kentucky, property, sells his furniture, and moves to Washington with his son Harry and daughter Hope. Without his knowledge, Senator Bingham, another party member, betrays him, and Marshall does not get appointed. Months of anxiety and frustration follow as he tries to collect the money he is owed by the government and his political party, destroying his health and speeding his death. Left on their own, Harry and Hope place their financial affairs in the hands of Senator Bingham's political manager and are soon reduced to penury and forced to leave Washington for the frontier. Fortunately, honorable people like themselves successively befriend them, and they are able to survive. After years of struggle and temporary reverses, they eventually regain financial security and social status by founding a town in Wisconsin, and Harry is elected to the U.S. Congress. Their suffering at the hands of self-interested politicians using political patronage to build fortunes while treating others ruthlessly have sensitized Hope and Harry to the needs of other victims whom they seek out and assist. Through their conversations and the stories of the people they help, the reader is instructed in the evils of political patronage and the need for a merit system in the appointment of government officials. In addition to this political message, readers can learn a good deal about social behavior, particularly social entertainments, and the living arrangements of the upper-middle-class Washington household.

205. Leighton, Frances Spatz. *The Memoirs of Senator Brown, a Capitol Cat.* New York: Fleet, 1965. 164pp.

In this playfully satirical novel, the main character, a cat from Montana, Senator Brown, tells how he was elected, his Washington experiences, and his legislative projects. Many references are made to political issues, social figures, and politicians of the period. Some of the people mentioned are Hale Boggs, Perle Mesta, Bobby Kennedy, Peter Townsend, and Adlai Stevenson. Since Lyndon Johnson is President, much is made of the popularity of Texas, and Senator Brown is asked to address the Texas Breakfast Club. In preparing his speech, the senator notes how useful phrases like "slum clearance" and "police action" are for establishing immediate rapport with political audiences. He also finds audiences receptive to his major piece of legislation: the Mouse-on-the-Moon Project. As is common with politicians, he has a wall filled with photographs in his office. Photographs of this "status wall" and enlargements of selected images are included and feature famous Washington cats and dogs (those of Jeane Dixon, Congressman Frank Annunzio, Patty Duke, President Johnson, Senator Harry Byrd, Drew Pearson, Perle Mesta, Patty Cavin, and John Brounas).

206. Leighton, Frances Spatz. *Patty Goes to Washington.* New York: Ace Books, 1964. 142pp. young adult.

During the Lyndon Johnson administration, reporter Martin Lane's newspaper sends him on a two-week assignment to Washington during Easter and the Cherry Blossom Festival to interview the city's fifty most interesting men. He takes his nine-year-old son, Ross, his sixteen-year-old daughter, Patty, and her look-alike English cousin, Cathy, along. They stay at the Georgetown row house of his friends Toni and Don Sherman who live on Dumbarton Avenue, NW. While Martin works on his story, the children tour the city and hear many anecdotes connected with the places they visit and the historic persons associated with them. The girls meet two congressional pages and hear about the page system, as well as receiving behind the scenes tours of the Capitol and seeing Senators Dirksen, Humphrey, Kennedy, and Saltonstall. Their pages also take them to an informal party at the house of some friends where they learn the local slang and new dances. When Toni

Sherman takes them to a tea at the Embassy of Iran, they learn some of the etiquette of attending such a function, as well as a little about Iran. They also attend a dance at the Naval Academy and learn about the traditions of the Academy and Annapolis. As a culmination of their trip, they serve as Junior Hostesses at the Cherry Blossom Festival, escorted by their pages.

207. Levy, Lewis [Stonewall, Cutter, pseud.]. *Senator Cashdollar of Washington.* Chicago: E. A. Weeks, 1899. 246pp.
    A Washington state banker is persuaded to run for the U.S. Senate by men who convince him that he will benefit financially, although their own financial interests are their primary motivations. The Cashdollar campaign builds momentum as his backers extract endorsements with promises of favorable legislation from a wide variety of interest groups, including timber and undertaking firms. When Cashdollar arrives in Washington he lives in great style, supporting his wife's ambitions to marry their daughter to a European nobleman. Although a willing nobleman is found, the daughter, who thought she wanted to dominate Washington society, decides to return home as the wife of her father's young, hard-working private secretary. In addition to this unexpected development, the fortune the senator expected from holding his office does not quite materialize, nor do his supporters make the amounts of money they had expected. Everyone still prospers, however, through his access to power in the federal government.

208. Lewis, Alfred Henry. *Peggy O'Neal.* Illustrated by Henry Hutt. Philadelphia: D. Biddle, 1903. 494pp.
    Written from the viewpoint of one of Andrew Jackson's associates, the novel takes the position that the historical figure Peggy O'Neal (Eaton) was a woman wronged. She was envied for her beauty, hated for her goodness, and despised for her humble origins.

209. Lewis, Alfred Henry. *The President.* New York: A. S. Barnes, 1904. 514pp.
    Richard Storms meets Dorothy Harley and her mother in Manhattan's Waldorf-Astoria when Dorothy catches her heel as she is walking down a staircase. Richard breaks her fall and is immediately smitten. Discovering that Dorothy lives with her family in Washington, Richard decides to move there and court her. He possesses significant wealth (mostly inherited from his parents) and respectable social connections and has spent most of his young adulthood in Europe. Unlike other affluent people, he conceals his wealth, fearing that people will like

him only for his money. When he arrives in Washington, people assume that the very distinguished English gentlemen living with him, Mr. Gwynne, is his patron; in fact, Gwynne is Richard's butler. When Richard discovers that Dorothy's father had built his wealth by using inside information and preferential business contracts secured through his senator brother, he secretly buys a newspaper and has Gwynne to offer the paper's columns to the senator as well as the services of Richard, as columnist. Although the senator and his brother immediately begin to take advantage of the situation to promote various schemes, and Dorothy is already in love with Richard, his suit does not progress far because of the antipathy of Dorothy's mother to her daughter's marriage to a poor man. She prefers Dorothy to encourage Storri, a Russian Count, who is wealthy from underhanded business schemes. When Storri presents a grand scheme to Harley that involves railroads and gold in China and building a railroad and Great Lakes shipping company in the United States, the prospect of gold-based wealth excites him, and he quickly garners his brother's support. The brothers work with a syndicate of moneyed schemers on the project, and through their planning the author exposes the corruption of Washington and Wall Street. Richard makes certain that the syndicate's stock manipulation fails, destroying Storri, while Richard remains an impeccable gentleman and never publicly exposes the corrupt brothers. With Storri out of the way, Dorothy's parents finally yield before her love for Richard, and the two marry without his revealing his wealth—a revelation that would have made Dorothy's parents, the senator, and the rest of Washington obeisant to him. After the wedding Dorothy and Richard sail to Europe to live a far grander life than even the wealthiest senator can live in Washington.

210. Lincoln, Jeanie Gould. *A Genuine Girl.* Boston: Houghton Mifflin / Riverside Press, 1896. 264pp.

Lieutenant Theodore Frost, who has had a long career as an Indian fighter, has been recalled to Fort Myer and reenters the social circle of his friends and patrons Senator and Marjorie Gray. He is soon joined by his cousin, Penelope Frost, who comes to Washington to go to school with the Grays' daughter, Phylis [*sic*]. A short time later, Gerald, the Grays' son, who is studying at Yale, returns for Christmas and the beginning of the social season. The novel recounts the social activities in which the young people engage, some of which are specific to the Washington military community. One chapter concerns amateur photography using a large format camera that a servant carries about for the young ladies. Although there are general references to Washington places, the main focus is on the developing romances of the young people.

211. Lincoln, Jeanie Gould. *A Javelin of Fate*. Boston: Houghton Mifflin / Riverside Press, 1905. 295pp.

Set during the Civil War, the novel captures the peculiar nature of social life in Washington and Baltimore, as border areas in the conflict and where many residents still maintained ties to the South. People living in these cities had relatives who traveled back and forth across the Mason Dixon Line to visit them and, sometimes, carried secrets useful in the war effort. The main focus is on the home of Baltimore resident Evelyn Vansittart which is the center of a counter-espionage ring, but some scenes are set in Washington.

212. Lincoln, Jeanie Gould. *Her Washington Season*. Boston: James R. Osgood, 1884. 207pp.

This epistolary novel features Dolly Oglethorpe's letters to friends in the Northeast and relatives in London, describing a visit to her aunt in Washington and her first social season in the city. The Oglethorpe family house in which she stays was built during the construction of the Federal City and is located at 1700 K Street, NW. She contrasts etiquette in New York, London, and Washington and details the forms of socializing popular in the city (tea, dancing receptions held before dinner, formal dinners, informal receptions after dinner, the "germans" held by the Bachelors' Club, private balls, private theatricals, breakfasts, and luncheons for ladies). She comes to realize that intelligent conversation is the hallmark of "resident society" (a term used to distinguish those social figures with long-term standing in the city) and that the city fascinates Northerners for combining picturesque beauty with the best cosmopolitan society. Many historical characters appear in the novel, including Aristarchi Bey, George Bancroft, and W. W. Corcoran.

213. Lincoln, Natalie Sumner. *13 Thirteenth Street*. New York: D. Appleton, 1932. 293pp.

The novel's protagonist, Colonel Wayne Campbell, is a widower who lives on Massachusetts Avenue, NW, in a floor-through apartment in an old house. He recently inherited a colonial house, known as the Apthorpe Mansion, that originally had grounds reaching from Tiber Creek to the Potomac River. Its current address is 13 Thirteenth Street, and when Countess Ilda Zichy, a world famous Hungarian dancer, is found stabbed to death in the empty house, the event seems in keeping with the ominous address. Campbell tries to solve the crime. Descriptions of the neighborhood in which the house is located are of interest since the area is still filled with houses. The novel includes negative portrayals of African Americans, French, and Japanese.

214. Lincoln, Natalie Sumner. *The Blue Car Mystery*. New York: D. Appleton, 1926. 314pp.

The last Whitney of his line, a retired naval commodore named James Whitney has been murdered in his colonial mansion at New Jersey Avenue and N Street, SE. The house is named "Whitney's Folly" after a long-dead Whitney who refused to move to a more fashionable area during the establishment of the Federal City. The suspects are numerous, although the only person who might have some plausible motivation is the niece of the deceased, Harriet Whitney, the beautiful daughter of James' estranged and impoverished brother, who inherits his estate. Although summoned to spend New Year's Eve with her uncle, she was also on a mission to obtain money from him to help relieve her family's financial difficulties. A family friend and lawyer tries to find the real murderer and free Harriet. From descriptions of Harriet and the way she is contrasted with other female characters the reader gets a sense of the author's understanding of the role of women in society. Furthermore, attitudes toward physical deformity and mental illness are revealed through the roles a "hunchback" and characters with emotional problems (some of them veterans) play in the story. Domestic servants, some but not all African American, also play a major role in the novel and are portrayed with clear distinctions as to relative social status. The Washington setting includes references to specific locations in the District and actual businesses and local landmarks, such as the Bethlehem Chapel at the National Cathedral, Walter Reed Hospital, and Rock Creek Parkway. Because the plot, in part, revolves around automobiles, information is presented about licensing, traffic and parking in the District, and the interiors and construction of cars. Some information is included that indicates the activities, household arrangements, and social tensions that existed in an upper-class household.

215. Lincoln, Natalie Sumner. *The Dancing Silhouette*. New York: D. Appleton, 1927. 277pp.

Arnold Winslow has hired a private detective named Thorne to investigate the mystery of his adopted son John's fiancée. John, the birth son of Winslow's brother, had been in a car accident, and the other vehicle contained Elsa Chase. She was paralyzed by the accident, and, to his stepfather's bewilderment John fell in love with Elsa. Winslow is concerned because he has been unable to find out anything about the girl. When a doctor brought by Winslow to examine Chase is found dead, Thorne's task becomes more complicated. The Winslows live on an estate named Oaklands beyond Congressional Country Club. Other Washington places mentioned include the Cosmos Club, a seedy Dupont Circle, and the Lock Tavern Club on the C & O Canal. Mental illness and cocaine smuggling play roles in the plot.

216. Lincoln, Natalie Sumner. *The Lost Despatch.* New York: D. Appleton, 1913. 309pp.

Captain Lloyd has been called back from the front lines of the Civil War to search for a spy who is sending information about troop movements to the Confederates. A woman is the suspect. As the novel recounts Lloyd's search, it describes Washington and includes accounts of historical figures of the time. Wormsley's Hotel plays a major role, and the lyrics of several war era songs are included.

217. Lincoln, Natalie Sumner. *The Man Inside.* New York: D. Appleton, 1914. 303pp.

When Cynthia Carew leaves a ball on Massachusetts Avenue in the landau of her father, Senator Carew, she comes to the startling realization that a man is slumped onto the other seat of the darkened interior. When he will not answer her, she assumes he is drunk and has passed out. At the end of the short drive home, she has the butler look into the coach, and he finds the dead Senator Carew. In the ensuing investigation, it soon becomes clear that the murder is connected to international espionage. The Carews live on Massachusetts Avenue, NW, east of 14th Street, NW. Descriptions of Washington focus on the vulgar new mansions constructed in the city by recent arrivals that one character believes give it the appearance of a suburb of New York or Chicago. Some scenes are set in the State Department and others in the White House.

218. Lincoln, Natalie Sumner. *Marked "Cancelled."* New York: D. Appleton, 1930. 285pp.

In this murder mystery, eccentric Washington millionaire Albert Reade is found dead, and in his supposed suicide note is a marriage license marked "cancelled." Although entirely set in Washington, beyond some references to apartment buildings (Alamo House and Studio House), there is little content specific to the city.

219. Lincoln, Natalie Sumner. *The Meredith Mystery*. New York: D. Appleton-Century, 1934. 279pp.

The mansion Ten Acres, not far from Washington Cathedral, dates from the Colonial period and offers views over the entire city. The owner of the house is found murdered, and one of the weekend guests, David Curtis, a blind physician, undertakes to discover the murderer. The police suspect Anne Meredith, the murdered man's niece, but David has fallen in love with Anne and cannot believe the circumstantial evidence against her. The novel includes little description specific to Washington except for the fact that the funeral is held at Oak Hill Cemetery.

220. Lincoln, Natalie Sumner. *The Official Chaperon*. New York: D. Appleton, 1915. 331pp.

Marjorie Langdon lives in reduced circumstances with her great-aunt, Madame Yvonett, in a small house on 13th Street, NW, (opposite Franklin Square) and works as a secretary for Rear Admiral Lawrence. However, after Yvonett dies, Lawrence dismisses her because he suspects that she has purloined a codicil to his wife's will that would have cut out Marjorie's boyfriend Chichester Barnard. Although she did not steal the codicil, the loss of her job and recent news of the failure of the bank in which her great-aunt had deposited her money mean that she needs to figure a way out of her financial crisis—something that she wants to do before she marries. After a time, she finds work again as a secretary and later as a chaperon. Eventually, she finds a new suitor more honorable than Chichester, who was directly involved in the codicil business. The novel includes references to hypnotism, bank failures, fortunes made by opium importers, the vulgarity of the newly rich, mental illness, a cavalry drill sponsored by the Woman's Army Relief Society in a riding hall, Rigg's Bank, Turkish baths, and Brentano's. Several characters in the novel are concerned about the new lack of manners in Washington, which is considered uncharacteristic of the "resident circle" and is be attributed to vulgarly ostentatious newcomers.

221. Lincoln, Natalie Sumner. *P.P.C.* New York: D. Appleton, 1927. 259pp.

A cab driver picks up a fare on 7th Street, SW, near the city wharves. Reaching the requested destination, he finds that his fare has died in the back of his cab and, despite being garbed in men's evening clothes, is a woman. When the police arrive, they realize that the woman is the fiancée of Senator Barry Langhorne and a high-level investigation follows. One of the areas described in the novel is Massachusetts Park, a term for a new residential neighborhood near Washington Cathedral; another is the area around the National Zoo.

222. Lincoln, Natalie Sumner. *The Trevor Case.* Illustrated by Edmund Frederick. New York: D. Appleton, 1912. 332pp.

Beatrice Trevor is found murdered inside the silver safe of her husband, the United States attorney general, and this novel traces the solution to the mystery. Trevor's house is at the corner of Massachusetts Avenue, NW, and Dupont Circle. The novel includes descriptions of houses and social events, including a woman's luncheon club, a Bachelors' Club dance, a charity ball, and references to the battle between old Washingtonians and the nouveaux riches. One scene takes place at St. Elizabeth's Hospital and describes the view of the city from there.

223. Lipton, Lew. *Ideas.* New York: Chatham, 1937. 344pp.

The book provides several motion picture synopses as examples for writers and the general public of précis that would be presented to movie studios. In one of the synopses, "Washington, D.C.," John Randolph, a Virginia planter, is ambitious that his child will live in the White House. When the child turns out to be a girl (Carolyn), his ambition is undimmed, and with his support she matures into an engaging social hostess with powerful suitors. Her father insists that she reject her true love, Matt Richmond, and marry Stephen Elgin, a wealthy political lobbyist. At first, Carolyn is crushed by her exposure to the crude society of purchased congressmen and lobbyists. However, she soon adapts, and, after Elgin's death, she continues to live in Washington as a very wealthy widow with a house on S Street, NW. Richmond becomes the legal advisor in charge of her investments, but given a second chance to marry him, she marries a senator, instead, to aid her campaign to enter the most exclusive reaches of Washington society. Richmond goes back to Virginia to return to the gentility of his youth, sickened by Washington society. Carolyn realizes her mistake too late; by the time she pursues Richmond he has married another.

224. Litchfield, Grace Denio. *In the Crucible.* New York: G. P. Putnam's Sons, 1897. 344pp.

Leigh Cameron is the niece of Mrs. Everett, a woman who reigns at the center of Washington society from her home on Farragut Square. When Leigh arrives in the city for her first social season, she immediately wins the devotion of two young men, Lloyd Gilfillan and Russell

Olney. Even though they have been raised as brothers in the Massachusetts Avenue, NW, mansion of General Gilfillan, they are actually
cousins, Olney being an orphaned son of the general's brother. As the
season progresses, Leigh experiences all the excitement of a Washington season, but is also forced to follow expected social obligations and
marry either Lloyd or Russell. Equal heirs to the general's fortune,
Lloyd shows promise as a lawyer and Russell as an ensign, so which
one Leigh chooses seems immaterial to her aunt. The choice is of great
import to the men involved, of course, and when Russell seems fa-
vored, Lloyd pledges to do all in his power to win Leigh. Fate gives
Lloyd a weapon. He comes upon Russell arguing with a dishonorable
cousin who is demanding money to cover a gambling debt. When the
cousin lunges toward Russell, Lloyd trips him, sending him to his death
from a high wall. Lloyd convinces Russell that Russell caused the
death, and that to tell anyone would surely lead to the death of his beloved cousin Dorothy, who has a heart condition. Believing that he is
no longer worthy of his office, Russell resigns his naval commission.
Lloyd's claim to the general that the resignation was forced by dishonorable behavior leads him to disinherit Russell. Lloyd also tells Leigh
that Russell was responsible for the death of his cousin, causing an un-
breachable estrangement between the two. After Lloyd tricks Leigh
into marrying him, he sinks into a life of greed and gambling. Leigh,
feeling she will never love anyone again, works hard at her role in society, becoming the perfect wife, a role that she continues even after she
learns the truth about Lloyd. In the end, Lloyd kills himself rather than
be publicly discredited as a cheat and debtor. Russell redeems himself
through his hard work as an architect and finally marries Leigh. The
author's efforts at moral uplift rely not only on the plot, but also on the
speeches of Mrs. Everett, the long-suffering Dorothy, and other characters as they talk about the role of women in society, the purpose of
marriage, the nature of personal redemption, and the meaning of life.
Washington is used as an appropriate backdrop for these discussions.
Social events are detailed, including balls, dinners, teas, a presidential
reception, and an inaugural parade.

225. Lockling, Lydia Waldo. *The Adventures of Polly and Gilbert in
Washington, D.C.* New York: Cosmopolitan Press, 1912. 130pp. young
adult.
        Gilbert Thompson is sent to Washington to visit relatives while his
father and mother travel to a resort in the hope of restoring Mrs.
Thompson to health. His cousin Polly meets him at Union Station, and
the two explore the city together accompanied by Polly's older brother,

Walter. During their visits to the major sites in Washington, Alexandria, and Mount Vernon, Gilbert learns about the history of the area and the workings of the United States government. Although Gilbert does not go there, St. Elizabeth's Hospital is pointed out to him, and he hears from Polly how sad it is to tour the facility. When Gilbert and Polly travel to Anacostia a "lunatic" attacks them and they have the excitement of seeing him captured and put into a strait jacket. At the Soldier's Home, they visit the original farmhouse on the property and learn about the spiritualist who paints pictures on the walls at night in total darkness. Gilbert's visit ends when his father comes to retrieve him with the good news that his mother has recovered.

226. Longstreet, Stephen [Burton, Thomas, pseud.]. *And So Dedicated.* New York: Harrison-Hilton, 1940. 416pp.

Longstreet's novel is primarily set in the imaginary town of Corinth. However, one of the townspeople rises to political importance in the Harding administration, and, through him, his son-in-law Tom Raleigh, the novel's protagonist, is appointed the Associate Director of Veterans' Hospitals and moves to Washington. Raleigh and his wife settle into a luxurious seven-room apartment. Descriptions of the city mostly focus on "The Great Grab" as political insiders jockey to translate their connections into financial gain. Because he makes decisions about where veterans hospitals are built and how they are staffed and supplied, Raleigh is a witness to political graft. To his dismay, the society of 1920s Washington is centered on sex and alcohol. Even though he vacillates between opportunism and morality, morality wins out in the end, and he decides to leave the city. However, Raleigh cannot persuade his wife to move back to Corinth with him, and she stays on to live the life of a socialite. In the rest of the novel Washington plays only a minor role as a setting, as the book focuses on Corinth to delineate the social impact of 1920s historical events on the general population of the United States.

227. Loring, Emilie Baker. *Across the Years.* Boston: Little, Brown, 1939. 298pp.

An inventor has developed a new system that will improve aviation and save many lives. Senator Teele has made possible its secret testing on government lands and been assisted by his legal advisor Duke Tremaine, a wealthy Georgetown lawyer. When Faith Jarvis, the sister of Ben Jarvis, Tremaine's legal partner, returns to the United States after eight years in Europe, deciding to do more with her life than drawing her inheritance, Duke is entranced with her. However, he is puzzled by what appear to be entanglements with other men, including a count. There are also puzzling connections among other men and women, including the daughter of Senator Teele, Ben Jarvis, and Wayne Marshall, the senator's new secretary. An espionage plot surfaces when the senator's safe is rifled. The novel is filled with servants, mostly "dusky-skinned," but occasionally French, elegant dinner parties, and chauffeured cars. Despite the tension of international espionage, the novel ends with the senator pleading a form of isolationism. He also claims that the United States must take the role of peacemaker to end disputes in a world in which war is on the decline.

228. Loring, Emilie Baker. *Love Came Laughing By*. New York: Grosset, Dunlap, 1949. 274pp.

Wendy Adair has fled political unrest in a South American country to rejoin her divorced mother, Mrs. Joshua Crandon, who lives in suburban Virginia comfort attended by servants. Wendy has been entrusted with official papers to deliver to Washington. On the final leg of her journey, she meets Congressman Vance Tyler aboard the train, and he pledges to help her with her mission. What follows is a romance that includes espionage and international intrigue. When Wendy meets her new-stepfather, who is focused on money and power and has no regard for literature or art, except as symbols of social status, she dislikes him, but is fair-minded and decides that he is an honorable man. As Wendy participates in her mother's life, a good number of upper-middle-class social details are provided, including information about room furnishings, forms of socializing, clothing, food, and drink. Specific Washington locations are mentioned, including Ford's Theater, Constitution Hall, Rock Creek Park, the Shoreham, and the Swedish Embassy.

229. Low, Alfred Maurice, Sir. *The Supreme Surrender*. New York: Harper & Brothers, 1901. 329pp.

Laura Olive Wentworth is the daughter of Sidney Ernest Wentworth and his devoted wife, Amelia. Although they are related to the Wentworths of New York and Boston, these Western Wentworths have had little contact with the more prominent branch of the family. Sidney inherited a profitable law practice from his father, as well as real estate that brings in good returns. He has occupied public offices, including that of governor, but has always simply done what was expected, never making great contributions in any position, but also never doing anything wrong. His wife has been equally staid. Their daughter, whom they have indulged, has, however, always done what she wanted without a thought for convention. When a newly elected President appoints

Sidney Wentworth to the Cabinet, Laura quickly attracts attention in Washington and is taken up by the beautiful, socially connected, but intellectually independent daughter of the secretary of state, Edith Chester, and falls in love with a married senator, Montgomery Laughton. Laura shatters the world of Laughton, who has never before known real love, but married his wife out of a sense of propriety. Even though he is considered one of the most important politicians in the country and thought of as the next President, he is willing to give up everything to marry Laura. On the night that he resigns his position and is awaiting word from his wife that she has filed a motion for divorce, he learns that Laura has decided that she cannot let him ruin his career. Fearing that after they marry he will resent her for all that he has given up, she has eloped with another man. When a final tragedy strikes, Laughton's reputation is preserved, although his life is not.

230. Lowe, Samuel E. [Hart, Helen, pseud.]. *Mary Lee at Washington.* Racine, Wis.: Whitman, 1930. 124pp. young adult.

Despite the title of this work, most of the novel is set in New York City. World War I is in progress, and Mary Lee, an orphan, lives with the Saunders family, since she is a friend of one of the daughters, Letty Saunders. Their friend Ruth's father is appointed to a position in the Quartermaster's Office in Washington, and the girls suddenly take more interest in the war effort and Washington. Through their Red Cross group, they learn the importance of buying Liberty Bonds rather than spending their money on clothes. They economize and buy as many bonds a possible. As a result of their activities, they are invited to address a conference of girls meeting in Washington. In addition to hearing other girls talk about their war efforts, they take special tours of Washington and visit with their friend Ruth. In the end, Mary Lee is named to the Executive Board of the Girl Workers and anticipates future trips to the city.

231. Ludlow, Louis. *Senator Solomon Spiffledink.* Illustrated by Ray Evans. Washington, D.C.: Pioneer, 1927. 430pp.

Ludlow, a journalist covering Congress, sets out to describe the personality and behavior of a Washington type: the corrupt politician. As his example, he uses Solomon Spiffledink who is convivial, a skilled orator, respected, and, due to his success in attracting press coverage, known throughout the country. Although his campaigns make a great deal of the fact that he was born on an Indiana farm, Spiffledink has always been affluent and was tutored in Latin and graduated from Yale. Prominent in Indiana society, Spiffledink and his wife realize that only the national social prominence that might be won in Washington will satisfy their belief that wealth can easily secure congressional office. Much of the novel recounts the way Spiffledink's staff manipulates the electorate and stuffs ballot boxes when necessary. The Washington portion of the novel details the methods Spiffledink and his associates use to keep him in office. These techniques combine influencing Indiana voters through the manipulation of news outlets, use of form letters, and circulation of distorted biographical sketches with gifts and parties to woo key people in Washington. The legislative discussions that play a role in the novel include the battle over Prohibition and debate on the extension of Massachusetts Avenue.

232. MacGrath, Harold. *The Man on the Box.* Illustrated by Harrison Fisher. Indianapolis: Bobbs-Merrill, 1904. 361pp.

Robert Warburton, a West Point graduate serving as a U.S. Cavalry lieutenant in the West, is shot in the ankle during a skirmish and decides he has had enough of the frontier. He resigns his commission to travel in Europe for nine months. On his return cruise, he becomes smitten from a distance by a young woman, Betty Annesley. Her father, Colonel Annesley, is traveling with her and has given orders that no one is to be presented to her. So, Warburton is left to pine from afar. Once he lands in New York, he tries, unsuccessfully, to be introduced through acquaintances. With some frustration he leaves for Washington where he plans to stay with his brother. He barely settles into the Scott Circle mansion of his relatives when he decides to play a prank by disguising himself as a coachman and picking up the family at a British embassy ball. Unfortunately, his reckless driving attracts the police, and when the carriage door opens it is not his family members inside, but Betty Annesley and a friend. Fearing disgrace should his name appear in the papers, he allows himself to be arrested, but uses an alias. Soon after he is convicted, he discovers that Betty Annesley got him freed by paying his fine and she subsequently hires him as a coachman. Thrilled at the prospect of close proximity to the woman he loves, Warburton continues the charade, which turns out to be fortunate for Annesley and her father. While in Europe, Colonel Annesley, the trustee for Betty's vast estate, had gambled away her money in the hope of increasing the fortune. A Russian count witnessing his losses loaned him money that he also lost. To cancel his debt and recover his daughter's fortune, he agrees to sell plans of United States fortifications to the count. Warburton intervenes in the nick of time to save Betty and her father from disgrace. The action of the novel is set in Chevy Chase, Scott Circle, and the fashionable residential neighborhoods of late nineteenth-century Washington, and concerns with attire, etiquette, and reputation dominate the plot.

233. Magruder, Julia. *Across the Chasm.* New York: Scribner's, 1885. 310pp.

Margaret Trevennon leaves her parents' home in a small Southern town to visit her married cousin in Washington. She is exposed to new social situations and meets people who force her to speculate on the nature of gentility and regional differences. When, of all of her suitors, she chooses a Northern-born architect, she announces that their union bridges the "bloody chasm" between Yankee and Rebel. With Trevennon as her foil, the author examines regional differences in manners and allegiances, capturing the social tensions of Washington in the post-war 1880s.

234. Malloy, John Edward. *Potomac Poppies.* New York: Pageant Press, 1953. 198pp.

Because she is still torn between the spiritual and the worldly, and preparing to enter a convent, twenty-four-year-old Ursula Cunningham has decided to see something of the world by living and working in Washington for a time. On the train to the city, she meets an employee of the Central Intelligence Agency, where she will also be working. This chatty fellow talks about the indiscriminate hiring by the CIA and reveals his alcoholism which he blames on Washington, the city with the highest per capita alcohol consumption in the United States. In his view, the city is an unhealthy place because so many people go there for selfish reasons, including an escape from small-town America, the social insurance of a federal paycheck, and political power. Upon arriving, Ursula moves into a house with Judith, Fern, and Teresa. Judith is from Providence and was having an affair with a wealthy man when a detective hired by the man's wife discovered the two of them at a hotel. To avoid scandal, Judith got five hundred dollars, a plane ticket, and a government job in Washington. Eighteen-year-old Fern was offered a government job based on her civil service examination results. When the job offer came, she wept for joy at the opportunity to escape her backwoods North Carolina town. Teresa moves to Washington to continue to explore her art and her sexuality in a more anonymous, less judgmental environment than her small town could offer. She uses her sexual encounters as the basis for her art and, at twenty-four, she has already had an illegal, traumatizing abortion. The women are friends with a cab driver, George Wilson Priest, who fondly refers to them and other women of their ilk as "Potomac poppies." He eventually intro-

duces them to various men, including a man from the poetry department at the Library of Congress working on a doctoral dissertation
about female government workers, a physicist, a priest, and some of
Judith's many eventual conquests (including sailors, millionaires, and
congressmen). By the end of the novel the women have experienced
dramatic personal crises in the city. Fern has a nervous breakdown and
must spend time in a mental ward before marrying an asexual physicist
after the marine she knew from back home makes sexual advances.
Judith marries a millionaire and moves to Maryland. Teresa, who had
been pursuing a black man she referred to as her "Samson," is murdered by him. Ursula, having witnessed the world in Washington, takes
her vows and becomes a nun. As one of the characters observes, each
woman found her own resolution to the problem of female sexuality in
a city that the whole world looks to for answers.

235. Maltz, Albert. *A Long Day in a Short Life.* New York: International, 1957. 350pp.
    Set in the Washington, D.C., jail on one day in October 1946, the
novel illustrates the impact of racial and economic inequality on people's lives. Although the setting is entirely within the jail, conditions
outside the jail are the real theme of the novel. Through accounts of the
ways the inmates ended up in jail and their reflections about life on the
outside, the reader learns about work lives, social activities, and living
conditions. Most of the information on racial politics is presented
through the story of Huey Wilson. Recognized as a marcher at a school
integration demonstration, the eighteen-year-old was attacked by some
whites and unfairly arrested for brawling. He had wanted to become a
lawyer and cannot grasp the injustice with which he is being treated,
although his fellow black prisoners regard his situation as a commonplace story. He resists the idea of a plea bargain in order to fight the
injustice, and by the end of the novel it looks like the NAACP will support his difficult fight.

236. Malvern, Gladys. *Mamzell: A Romance for Teen-Age Girls Set in
the Days of Dolly Madison.* Philadelphia: Macrae Smith, 1955. 208pp.
young adult.
    In 1814, because her father believes that New Orleans will be at-
tacked by the British, Jeanne Siousat is sent to her father's uncle, Jean
Pierre Siousat, who lives in Washington as the footman at the White
House. Her servant, Praline, accompanies her, as does an emissary of
the governor, Kent Claiborne. When the party arrives after the long
journey by riverboat and stagecoach, the unmarried Jean Pierre is ill-

prepared to receive Jeanne, and she gets to live in the White House with Dolly Madison as a mentor. She is courted by Kent but spurns him until the dramatic incidents during the burning of the Capitol transform her feelings. The novel includes descriptions of the unfinished Federal City, as well as detailing events of the War of 1812 and the capture of Washington. In addition to the Madisons, other famous residents of Washington, such as Dr. William Thornton and Francis Scott Key, play a role.

237. Mazor, Julian. *Washington and Baltimore*. New York: Alfred A. Knopf, 1968. 212pp.
     Of the six short stories in this book, three are set in Washington. In "Jack Kelsey's All-Stars" some eighteen-year olds on a semi-pro base-ball team pass through Washington at the end of their season. In addition to the typical tourist sites, some of them visit a whorehouse. In "Rock Creek" and "The Boy Who Used Foul Language," an upper-middle-class boy living near Rock Creek deals with his emotional reactions to the deaths of two childhood friends and the prejudices his family's African American maid experiences. Although the other stories in the book are not physically set in Washington, they deal with characters who live in Washington and with themes (race relations and prejudices Southerners experience in the North) common to the Washington experience.

238. McAdoo, Eleanor Randolph Wilson. *Julia and the White House*. New York: Dodd, Mead, 1946. 187pp. young adult.
     Through her fictional creation, Julia Lane, President Wilson's real-life daughter presents her view of White House life. Julia's father, Jonathan Lane, a successful midwestern farmer, got involved in politics to advance the cause of farmers. He allowed his name to be forwarded at his party's national convention since he assumed he had no chance of being nominated for President. When he wins the nomination, his family realizes they must play a role, since families can aid or harm the popularity of a candidate. Fictionalized accounts of events in the campaign, the wait for election returns, the reaction of townsmen in the President's hometown, the journey to Washington, the inauguration, and the first tour of the White House as residents all presumably reflect the author's own experiences. Once the Lanes are residing in the White House, McAdoo presents information about the executive residence's history, internal operations, and conduct of official receptions and dinners. The challenges Julia faces in interacting with Washington society members and important political figures are also described. Julia's life

in the executive mansion ends just as the author's did, with a White House wedding. However, while Eleanor Wilson married U.S. Treasury Secretary William Gibbs McAdoo (a match that ended in divorce), Julia weds a poor country doctor, who had been her hometown fiancé.

239. McCutcheon, John T. *Congressman Pumphrey the People's Friend.* Indianapolis: Bobbs-Merrill, 1907. 126pp.

In this gently humorous, satirical work by a political cartoonist, words and drawings combine to show what happens when the idealistic, but naïve, E. Joseph Pumphrey of midwestern Minerva Junction is elected to Congress. To his delight, an important railroad lawyer, Colonel Harrison K. Bunker, and the powerful Senator Octopus go out of their way to become his friends. They help him find a house for his family, see that he is invited to parties, play card games with him that he always seems to win, secure a trustworthy valet for him, and even find a job for his son. They also teach him the power he has as a congressman to control the press back home. At the end of the novel, Pumphrey is left debating whether to carry out the wishes of Senator Octopus, despite their politically disastrous consequences. Although Pumphrey is hesitant, it is clear that Octopus will get his way.

240. McGerr, Patricia. *Pick Your Victim.* Garden City, N.Y.: Crime Club / Doubleday, 1947. 222pp.

Bertha Harding creates the Homemakers' Information Bureau in 1939. Individual women subscribe to the service to get answers to their housekeeping inquiries and newspapers subscribe to reprint material. Paul Stetson believes that with the right public relations department the organization could be lucrative and play an important role to give the disenfranchised a voice. Pete Whipple also goes to work for the firm as part of the public relations team and comes up with the name Society to Uplift Domestic Service, yielding the catchy acronym "SUDS." The natural headquarters for such an organization is in Washington, and the novel recounts the workings of the public relations industry, legislative lobbying, and office bureaucracy and politics. Although little physical description of the city is given, the novel captures an important aspect of Washington as the home for so many national associations. The plot of the novel revolves around a mysterious string of physical injuries, usually claimed to be accidents, which culminate in a murder.

241. McLaughlin, Nathan Monroe. *The Last Man.* Washington, D.C.: Neale, 1900. 221pp.

McLaughlin presents his vision of the means to reunify the North and South by focusing on the prominent role the South played in the founding of the country and the fact that George Washington, the first President, was a Southerner and that he planned the Federal City as a symbol of the unity of two very different regions of the country. The novel tells the story of a Northern man and Southern woman. Lieutenant Alfred Boyd enlists in the Army of the Potomac. While his regiment is boarding with families near Gramercy, West Virginia, he meets Alena Long. Although she is a Confederate sympathizer, he considers her political convictions just as honorable as his, and the two development a romantic attachment. When Boyd is wounded and captured at the Battle of Chancellorsville (May 1863), by a remarkable coincidence Alena Long becomes his nurse, and he is chosen for a prisoner exchange through her influence. At the end of the war, he helps his black servant Sam purchase land in Northwest, Washington and seeks out Alena, courts, and marries her. The two decide that Washington, the city that symbolizes the Union, should be their honeymoon destination, and they marry in Alexandria in the church where Washington worshipped. After their marriage, the couple travels to the Ohio River Valley where Boyd becomes a principal in a coal company. He later makes other investments, including some in the South, and becomes an active churchgoer and a GAR member. As he becomes affluent, Boyd founds a colony in Alabama of Union and Confederate veterans. By the 1880s, he is living in Washington and devoting himself to civil service reform to overturn a political patronage system that still punishes former Confederate sympathizers. He also becomes active in many causes such as an upgraded transportation network to improve the city, for which he feels such a deep emotional attachment. In the end he is buried in Arlington Cemetery, something of a national hero for the ways in which he worked for reunification. His story is clearly meant to demonstrate the path that other Northerners should take. Although the novel does not include extensive descriptions of Washington, the city plays an important role as the symbol of national unity.

242. McLaws, [Emily] Lafayette. *The Welding.* Boston: Little, Brown, 1907. 360pp.

McLaws dedicates her book to General Lafayette McLaws, C.S.A., and the work presents a distinctly Southern viewpoint of the United States before and during the Civil War. David Twiggs Hamilton is the son of a poor Georgia farmer; however his intelligence attracts the attention of wealthy plantation owner and senator Alexander Stephens, who eventually makes him his page and pays for his schooling at the preparatory school of Columbian College (Washington, D.C.). By the time he arrives in Washington, Twiggs has been exposed to the evils of some slaveholders and the nobility of others. Through a schoolteacher in his native Georgia, who secretly helps slaves escape, Hamilton has also been exposed to the abolitionist viewpoint. When he arrives in Washington, he hears the arguments of Northern politicians concerning slavery and the Secession movement. Having heard all the arguments on both sides, when war commences, Hamilton returns to fight for Georgia, as a loyal citizen of his state, even though he believes slavery is ultimately wrong. In the same way, his mentor Senator Stephens remains loyal to his region and becomes Vice President of the Confederacy. The author shapes his narrative to show that through Lincoln's guidance the war welded disparate states into a nation, and by the end of the novel Hamilton is poised to take his place in that nation. Most of the novel's Washington scenes concern historic events such as the great floor debates before the war, the Buchanan inauguration, the trial of John Brown, the Lincoln inauguration, reaction to the firing on Fort Sumter, wartime hospitals, and the Lincoln assassination. The author conveys the smallness of Washington in the 1850s and 1860s that fostered a great degree of social interaction among politicians and their families.

243. Medora, Marie. *Patty McGill, Investigator.* Philadelphia: Penn, 1936. 206pp. young adult.

Seventeen-year-old Patty McGill is the daughter of Mason McGill, the owner of the *Washington Sun* newspaper. Her father agrees to employ her as a reporter, though initially she is only assigned to cover social events, including diplomatic receptions. Her chance at a major story comes when the secretary of state disappears. In the course of the novel she rushes around 1930s Washington following leads. Her family lives in Chevy Chase and she visits Chinatown, Connecticut Avenue nightclubs, the Potomac, and a tenement district composed of mansions converted to boarding houses where African Americans and Chinese live side-by-side. In the course of her investigation, she is kidnapped, falls off a boat and nearly drowns, and crashes her car as she deals with villains that include Chinese narcotics smugglers, South American smugglers, and white-collar stock manipulators. In the end, she solves the disappearance and gets her "scoop." The novel is filled with cultural references, including a description of the big announcement boards maintained outside newspaper offices to proclaim breaking stories, references to the landmark apartment buildings on upper Connecticut Avenue, NW, and the uniformly denigrating tone of discussions about "colored" people.

244. Mellett, Berthe K. *The Ellington Brat.* New York: Dodd, Mead, 1928. 340pp.

Loretta Ellington, the daughter of a rich Washington resident, earned the title "brat" in childhood for her lack of conscience and ruthless selfishness. As Loretta reaches a marriageable age her father has no control over her or her choice of a husband. She quickly sees through one man, since she recognizes her own selfishness in him, which, in his case, makes him a fortune hunter and philanderer. She has known her other suitor from childhood. The latter's outrage over social inequities almost entirely conceals his romantic interest in Loretta. Seeing that Loretta will never give up her money, he leaves Washington, and Loretta, realizing she will never marry, resigns herself to her fate to become a significant Washington hostess, even though the activity fills her with boredom.

245. Mellett, Berthe K. *Wife to Caesar.* New York: Brewer, Warren, & Putnam, 1932. 312pp.

In 1913, Blount Marvel is a new congressman from the South. His wife, Leda, was raised on a Caribbean island that was a British protectorate. A romance in her youth ended with the abrupt departure of her suitor, Garry [sic] Clune, and subsequently her widowed father left with the Resident Commissioner's wife. Marvel, a lawyer who was given control of a glass factory, fell in love with Leda when he came to the island looking for a supply of silicates. Soon after Marvel is sworn in, Leda is visited by Clune, now a married man of significant wealth living in the Virginia horse country. Clune believes he owes his wealth to Leda's father who had shared a formula he had developed for the use of palm oil in food products on which Clune subsequently built an industry. Since for years Leda has not known the location of her father, Clune suggests that he give her father's share of the money to her. Leda, perceiving Clune as a ruthless capitalist, is afraid of having any contact with him since her husband was elected to Congress on a platform of helping the disenfranchised. However, Marvel is entranced by Clune as an example of the American dream fulfilled and encourages a friendship with him. Even Clune's wife, Kathy, fearful of Garry's dissatisfaction with his life and marriage, begs Leda to be as intimate as she wishes with Garry, short of sleeping with him. Through Garry's connections, the life of the Marvels is transformed, particularly when a business acquaintance agrees to turn around the glass factory that had been a drain on Marvel's income. Marvel's factory begins manufacturing high-quality headlights for automobiles at the suggestion of one of Marvel's friends, and his fortune is soon made. The plot follows the temptations the Marvels endure and the gradual readjustment of their ideals. By the end of the book they are living in a mansion on the heights of Georgetown enriched by the war that Marvel had so outspokenly advocated. The novel includes numerous details about domestic and social life in Washington prior to and during World War I. Since the novel was written during the Depression, it is not, perhaps, surprising that the physical descriptions are so rich.

246. Mertz, Barbara [Michaels, Barbara, pseud.]. *Ammie, Come Home.* New York: Meredith Press, 1968. 252pp.

Inheriting a house in historic Georgetown gives Ruth Bennett the chance to establish a new life after a brief marriage that ended with the death of her husband. The tranquility for which she yearns, however, is disrupted when her young niece, Sara, comes to live with her. Sara introduces her aunt to a whole range of new ways of thinking as well as to her attractive anthropology professor. Sara also involuntarily becomes the medium for the spirit of a female eighteenth-century ghost who can only be exorcized when the historical mystery she presents is solved.

247. Merwin, Samuel. *The Citadel: A Romance of Unrest.* New York: Century, 1912. 409pp.

Congressman John Garwood makes a speech against the U.S. Constitution, referring to it as reactionary and restraining and created to hold the American people in subjection. The novel traces the reaction in Washington that results in his being driven from Congress and then recounts his campaign to regain his seat. The book has the villains typical of such political novels (a railroad attorney, a banker, an industrialist, and a political boss based on Mark Hanna). The romance of the title is with a politically aware woman in sympathy with Garwood's views whom he finds after breaking off an engagement with a woman who cannot embrace his cause.

248. Miller, Merle. *The Sure Thing.* New York: William Sloane Associates, 1949. 341pp.

Brad Douglas works for the State Department in the late 1940s. He and his wife Laurie have a modest, but interesting, Washington lifestyle, with social connections through her family and political connections through his job. Laurie has affluent parents, and her first husband, Jay Seaver, was wealthy. Brad had a more modest upbringing, although he got a good education and his first wife had a Park Avenue childhood. Without warning, Brad is accused of being a Communist, and his and Laurie's lives are scrutinized. Because the couple has so many acquaintances, the authorities find many damning connections. Interestingly, these past acquaintanceships are considered incriminating not only because of the political convictions of the individuals, but also because some of them were African American, others Jewish, and still others labor organizers. Much of the novel recounts the backgrounds of Brad and his friends and their current lives in Washington. In doing so, a whole stratum of lawyers, intellectuals, and upper-level civil servants are presented, as well as the clothes, food, drinks, dwellings, and social activities that form the background of their lives.

249. Miller, Mrs. Alexander McVeigh. *The Senator's Bride*. New York: Street & Smith, 1887. 211pp.

At the beginning of this novel, Bruce Conway decides that his love of ease and luxury is greater than his love for Grace Grey, his Aunt Conway's paid companion. Grey, the impoverished daughter of a family who suffered Civil War losses, is shocked when Conway tells her he is going on an extended European tour, although he does not tell her the reason. His aunt has forbidden him to court Grace, and as her sole heir he cannot imagine ignoring her wishes. During the years he is abroad, he realizes his mistake, and when he returns immediately proposes to Grace. However, she has married Senator Winans from Louisiana, and when Winans hears of Bruce's very public proposal he informs her that he will begin maintaining a separate household from her and their infant son and challenges Bruce to a duel. Although the senator wins the duel, he does not mortally injure Bruce. Ignoring Grace's assertion that there had never been anything serious between herself and Bruce, the senator moves to Washington for the season, leaving Grace in Norfolk, Virginia. Desperate to see her husband, Grace finally travels to Washington in secret, remaining veiled in public. However, the senator eventually discovers her presence and cannot resist seeing his infant son. While the boy is in his care, Winans is called away momentarily, and when he returns the boy is gone. Much of the rest of the plot is occupied by describing the search for the boy and Grace's emotional collapse and recovery. During the years that their son is missing, Winans resigns his office and searches for him in England; then, having given up hope, fights in the Franco-Prussian war. Grace recovers her mental and physical health by reestablishing her friendship with Mrs. Conway and making friends with a young woman who invigorates her religious faith by helping her see the importance of acts of charity. In the end, the missing boy, who has been adopted as the heir to an English nobleman, is reunited with his parents, who reconcile. Although much of the novel is not set in Washington, some of the most important action of the plot is enacted there. Furthermore, although the Southerners who are the main characters may have rural estates, and social lives in small Southern towns and cities, Washington is the focus of their social season. Physical descriptions of Washington focus on hotels and the Capitol.

250. Miller, Mrs. Alexander McVeigh. *The Senator's Favorite*. New York: Street & Smith, 1883. 215pp.

Sixteen-year-old "Precious" Winans is the favorite of her senator father to the resentment of her older sister Ethel. When the family attends an inaugural ball, Precious is kidnapped by her drawing master who conceals her in a ramshackle house in Southeast Washington watched over by his mother, claiming he will not release her until she marries him. As the rest of the family is frantic with anxiety and private detectives search the city, Ethel is most concerned about enticing Lord Chester into proposing to her. Upon the advice of her black maid, she visits a fortuneteller who turns out to be her sister's jailer. Locked in with her sister, she devises a plan for their escape involving breaking a window and sliding down a rope made of sheets. Before the plan can be executed their captors set the building on fire. Ethel goes out the window first and, when Precious does not join her, realizes that her sister has been overcome by smoke. Instead of getting help, Ethel decides her sister has already perished and she runs away. Fortunately, Earle Winans, the girls' brother, happens by the burning house with Lord Chester and hears sounds from inside. Lord Chester saves Precious with whom he is immediately smitten. However, he feels honor bound to remain loyal to Ethel. After a number of plot twists, including a poisonous snakebite, a shipwreck, a duel, the return of the evil drawing master, and a bizarre accident that kills him, Ethel finds humility and goodness in herself and becomes a nun, and the true lovers, Precious and Lord Chester, are free to marry.

251. Mixon, Ada. *Washington Shadows*. Philadelphia: Dorrance, 1942. 284pp.

Amelia Blomer, who has worked as a civil service secretary for years, resents the influx of "minxes" who have rushed to wartime Washington. To escape from the overcrowded city, she and a friend take a weekend trip to Old Point Comfort, Virginia. On the last day of her trip, Amelia decides to be innocently adventurous and strikes up an acquaintance with a man to whom she has not been introduced. They have a pleasant dinner together, although, in her nervousness, Amelia asks many questions to maintain a conversation. Furthermore, when the man asks for her name and address, she decides to be cautious and gives him the name of Corinne Caruthers, her eighteen-year-old niece, and a false address. When he cannot find Amelia the next day and a ship that had been in port at Old Point Comfort goes missing, he becomes suspicious and, as the member of a government spy service, begins an inquiry. His suspicions seem to be confirmed when he cannot find Corinne's name in the hotel register and a letter he sends is returned. As a result, the search for the mysterious woman who pumped him for information and could speak French becomes more serious. In the meantime, the real Corinne Caruthers, bridling at having to stay home with her aunt and knit socks for troops while the rest of her family is abroad with the Red Cross, runs away to Washington. En route, she sees an information wanted notice for "Corinne Caruthers" and decides to assume a false identity. While tracing the confusions and dangers to which the subterfuges of Amelia and Corinne lead, Mixon provides a detailed account of what it was like for a single woman to live in Washington during World War I and work in a government office. She also conveys a sense of spy-obsessed Washington and details public entertainments, restaurants, housing shortages, and actual legislation and events that affected wartime workers, including the influenza epidemic and the Armistice Day celebrations. Physical descriptions in the novel tend to focus on Union Station, Potomac Park, and downtown areas along F, G, and N Streets, NW.

252. Moore, Olga. *I'll Meet You in the Lobby.* Philadelphia: J. B. Lippincott, 1950. 250pp.

This fictionalized memoir traces the life of the protagonist, Olga, a woman born in Johnson County, Wyoming, from her childhood in the early twentieth century through middle-age. The daughter of a Southern Democrat who was politically engaged on the state level, she attended the University of Wyoming and married a local man who earned a Harvard law degree and was soon the dean of the law school at the University. When he gets appointed to the legal staff of the U.S. Maritime Commission in 1941 the two move to Washington and live at 2615 Connecticut Avenue, NW. During the first year they live there, Olga's father, mother, and, finally, her husband all die. The attack on Pearl Harbor pulls her out of her bereavement and into a flurry of volunteer work. Soon realizing that she needs to support herself, and having been rejected by many government agencies, she lands a job as a lobbyist with Best Foods, Inc., to work on overturning the tax on oleomargarine. Her accounts of wartime Washington vividly outline the impact of the housing shortage, the influx of highly skilled people that made obtaining a job challenging, and the forced camaraderie that stemmed from as many as six people having to share a cab. She meets several prominent people, including Evalyn Walsh McLean and Mary Chase, who was followed by a large, imaginary white rabbit long before she wrote the successful play *Harvey*. When Olga is offered a job with the Office of War Information, she jumps at the chance to work as a reporter as she had in her youth. After a posting in New York City, she is sent to London where she works until the end of the war. Returning to Washington, she moves into an apartment on the top floor of a house on 34th Place in Georgetown and begins working as a lobbyist, promoting such causes as acceptance of the Marshall Plan, establishment of the Voice of America, and Reciprocal Trade Agreements.

253. Morris, Charles. *The Stolen Letter; or, Frank Sharp, the Washington Detective.* Patrol Detective Series. Chicago: Continental, 1891. 199pp.
No additional information available.

254. Morris, Willie. *The Last of the Southern Girls.* New York: Alfred A. Knopf, 1973. 287pp.
In the character of Carol Hollywell, Morris presents an intelligent, sensual, elegant woman who knows how to get her own way—the kind of woman who has received the fascinated attention of society in many eras. Through Hollywell's adventures in Washington, mingling with ambassadors, politicians, and society people, Morris conveys a sense of what social life was like in the city in the 1970s.

255. Morrow, Honoré Willsie. *Black Daniel: The Love Story of a Great Man.* New York: William Morrow, 1931. 370pp.
Although much of this book is set in Boston and New York City, roughly the final seventy pages are set in Washington. Throughout the novel, Daniel Webster reassesses his life, longing for retirement to a country estate he is building and for marriage to Caroline Le Roy. Cases he has promised to argue before the Supreme Court and political crises prevent his retirement from public life, but his difficult courtship of Caroline ends successfully, and the couple travels together to Washington in January of 1830. In addition to fully articulating the major political issues of the era through the words of Webster and notables such as John Marshall, John Benton, and John C. Calhoun, Morrow uses Caroline's introduction to the city as a reason to provide descriptions of Washington and its social life. Included in the descriptions are

the unfinished Capitol dome, the uncultivated landscape along Tiber Creek, entertaining in rented rooms, the Jackson White House, and the role the Capitol played for affluent Washingtonians as a place to meet and be seen.

256. Morrow, Honoré Willsie. *Forever Free: A Novel of Abraham Lincoln.* New York: William Morrow, 1927. 405pp.

This historical novel begins with the inauguration of President Lincoln, after which Annabel Ford, a Virginian living in Washington, receives a request from Jefferson Davis to spy on the Lincolns. Ford plays upon Mrs. Lincoln's social insecurity and her desire to establish herself with the Southern women who control Washington society. Soon after their meeting, Miss Ford proposes herself as a White House social secretary, a position she retains after war breaks out, despite her open advocacy of the Southern cause. Her success with Mrs. Lincoln encourages Ford to win over the President. Even though she eventually falls in love with him, she still works against him politically and becomes a supporter of McClellan. For Lincoln, her declaration of love is just as distasteful as the evidence he receives of her spying, and he sends her away, suggesting that if she would go to Richmond and love Jefferson Davis the way she had loved him the Confederacy would fall within a month. However, Ford does not stay out of Washington long and finds other means to continue her career as a spy. Her fixation with the Lincolns climaxes when she returns to the White House and tries to shoot Mrs. Lincoln. The novel ends with the signing of the Emancipation Proclamation. Morrow presents a good deal of historical information concerning wartime events through conversational exchanges and depicts wartime life in Washington. She includes a list of the sources upon which she based her account.

257. Morrow, Honoré Willsie. *The Last Full Measure.* New York: William Morrow, 1930. 340pp.

Morrow fictionalizes the activities of Abraham Lincoln and John Wilkes Booth from September 1864 through April 14, 1865, capturing the atmosphere of Washington as the Civil War was ending. Many of the characters talk of kidnapping and assassination plots that fail to materialize, although Lincoln's death seems inevitable. Morrow includes many poignant details of Lincoln's family life and accounts of his exchanges with a large number of historical figures.

258. Morrow, Honoré Willsie. *With Malice toward None.* New York: William Morrow, 1928. 342pp.

Covering the period from the Spring of 1863 through the fall of Richmond. Morrow treats Washington as a small town in which Lincoln is a highly visible and beloved figure. As in her other Lincoln novels, his family life, including the extended "family" of his personal secretaries, is a major focus. One of the major themes is the complex relationship between Lincoln and Charles Sumner that includes periods of friendship and admiration as well as distrust and serious political disagreements.

259. Murray, Charles Theodore. *Sub Rosa: A Novel.* New York: G. W. Carleton, 1883. 419pp.

By tracing the adventures of an innocent young man from Simpsonville, Indiana, Murray presents a dark view of a Washington filled with lobbyists, graft-motivated politicians, and manipulative women. His story includes descriptions of the civil service, hotel and boarding house life, "Rum Row," "Newspaper Row," "Murder Bay," and the fashionable West End. His descriptions of an Inaugural Ball and parade, sessions of Congress and the observers' gallery, a gambling club, and day-to-day operations in the U.S. Treasury Department are highly detailed.

260. Neill, Esther W. *The Tragic City: A Story of Washington in the Eighties.* Notre Dame, Ind.: Ave Maria, 1931. 290pp.

Set in Georgetown in 1884 and 1889, during the course of the novel Elizabeth Patterson Crowder, whose mother had died years before, ages from twelve to seventeen. Her father, Tom Crowder, who had been a U.S. senator, has been out of office for three years at the beginning of the book, but continues to support himself by selling access to political influence. He had gotten elected by appealing to his gentlemanly antecedents, correctly believing that the Civil War had not ended the voters' reverence for "aristocracy." His career ends abruptly after a public outcry over political corruption brings to light the personal fortune he built through under-the-table deals. Out of office, his access to power is mostly through political party machinery, and, although he is still given assignments that take him around the country, his grip on power weakens during the course of the novel. While Crowder is on business trips, he leaves Elizabeth alone in the towering Georgetown house he inherited from his father-in-law. Living on his shaky credit, she barely sustains herself and is left to manage with her elderly and ill "mammy," Zeila. Elizabeth's life changes when a new family moves in next door. The wife, Joan, is the descendent of an old and affluent Maryland family that had been closely connected to the Bromleys, the family of Elizabeth's mother. Out of a sense of family obligation, Joan married a "rich Yankee" to replenish her family's fortune that had been destroyed by the Civil War. Her new husband had investments in South America, and she went to live there with him. Widowed soon afterward, she married a South American nobleman who could manage her now vast fortune and serve as a father to her two children. Joan becomes an important influence for Elizabeth, paying for her to go to a convent school near Georgetown (i.e., Visitation Preparatory) and launching her into society. She also encourages Elizabeth's talent as an actress in amateur theatricals. However, Elizabeth rejects an important New York City producer's offer of a coveted spot in his company, out of an obligation to look after her father, who has become increasingly despondent and prone to drunkenness. By the end of the novel, Tom Crowder is dead, and Elizabeth is free to begin her adult life. Although the direction she will take is left unclear, she will probably marry Joan's son and move with the rest of the family (minus the South American nobleman who turned out to be an embezzler) to a large, historic house on the Eastern Shore. This novel presents a convincing portrait of daily life in late nineteenth-century Washington and Georgetown through descriptions of shops, tradesmen, and street scenes, as well as parties and receptions (including an Inaugural Ball at the Pension Office). Some of the issues raised by the novel include race relations in post-Civil War Washington, social roles of women, influence peddling, and the evils of alcohol. In general, the novel is pervaded by nostalgia for the antebellum era.

261. Nichols, Laura D. *Nelly Marlow in Washington.* Boston: Lothrop, c. 1886. 296pp. young adult.
    When the father of a friend is elected to Congress, sixteen-year-old Nelly gets invited to Washington. After detailed preparations and much excited anticipation, Nelly arrives in the capital. In addition to sightseeing, she participates in popular entertainments such as going to church, tableaux-vivants, writing and reading poetry, and sailing on the Potomac.

262. Noble, Hollister. *Woman with a Sword: The Biographical Novel of Anna Ella Carroll of Maryland.* Garden City, N.Y.: Doubleday, 1948. 395pp.
    This fictionalized account of Anna Carroll's life focuses on 1860-1865 and draws on archival sources. Carroll was a well-connected

Southerner who used her contacts with Jefferson Davis, John Breckin-
ridge, Senator Toombs, and other Southern policy-makers to gather
information to aid the Union cause. The novel includes specific details
about wartime Washington and historic events, although most of the
Washington scenes occur in the offices of politicians and the novel is
not concerned with conveying a general sense of the city. Places that
are mentioned include Shillington's Bookstore, the Willard Hotel, the
Washington House, Rock Creek, District bordellos, and numerous government buildings. Abraham Lincoln, Edwin Stanton, William Seward,
and Ulysses S. Grant all appear in the novel.

263. Parker, Maude. *Secret Envoy.* Indianapolis: Bobbs-Merrill, 1930.
303pp.
  Diane More, the daughter of a senator and Cabinet member and
granddaughter of the U.S. Ambassador to Austria, has returned to live
in her family's Georgetown house by herself. Everyone in her family is
dead, except a brother, recently ill with tuberculosis, but recovered
enough during a Swiss sanatorium stay to begin college. The death of
their parents years before and a subsequent crash of investments in
Europe left the siblings dependent upon an aunt. She dies suddenly
before revising her will to take into account her dependents' new circumstances. Diane is devoted to providing for her brother, whose tuberculosis flares up during the course of the novel, requiring a stay at
an expensive sanatorium. As a woman of high social standing, which
she preserves by concealing her impoverishment, the only option seems
to be to marry well. Phil Lamond, a suitor of long-standing is, "highly-
placed" in the State Department and is very wealthy, but Diane believes
she can only marry for love and does not feel that Lamond is the "one"
with whom she is to spend the rest of her life. An opportunity to pay
immediate expenses and possibly gain real wealth comes when she
meets Edgar Justinian. Justinian, a lawyer, works with a syndicate that
covertly gathers information about pending federal legislation. Through
stock investments those associated with the syndicate can make huge
sums of money. In desperation, Diane agrees to cooperate, but only if
she does not need to lie or take advantage of her friends. Although she
has many qualms of conscience, Diane begins reporting back her inter-
pretations of seemingly innocent details of what she has witnessed at
social gatherings that include members of the State Department and the
diplomatic community. After a number of plot twists involving a Russian prince, a politically powerful newspaper editor, and political intrigue in South America and Russia, the novel ends with financial
security for Diane's brother and a love match to a senator for Diane.

Descriptions of social events, clothing, interiors, and Washington neighborhoods are convincingly detailed. There are also observations about the nature of social status, motivations of people active in society, the wealth that can be gained through inside information, and a great deal of discussion of the role of women.

264. Paynter, John H. *Fugitives of the Pearl.* Washington, D.C.: Associated Publishers, 1930. 209pp.

This novel fictionalizes actual incidents and photographs are included of a number of historical characters. The slave, John Brent, has an enslaved mother and unacknowledged father, who is a master with "aristocratic connections." As he grows older, he has the chance to work away from the plantation and keep a percentage of the profits. Starting in 1835, he works as a laborer in the War Department and in the evenings as a servant at social functions. By the time he is twenty-five-years-old, he is able to buy his freedom and begin saving to buy the freedom of other family members. He lives in Washington where he comes into contact with other freedmen and they work together to free slaves. Their largest scale attempt is to utilize a boat called "The Pearl." The scheme fails due to the work of a spy and everyone aboard is returned to the District to face trial. After many struggles, and with the help of Anti-Slavery societies, a number of the fugitives are freed and end up living in the Washington area.

265. Pearson, Drew. *The Senator.* Garden City, N.Y.: Doubleday, 1968. 447pp.

From the perspective of Edward Deever, personal secretary to Senator Hannaford, one of the most powerful figures in Washington, Pearson relates a tale of high-level graft and political corruption. Pearson, a long-time Washingon insider, convincingly presents a portrait of the city and its politicians. He describes popular activities, such as canoeing on the Potomac and attending Army Band concerts, as well as providing insider details about Georgetown, the Cosmos Club, and the Senate. However, the novel mostly relates political conversations focused on influencing legislation. The main topics of political debate are the Civil Rights Movement, the Communist threat, and environmentalism. Much of the plot centers on Hannaford's sponsorship of a bill that will open up national park lands to timber harvesting, the drilling of oil wells, and mining. Hannaford ends up being investigated for influence peddling and resigns from the Senate.

266. Pendleton, Don. *The Executioner: Washington I.O.U.* New York: Pinnacle Books, 1972. 187pp.

In a prologue, Pendleton provides background on Mack Bolan and the twelve previously published Executioner books that are not set in Washington. Bolan became a "death expert" while serving in the Vietnam War and was considered a phenomenally successful soldier. However, when members of the Mafia killed his teen-aged sister, father, and mother, Mack left the army and began his own war on the home front, traveling across the country executing prominent Mafia leaders. By taking the law into his own hands, he was soon given an unofficial "shoot to kill" designation by the police. Tracking Lupo, one of his most important targets, he arrives in Washington only to uncover a plot by the Mafia to take over the federal government by blackmailing key government figures into resigning and replacing them with Mafia-controlled politicians. Their final target is the office of President. When Mack saves the life of Claudia Vitale, whose charms have been used by the Mafia to lure politicians into photographically documented liaisons, she becomes his informant. The descriptions of car chases in the novel have the secondary effect of providing most of book's physical description of Washington; however, there are fairly specific references that detail crime and law enforcement in the city. The Mafia headquarters is in the Embassy District and disguised as IMAGE (Institute for Minority Action Group Encounters), a civil rights association for ethnic minorities. By the end of the novel, Bolan has destroyed the plot, killed many of the men associated with it, burned down their headquarters, and provided enough evidence to convict any survivors.

267. Perry, Eleanor [Bayer, Oliver Weld, pseud.]. *Brutal Question.* Garden City, N.Y.: Crime Club / Doubleday, 1947. 190pp.

Shortly after Alec Pike learns of the suicide of his boyhood friend Harvey Benson, a news analyst, he begins work as a radio master of ceremony for Mrs. Martha Finchley, an old acquaintance from World War II France. Benson's death in Italy seems unbelievable to Pike, and when people connected with the death begin appearing on Martha's broadcasting schedule he becomes suspicious. The new, live radio show airs from Finchley's S Street, NW, house in Georgetown and capitalizes on the fame her Sunday evening house parties had achieved, even in New York, for her politically and socially prominent guests' conversation. The show is an opportunity to bring some of the witty conversation to a nationwide audience. Pike's effort to solve the mystery of Benson's "suicide" becomes a life and death struggle after he witnesses the murder of Benson's widow at a the Volga Room, a Russian restaurant, where she is skewered with a sword by one of the floor-show entertainers. Shortly afterward an attempt is made on Pike's life. The author includes many details of Washington life in the 1940s including descriptions of nighttime F Street, Northwest's movie theaters, Dupont Circle, Connecticut Avenue, the Shoreham and Mayflower hotels, social events, Southwest seafood restaurants, Georgetown, clothing, and horseback riding in Rock Creek Park.

268. Peterson, Bettina. *Washington Is for You.* New York: Washburn, 1962. 63pp. juvenile.

Nine-year-old Toby Winthrop and his seven-year-old sister Pam travel with their parents to Washington over Easter. During their trip they visit the federal monuments and Mount Vernon. At the Lincoln Memorial they overhear a black woman telling her child that the President had freed their people when they were slaves. Toby reflects on Lincoln's identity as everyone's friend. As a climax for their trip the children participate in egg rolling on the White House lawn.

269. Philips, Melville. *The Senator's Wife: Being a Tale of Washington Life.* New York: F. Tennyson Neely, c. 1898. 240pp.

The only admirable people are journalists in this account of a Washington in which women wield power. The women drink hard liquor, smoke, and read lubricious novels and, through marriage, barter their looks for money and political control. For men, emotional distress, public disgrace, political downfall, and suicide result, although such outcomes might be considered appropriate recompense to creatures so bankrupt of moral character. After the men are tearful and despairing, the women, like the wife of the title, leave town for Paris. They will return, however, to take advantage of the next social season in the nation's capital.

270. Philips, Page. *At Bay.* Based on the drama by George Scarborough. Illustrated with photographs from the production. New York: Macaulay, 1914. 253pp.

This novel recounts a dramatic few days in the life of twenty-five-year-old Aline Graham. She lives in Washington with her father, U.S. District Attorney Gordon Graham, and is a popular society figure, with numerous suitors. To his puzzlement, she has told her father that she will not marry. He wants her to make a good marriage but opposes her most ardent suitor, thirty-eight-year-old Captain Lawrence Holbrook. Initially, his opposition is grounded in doubts about Holbrook as a provider. However, when Holbrook makes his case to Graham for Aline's hand, he reveals that he owns bonds producing an income equivalent to Graham's own salary. When an engagement announcement appears in the society pages of the *Washington Sun,* Graham, believing Holbrook had something to do with it, is incensed. Holbrook, who had been involved in the Philippine conflict as a secret agent, investigates and traces the announcement to Judson Flagg. A divorce lawyer, Flagg also sells gossip items to local newspapers. The bulk of his sizable income is derived from blackmailing Washington society figures using private letters he obtains by purchasing them from servants and obtains by other illicit means. Flagg has material on Aline, and, right after Holbrook's visit to his office, he sends a letter to her threatening to reveal a secret marriage she had made with a man named Tom Woolworth when she was still a student at Georgetown University. Aline goes to Flagg's office, slipping into his house after his assistant, who is also his nephew and heir, has gone to bed. When the price she offers for the incriminating letters is not sufficient she scuffles with Flagg and stabs him with the sharp point of a paper file spindle. She flees and later learns that Flagg had died. By a coincidence, at the time the crime is reported, Holbrook is visiting with the chief of police, an old friend. One of the first men on the scene, he immediately realizes that Aline committed the crime and tries to cover up and destroy evidence. For a brief time, the police accuse him of the crime, but quickly realize that Aline was involved. As explanation for her struggle with Flagg, she tells her father about her secret marriage. Infatuated with Woolworth, she had traveled to Baltimore with him where the two were married and then spent three days in Atlantic City. However, Woolworth abandoned her immediately afterward and has since disappeared. When Holbrook informs Aline that an autopsy revealed that Flagg died of a heart attack, Aline also confesses her previous marriage to him. He exclaims that he knew Woolworth as a war correspondent covering the Philippines and that he died of an illness in Holbrook's arms. No longer accused of a crime and with Woolworth dead, Aline finally accepts Holbrook's proposal with Graham's approval.

271. Phillips, David Graham. *The Cost.* Indianapolis: Bobbs-Merrill, 1904. 402pp.

The depiction of Washington in this novel is tightly focused on the workings of the U.S. Senate. Phillips was a college friend of Albert J. Beveridge and modeled the character of hard working Senator Hampden Scarborough on him. Scarborough uses his skills as an orator to battle political machines and the corporations that control many aspects of the political and legislative process. Phillips represents the corruption of the system through the character of John Dumont who manipulates an impressive set of connections, including judges and legislators, to create a wool shortage from which he benefits while the poor suffer.

272. Phillips, David Graham. *The Fashionable Adventures of Joshua Craig.* New York: D. Appleton, 1909. 365pp.

Joshua Craig is a thirty-four-year-old assistant to the attorney general of the United States. He has already argued a case before the Supreme Court and is generally thought to be at the beginning of an important political career. When he begins courting Margaret Severence, she feels compelled by his social standing and political promise to accept his attentions and overlook his arrogance and eventually agrees to his marriage proposal. Through Margaret's lengthy discussions with her grandmother, who opposes the marriage because of Craig's arrogance toward Margaret, Phillips explores the tragedy of women's lack of political and social power and the narrative advocates for change. At the end of the novel, Margaret boards a train for Minnesota, where Craig is certain of his election as governor, and enters, what is for her, a horrible exile from society.

273. Phillips, David Graham. *The Plum Tree.* Indianapolis: Bobbs-Merrill, 1905. 389pp.

In this confessional novel, Senator Harry Sayler reveals the web of favors and payoffs that are standard in government at all levels, demonstrating how corporations control government for their own purposes, robbing the electorate of any real power.

274. Phillips, David Graham. *The Social Secretary.* Illustrated by Clarence F. Underwood. Indianapolis: Bobbs-Merrill, 1905. 197pp.

Mrs. Burke, the wife of a Western senator, hires Miss Talltowers to be her social secretary and aid her family's entrance into Washington society. Senator Burke's political career is advanced by these activities, as well, and Phillips explores this relationship between social influence and national politics. The story is told through Miss Talltowers' diaries, which provide detailed accounts of political strategy breakfasts, dinners, balls, at homes, and the daily round of making calls. Her entries also comment on etiquette and even provide menus.

275. Phillips, David Graham. *A Woman Ventures.* New York: Stokes, 1902. 331pp.

Emily Bromfield has lived as a member of Washington society since she was born. Her father was an assistant secretary in the U.S.

State Department. However, when he dies she is reduced to poverty and needs to quickly find a way to support herself. She rejects marriage as a solution and moves to New York City, quickly becoming a successful journalist. When she does marry Edgar Wayland, she fears an end to her independence and stipulates that they live in separate apartments and divorce if their love should ever weaken. When the two fall out of love, Wayland moves to South Dakota seeking a quick divorce. Emily later falls in love with a married minister, who, despite his love for her, cannot bring himself to divorce his wife. Although very little of this novel is set in Washington, it does provide one perspective on the limited options for society women in the city.

276. Pierce, Gilbert A. *Zachariah, The Congressman; A Tale of American Society.* Chicago: Donnelly, Gassette, & Lloyd, 1880. 440pp.

The protagonist, Zachariah Martin, is the twenty-seven-year-old son of a prosperous farmer in the Western town of Martin's Corners when he secures a nomination to Congress through a local political boss "Spiker" who wants to be appointed a tax collector. Martin is honest and does not run for office to enrich himself. With the support of his party, he is easily elected. His experiences as a naïve, newly appointed rural congressman are recounted, as are those of the innocent Timothy Bobbin, who Martin got appointed to a clerk position in the U.S. Treasury in return for his campaign work. Martin's hometown, parents, and fiancée, quickly fade from his mind, as he becomes acclimated in Washington and begins to frequent the home of Mr. and Mrs. Marmaluke and their beautiful daughter Belle, with whom he quickly becomes infatuated. Mrs. Marmaluke tolerates him as a suitor because of his office and the general consensus that he is a man on the rise. Belle pretends to be interested in him for the sake of her mother, while secretly being devoted to Richard Hartwell. She and Hartwell believe that Martin will not be a success for more than a few years, and, if he is, Hartwell pledges to destroy him. During Martin's second term, Hartwell acts, setting in motion a plot to make it seem as though Martin made an appointment in return for a bribe. Martin is eventually saved through the efforts of his first love, Peggy Clover. Clover, an orphan, the daughter of an itinerant portrait painter, grew up in the Martin household. When Martin writes from Washington to break off their engagement, she sets out for Philadelphia where a wealthy brother and sister hire her to be a maid. However, they discover her artistic skill and use their resources to have her trained in Philadelphia and Europe. Eventually, they adopt her and are with her when she returns to Washington for the unveiling of her portrait of the President, which is enthusiastically praised. Reconciliation, although not immediate, does occur and Zachariah and Peggy are married and retire to the Martin farm happily resisting any calls to reenter the life of politics and society.

277. Pierson, Eleanor. *The Defense Rests*. New York: Howell, Soskin, 1942. 229pp.

Lila Donnelly is found stabbed with a silver paper knife at the conclusion of a party held by John Hadley, the lawyer who had successfully defended her in a recently concluded murder trial. The murder, of which Donnelly had been found not guilty by reason of accidental self-defense, was that of her boyfriend, George Adams. Donnelly and Adams had attended a dinner dance at the Chevy Chase Club. The drunken Adams forced himself on Donnelly, and, when other resistance failed, she pulled a small handgun from her purse. In the ensuing struggle, the gun fired, killing Adams. All of Washington society attended the post-trial party organized by Hadley and his wife Susan as part of a scheme to get Lila readmitted to her rightful social circle. Her deceased father, Senator Donnelly, had been widely admired for his conservative politics and wealth (he owned the Donnelly Mining Company for which Hadley served as chief counsel). As the investigation of Donnelly's murder unfolds, the prime suspect in what turns into a string of murders (that includes a society reporter) is a "Soviet," Vladimir Lorski. Except for fleeting references to the Mayflower and Shoreham hotels, St. Stephens Church on G Street, NW, grand Connecticut Avenue apartments, and mansions in Georgetown and on Rock Creek, there is scant physical description of Washington. There is a more detailed account of the State Department Building that notes improvised attempts to retrofit the structure with electricity. There are also details about traveling to the Eastern Shore by ferry to track down the killer (not Lorski, as it turns out) at the house and grounds of a former plantation house expensively converted for use as a "hunting camp." Descriptions of a cocktail party, diplomatic reception, and funeral indicate how public such events were during the 1940s. Large audiences gather on the streets to watch and comment upon the arrivals, and the newspaper coverage even includes details about clothing. The novel also demonstrates the social divide in New Deal Washington between the old guard and the influx of newcomers.

278. Plum, Mary. *State Department Cat*. Garden City, N.Y.: Crime Club / Doubleday, Doran, 1945. 208pp.

George Stair, the son of a career diplomat, was imprisoned with his father by the Japanese at the beginning of World War II. His father did not survive, and George returned to the United States nearly starved to death. He makes several attempts to enlist in the armed forces but fails due to his compromised health. His last hope at service is with the State Department. On the day of his oral examination, a cat brushes against him in the hall of the State Department Building. A beautiful young woman, Nancy Colman, witnesses the cat incident and rushes to explain that the cat, named "Trouble," lives in the basement and is said to appear only when something bad is about to happen. She helps him remove the cat hair from his trousers before his interview. Later her uncle, a State Department official who knew his father, provides the influence that turns his rejection into an appointment. When he starts his new job, George becomes enmeshed in political intrigue stemming from the efforts of General Cavala to use the United States to gain legitimacy for his corrupt presidency of a South American country. The senior George Stair had been on assignment to the general's country years before and wrote a scathing report of Cavala's brutal rule. When Stair is sent to a diplomatic reception with a secret-filled dispatch case that he is to deliver to one of the guests, he finds he knows several people there from his time in Cavala's country. He never finds the man to whom he is supposed to give the dispatch case, and the case is stolen from him. He becomes increasingly embroiled in the intrigue surrounding Cavala, and Nancy Colman reappears to help him unravel the mystery. Although there are some descriptive passages that try to get at the ways the District is different from other cities, on the whole, the work focuses on international political intrigue.

279. Plum, Mary. *Murder of a Red-Haired Man.* New York: Arcadia, [1952]. 220pp.

Dispatched by his employer, Congressman Meriden, to investigate his future son-in-law Russ Odden, Jerry Vane finds himself in a remote part of the Florida Everglades where he happens to witness a murder attempt on Deborah Todd. The young woman who lived all her life with her Aunt Neely has recently been thrown upon her own resources by the death of her benefactress. Vane suggests she return to Washington with him to work as a typist in Congressman Meriden's office. Through the experiences of the innocent newcomer, Plum is able to describe post-World War II Washington from the perspective of a single woman working in a government office and living on a modest income. She includes descriptions of clothing and life in a shared apartment. Because she makes friends with Congressman Meriden's daughter Sally she is invited to embassy parties and quickly makes friends with young people intrigued by her very proper speech and manners and her innocence. Violence follows Deborah to Washington leaving Meriden and Vane with a mystery to solve that involves property in Florida, a religions sect called the Prophets of Tomorrow, and a plot to smuggle Russian spies into the United States. During his search Vane follows leads in seedy parts of the city, such as H and 9th Streets, NW.

280. Popham, William Lee. *Washington Monument Romance.* Seven Wonders of the World Series (American) 7. Louisville, Ky.: World Supply, 1911. 109pp.

Bildad, a farmer from Mountain Creek Valley, Tennessee, visits the capital to see the Washington Monument. During his stay he meets Daisy Sunflower, a restaurant cashier, and falls in love. During his brief time in the city, he courts her by taking her to the theater and eating in the restaurant where she works. After his departure, she remembers Bildad and thinks about how pleasant he is compared with the pawnbroker who forces himself on her attention. When she rejects the pawnbroker's advances, he vows revenge and pressures her boss to fire her for supposedly making incorrect change. Receiving a postcard invitation from Bildad to visit Mountain Creek Valley, she decides she needs a vacation from the city. Bildad proposes marriage, and she happily escapes Washington for the friendly, healthful countryside and the love of a respectful man. Although there is little description of the city in the novel, except for facts and figures about the Washington Monument, this work does present Washington as a national destination which brings together people who would never otherwise meet.

281. Porter, Duval [Slick, Sam Jr., pseud]. *Adventures of an Office Seeker.* Richmond, Va.: Everett Waddey, 1904. 159pp.

This political satire focuses on politicians and policy debates during the period from the Grant through Cleveland administrations. The protagonist is a newspaperman, and the novel describes the locales of the local and national newspaper offices and well-known publishers, editors, and reporters. There are also extended accounts of politicians and floor debates. The work also describes attempts to obtain a government job through political influence and is filled with details of boarding house life, saloon and restaurant dining, office work in the Government Printing Office, and interactions among people from various regions. Issues such as civil service reform, the Hawaiian territory, currency reform, the treatment of Southerners, and office-holding African Americans all receive attention.

282. Price, William. *Clement Falconer; or The Memoirs of a Young Whig.* 2 vols. Baltimore: N. Hickman, 1838. 229pp. 192pp.

The orphaned Clement Falconer, whose father was killed in a duel and whose mother died of heartbreak, is adopted by his wealthy bachelor uncle and lives in comfort on a two thousand acre farm in western Maryland, benefiting from all of the trappings of Southern aristocracy. Educated at Princeton, he reads law and takes a western tour that includes points as far away as Wisconsin, before ending up in Saratoga during the summer season. There, he meets a young Philadelphian who, after numerous setbacks, becomes his bride at the end of the novel. His career in Congress ends in a duel, but only after many pages devoted to satirical descriptions of the main figures in the Jackson administration, and dialogue that evinces the author's views on everything from abolitionism, to mismanagement of the post office, to the evils of dueling, and to the franking privileges of legislators. One of the most surprising and extended satirical passages describes Anne Royall (1769-1854). Descriptions of Washington scenes include the etiquette in force at the Jackson White House and life in a political "mess" (a domestic arrangement in which several politicians set up a household together to avoid the dismal existence of a boarding house or the expenses of a private household).

283. Ragan, Emily Lee Sherwood. *Willis Peyton's Inheritance: The Story of a Claim.* Boston: Universalist Publishing House, 1889. 237pp.

The Peyton family lives in Virginia and has owned land close to Munson's Hill for generations. Their land is one of the highest points in the area with a commanding view of the Capitol and was used by the federal government during the Civil War, so after the war the family filed a claim for its use. Before his death, Judge Peyton asks his son Willis, who is about to graduate from Columbian Law School, to devote himself to the resolution of the claim so his sisters, Jessie and Georgia, can enjoy the family's antebellum level of affluence. After Peyton dies in 1876, the children lease their family home and move to a house in Washington. In order to help with expenses, Georgia takes up arts and crafts work and Jessie begins a kindergarten, funded by selling family heirlooms to take advantage of the popular interest in all things Colonial. In addition to describing middle-class socializing, courting, and marriage during the time period, the novel gives a full account of the claims system and its frustrations. Eventually, anxieties over the claim drive Willis insane, and he commits suicide. Because he had been a Confederate during the war, his death actually eases the settlement of the claim, and his sisters use the payout to begin a new life in Washington and marry the men with whom they have fallen in love.

284. Raphael, Chaim [Davey, Jocelyn, pseud.]. *A Capitol Offense: An Entertainment.* New York: Knopf, 1956. 252pp.

Ambrose Usher, an Oxford don, arrives in Washington to uncover a spy on the British Embassy's staff. Public sentiment toward Britain has suffered a dramatic reversal in the United States since World War II and has further deteriorated because of a recent diplomatic crisis over the Falkland Islands. Everyone at the embassy, including Usher, wants to re-inspire admiration for Britain and advocate the country's interests. Usher has many chatty conversations about the United States and world affairs with diplomats from Canada and France. His espionage investigation becomes more complicated when Maurice Hewitt is killed at the embassy during a Guy Fawkes Day celebration. Hewitt was a British agent assigned to infiltrate Communist groups in the United States, but the British had started to suspect he was a double agent. Further crimes occur, and for a time Ambrose thinks he is on the trail of misappropriated atomic secrets. However, he learns that a wronged lover committed the crimes. Not surprisingly, the novel includes a good deal of physical description of the British Embassy and Ambassadorial Residence. In addition, since the sociable Ambrose dines out, the author also describes some restaurants in Georgetown and Woodley Park.

285. Reed, Sarah A. *A Romance of Arlington House.* N.p., 1905. 116pp.

In the preface, the author claims that the letters that make up this work are those of Virginia Colton, found in a hidden compartment in an old desk by a Washington woman residing on I Street, NW. The letters, written by Virginia to her mother, tell the story of Colton's stay at Arlington House in 1824 when General Lafayette was visiting Washington. The Custis family, including future in-law Robert E. Lee, is described in some detail, as well as their house and family portraits and heirlooms from Mount Vernon. Virginia also describes the celebrations and receptions held for Lafayette in Washington and her own romance with Captain Harry Worthington, who is one of Lafayette's American escorts.

286. Rennert, Maggie. *A Moment in Camelot.* New York: Grove Press / Bernard Geis, 1968. 713pp.

This novel tells the story of a circle of Georgetown residents in the decades following World War II. Rennert lived in Georgetown for many years and, in an afterword, notes her goal to describe daily life in nearly "anthropological" detail. The novel was criticized for the way narration and transcriptions of conversations impeded the pacing of the plot. Social historians, however, will find these very features useful, especially when Rennert turns her attention, as she often does, to embassy parties, art exhibitions, White House parties, holiday celebrations, shopping, food, and clothing. In the Georgetown circle of the novel are Gil Kimball, a reporter and editor at the *Washington Tribune*, and his wife, Betty; Marian Farland, art critic of the *Washington Tribune*, and her husband, Will, a State Department official; Andrea Langwith, a young, attractive, wealthy widow; and Senator Alec Girard of Vermont. Girard, who marries Andrea, is eventually elected President, and all of the steps leading up to his taking office are recounted. A subplot involves how Andrea deals with the intrusiveness of journalists' human-interest stories, a particular concern as she tries to protect her infant children from public exposure and later deals with a miscarriage and her daughters struggle with leukemia. The greatest political challenge Girard faces stems from increasing civil unrest over racial prejudice. The crisis comes in the form of a dramatic challenge from a town in the deep South concerning the power of the federal government over states and municipalities.

287. Riddle, A. G. *Alice Brand: A Romance of the Capitol.* New York: D. Appleton, 1875. 384pp.

Alice Brand, heiress to a Tennessee plantation, arrives in Washington to pursue claims for war damages to her property. During her stay, she experiences boarding house life and political corruption, while working in a civil service job. Attempts to get her claims addressed are thwarted by a circle of dishonest men who collect money without transferring it to the rightful owners. Her natural gentility preserves her in a Washington filled with crude arrivistes and wins her the love of a true gentleman who successfully prosecutes her claims, enabling her return to her rightful place as chatelaine of Magnolia, her family home.

288. Rinehart, Mary Roberts. *The Man in Lower Ten.* Illustrated by Howard Chandler Christy. New York: Review of Reviews, 1909. 282pp.

Lawrence Blakeley is a partner in a law firm and lives an affluent Washington life with two servants, a stableman and Mrs. Klopton, his over-solicitous household manager. He must travel to Pittsburgh as part of his preparation for a forgery trial. On the way back to Washington, all of his possessions, including evidence crucial to the case, are stolen, and the man occupying the berth he was to sleep in is murdered. Soon afterward, an investigation begins in which Blakeley is the prime suspect. However, the train crashes, and Blakeley escapes with the help of Alison West, the granddaughter of wealthy John Gilmore, the man with crucial evidence in the forgery case. West was a friend of the accused in the forgery case and seems to be involved in the mystery. The only other survivors of the crash are Wilson Budd Hotchkiss, a government employee and amateur detective (who turns up while Blakeley is recovering from his injuries), and the unknown man who seems to have committed the murder. Most of the narrative is occupied with a complicated plot, variously set in Baltimore, Richmond, the shores of the Chesapeake Bay, and the Virginia countryside. However, there is some description of summertime in Washington, including a theater performance that incorporates a newsreel, boarding houses off Washington Circle, a restaurant where food is served in chafing dishes, bachelor apartments, and American plan hotels.

289. Rollins, Montgomery. *The Village Pest: A Story of David.* Illustrated by J. Henry. Boston: Lothrop, Lee & Shepard, 1917. 360pp.

Although the names have been changed, the author notes that the novel is a fictionalized account of true events, centering on the mischief of ten-year-old David Hamilton. Rollins, the son of Senator Edward Henry Rollins, seems to be presenting an account of his own experiences or those of a brother. David, the son of a senator, lives in Washington when Congress is in session. The rest of the year, he and his family live on a Southern plantation ("little changed by the sixties") in the winter and at a long-held New England family property in the spring and summer. During one Washington season, the family lives with the Lawrences, a retiring couple whose large house on East Capitol Street, NW, stands where part of the Library of Congress stands now. David's games and highjinks with the sons of other legislators and his "big yaller dog" terrorize the Lawrences. His adventures include fights with the sons of ambassadors, playing tricks on tourists at the Capitol, and trying to fulfill a dare to steal an ivory key from a harpsichord at Mount Vernon. The author also includes incidents that show that, despite his mischief, David is essentially a good boy. He helps save horses during a fire and keeps a friend from drowning during a canoeing accident. The fact that his father is chair of the District Committee and has held office for many years means that David has become a familiar figure and people make allowances for his behavior. To keep him under watchful eyes, he is made an honorary page and given the run of the Senate floor, a privilege he retains, despite shooting spit wads from the Senate Gallery.

290. Roosevelt, Alice. *Scamper, the Bunny Who Went to the White House.* Illustrated by Marjorie Flack. New York: Macmillan, 1934. 72pp. juvenile.

Mrs. Whitby mails "Scamper," a bunny dressed in a red suit with shiny brass buttons, to the White House as a gift for the President's grandchildren who are to visit over Easter. His new family is delighted with him and show him all around Washington, making him try to guess the buildings they will see next (Washington Monument, Treasury Building, Capitol) by the rhymes they recite. After an exciting day at the White House Easter Egg Roll, the children explore the White House kitchen for a snack and spy on a formal dinner party until the screen they are hiding behind falls. The following day they take a boat trip to Mount Vernon. Playing tag on the grounds, Scamper falls into a rose bush and ruins his suit. The children conceal him in their grandmother's sewing bag, knowing that she will make him a new one. However, they do not know that she is leaving on a trip. So, Scamper gets a ride on an airplane before he is mailed back to the children to return to life at the White House.

291. Roosevelt, Eleanor. *A Trip to Washington with Bobby and Betty.* [New York]: Dodge Publishing Company, 1935. 91pp. juvenile.

Nine-year-old Betty and twelve-year-old Bobby have birthdays in the same month. As a treat, their father takes them to Washington. They fly from the Newark airport and receive an aerial view of D.C. as they arrive at National Airport. They take a driving tour of the city that includes Georgetown, and their father tells them about the city's history. They also visit the Capitol to learn about the workings of government and the Library of Congress, where they are introduced to Mr. Herbert Putnam, the director, who is a friend of their father. In addition to Washington sites, they travel to Arlington, Mount Vernon, and Fredericksburg. As a special treat, they have lunch at the White House and get a tour that even includes the kitchen. This book is extensively illustrated with black and white Underwood and Underwood Company photographs.

292. Roudybush, Alexandra. *A Capital Crime.* Garden City, N.Y.: Doubleday, 1969. 192 pp.

A pretentious, publicity-seeking television journalist, Theodulus Suttler, is based in Washington and travels about the city in an ambulance that has been converted to an office with space for his secretary. Suttler speaks with an Oxford accent, wears British-tailored suits, and lives in a castle-like house. During the New Deal era he had been able to buy the house as a white elephant and rented out rooms to some of the large number of serious bachelors who descended on Washington to take jobs with the Roosevelt administration. Through these men, who became highly placed administrators, and through a good deal of manipulative public relations, Suttler built fame and fortune as a media entrepreneur. One well-guarded key to his success has been his use of an employment agency to place secretary-spies in offices all over town. When the head of his agency is murdered, several female reporters pursue the story. The novel includes physical details of 1960s Washington but is perhaps of most interest for conveying the cosmopolitan nature of the city that made it fertile ground for gossip columnists.

293. Runbeck, Margaret Lee. *People Will Talk.* Chicago: Reilly & Lee, 1929. 334pp.

A family originally from Des Moines, Iowa, moves into a modest house on 2nd Street, SE, near Garfield Park in 1906. The father, Peter Lauren, is a machinist who works in the Navy Yard and Sally, the mother, a homemaker. They have two young children, Nancy and Eric, on whom their ambition focuses. Throughout the novel, Sally promotes social uplift and influences her family to set reasonable expectations for each other and accept what they cannot change. When she goes back to Des Moines to help Peter's estranged father, Mrs. Swan, a wealthy, widowed neighbor woman, uses the opportunity to establish herself at the center of Sally's household. Instead of attacking her, Sally befriends the woman upon her return. Later, when Peter is cheated by a patent lawyer out of the rights to an invention, Sally influences him to simply forget the disappointment and focus on his work at the Navy Yard, where he gradually advances and earns a particularly good wage during World War I. Eric marries out of moral obligation rather than love, and Sally helps him make the match work. Nancy comes closest to abandoning Sally through her continuing devotion to Mrs. Swan, who has become very wealthy through an inheritance and moved away to live in high society. Mrs. Swan encourages Nancy's writing, and she becomes a financial success writing novels and plays. When a former much younger beau of Mrs. Swan appears, Mrs. Swan encourages a friendship Nancy and him. It blossoms into love, but the man is unable to secure a divorce. Nancy has the option of acting like Mrs. Swan's sophisticated friends and simply living with the man. She even plans to go away with him on a trip to South America and simply say they had eloped and married there. However, she has come to appreciate the value of her parents' morality and realizes deception would not only be morally wrong but would weaken the love she feels. After Nancy makes her decision, she learns that Mrs. Swan has successfully persuaded the man's wife to give him a divorce, and Nancy marries him. The novel ends with all of the Laurens gathered together at Christmas time content with each other and aware that they have made the right choices.

294. Sanborn, Mary Farley. *Lynette and the Congressman.* Boston: Little, Brown, 1905. 396pp.

Lynette, daughter of James Pralier, was born in Richmond but grew up in New Orleans, Chicago, San Francisco, and New York City. Her father had no money of his own but spent his wife's freely. Upon his death twenty-one-year-old Lynette and her mother find themselves impoverished and move to Washington to live in a boarding house, surviving on Lynette's wages as a government office worker. Lynette is courted by one of their boarding house acquaintances, Gerald Wyndham, who is completing law school and working for a congressman. Although Lynette realizes marrying Wyndham would be a safe choice and eventually lead to some financial security, she becomes interested in Congressman Cartwright of Michigan. Her senior by seventeen years, Cartwright is also a widower with two sons, ages twelve and fifteen, so marrying him does not seem a possibility. However, through talks with him, her intellect and personal ambitions are awakened, and she begins to dream that she might enter some career. Wyndham despises careers for women, and Lynette realizes that she sees too many examples of older women in her office who make good wages but have no goals and live empty lives. Lynette assumes that Cartwright will eventually marry Mrs. Belmont, a twenty-six-year-old widow whose husband left her a substantial fortune. She does not understand the life of someone like Belmont and allows the widow to hire her as a maid in order to learn about Washington society ladies. The two women become friends, and Lynette discovers Belmont's deep unhappiness, which she believes is in part due to being spurned by Cartwright. Not wanting to be the cause of a break-up, she flees to visit friends in Richmond and later takes a summer trip with an aunt on the Great Lakes. It is there that Cartwright catches up with her and reveals that Belmont had been lovesick over another man and merely considered him an acceptable substitute. Lynette is relieved to discover that she can marry Cartwright without hurting Belmont. The novel is filled with social details concerning food, boarding house life, race relations, upper-middle-class household life, and the relationship between maid and mistress. The Washington setting includes descriptions of the National Zoo, Library of Congress, market day, F Street shops, Rock Creek

Park, Dupont Circle restaurants, vesper service at St. John's Church, and the Corcoran Gallery.

295. Schneider, Martha Lemon. *A Government Countess: A Novel of Departmental Life in Washington*. Washington, D.C.: Neale, 1905. 221pp.

This book provides strong descriptions of daily work in government offices, as well as the diversions popular with Washingtonians of all classes during the early 1900s, including fishing trips to Great Falls, excursions to Mount Vernon, listening to the Marine Band, promenading on Connecticut Avenue, shopping on Pennsylvania Avenue, and walks in the countryside at the edge of town. The hazards of government employment are told through the experiences of a circle of young people who live in a newly improved Washington with newly paved streets and sapling-filled parks. Protagonist Ralph Dennison arrives from his small town with letters of support secured through his village postmaster, a dominant force in local politics. Despite his contacts, Ralph experiences difficulties in getting an appointment and struggles ineffectually until the postmaster himself appears and bullies an elected official. Through another man, Jim Donovan, from his hometown, who is married and has a government job, Ralph meets Jean Ainslie, an orphan who boards with the Donovans. Jean works in the U.S. Treasury Department counting sheets of banknotes, a job she "inherited" at the death of her aunt and that she and her fellow workers refer to as being a "government countess." Despite the tedious work and low pay, Jean makes the best of her lot, working hard, transforming her modest room into a plant-filled bower, and taking pleasure in aspects of her environment that others might overlook. Developing an acquaintanceship with Ralph through his visits to the Donovan household, Jean is quickly smitten by the young man. She is also thrilled by a friendship she develops with a new "countess," Dora Hart. Dora is also an orphan, however, her mother had been a popular singer of light opera, who enjoyed fine clothes and being courted for her beauty. Her daughter inherited both of these tendencies, and Jean must work hard to influence Dora to focus on her work. Dora is soon living in the room next to Jean's as a fellow boarder. To Jean's dismay Ralph soon focuses his attention on Dora, as does his newfound friend, an affluent lawyer from the West. Dora also attracts the attention of a prominent government official. Despite Jean's warnings she accepts his patronage and is soon promoted to a clerkship not realizing the high cost she will pay.

296. Scott, John Reed. *The Cab of the Sleeping Horse.* New York: G. P. Putnam's Sons, 1916. 361pp.

Most of the action in this mystery/espionage novel occurs in apartment hotels, particularly the Collingwood near Dupont Circle and the Chateau on F Street, NW, as well as on the streets of Washington, which are closely described in a series of chase scenes. The work apparently presents the author's view of the diplomatic corps as composed of spies and people who would do anything to advance the interests of their countries. The action begins with a bizarre incident involving an empty cab with a horse asleep between the shafts, which Harleston (most people in the novel have only last names) of the State Department discovers on his way home from a club. Upon investigation he finds three puzzling items: a clutch of American Beauty roses, a sealed envelope with no address, and a woman's handkerchief. The mystery of these items quickly deepens, and Harleston is involved in locating a diplomatic letter, the key to a ciphered message. He eventually discovers that the message warns that a female spy is carrying a scientific formula for creating smokeless ammunition for high-powered artillery pieces. From then on, the chase is on to retrieve the formula.

297. Scott, John Reed. *The Man in Evening Clothes.* New York: G. P. Putnam's Sons, 1917. 387pp.

Many Washington locations are mentioned in this novel, as well as apartment buildings and restaurants; for some the author uses real names. Through anecdotes and observations, nouveaux riches characters that are not part of the diplomatic set are subjected to ridicule. The main character, Colin Marjoribanks, the youngest son of the Earl of Warrington, is in Washington as part of the British legation. His duties are light, and he spends most of his time at social functions and romancing women, particularly wealthy, attractive widows. When he finds a pearl pendant in his evening clothes upon returning home one evening, he thinks it has accidentally fallen there during a passionate embrace. The value of the pearl weighed against his poverty convinces him to keep the jewel, and he takes advantage of other surprising opportunities to add to his hoard. However, soon another man in evening clothes is also stealing jewels. Colin is approached by the other thief, who is chauffeured about in a limousine, and learns that he will be turned over to the police for his thefts if he does not cooperate with the other thief's plans to steal a famous jewel collection, soon to arrive with the wife of an English lord. Marjoribanks' conscience is finally awakened, since he has been in love with the lord's daughter for years and she is accompanying her mother. He is able to anonymously return the jewels he has taken and successfully lay a plot to capture the real thief. He also proposes to the lord's daughter, because two accidental deaths in his family have made him the heir to his father's title and the match will no longer be considered inappropriate.

298. Scott, John Reed. *The Red Emerald.* Philadelphia: J. B. Lippincott, 1914. 352pp.

This novel makes great efforts to be current and includes references to telephones, criticisms of State Department appointments based on wealth (with references to actual appointees), smoking in social settings, apartment suites, Egypt (picking up on the "Tut" craze), auction bridge, gentlemen's clubs, automobiles, and air-ships. The main character, Orme Vendome, newly appointed Ambassador to Spain, has returned to Washington on leave after a five-year absence. He is updated on changes in society and told about an unusual newcomer, Natalie Tremaine, a twenty-five-year-old divorcee, whose radiant beauty is matched by her refined social bearing and delightful conversation. She has maintained her social position, despite her divorce, because she had no children, separated from her husband so discreetly that no one knows the reason, and remains on cordial terms with him. Much of the novel is set in Virginia hunt country, and it is there that the romance between Vendome and Tremaine plays out with some competition from an Englishman who has become wealthy in the West and is the master of the local hunt. He and Natalie had had an infatuation in London before she was of age. A sub-plot involving the Crown Jewels of France that were hidden in the eighteenth century on a nearby Virginia plantation introduces additional drama. The African Americans on the plantations are described as knowing their place and possessing all of the appealing qualities they had before the war, except that if they desired they could choose another life for themselves, far from the pleasant plantation.

299. Seawell, Molly Elliott. *Despotism and Democracy.* New York: McClure, Phillips, 1903. 311pp.

The author of this novel exhibits a Washington society filled with people who came from nowhere with humble backgrounds and have only recently become wealthy. There is also a good deal of discussion in the novel of "Negro" servants and how to deal with them. At the center of the story is Congressman Julian Crane from the fictional Circleville, Buncombe County, who is entranced by Washington society. His wife, Annette, gave up breaking into it after her first season in Washington and now stays home during legislative sessions. His friend,

Geoffrey Thorndyke, who has been in office eighteen years, also generally ignores society, despite his wealth. He lives modestly, while Julian lives in a fashionable hotel he can barely afford and courts society arbiters. One of the newest of these society women is Constance Maitland with whom Crane has become infatuated. Thorndyke, himself, had romanced Maitland eighteen years before, but Maitland's family disdained his courtship. In fact, the will through which she would receive a fortune was re-written so that she would receive almost nothing if she married an American, and Thorndyke withdrew to the United States. He says nothing to Crane of his former attachment to Maitland, although he does help his political career by ghosting a speech for him that receives national attention (Crane is the Chair of Foreign Relations). However, in Crane's moment of triumph, senators to whom he owes the money he had borrowed to finance his society life demand that he aid them in deceiving the senator to whom he owes his political career. Perceiving how troubled he is, Thorndyke encourages him to bring his wife to Washington. When Annette Crane arrives in the city, her beauty and demeanor charm everyone she meets. She even befriends Maitland, although she knows of Crane's interest in the woman. Despite her social success, Crane imagines that she is embarrassing him with her simplicity and honesty about such things as making her own gowns. Even though Crane yields to temptation and agrees to betray his senator patron, by the end of the novel he has realized his good fortune in being married to Annette and has renounced his alliance with the plotting senators by confessing to his patron. He has the strength to act despite the political and financial costs because of the support of Annette. Thorndyke also makes a confession when he announces to Maitland his continued love for her. When he does, he learns that she will be able to marry him and keep her fortune after all.

300. Seawell, Molly Elliott [Davis, Foxcroft, pseud.]. *Mrs. Darrell.* Illustrations by William Sherman Potts. New York: MacMillan, 1905. 391pp.

Many sections of this novel are disquisitions on the nature of true gentility. The newly moneyed class flooding Washington also receives a great deal of attention. The first section is set, as the narrator points out, "before the Deluge"—that is, before the newcomers supplanted the "cave dwellers" who had controlled society in the city since its founding. General Brandon is well connected to the cave-dweller set. He had been a brigadier general in the United States Army before the war but resigned his position to join the Confederate Army and lost almost everything after the conflict. Instead of the Virginia plantation that had been his ancestral home, he lives in a mortgaged house in Northwest Washington and works as a government clerk. Although generations of distinguished ancestry do not translate into financial security, he is still very much in society and remains genteelly resigned to his lot. A widower, he has a twenty-one-year-old daughter, Elizabeth, for whom he has made every sacrifice so that she may be properly launched into society with the help of his old friend Mrs. Luttrell. Given his circumstances he might have tried to make certain she married well, but, when she chooses a British officer, Captain Darrell, stationed in India and visiting the United States with his relative Captain Pelham, he embraces the choice as a love match and wishes the couple well. Pelham realizes the marriage is a mistake, since Darrell, although his closest friend, is a shallow, if attractive, lady's man. Pelham also has no real prospects; his pay is modest, and, although an elderly relative's estate will come to him, he will have no title.

Back in India, Elizabeth quickly becomes closer to Pelham than to her husband. After nine years, the elderly relative dies, and Darrell comes into money. However, because he has failed to produce an heir and is now forty and in poor health, the London house, and even the jewels with which he adorns Elizabeth, are a life trust and will transfer to Pelham should he die. Confused by her feelings for Pelham, when he is offered the opportunity to take command of an expedition to West Africa for a year, Elizabeth encourages him to go, and she and Darrell devote themselves to society life. However, Darrell dies suddenly, and Elizabeth cannot reach Pelham in the jungle. So, within a few months Elizabeth must return impoverished to Washington.

The nouveaux riches have transformed the town in her absence, and mansions, just being opened for the social season as she arrives, now surround her father's humble dwelling. The house closest to theirs is that of Senator James Clavering. The senator started with nothing and made a fortune in mines. Then, he got elected in order to enlarge his fortune even further through the land grants and other chicanery available to an office holder. He pledged long before that when the moment was right he would divorce the woman he had married when he was poor and marry the beautiful and refined Elizabeth. Even as an investigative committee begins to look into the complex web of his thefts, he becomes acquainted with Elizabeth and sets his plans in motion. Pursued for repayment of debts by a lawyer for the life trust from which her husband had benefited, for a time it looks as though she will be forced to marry Clavering. However, she is saved at the last moment when Pelham finally returns from the jungle.

301. Seawell, Molly Elliot [Davis, Foxcroft, pseud.]. *The Whirl: A Romance of Washington Society.* New York: Dodd, Mead, 1909. 306pp.

As its title implies, this novel captures the excitement of a turn-of-the-century Washington filled with titled foreign diplomats and wealthy Americans. The endless descriptions of social events and clothes are generally unimpeded by a plot.

302. Seifert, Shirley. *The Senator's Lady.* Philadelphia: Lippincott, 1967. 377pp.

This historical romance begins by tracing the reaction of Washington society to the betrothal of Adele Cutts (1835-1889) to Stephen A. Douglas (1813-1861). However, in the course of the novel, both Cutts' and Douglas' earlier lives and the full story of their romance is described. In addition to detailing political history during the period from 1856 to 1861, Seifert provides full descriptions of social and domestic life in Washington, as well as attempting to bring all the historical figures of the time to life. In a postscript she details her research and sources, pointing out that she used a journal kept by Mrs. Elizabeth Lindsay Lomax (b. 1796) to reconstruct life in Washington during the time period, right down to the day on which social events occurred and the weather.

303. Seifert, Shirley. *Three Lives of Elizabeth.* Philadelphia: Lippincott, 1952. 287pp.

Seifert's story alternates between Boonslick, Missouri, and Washington, D.C., as she recounts the life of Elizabeth Moss, an actual historical figure. In 1820, Dr. Daniel P. Wilcox arrives on the Missouri frontier and eventually marries Elizabeth, daughter of Dr. James Moss. The couple moves to Columbia, Missouri, where he builds a medical practice and gets involved in politics. However, Wilcox dies at a young age, and General William Henry Ashley, a congressman who had made himself odious to Wilcox through a legal conflict over a tract of land, courts the widowed Elizabeth. Ashley's sincere attentions and his wealth eventually win Elizabeth over. She becomes his wife and moves to a mansion in St. Louis. However, Elizabeth's life as Mrs. Ashley truly begins when the couple moves to Washington, a city that makes life anywhere else seem impoverished for her. Life there appeals to her so much because she is treated with respect as the wife of a man with both money and political influence. Her own ancestry as a member of Virginia's Randolph family, of little consequence in Missouri, enhances her status in Washington. Seifert provides a fairly detailed account of the city in the early 1830s as various well-connected people explain Washington to newcomer Elizabeth. Ashley, intent on creating an even larger fortune to support his wife's awakened social aspirations, only lays the groundwork before his death. Within a few years, however, his foresight has made his widow very wealthy, and she enjoys the migratory life of the East Coast, following the social season from New York, to New Orleans, to Saratoga, to the winter season in Washington. By the 1850s, Elizabeth is being courted by John Jordan Crittenden, a senator. He wins her hand and later becomes attorney general of the United States. In her account of this courtship, Seifert presents details of early 1850s Washington. She also elucidates Crittenden's political stances of the late 1850s and early 1860s and the social tensions and changes in Washington during this period. By the time of Crittenden's death in 1863, Elizabeth has wearied of Washington social life and returns to Missouri to live until her own death in 1873. Although Seifert presents no bibliography, she does provide notes on her research as a postscript to the novel.

304. Seton, Anya. *My Theodosia.* Boston: Houghton Mifflin, 1941. 422pp.
      This fictionalization of the life of Theodosia Burr Alston attempts historical accuracy and presents a theory to explain Theodosia's disappearance that members of the Alston family members known to the author considered the most likely. Theodosia spent most of her life at her father's estate in Albany and on her husband's plantation in South Carolina. However, she and Burr lived in Washington off and on for almost ten years, and she visited her father there, even after her marriage. The Washington chapters of the novel are mostly concerned with the affair that the married Theodosia had with Meriwether Lewis, Jefferson's secretary and the man she had loved but could not marry. Some attempt is made to convey physical conditions in the Federal City, the political gossip about Jefferson's Louisiana Purchase, and public opinion of Burr. The novel ends with an account of the disappearance of the ship upon which Theodosia was traveling to visit her father in New York City during the 1812 holiday season.

305. Smith, Ellen Hart [Revell, Louisa, pseud.]. *The Men with Three Eyes.* New York: MacMillan, 1955. 188pp.
      Julia Tyler, an elderly ex-schoolteacher who used to teach Latin, visits Washington as the guest of wealthy Ruth Gibson. While Gibson's husband is on active duty in the U.S. Navy, she is living in a settlement house as a social worker. Her employer, the Neighborhood House, is located near Stanton Square on Maryland Avenue, NE. The plot of this

novel focuses on the death of a prominent neighborhood man, Victor Caprio, an organized crime figure who is found in his yellow Cadillac convertible. Although a murder mystery, through the Gibson character the author provides a great deal of information about poverty and crime in Washington. In statistical and narrative format Gibson presents details about residents living in poverty and touches on the discontent bred by inequalities of wealth, indicting Congress, which controls the District, for not correcting the problems that foster the slums of Washington. In addition, Gibson analyzes crime in Washington, pointing out the small percentage of police officers who walk the beat and the connection between poverty and crime. She notes the inequalities of wealth that even exist in a criminal world in which "overlords" of crime reap the profits and the "foot soldiers" like those that reside in the Stanton Square neighborhood rarely climb out of poverty. Much of her discussion of crime focuses on the politics of prostitution and the nature of the drug trade (heroin). Because most of the Stanton Square families are Italian, a social group that experiences prejudice, Gibson makes some efforts to increase Tyler's cultural awareness of Italians. She also tries to influence the police to be more sensitive in dealing with these and other recent immigrants. The realistic Washington setting of the novel includes mentions of actual jewelers, department stores (where many of the women in the neighborhood work), Roman Catholic churches, hotels, and restaurants. The settlement house's classes and social events are also described.

306. Smith, Margaret Bayard. *A Winter in Washington: or, Memoirs of the Seymour Family.* New York: E. Bliss & E. White, 1824.

In a preface, Smith notes that the anecdotes and physical descriptions in her fiction are accurately written and based upon her familiarity with Washington from the time of the city's founding. She recounts seeing and admiring the natural beauty of the site that would become Washington from Capitol Hill before the Capitol was constructed. At the center of her story is the Seymour family, which is presented as exemplary in demonstrating intellect, culture, patriotism, simplicity, and disdain for worldly vanities. Their way of life is contrasted with other people in the city and elsewhere in the country, as characters tell each other long and instructive moralistic anecdotes set outside Washington. The family and their guests also discuss literature, philosophy, and politics and celebrate American cultural achievements, particularly Joel Barlow's epic poem "The Columbiad." In fact, they recite from the work, taking special delight in the "Hasty Pudding" section of the poem for the way it celebrates this symbol of American wholesomeness and simplicity.

Romance is at the center of the novel's plot, which revolves around the question of whom Louisa Seymour should marry. Local examples of flirtatiousness in women leading to despair are described. Louisa, herself, eventually recovers from her fascination with New York City adventurer Frederick Wilmot to become engaged to a down to earth family friend. The Washington of the novel is filled with people from all over the country and the world. Much is made of the number of foreign dignitaries in the city. However, the largest numbers of people at receptions and social events are residents of the city, Georgetown, and Alexandria. Public worship in the Capitol building, walks in the woods that fill and surround the city, the climate, and a July 4th celebration are all described in detail. Although Washington is treated enthusiastically, the Seymours consider it a part-time home, retreating to their country cottage as their real abode, and the novel ends with Jefferson leaving office to retire to his Virginia farm. Throughout the work, nature is celebrated above wealth and fashion.

307. Smith, William Russell. *As It Is....* Albany, N.Y.: Munsell & Rowland, 1860. 260pp.

General Jack Sterling is a newly elected Southern congressman traveling to the Federal City for the first time. He meets long-time Senator Burton, as well as Colonel Walker and his daughters (the young Mrs. Beatrice Curtis and Helen). Sterling is immediately attracted to Mrs. Curtis and is disappointed that she is, seemingly, married. Soon after Sterling and Burton check into Gadsby's Hotel, Burton leads them in an evening of entertainment that includes a visit to a "house of gaiety," where many unattached women are eager to meet the new congressman. He also meets the young orphan girl Lily in the house and spirits her away for her own protection. Not knowing how to support her without causing scandal, he convinces Lily to dress as a boy and gets her appointed as a House page. Both Sterling and Lily have contact with numerous politicians against whom a great deal of satire is directed. They have names like Blunderbuss, Pustlepouch, and Clodhead and are lobbied by Huron and others. Political discussions center on the threat of dissolution and the power of Tammany Hall. "Hells," or gambling houses, receive much attention in the novel, not only because Burton frequents them, but also because Dr. Curtis, the husband of lovely Beatrice, gambles away the fortune that Colonel Walker has settled on the couple. While Curtis is at the gaming tables, Sterling visits Beatrice, and the two discuss philosophy and literature.

The author contrasts their interests in European culture and attainments with the sordid interests of other Washingtonians, like Burton and Curtis. Although Sterling cannot openly escort Beatrice to social events, they attend the same entertainments, including "Assemblies" and "Hops." Curtis, who professes love to both Beatrice's younger sister Helen and a female lobbyist, is eventually shot in a gaming house after he correctly accuses the dealer of cheating, and the way is opened for Sterling and Beatrice to marry.

308. Southworth, E.D.E.N. *Ishmael; or In the Depths.* The Companion Series. New York: R. F. Fenno, [1904]. 549pp.

The heir to a large plantation makes a secret, false marriage with a poor woman. Ishmael is born to the union after his father has abandoned his mother. She uses a modest economic settlement to move, but Ishmael's youth is still constrained by poverty. However, he takes every opportunity to improve himself. He meets Claudia, the daughter of Judge Merlin, and falls in love. When he saves Claudia from accidental death and is injured, he is invited to recuperate in the Merlin household and use the judge's large library. Ishmael makes such a positive impression that when the judge is appointed to the U.S. Supreme Court and moves his family to Washington, Ishmael is invited along. The large house in which the Merlins live is north of the Capitol, located on a rise that affords views of downtown and Georgetown. Through his self-study and work with the judge, Ishmael prepares for and passes the bar examination and rapidly becomes the city's leading attorney. Many of his legal cases are suits to redress wrongs that have been done to women. Meanwhile, Claudia has become absorbed by Washington society. She meets a viscount and, determined to be an English peeress, agrees to marry him, despite the fact that she finds him repugnant. The novel, as part of a projected series, ends inconclusively.

309. Spofford, Harriet Prescott. *Old Washington.* Boston: Little, Brown, 1906. 279pp.

Two elderly ladies, Miss Veronica and Miss Sedley, live west of the White House, only a few blocks from the most fashionable section of Connecticut Avenue, in a house surrounded by a grove of trees and filled with family treasures from the earliest days of the country. For more than forty years, they have rarely left the grounds and taken little interest even in happenings like the Civil War and the emancipation of their slaves that have struck so near to them. Only recently has the world begun to intrude as houses on some of their rental properties are being destroyed to widen streets during the great improvements of the

District under Alexander Shepherd. Without quite realizing it, they have become dependent upon their former slaves, who, having squatted on and sold land in the District, now have far more money than the sisters and out of respect for the past provide food for their table and take no salary.

Their first caller in many years, who is treated to a long afternoon of visiting, in which the family history is related, and all the family treasures shown, turns out to be a journalist. When the woman returns with clippings of the newspaper article she wrote about the sisters, they are mortified, although they begin to experience more of the world as the journalist introduces them to actresses and women who work in various government offices.

The newspaperwoman lives at Mrs. McQueen's where a widow, Mrs. Gilroy, and her daughter, Connie, impoverished Southerners who had lived on great estates before the war, also live. They have salvaged only the harp the daughter plays and the services of one of their former slaves who has established herself in the District. The daughter, who works as a clerk in the Government Printing Office, is very beautiful and attracts the attention of a wealthy senator. Despite the great lengths to which he goes to buy her hand, she rejects him for a clerk in the Treasury Department who also lives in the boarding house. Through the senator's ill will both of them lose their positions. They are saved from poverty only by a former slave who engineers a position for the woman to teach harp to the African Americans in Washington so they will know how to play when they arrive in heaven. A woman who spends years trying to get the government to pay reparations for the house and lands of her husband that were destroyed by Union troops, a general and his daughters, and a Cuban beauty lobbying for United States involvement on the Island who eventually marries a congressman also live at Mrs. McQueen's. In the end, a wealthy, self-made man has a carriage accident on the improved street outside Mrs. McQueen's and must recuperate in the household. He falls in love with the widow, and, by the end of the book, she and her family have been removed to his country estate and the boarding house has been closed.

310. Stacton, David. *The Judges of the Secret Court.* New York: Pantheon, 1961. 255pp.

Stacton tells the story of John Wilkes Booth and the Lincoln conspirators beginning with the day of the assassination. He focuses narrowly on personalities and historical events with little description of Washington.

311. Standish, Hal. *Fred Fearnot and His Dog; or, The Boy Who Ran for Congress.* Work and Win Series 278. New York: F. Tousey, 1904. 28pp. juvenile.

This volume is one of more than fifty books for boys that follow the adventures of Fred Fearnot in stories set everywhere from the Western frontier to Wall Street.

312. Standish, Hal [Shackelford, Harvey King, pseud.]. *Frank Fair in Congress; or, A Boy among Our Law Makers; a Thrilling Story of Washington.* New York: F. Tousey, 1899. juvenile.

This book is part of a series of Frank Fair books for boys with various settings, although this is the only one set in Washington.

313. Stanley, Caroline Abbot. *Modern Madonna.* New York: Century, 1906. 401pp.

This story hinges on a law, repealed in every state but still on the books in the District, that enables a father to will away even unborn children from their mothers. Although primarily concerned with describing how important the mother-child relationship is in shaping a person's entire life, the political status of the District and the legislative process to change District law plays an important role in the plot. Though perhaps not specific to the District, race relations and the role of women in society are also important themes.

Protagonist Margaret Varnum marries Victor De Jarnette in St. John's Church, worrying her friends, since his mother caused a scandal by deserting her family to live with a lover, and the wealthy Victor is reputed to be a ladies' man. The couple settles into a Massachusetts Avenue mansion, and Margaret spends her days arranging the household to give her husband the greatest comfort. A few months after their May wedding he proposes an extended stay at the seashore, only to spend all of his time with a fast crowd from Baltimore, and, soon after the couple returns to the city, Margaret discovers him riding in a carriage with another woman when he was supposedly out of town. When she forces Victor to choose between his marriage and his life as a romancer, he leaves for Paris. Throughout the separation, Margaret, now pregnant, maintains the pretense that Victor is away on business. When Victor does return, tragedy soon follows. He is discovered dying from a gunshot wound in his own office. At the reading of his will, written on the same day that he had left the city for Paris, Margaret discovers that he has left all of his money to her but willed her child to his brother Richard De Jarnette, who soon takes the child to live with him. Margaret's court battles compose much of the remainder of the novel.

314. Starnes, Richard. *Another Mug for the Bier.* Philadelphia: J. B. Lippincott, 1950. 248pp.

Barney Forge, a newspaperman in the Senate press corps, finds the dead body of Courtney Mandel, a hated broadcast journalist, in the vacant office of Bowie Culpepper, a lawyer with the Public Power Committee, chaired by Senator Philander Chance. Forge, whose animus for Mandel is widely known, removes the body and places it in the grounds of the Capitol out of fear of incrimination. Investigating Mandel's murder, he finds a payoff list the journalist kept to show the amounts of money people gave him in return for information. He also discovers the script for a broadcast Mandel was about to deliver in which he would have reported that Senator Chance had been seeking millions in taxpayer funding for a pipeline to an oil field known to be dry. As Forge tries to unravel who killed Mandel, he encounters several Washington types, including society hostesses, lobbyists, and crooked political staffers eager to leak information to the press for a profit. The city, particularly its hotel dining rooms, bars, and expensive apartment buildings, form a backdrop to Forge's investigation. Forge resides in Alexandria, and physical settings in the novel are often outside the District. An Alexandria physician named Dr. Peachy lives in an eighteenth-century Alexandria house and provides the medical information that solves the murder.

315. Starnes, Richard. *The Other Body in Grant's Tomb.* Philadelphia: Lippincott, [1951]. 249pp.

Barney Forge, a well-paid senior writer for *Palm,* a pocket-sized news magazine, arrives in Washington to write an investigative piece on the influence of organized crime on the city's municipal government. Although there is much evidence of wrongdoing, he is not optimistic that investigative reportage will bring change. One of his informants is Hack Harper, a disgraced journalist with detailed information but no venue for publication. Forge spends most of his time in disreputable areas of the city and gets embroiled in discovering a murderer when one after another of his informants is killed, including Kay Tinsel and an embezzling lawyer named Civet. The only neighborhood given any description is the tenderloin area near the intersection of "Ocean Avenue and Paradise Alley." Here Barney discovers the Golden Cockroach Bar and the Grant's Tomb of the title, a Turkish bath that serves alcohol.

316. Starnes, Richard. *And When She Was Bad She Was Murdered.* Philadelphia: Lippincott, [1950]. 224pp.

Barney Forge, a newspaperman, recounts how his friend, St. George Peachy, M.D., solved a murder. Both men live in Alexandria, Virginia, on Prince, a street mostly inhabited by upper-level civil servants, Washington-based journalists, retired military men, doctors, lawyers, and a few millionaires. The plot is set in motion by the aftermath of a cocktail party hosted by a sculptor who has set up a studio in the neighborhood. At the party, his attractive blonde model was a bit too flirtatious with married men. Soon afterward Forge discovers the body of the dead model. Her throat has been slashed, and he and Peachy begin an unofficial investigation. Although the physical setting of the work is mostly Alexandria, the social setting is Washington since the characters described are Washington types (i.e., a lawyer who had been the enfant terrible of the New Deal cocktail circuit, Georgetown hostesses, apartment-dwelling newspaper women, silver-haired senators, and District police detectives).

317. Stead, Christina. *The Man Who Loved Children.* New York: Holt, Rhinehart & Winston, 1965. 527pp.

Stead used information gathered on a three-month stay in Washington to create a setting for her story about the Pollit family, which is destroyed by the egocentric father, Sam. Neighborhoods in Georgetown and other parts of the District provide a background for this story of a government scientist and his family; however, the book does not present any significant description of the work life of a Washington bureaucrat.

318. Stoddard, William Osborn. *Long Bridge Boys: A Story of '61.* Illustrated by I. B. Hazelton. Boston: Lothrop, 1904. 344pp.

Through the boys William Putnam and Oliver Mason, the author relates the arguments leading up to the Civil War and recounts events in and around Washington during the first days of the conflict. Because the Mason family is prominent and Putnam's father (Sam Putnam of Connecticut) works in the U.S. Treasury Department, the boys know many of the great statesmen of the day. Some of the public scenes fictionalized here are election crowds in Washington in 1860, the Buchanan White House, the open controversies in Congress and elsewhere as secession begins, the Lincoln inauguration, the rush for political appointments after the inauguration, and popular reaction to the firing on Fort Sumter. While visiting his friend, Putnam overhears a plot to take over Washington by smuggling troops over from Alexandria on the ferry and taking over the Navy Yard and White House. While Putnam is reporting this information in Washington, Mason is acting as a courier on behalf of the conspirators and eventually boards the early morning ferry with them. Putnam is a part of the militia that makes a surprise capture of the ferry as it lands. The novel ends with the capture of Alexandria by Union troops marching over Long Bridge in darkness. Putnam is a sentry on one side, and Mason reports the invasion on the other side.

319. Stone, Grace Zaring. *The Almond Tree*. Indianapolis: Bobbs-Merrill, 1931. 350pp.

Providing rich descriptions of social life in Washington, Stone tells the story of the three Gentry sisters who are reunited in Washington after several decades during which their lives took very different courses. At the end of their childhoods, they had moved to the city from Indiana when their father was elected to Congress. During his first term, their mother died and the oldest sister, May, took over the management of their large, elegant house. Their father's prominence and wealth increased until he was elected to the Senate and he was mentioned as a possible presidential candidate. After his death, May remained unmarried and maintained his house as a shrine to his achievements. Living her life in the golden past of her father's prominence she is perpetually courted by "young" Harry Ellington who moved to Washington as a very young man to take a job as a file clerk with the Internal Revenue Service in order to be close to her when the family moved from Indiana.

The other two Gentry sisters married. Leda wed Blair Brune, a career diplomat. Although the couple's social life was rich, Blair's salary was small. Deeply in love with each other and mostly concerned about living to the fullest, the couple spent Leda's share of the income from her father's estate to underwrite the costs of their diplomatic lifestyle. Their love for each other was so deep that everyone, even their daughter Marise, was kept at a slight distance. Brune died unexpectedly, and Leda and sixteen-year-old Marise now live with May and rely on her charity. The third Gentry sister, Susan, was married for ten years before divorcing her husband. She had always been prudent with the income from her father's estate and now, with alimony income as well, can live very well and fashionably.

Marise becomes a focus for all the sisters. She is excited by the prospect of living in a country where everyone has a chance to work and create his or her own future and admires Susan's focus on increasing her wealth and social prestige. Unlike May and Leda, Susan also lives on the cutting edge of fashion. Flattered by Marise's attention, Susan arranges for Marise to work as an apprentice to decorator Candace Page. Stone's descriptions of Marise's experiences as a working girl include vivid descriptions of daily life for ordinary Washingtonians during this time period. The novel's dramatic conflict arises when Leda meets Zachary West, a naval officer with whom she falls in love, although she feels powerless to act on her feelings. West is attracted to Leda, as well, but her reserve and Marise's obvious interest lead him to court Marise, instead. Susan encourages the relationship and launches Marise in society. With the exception of May, by the end of the novel, each character's relationship to her past and hopes for the future has been altered.

320. Stone, Irving. *Immortal Wife: The Biographical Novel of Jessie Benton Fremont.* Garden City, N.Y.: Doubleday, 1958. 456pp.

This work of historical fiction was researched in depth, and Stone presents his sources in a postscript. At the beginning of the novel, when Jessie, the daughter of Senator Thomas Benton, meets John Fremont for the first time, she is a student at Miss English's Academy in Georgetown. A number of scenes are set in the Benton household where guests include family friends like Samuel Morse and James Buchanan and a good deal of information is included about Senator Benton's career in Washington. Despite her father's opposition and the poverty and undistinguished family background of Fremont, Jessie secretly marries him. Due to her father's political importance, the couple is invited everywhere and she is a close friend of Countess Bodisco and Nancy Polk. When Fremont is named commander of the expedition to find a southern pass through the Rocky Mountains, the couple is feted by Samuel Morse, Stephen Kearny, James Buchanan, and President Tyler. After Fremont leaves, there are accounts of Jessie's work as secretary for her father, her pregnancy, and her social activities. When Fremont returns, she helps him write his report to Congress and, later, a report on his California expedition. She also takes an influential, behind-the-scenes role to struggle against his court-martial. After Fremont's resignation from the Army, the novel is only occasionally set in Washington as the Fremonts travel back and forth to California. Following the death of his wife and his electoral defeat, Thomas Benton's Washington house burns to the ground, and he begins living with the Fremonts. The primary settings become Manhattan, Staten Island, and St. Louis. However, near the end of the novel, the couple returns to Washington to live in a house on Dupont Circle and use the Library of

Congress while writing Fremont's memoirs; they remark on the changed Washington of 1886.

321. Stone, Irving. *Love Is Eternal: A Novel about Mary Todd and Abraham Lincoln.* Garden City, N.Y.: Doubleday, 1954. 462pp.

Stone extensively researched the Lincolns and includes a list of primary and secondary sources he consulted to create this work of historical fiction. He begins his story before Mary meets Abe, showing her surrounded by politicians in her father's affluent household. When she does meet her future husband, her social skills are contrasted with his awkwardness. Their difference in wealth is emphasized, as is Abe's resistance, even after they are married, to adopt the lifestyle that Mary can afford. In Stone's account, Lincoln is a hypochondriac and depressive, and Mary believes she can heal him through love. She later learns that her own psychological well-being is dependent upon Abe. The Washington sections of the novel recount the horrible emotional trials Lincoln and his wife endured, even when he was a congressman. A great deal of time is spent analyzing the varying emotional states of each of them in the context of historical events. The novel ends with Mary's delayed departure from the White House. The mansion's staff has departed, and vandals roam the public rooms stealing souvenirs. In Stone's account, she leaves in disgrace, heavily in debt, and accused of looting the White House.

322. Stone, Irving. *The President's Lady: A Novel about Rachel and Andrew Jackson.* Garden City, N.Y.: Doubleday, 1951. 338pp.

Despite this historical novel's title, very little of the book is set in Washington. Jackson's career is recounted through from the perspective of Rachel, but she dies before he is sworn in as President. Rachel does make a few trips to the Federal City with Jackson. Years pass in between the trips, and she comments on the changes in the streets and buildings. By her last trip, the Bulfinch dome on the Capitol has been completed.

323. Stone, Irving. *Those Who Love: A Biographical Novel of Abigail and John Adams.* Garden City, N.Y.: Doubleday, 1965. 650pp.

Only approximately eighteen pages of this novel are set in Washington. The Adamses arrive to take up residence in the new executive mansion in December 1800, and Abigail turns the house over to Jefferson in February 1801. Washington and Georgetown are described, and Abigail is credited with playing an important role in furnishing the White House and initiating social life there.

324. Stonebraker, Florence. [Branch, Florenz, pseud.]. *Passion on the Potomac.* New York: Phoenix, 1943. 256pp.

At the insistence of wealthy, but married, Senator George Haley, model Vicky Dawnes travels from New York City to Washington to take a government job. The two met at a party at the Waldorf-Astoria, and Haley courted her with gifts of expensive clothes and perfumes. She is shocked when she sees the apartment the senator's staffer has arranged for her in Southeast Washington. Despite Haley's claims that the furnished apartment is the best to be found during the wartime housing shortage, she believes he is trying to hide her and is outraged. His solution, proposed by a faithful staffer, is to introduce Dawnes as a relative and assign Bob Kenyon to escort her to social events attended by the senator. Kenyon is dependent upon Haley because he got him his job as a poster artist for the Office of War Information. Vicky and Kenyon immediately fall in love, although Kenyon is so innocent that he believes his interest in Dawnes is purely aesthetic and he uses her as the model for a mother in a poster. When Haley discovers the emotional attachment, he tells Kenyon the truth about Dawnes. He also imposes on a woman, with whom he previously had an affair and who cannot get over him, to come to Washington and marry Kenyon. Dawnes convinces Kenyon that she has no feelings for Haley, and the two secretly have an affair. However, Haley, who has been suffering politically for his isolationist stance before the war, decides not to run for re-election but plans to divorce his wife, marry Dawnes, and settle on a farm in Maryland. Kenyon hears of the divorce from Haley's wife and believes the worst about Dawnes, even though she had actually laughed in Haley's face at his proposal. In revenge, the senator has Kenyon dismissed from his job, claiming that he used a prostitute (Dawnes) to represent American motherhood in one of his posters. Kenyon is forced into the army and is about to marry the woman Haley had provided before he discovers the truth from Dawnes and they reconcile. In the Washington of this novel, beset by wartime deprivations, everyone is obsessed with meat, alcohol, and apartments.

325. Stonebraker, Florence. [Branch, Florenz, pseud.]. *Pay for Your Pleasure.* New York: Phoenix, 1937. 251pp.

The daughter of a K Street, NW, rooming house owner/manager, Donna Mountford, threw over her boyfriend, Jimmy Brandon, when she was nineteen because of the thrilling attentions of Clarke Middleton, a wealthy man twice her age who maintained a legal practice in a building at 14th and G Streets, NW, mostly as a place to pass the time, reading tastefully lubricious French novels and drinking expensive liquor. To mend his heartbreak, Brandon immediately left town for a job on a coffee plantation in South America and Donna settled into life as Middleton's secretary, passively accepting his reasoning that they should not marry, since he would not want to spoil her chances of finding a husband closer to her own age. However, Donna returns from an out of town trip to find Clarke and her mother in a passionate embrace on the living room sofa. This is the first of her experiences that reveal the true nature of the human male. When Jimmy reappears, she believes he is sincerely passionate about her and will marry her, only to discover, after she allows him to have sex with her, that he is about to marry someone else. Forced to find a job with no skills, she is soon working as a hostess for a powerful lobbyist, living at the Willard Hotel, charming politicians, and plying them with alcohol to ease her boss's business with them. When her boss presents Jimmy, now an officer with a New York transportation company, to Donna, the two are soon emotionally involved again. Claiming he will divorce his wife if Donna is patient, she gives up her job and rents a cabin on an overgrown piece of land in disreputable Georgetown. Seemingly abandoned by Jimmy once again, Donna falls in with Russian exiles, educated and formerly wealthy men and women who were forced to flee their country during the Revolution. One of the Russians becomes her lover and she becomes an "interpretive" dancer at a Russian restaurant named Club Morocco on the outskirts of Washington. Just as she is about to be arrested one night, unfairly charged with lewd dancing, Jimmy reenters her life. He saves her and later reveals that his wife has had the child of another man and asked for a divorce and that he is there to marry Donna and take her to New York. A number of Washington hotels, including the Powhatan and Occidental, are mentioned in this novel, and several nightclubs are described, including one with jungle murals painted on the walls that features "primitive" dancing by scantily clad African Americans.

326. Stonebraker, Florence [Stone, Thomas, pseud.]. *The Playboy's Girl.* New York: Phoenix Press, 1942. 250pp.

Stonebraker's book provides a thorough description of Washington's World War II "duration gals" through the story of Linda Terry from Fairview, Pennsylvania. Traveling by train to her fiancé, soldier Ward Ritter, twenty-year-old Linda meets Larry Bliss. Bliss is a senator's secretary, and he describes 1941 Washington as the nation's fastest-growing and most exciting city. In the course of their conversation, he also assures her that he can find a secretarial job for her. She resists at first but is quickly won over by the sophisticated Bliss. Up until this meeting, she had been on her way to live in an apartment in New Jersey while her fiancé is in camp in the area. When she sees the apartment near Ritter's camp, it seems dismal, and they quarrel over the impracticality of trying to marry on his private's pay. Within a few weeks she is on her way to Washington instead. She must quickly learn how the city operates. Due to the wartime housing shortage, she shares an apartment in the Wardman Park Hotel with Martha Jackson, a famous political columnist acquainted with Bliss. Jackson becomes her guide and protector and instructs her on how to live as an independent woman. Through Linda's experiences, readers learn about getting a civil service job, workplace politics, and the finances of a single woman in the city. Eventually, Linda moves into an apartment located at 13th and M Streets, NW, with several other women. They encourage her to take courses in typing and shorthand so that she can work her way up the civil service ranks. They also instruct her in wartime relationships between men and women. The other girls improve their lifestyles through dates with men who are passing through Washington. The men like having a woman to take to dinner or a show and keep their escorts provided with "cab fare." The really generous ones send flowers and bottles of champagne. Despite their mercenary behavior, Linda's apartment mates all seek true love and want to marry. Linda, herself, reconciles with Ritter, and they wed. In addition to telling the story of women like Linda, Stonebraker provides references to wartime events, such as Pearl Harbor, current opinion about the menace of Hitler, and descriptions of specific hotels and night spots (the Mayflower and Shoreham Terrace hotels, the Del Rio on 15th Street, NW, and the Troika on Connecticut Avenue, NW. She also describes people other than "duration gals" drawn to Washington by the war, including female newspaper correspondents, psychiatrists, government contractors, and diplomats.

327. Strizzi, Michele Cristofora. *All Came by the Sea.* Philadelphia: Dorrance, 1949. 414pp.

Strizzi's stated purpose is to show how people from England, Germany, Ireland, and Scotland collaborated in the creation of a new country and of a new type of person, the American. She covers the years 1800 to 1825, following the development of the Federal City through the experiences of Daniel Patrick McMallon's family. Historical figures come into contact with the McMallons, and a great deal of history is dramatized in the novel. A main focus is the challenge of creating a planned city and the problem of financing federal building construction. Later a detailed account is given of the capture of Washington and the burning of the Capitol. During the Jefferson administration, McMallon's son, Thomas, serves as Jefferson's private secretary in charge of diplomatic correspondence and foreign relations administration. Through Thomas' story, Jefferson's influence on Washington's development is revealed, and the debate over the form official entertainments should take gets aired. The novel concludes with an account of Lafayette's visit to the Federal City, which is described as fully realized with government buildings, church spires, bridges, and parks.

328. Strong, Armour. *Dear Days: A Story of Washington School Life.* Philadelphia: Henry T. Coates, 1901. 316pp. young adult.

This novel's plot mostly focuses on schoolgirl rivalries centered on competition over boys and differences in ethnicity, affluence, and religion. There are references to Washington locations and buildings (the National Rifles' Hall, Ford's Theater, the Botanical Garden, egg rolling on the White House, and Arlington Cemetery), and street life is described, particularly street vendors (ice wagons, fruit wagons, and an organ grinder). Although the city is shown to be composed of people from many national origins, the prejudices at work make it seem far from cosmopolitan.

329. Strong, Charles S. [Bartlett, Nancy, pseud.]. *Embassy Ball.* New York: Gramercy, 1938. 252pp.

Elvira Hathaway is the bereaved daughter of retired Marine Corps Commandant Major General John Hathaway whose long illness began shortly after her debut. In mourning ever since his death and living in seclusion in the Chevy Chase colonial mansion of her Aunt Corinthia, Elvira is pleased to receive a message from Garrett Preston, an undersecretary in the State Department, asking her to become his secretary. She is tired of her quiet life and of her boyfriend, Henry Grenville, who is absorbed in his studies of agricultural science at Johns Hopkins University. Using the commute and need to be on-call as an excuse, she accepts Preston's offer of accommodation in the Georgetown house he shares with his wife. On her first day at work, she meets many eligible young men, all of whom seem interested in her. One, Martin Denham, a student in the Foreign Service School, is particularly smitten. Although she finds him attractive, part of her duties involve showing Washington to visiting dignitaries, and she soon meets and falls in love with Prince Frederick. The Balkan royal, who is in the United States to study shipping canals that might be used as models for his country, invites her to go horseback riding in Rock Creek Park, give him a tour of the State

Department Library, attend the Army-Navy football game, sail on the royal yacht, be his guide as he participates in a Virginia fox hunt, and accompany him to a Presidential luncheon. Elvira is shocked out of her romantic reverie while buying a gown at Woodward and Lothrop's for the Embassy Ball. She overhears an elderly society woman claiming that Elvira is making a spectacle of herself over the prince and that he will ignore her at the ball. However, she takes a central role at the ball (that is described in some detail), when she is officially presented to the prince. The prince eventually proposes to her; however, at the ball her aunt hosts for the engagement to be announced, she finds out that the prince and his entourage are being forced to leave the country immediately on the grounds of espionage. Her admirer, Denham, is implicated as well. However, Henry, who had remained faithful to her, despite her romance with the prince, is revealed to be a hero. He has discovered a process for making nitrate from desert salt and electricity that the prince was trying to obtain, since nitrate supplies in Europe had been depleted by the world war. He also valiantly ignored the advances of a beautiful female spy. Henry and Elvira are immediately reconciled and look forward to a life in the Washington area; Henry will work as an assistant professor at Johns Hopkins and Elvira at the State Department.

330. Sutton, Henry Sidney. *Rhoda Roland: A Woman from the West in Washington.* New York: Abbey Press, 1902. 300pp.

Through her stenography business, a forty-year-old widow with a young daughter becomes acquainted with the congressman from her district. She acts on his encouragement to relocate to Washington where so many lawyers need stenographers. Thrown into the society of working women who live in boarding houses, she is given an initiation into boarding house life and learns the characteristics of various neighborhoods, places where a respectable lady can spend time by herself in public, opportunities in different government agencies, slang expressions, street car lines, popular weekend outings, department stores, and ways of preserving one's reputation as a single woman. Resentment against African Americans is open throughout the work. In addition to a rather exhaustive catalog of shops, entertainments, sites worth seeing, and advice, the book includes a large quantity of verses and anecdotes that are not set in Washington. A few of the stories are told by women Roland meets and tell how they came to be in their current circumstances (a palmist, vaudeville performer, and traveling saleswoman). Some of the adventures of the protagonist include buying and learning to ride a bicycle, being taken out in disguise for a night in

"Bohemia," catching an African American boy who had robbed her, and being courted by various gentlemen, some of whom are married. By the end of the novel, Roland's secretarial job has closed after a decline in business and she has been unsuccessful in securing another position through her congressman because of the jealousy of his female secretary. So, when the secretary offers to finance Roland's trip back to the West so long as she will have no further contact with the congressman, she accepts and decides to look upon her stay in Washington as nothing but an exciting adventure.

331. Tate, Allen. *The Fathers.* New York: G. P. Putnam's Sons, 1938. 306pp.

Largely set in Georgetown in 1860, the novel contrasts traditional rural life in the old South of Virginia with the new South of Georgetown where people live a town life focused on commerce. Prospect House, 3508 Prospect Street, NW, is the residence of the George Posey family to whom fifteen-year-old Lacy Buchan, Posey's brother-in-law, is sent to spend the Civil War by his father, Major Buchan, who remains at his farm, Pleasant Hill, in Fairfax County, Virginia.

332. Taylor, Mary Imlay. *The Impersonator.* Illustrated by C. Grunwald. Boston: Little, Brown, 1906. 392pp.

Mary Lang, who has been living as an impoverished art student in Paris, agrees to impersonate May Hadding, a student friend who has been invited to spend the winter social season with her aunt in Washington. Although Mary enjoys the comforts afforded her, she finds society filled with nasty gossips and schemers. The only honorable man she meets is a young politician, who is attracted to her for being so different from her peers. A period of uncertainty begins when the woman she is impersonating arrives unexpectedly; however the crisis ends when the aunt finds her real niece unlikable and sends her away. To everyone's delight, the impersonator learns her true identity as the heiress to a wealthy ambassador and is betrothed to the rising young politician.

333. Taylor, Mary Imlay. *The Reaping.* Boston: Little, Brown, 1908. 334pp.

Through this novel's plot, dialogues, and the internal reflections of the characters, the issues of the role of women in society, the good or evil of wealth, the relationship between politics and character, and other concerns about contemporary morality are raised. Physical descriptions of Washington are interesting for their focus on domestic establishments. The main character, William Fox, is a congressman with a national reputation for his powerful oratory and well-informed positions during legislative debates. The one love of his life, Margaret, years before married his Harvard classmate, Wicklow White, since Fox had no significant fortune and White did. Margaret grew up in affluence and could not imagine living the middle-class existence Fox could offer. Through his cousin, Bobby Allestree, a portrait painter, Fox meets Rose Temple, the daughter of an elderly judge, and soon falls in love. When Margaret discovers the discreetly enacted and chaste romance (Rose is a very traditional and religious young woman), she lets Fox know how unhappy she is in her marriage and becomes more scandalous in her public behavior. On one occasion she performs an elaborate dance in the style of Sandra Bernhardt, and at a costume ball she takes the part of Ophelia. Such performances are considered inappropriate, as is her habit of cutting down parvenus to their faces. Taking no pleasure in her elegant household, illustrious dinner parties, or her children (who remind her of the husband she has come to despise), she becomes more reckless and lets Fox know she plans to divorce Wicklow, who is having an affair with the divorcee Lily Osborne. Fox knows that once she is divorced, honor will oblige him to marry her and forget about Rose. Although Margaret abandons her children and sues her husband for divorce, during four hours on a rainy Washington afternoon, just before she dies of a heart attack, she makes some devastating realizations about herself and her behavior and pledges to become a mother to her children and give up Fox so that he can marry Rose.

334. Thomas, Katherine Elwes. *Not All the King's Horses.* New York: Cassell, 1896. 210pp.

Eight years before the action of the novel, Mrs. Oglethorpe Lyman arrived in Washington with a husband made wealthy by an invention. Through Mrs. Lyman's careful strategizing, the couple attain the pinnacle of society, becoming accustomed to entertaining notables at their Farragut Square house and receiving invitations to the White House. Then, Mr. Lyman dies, and Mrs. Lyman retires from society for three years of mourning. Just as this time is nearing its end, she learns that business reverses have destroyed her income. Her lawyer advises closing up her house and selling off her possessions. She, however, is convinced that for the sake of her young daughter she must find another solution. So, during the season of 1892 she abandons her mourning and begins her campaign to marry William Stone of the Dakota Territory, the least established, but wealthiest, of the bachelors in the city. The novel chronicles the dinners, receptions, and social events that bring Mrs. Lyman ever closer to her goal. Her campaign nearly loses its focus when she acknowledges her feelings for a man from her past, also successful, but not nearly as wealthy as Stone. However, her daughter's illness from diphtheria refocuses her, and her wedding to Stone occurs even sooner than anticipated.

335. Thomas, Ross. *The Money Harvest*. New York: William Morrow, 1975. 311pp.

William Makepeace Gilmore, advisor to six presidents, is shot to death at the age of ninety-three on the steps of his Georgetown house. His former law partner, Ancel Easter, suspects more than a mugging since Gilmore had an appointment to speak with him about the details of a plot that he had inadvertently overheard. He refused to discuss the details over the telephone. Easter calls upon Jake Pope, a friend of his and Gilmore's to investigate. With little evidence to go upon, except for the fact that Gilmore had overheard the plot at the Cosmos Club on a certain date, Pope uses his extraordinary skills as a private investigator to uncover a conspiracy to steal information from a report on wheat production by the Department of Agriculture before the numbers are released to the public. The novel rises above its genre by the details Thomas includes to present telling biographical summaries that flesh out even minor characters. In doing so, he conveys a great deal of social detail that presents what it was like to live in Washington in the mid-1970s for people from a range of social classes, including doormen, members of a commune living in Dupont Circle, mid-level civil servants, and the very wealthy. Settings include the Madison Hotel, the Cosmos Club, and the neighborhoods of Dupont Circle, Georgetown, and Kalorama.

336. Tibbetts, Edgar Alfred [Johnson, Ivar, pseud.]. *The Department Clerk; A Story of Civil Service Reform*. New York: F. Tennyson Neely, 1899. 216pp.

Tibbetts exposes the injustices of the civil service by tracing the experiences of Walter Ray, the offspring of impoverished parents who grew up in the West with a love of books and learning. The novel argues that despite past reforms, the civil service continues to serve the needs of a system of political patronage.

337. Tilden, Freeman. *Square Yards of Roofing*. Albuquerque, N.Mex.: Laugh O' the Month Book, 1936. 24pp.

This booklet satirizes the Civilian Conservation Corps.

338. Toombs, Alfred. *Good as Gold.* New York: Thomas Y. Crowell, 1955. 281pp.

Representative Jack Fairweather lives with his wife in George-town. John Henry Johnson from his home district petitions him in person for gold from the government to produce mercury isotopes in order to perform experiments on plants. Johnson demonstrates the beneficial effect of the isotopes on a prize-winning begonia of Fairweather's wife. Fairweather fobs him off to the U.S. Treasury Department, and, after Johnson explains his request, he is locked up in a psychiatric ward. Although Fairweather is able to arrange Johnson's release, the now radioactive demonstration begonia is still in his car. The plant grows so rapidly that its stems thrash like an octopus and Fairweather's parked car attracts the attention of the Capitol Hill security detail and an investigation begins, leading to accusations of a Communist plot.

339. Toomer, Jean. *Cane.* Foreword by Waldo Frank. New York: Boni & Liveright, 1923. 239pp.

This impressionistic novel, composed of poems, sketches, and stories with interrelated themes, leaves the reader with the feeling of having an experience, rather than following a unified narrative. Although the first section is set in rural Georgia, the second section is set in Chicago and Washington. The Washington setting is restricted to the African American neighborhoods of the time and emphasizes fast-paced urban life, as well as devoutness to traditional Christian religious beliefs. Although Washington does not play a prominent role in the novel, the work provides important insights into the experiences of African Americans in the city.

340. Tourgée, Albion Winegar. *Pactolus Prime.* New York: Cassell, c. 1890. 359pp.

The eponymous Prime is an African American bootblack at one of Washington's best hotels. Over years of working in the city, he has become a recognized figure and accumulated a great deal of knowledge about politicians and notable city residents. The main action of several chapters of the novel consists of Prime confronting his clients with uncomfortable truths about the continuing effects of racial inequality. In an ending meant to be sensational, we find out that Prime's father was a white plantation owner to whom his mother was enslaved, and his daughter has grown up thinking that she is the white daughter of the plantation owner.

341. Trumbo, Dalton. *Washington Jitters.* New York: Alfred A. Knopf, 1936. 287pp.

When Harvey Upp, author of the daily column "Washington Jitters," arrives unexpectedly at the office of Hamilton Dill, administrator of the Agricultural Survey Program (ASP), Dill has just left for dinner at the Cosmos Club, having fired his secretary so that he can give her job to the daughter of a politically powerful friend. The secretary is in tears, and Henry Hogg, a sign painter with government contracts, is comforting her. When Upp asks about irregularities in the office, Hogg goes into a tirade against Dill that Upp prints in his column, without any statement from Dill. The political fallout from the column spreads as important men jockey to take positions on what would otherwise be a minor incident in a department concerned with surveying people on such matters as whether they breakfast at home. Within twenty-four hours, Hogg is appointed coordinator of the ASP. The power exhilarates him after a lifetime of being told what to do, and people who believe Upp is Hogg's patron line up to increase Hogg's authority and power, including a Harvard-educated lawyer who becomes his paid assistant and works to advance Hogg in order to advance himself. Soon, important politicians are using Hogg's new prominence to forward their legislative agendas. Although Hogg's supporters and manipulators want him to run for President, he eventually rejects Washington officialdom and goes back to sign painting. Men in power are unconvinced by his decision, believing it is some ploy. Fearing his political power, they offer him a federal job in Europe with no responsibilities, and Hogg, always looking out for his own interests and tired of Washington, accepts. Although the novel provides little physical description of Washington, Trumbo satirizes emblematic Washington professions, such as ghostwriting, public relations, and lobbying, as well as skewering Washington socialites.

342. Tuel, John E. *St. Clair, or The Protégé: A Tale of the Federal City.* New York: W. Taylor & Company, 1846. 142pp.

Henry St. Clair, orphaned at an early age, is raised by a family friend, Richard Wilmont, who becomes his patron. Upon entering adulthood, Henry practices law and participates in Washington social and political circles. His closest friend is Claude Alden, with whom he shares the triumphs and heartaches of his love life. Tragically, the two men pursue the affections of the same woman—Virginia Wilmont (niece of Henry's patron). An embittered Alden challenges St. Clair to a duel, and St. Clair, defending his gentlemanly honor, shoots Alden dead and marries Virginia.

343. Tully, Andrew. *Capitol Hill.* New York: Simon & Schuster, 1962. 412pp.

Despite the Cold War threat of nuclear annihilation, the men at the summit of United States political power are preoccupied with sexual alliances, racial and religious prejudices, and internal power struggles. Much of the plot focuses on John Thurston, assistant secretary of Defense, and his wealthy, sexually promiscuous wife, Anne. John is having an affair with Alicia, and Anne wants a divorce. John resists a divorce since he will only get a cabinet position in the administration of President Dan Williams if he is perceived to be morally irreproachable. No matter what John offers as blandishments or rationales, Anne presses to end the marriage, not only because of John's affair, but also because of her distaste for John, who, despite his avid patriotism, will do anything to promote his career. She is also in love with another man—Charles Sturges, a Foreign Service officer. In addition to the Thurstons, the novel reveals the preoccupation of other politicians with the Communist threat, global political alliances, and, on the domestic front, civil rights for "Negroes." Each of the novel's politicians is carefully weighing this issue based upon how it will translate into votes and political power. One presidential candidate believes the issue has campaign value and promises to appoint "Negro" physicist Norman Miller to a high administration position at the Atomic Energy Commission. To be appointed, however, Miller must end his relationship with the white woman he loves so that it will not become a press scandal in an environment in which the Washington press corps focuses on the human angle to every story and the unblinking eye of television has a power that even the most senior politicians must acknowledge. The novel is filled with references to Washington locales and establishments that were trendy during the early 1960s (i.e., the F Street Club, Georgetown, Burning Tree Golf Club, Goldie Beck's, and the Ace of Spades).

344. Tully, Andrew. *Supreme Court: A Novel.* New York: Simon & Schuster, 1963. 409pp.

President John Alden Hughes, III, was re-elected to office by carrying forty-six states. In his first term, the public worshiped him and Congress tended to obey his every request. Now, with even more of his party in office, he can get any legislation passed. He decides he wants to increase the number of justices on the Supreme Court to eleven, with the stated rationale that there is too much work for nine. However, he actually wants to pack the court with men who will be less concerned with the rights of individuals and let the federal government have more power to battle Communism. With his appointees, cases like those brought against the Sons of Slaves, an African American civil rights group, would go Hughes' way. So far, each time members of the group refused to reveal their political affiliations before the House Un-American Activities Committee the court vindicated them. Furthermore, the President looks forward to judicial support for his belief that individual states should make decisions about integration. The story of Hughes' efforts is told from a number of viewpoints besides that of the President, including those of Senator Frank Hoar of Ohio (who opposes the plan) and Justice Francis Copley Dalton, a Hughes appointee and confidante. The private lives, character traits, and moral convictions of these protagonists have a major impact on the story. The novel's action is set inside government buildings, at official functions, and in relatively anonymous social settings.

345. Tweed, Thomas Frederic. *Gabriel Over the White House: A Novel of the Presidency.* New York: Farrar & Rinehart, 1933. 309pp.

The President, Judson "Jud" Cummings Hammond, is seriously injured in an automobile accident, inspiring his confidential secretary, the narrative voice in the novel, to reflect on Hammond's life and political career, as well as the accident and its surprising impact. Hammond grew up in Milwaukee, Wisconsin, the son of an entrepreneur who founded a chain of stores, innovative for the local shared ownership structures they encouraged. Jud made his father's business even more profitable and sold his shares to become a very wealthy man. After World War I, he embarked on a political career and was elected to the U.S. Senate. In office during the financial crisis of the early 1930s, he participated in the dramatic formation of the National Party, composed of the former Democrat and Republican parties and embracing isolationism as its central tenet. The opposing party that emerged, the Progressive Party, was a loose alliance of dissenters, reformers, and radicals, and when Hammond, known for his oratory and considered a man of the people, got the National Party nomination he was guaranteed the Presidency. His administration runs smoothly until an automobile accident mysteriously transforms the President's personality. He decides that corporate America and the country's financial and political institutions should be held accountable for the economic crises facing the nation. Already in control of political institutions, he creates legislation to nationalize manufacturing and financial institutions. After he succeeds in transforming society to give himself absolute control, he then responds to direct appeals from the citizens of the United States, mostly through a television-like medium.

346. Tybout, Ella Middleton. *The Wife of the Secretary of State*. Philadelphia: J. B. Lippincott, 1905. 359pp.

Political intrigue and private secrets swirl around a large cast of characters at the height of the social season in Washington. At the very center is Estelle Redmond the young and beautiful wife of the secretary of state and a Russian, Count Vladmir [*sic*]. The count, working to obtain secret U.S. documents for his country, has Estelle under his control because he knew her when she was living in Berlin with her father, a notorious spy willing to sell his services to the highest bidder. When documents that could start a world war are stolen from the secretary of state's office, suspicion is cast in a number of directions, and the race is on to find the papers that have gone missing in a bizarre fashion. Other characters include senators (one of whom is rich and laughably uncouth), a beautiful senator's daughter being forced to marry to advance her father's career despite her love for another man, several rival congressmen (one of whom will do anything for advancement), the secretary of state's private secretary, Estelle's father (Colonel Albert St. John), and the residents of a Washington boarding house. In addition to official residences and public buildings, the Octagon House and Roslyn are important settings.

347. Tyson, J. Aubrey. *The Scarlet Tanager*. New York: Macmillan, 1922. 340pp.

The novel is set eight years in the future (1930) when a modern-day buccaneer, Seafalcon, is terrorizing ocean shipping with submarines. He has also formed a secret society, the Brotherhood of the Scales, which has hundreds of thousands of members in the United States. When Oliver Channing, an inventor who created a system for tracking boats and submarines, is murdered, the U.S. government fears that Seafalcon is responsible and that the invention will make him invincible. George Rennison, a military intelligence officer, is assigned to investigate. In his early thirties, Rennison is the son of a brigadier general who had married a Washington society belle. Both of his parents are dead, and he inherited a small fortune before attending West Point and fighting in World War I. He is known for solving mysteries but never brings people to court. Instead, the guilty parties are always found dead, seemingly at their own hands. Rennison's investigation of Channing's murder quickly leads him to the culprit, Miriam Warburton, the twenty-five-year-old daughter of Lord Rothinghithe, who lost his fortune, forcing Warburton to earn her living on the stage, where she is known as the Scarlet Tanager, after one of her best-known roles. However, Warburton is surprised to learn that Rennison was working as a U.S. secret agent, carrying out the plans of a high-level Navy officer who claimed Channing was a spy in league with Seafalcon. In fact, Channing was not a Seafalcon ally, but those who planned his death were. By the end of the novel, the government officials collaborating with Seafalcon have died by their own hands, as has Seafalcon himself, not, however, before he reveals his secret to Rennison. He had been attempting the rehabilitation of the American republic, protecting its Anglo-Saxon culture from internal defeat by immigrants of other races and ethnicities. Pretending to be a traitor, Seafalcon surfaced real traitors and documented their activities, keeping the evidence in a vault in New York City to which he gives Rennison the combination. The novel is more concerned with intrigue than setting, but seedy Washington hotels and a teashop where men and women have assignations are described, and the neighborhoods of Columbia Heights, Lafayette Square, and Georgetown are mentioned.

348. Vanderbilt, Cornelius Jr. *A Woman of Washington.* New York: E. P. Dutton, 1937. 282pp.

Senator William W. Harrow of Oklahoma has proposed a bill to nationalize the public utilities industry. His son, Jim Harrow, is about to propose to Constance Bacon, a personal secretary to Joan Glenarm, a socialite. Without the knowledge of anyone, Joan Glenarm is the secret lover of Stanley B. Rutherford, a fabulously wealthy capitalist who finances her Massachusetts Avenue lifestyle. Through her, he is trying to influence Senator Harrow by feeding Harrow the information that stock investors are buying short on utility shares so that they will make a fortune if his bill passes. As a result, he takes the action Harrow, a utility company owner, wants and begins opposing his own bill by carrying out a filibuster. Even though his cousin becomes so distraught by Harrow's behavior that he tries to assassinate him, Harrow holds to his course day after day. However, Constance discovers the Rutherford-Glenarm plot and gets a note to Harrow. Realizing that he has been made a pawn of Rutherford, he ends his filibuster. Although most of this novel is focused on political machinations, there are several passages that sum up the essence of Washington as a place where personal integrity can influence the entire country.

349. Vidal, Gore. *1876.* New York: Random House, 1976. 364pp.

Charles Schemerhorn Schuyler, a respectable writer and social figure, bears the secret knowledge that he is the illegitimate son of Aaron Burr. He returns to the United States after an absence of thirty-nine years with his daughter Emma, who is the widow of Prince d'Agrigente. Schuyler left America when he was appointed vice-consul at Antwerp by President Van Buren in 1837 and returns in the country's centennial year to re-enter society for the benefit of his daughter. A writer and journalist, he uses his impressive social connections (that include everyone from the Astors to Washington's most powerful politicians) to gather information for pieces commissioned by the most important publications of his day. His election year reportage has great political import and includes coverage of investigations of James G. Blaine for financial impropriety. Although significant portions of the novel are set in New York City, Philadelphia, and Newport, Rhode Island, Vidal conveys important aspects of Washington during final days of the Grant administration when political corruption was on everyone's mind. One of the most extended sections with a Washington setting focuses on the Electoral College fight between the supporters of Governor Tilden and Rutherford B. Hayes. Although Schuyler and his daughter are fictional characters, in a note to the reader Vidal touts the historical accuracy of his work.

350. Vidal, Gore. *Burr.* New York: Random House, 1973. 430pp.

In this first-person narrative, young Charles Schemerhorn Schuyler (a fictional character who assures inquirers that he is not related to either prominent New York family whose names he bears) works in the law office of Aaron Burr and writes about his friendship with Burr beginning with Burr's marriage, at the age of seventy-seven, to Madam Jumel. Schuyler freelances as a journalist, and his editor encourages him to investigate if Burr is, as has been claimed, really the father of Martin Van Buren, who is running for President. Schuyler's indirect questions about the past lead Burr to recruit his help with his memoirs, which become a significant percentage of the novel. Although a small portion of the whole work, several chapters of the novel are set in Washington, including a section that depicts the city site before construction, when investors, including Washington and Burr, rode around the heavily wooded land deciding which tracts to purchase.

351. Vidal, Gore. *Washington D.C.* New York: Random House, 1976. 377pp.

The novel covers the years from July 22, 1937, through the early 1950s and touches on all of the major historical events of the period from the perspective of powerful, or striving, Washingtonians. Blaise Sanford has enormous inherited wealth that makes senators hang on his most trivial observations. One of his acquaintances, Senator Day, is strategizing years and years in advance of a presidential bid and courts

Sanford. In the meantime, Sanford's secretary, the classically hand-some Clay Overbury, is courting Day's daughter, while secretly having sex with Sanford's daughter. Overbury was born into humble circum-stances and does everything he can to aid the senator because of his own dependence on the politician for his social and political status. He also takes every opportunity to independently advance his own career. All of the novel's characters have similar attitudes. Marriages, friend-ships, and social alliances are all manipulated for political power. When World War II breaks out, Clay immediately enlists in the hope of coming back a war hero. He does just that, but only through a nation-ally covered news story fabricated by a homosexual reporter of his ac-quaintance who is smitten by him. With the financial backing of Sanford, who finds in Clay an opportunity for the active, public life in which he never engaged, Clay is elected congressman and, later, sena-tor, even after Sanford's son, who has become an editor of a left-lean-ing magazine, exposes the truth about his "heroism." Throughout the novel, Vidal's subject is not only the political world, but also the social world to which it is so intimately connected in Washington, as he dem-onstrates how newcomers establish themselves over time.

352. Vingut, Mrs. Gertrude (Fairfield). *Irene: or, the Autobiography of an Artist's Daughter and Other Tales*. Boston: Damrell & Moore, 1853. 383pp.
   In this book of novellas, only one, "The Vice President's Daugh-ter," is set in Washington at the beginning of a presidential administra-tion. In the work, British aristocrat Lord Falmouth meets the vice president's daughter, Ariadne Kedar, and her cousin, Alexandrina Ke-dar. Initially, he is attracted to Alexandrina for her quiet inner beauty, and he becomes engaged to her. However, when Ariadne shows interest in him, her greater beauty turns his head. He asks Alexandrina to re-lease him from their engagement. Only after marrying Ariadne and taking her back to England with him does he realize his mistake as she becomes indolent and temperamental, caring only for parties and new dresses. Eventually, Ariadne abandons him for an Italian count, and he returns to America to find and marry Alexandrina.

353. Vrooman, Julia Scott. *The High Road to Honor*. New York: Minton, Balch & Company, 1924. 299 pp.
   From her youth, Mathilde Ogden has had the power to evoke the best in men. She influences Charleston Bryce, a young man with a pri-vate income, to labor as a medical researcher, instead of living the life of leisure his fortune could purchase. While studying in Paris and

achieving extraordinary advances in his research, he nurtures his love for Mathilde. However, when he travels to Cleveland, Ohio, to propose, he discovers that she is engaged to marry David Brandon, an affluent man fifteen years her senior. Brandon has devoted himself to staving off class warfare through progressive politics and attacking political corruption and the power wielded by lobbyists. Mathilde has fallen in love with him because he has helped her grow through presenting stimulating ideas about how society could be. Through Mathilde's supportive love, Brandon has found new inspiration to pursue his reform agenda. Emotionally devastated by Mathilde's announcement of her engagement, Bryce secretly pledges to always be worthy of her high opinion of him and returns to his research laboratory. The novel traces Brandon's political struggles and the way his wife aids him by getting some politicians to act from their higher nature, rather than their own self-interest. After successful campaigns for the Ohio legislature and the governor's office, Brandon goes to Washington as a senator. In Washington, Mathilde establishes their residence as a salon where the important ideas of the day are discussed. She has influence on the course of public life, just as Brandon does from the floor of the U.S. Senate. He has focused on ending the power of the railroad lobby, and, just as he is introducing a crucial bill, Mathilde learns she is pregnant. The difficult birth of the baby (during which Bryce saves her life) and the passage of the bill provide the dramatic climax of the novel. The novel includes some loving descriptions of Washington and a good deal of observation concerning the workings of society, particularly the "social lobby" and its effect on the political process.

354. Walker, Mannix. *Everything Rustles*. Illustrated by Helen E. Hoskinson. New York: Dodd, Mead, 1945. 242pp.
    Two Boston society women, the widowed Agatha Dowell and her maiden sister Charlotte Adams, are inspired after Pearl Harbor to volunteer for the war effort. They join the air raid patrol on the streets near their Beacon Hill house wearing evening gowns and carrying antique armaments in their purses, observing everything through their lorgnettes. One night they detain Sheldon Burke of the War Department, forcing him back to their house to examine his papers, which they falsely believe are forged. From him, and people in their circle who leave for Washington, they come to the startling realization that Boston is not the center of the country and that they should go to Washington if they wish to make the greatest contribution. Through Mrs. Prendergast, whom Charlotte had known at Radcliffe, they quickly make acquaintances in Washington, and these society people are described in great

detail. The novel is also filled with humorous descriptions of wartime life in the District from the perspective of the very affluent. Much of the conversation occurs around mahjong tables and over drinks. Initially, because of the housing shortage, Charlotte and Agatha stay with Mrs. Prendergast in her 1888 house on Farragut Square. Eventually, Agatha discovers Georgetown and rents a house there (the author includes descriptions of the shops and streets and actual businesses in the neighborhood). Like the rest of Washington, the women are obsessed with spies, and Agatha pursues her connections to unsuccessfully propose herself as a counter-espionage agent at a number of government departments. The sisters suffer fits of jealousy when their friend Baby Blossom captures a spy. However, they finally get their chance and capture a whole spy ring.

355. Wallace, Irving. *The R Document.* New York: Simon & Schuster, 1976. 383pp.

In this political thriller, Attorney General Christopher Collins suffers personal attacks and attempts at extortion as he battles with the FBI Director Vernon Tynan over his proposed 35th Amendment to the U.S. Constitution, which would make it possible to suspend the Bill of Rights in cases of national emergency. The amendment was prompted by the dramatically increasing crime rate and has the support of the President. In the course of the novel, the fight proceeds until the amendment is about to be ratified or defeated by the vote of one state.

356. Walworth, Mansfield Tracy. *Lulu: A Tale of the National Hotel Poisoning.* New York: Carleton, 1863. 367pp.

During President-elect James Buchanan's stays at the National Hotel, a few weeks before his inauguration, and again immediately prior to his taking the oath of office, many hotel guests became seriously ill. Rumors abounded that an attempt had been made to poison Buchanan; however, an official investigation concluded that the illnesses had been caused by the unsanitary condition of the hotel's drainage system. Walworth was staying at the hotel when the illnesses occurred and later wrote this fictionalized account. The book gives insights into what it was like to live in a Washington hotel, as many politicians did at the time.

357. Walz, Audrey. [Bonnamy, Francis, pseud.]. *Dead Reckoning.* New York: Duell, Sloan, & Pearce, [1943]. 248pp.

Arabella Fly lives with her mother and works in the Map Division of the Library of Congress. In the basement of the stacks one day, she comes across the body of Hugh Mattson, a young man who worked for the Census Bureau preparing maps for census takers. At first, the police believe Mattson accidentally fell down the corkscrew stairs onto the concrete floor, then a janitor discovers hair and blood on a brass fire nozzle, and a murder investigation begins. The novel recounts the investigation conducted by Peter Shane, former head of the Department of Criminology at the University of Chicago, and his assistant Francis Bonnamy, who are visiting the city for a forensics conference (the District police are preoccupied by other unsolved cases). They are asked to take the case by Orson McCullough, an old student of Shane's. As information is gathered, the reader learns about the inner workings of the Library of Congress and the lives of bank clerks and civil servants living in rooming houses and sharing apartments. The middle-class life of McCullough provides a contrast to these modest lives, as do the descriptions of the more affluent environs of some of the suspects. Specific places are mentioned, including Willard's Hotel, Hains Point, Brentano's, the Mayflower Hotel, and many government buildings.

358. Walz, Audrey. *The King Is Dead on Queen Street.* New York: Duell, Sloan, & Pearce, 1945. 198pp.

Peter Shane, former head of the Department of Criminology at the University of Chicago, and his assistant, Francis Bonnamy, are in wartime Washington to support the war effort. They find the city overcrowded, and Shane despairs of eating every meal out in a crowded restaurant or at parties where buffet-style suppers have become the rage since maids can no longer be found. The only apartment they can find is in Alexandria's Queen Street. Although it is considered second best to Georgetown by those who arrived too late to live in that fashionable area, they take an apartment in the house of a well-connected woman who introduces them around. Two of the people they meet are Joe Long and his wife. Long had made popular movie travelogues until the war broke out and is now a colonel serving at a desk job. He is killed at a party, and the rest of the novel is devoted to solving the mystery of his murder. Although mostly set in Alexandria, the novel conveys an impression of the social scene in wartime Washington.

359. Walz, Audrey. *Murder as a Fine Art.* New York: New American Library, 1949. 160pp. First published as *Portrait of the Artist as a Dead Man* in 1947 by Signet / Duell, Soan & Pearce.

When Captain McCullough of Washington's Homicide Squad is called in to investigate the death of a famous painter, he can find no evidence of wrongdoing. However, the scene of the apparent suicide by hanging has enough puzzles to rouse his suspicions. Not wanting to add an investigation to his squad's workload when a good deal of work might only prove that no crime had been committed, and also fearing that if murder was committed, a famous and powerful general may be the culprit, he calls in his old criminology professor, Peter Shane, to work off the record. Shane, who had worked in Army Intelligence during the war, is still in Washington since the military has proved reluctant to give up his expertise and let him return to the University of Chicago. In the suicide case, he and his assistant Francis Bonnamy piece together an elaborate plot that involves art theft, as well as homicide. The dead painter, José Jimenez y O'Donnell, was a portraitist for whom every woman of prominence in Washington had sat. Loyal to the Spanish Fascists, he was aiding them in smuggling famous artworks out of Spanish museums and into the hands of American collectors so that the Spanish leaders could secretly accumulate currency. The society women had their roles to play, although mostly unwittingly. The novel includes descriptions of affluent Washington households and of five different women who might be considered social types (an unmarried society reporter, a wealthy widow, and the wives of a general, a diplomat, and a senator). People of more modest means in the novel (like McCullough and an art restorer) live in Georgetown apartments and boarding houses. Shane and Bonnamy typically travel around Washington by streetcar and only occasionally by cab. Although not, perhaps, specific to Washington during this time period, the recently concluded war is a continuing presence in the lives of many, particularly the art restorer who survived a concentration camp.

360. Ware, Richard D. *Rollo's Journey to Washington*. Boston: L. C. Page, 1919. 170pp. young adult.

Mr. Holiday and his young son Rollo travel to Washington during World War I since Mr. Holiday has not found work elsewhere and he believes the Ordinance Bureau of the War Department will hire him. On the way to Washington they spend some time in Boston and New York and discuss the origins and current conditions of the country. Throughout the work there is criticism of the Wilson administration and also of the wartime restrictions enforced to thwart spies. As an example of the unreasonableness of the latter, one of the letters Rollo sends to his mother gets heavily censored and his Aunt Sarah has been imprisoned for using a hatpin on a guard at a White House demonstration.

361. Warren, Stanley Sevier. *In Defense of His Excellency.* New York: Broadway, 1904. 118pp.

When Stephen Ridgway arrives in Tennessee as a newly elected congressman, he comes with a two-fold mission: to oppose higher education for the masses and to encourage respect for accomplished men and elected leaders. Through conversations with his Harvard Law School friend Edward Parkins Carter, a congressman from Massachusetts, and the people to whom Carter introduces him (including members of the affluent New York Du Mauriac family), Ridgway gets an opportunity to explain his ideas. He claims that people not as advanced by evolution are being filled with ambition to rise above the social status for which nature has prepared them. Through education they become unfit for the work in field and factory to which they are best suited and are made unhappy. His prime examples are African Americans and immigrants who have only recently begun to benefit from the civilization that has shaped most white men for generations. Educated above their stations, these people are apt to become socialists and anarchists and hate society's leaders. Newspapers that publish every scandalous rumor fuel their dissatisfactions. This situation led to the assassination of Lincoln, Garfield, and McKinley, the "martyred three" to whom the book is dedicated. Ridgway gets his chance to voice his ideas on the House floor during a debate on providing institutions of higher education for American Indians. He speaks at length about why he is opposed, and the newspapers are filled with denunciations of his speech. However, the men in power consider him a visionary, and, by the end of the novel, the President has appointed him ambassador to England and his marriage proposal to Miss Du Mauriac has been accepted.

362. Wartofsky, Victor. *Meeting the Pie Man.* New York: John Day, 1971. 314pp.

When carpenter Simon Farber can no longer find work in his trade, he is talked into buying a small grocery store in a predominantly African American Washington neighborhood. This novel traces the struggles of Farber and his family as the various members are subjected to assault, robbery, rape, arson, murder, and a riot.

363. Wartofsky, Victor. *Year of the Yahoo.* New York: John Day, [1972]. 223pp.

War in Panama and accompanying internal unrest has fostered intense debate in Washington over the proper level of national defense to be focused on foreign versus internal threats to national security. Characters with a range of perspectives on the issue, from a number of different social classes, are used to tell the story. Attorney General Clayton Osborn and his friend Congressman Hessie believe the President (who happens to be an African American) is too lax on defense and should do more to prevent internal conflicts like protest rallies. The congressman's sister, Irma, is devoted to socializing and tries to bring peace among powerbrokers with opposing viewpoints. Henry Plimsoll, a journalist nearing the end of his career, opposes the President. Donald Ansberry is a college professor whose accidental arrest at a demonstration radicalizes him. Steve Golinka is a veteran and District patrolman who wins promotion after promotion as he employs the increasingly aggressive law enforcement tactics the government sanctions to prevent civil unrest. The plotting of Osborn and Hessie eventually leads to the curtailment of civil liberties, and the Washington metropolitan area is filled with detention camps where Golinka and his forces are given free reign to torture prisoners. Although Osborn's covert power seems absolute, he plots for even greater control. In his final successful plot, he gets the President committed to an insane asylum so that his own man, the vice president, can ascend to the Oval Office. The characters who are honorable have no options in this novel, other than to flee the United States for Canada, leaving behind a country that is erecting huge walls and barriers to keep its citizens from escaping.

364. Watterson, George. *The L... Family at Washington; or, A Winter in the Metropolis.* Washington, D.C.: Davis & Force, 1822. 159pp.
    The L family of Hartford, Connecticut, journeys to Washington for the social season that coincides with the sitting of Congress. Mr. L has letters of introduction to President Monroe and an unrealistic hope of being made ambassador to the Court of St. James. He and Mrs. L also believe their visit will benefit their children, giving their son Richard the chance for a government office, and Barbara and Letitia the opportunity to marry men of consequence. The experiences of the L family (including the trip to Washington and stays in New York City and Philadelphia) are related through letters each of the children writes to acquaintances. The Ls' season in Washington includes visits to many of the sites still popular with tourists today. However, they are able to mingle directly with legislators and other office holders who are described under their real names or satirized under false ones. When they go to the Capitol, every room is open to them, and Richard spends an afternoon at the Library of Congress, attempting conversation with legislators and casual visitors. When the family goes to see the Supreme Court, they walk about and look at the judges in their alcoves working

on cases. They also attend "drawing rooms" at both the White House and the residence of Vice President John Adams, learning that these events are meant to be "conversation parties." They are also invited to a "birth night ball," hosted by the President and held to honor the anniversary of George Washington's birthday. Although they are not surprised that they can go everywhere, they are surprised that others are not excluded. Richard, in particular, is shocked at the people he meets in government buildings. He comments on the African Americans in the House Gallery and is aghast when he realizes that some beautifully dressed ladies there are actually "filles de joie." When he comments on this to an acquaintance he is told that in a free country free access to everyone is appropriate. Despite their ability to meet everyone in the city, the family does not have much social success, nor does Mr. L receive his ambassadorship. However, the children all become engaged. Richard marries an adventuress, whom he abandons to plan a trip to South America where he expects to be better appreciated. Letitia elopes with her beau and is abandoned by him before they marry when he discovers she is not wealthy. Only level-headed Barbara weds successfully by choosing a Westerner and moving to Kentucky.

365. Weaver, John D. *Another Such Victory.* New York: Viking Press, 1948. 250pp.
This historical novel tells the story of the Bonus Marchers, using fictional characters and dramatizing life in the marchers' Washington tent city. Weaver relates personal stories of the marchers to explain why they came to Washington, illustrates the relationships between husbands and wives in the tent city, and describes the ways in which the marchers tried to maintain their sense of personal dignity. Through conversations among the protestors, Weaver is able to capture some of the rhetoric, political views, and resentments of the marchers. The novel also captures the antipathy of Washingtonians toward the marchers, reportage on the March, and the visits by the curious to see the tent city. The novel ends with the clearing of the tent city by the military under the command of General MacArthur.

366. Weidman, Jerome. *The Captain's Tiger.* New York: Reynal & Hitchcock, 1947. 230pp.
A number of the short stories in this book are set in Washington. "The Third Alphabet" is about women working as "typewriters" during World War II. "Everybody and His Brother" also depicts office life in wartime Washington, but from the perspective of an agency office manager who chafes at his trivial achievements and awards compared

to the significance of those of actual soldiers. In "The Neat Mexicans," a senior economist and planner, who has stayed in Washington after his wartime service, reflects on his frustrations and decides to leave his government position for a college professorship. The protagonist of "A Lodging for the Night," Lieutenant Driscoll, visits wartime Washington to stay with the sister of one of his troop mates. He is repulsed by the loose morals she and her Glover Park housemates practice. When he realizes he is being forced into a liaison, he flees. In "The Pleasure of the President," the frustrations of bureaucratic politics in Washington are detailed.

367. Wheeler, Mrs. William Lamont. *A Washington Symphony*. New York: G. P. Putnam's Sons, 1893. 194pp.

From her H Street, NW, house, the beautiful, talented widow Mrs. Leigh-Scott helps a number of people find love and assists a new, rural congressman make his way socially. Focusing on intellect and artistic vision, she socializes without regard for the money or social position of her acquaintances. Her tastes and interests reveal controversial topics of the day, in particular the wearing of cosmetics by women, how guests are to be properly received, and the inappropriateness of May-December romances. The novel includes descriptions of typical Washington activities, including receptions, musical evenings, a flower lunch, balls, and egg rolling on the White House lawn. The titles of popular music, musical lyrics, poems, and descriptions of interiors, attire, and menus will be valuable to the social historian.

368. Wheelwright, John Tyler. *A Child of the Century*. New York: Charles Scribner's Sons, 1887. 346pp.

Thomas Sewall, a Boston lawyer who has lived within five miles of the Massachusetts State House dome most of his life, finally accedes to the urgings of a friend who has been living the artistic life in Paris for years, and he boards the "Cumbria" for France. By a strange coincidence his sister-in-law is aboard seeing off Miss O'Hara from Cincinnati, a young lady to whom she had been trying to introduce Sewall. After only a very brief acquaintance, Sewall realizes his attraction to Miss O'Hara, whose father's fortune was made running a "one-price" clothing store. When they arrive in France, Sewall's friend and other young men in his circle are also smitten by the Cincinnatian, and he retires from the field, deciding to return to his familiar round of duties in Boston. O'Hara, however, believed him to be far more marriageable than the young men, whose appeal was merely superficial. When Sewall is elected to the U.S. Congress, she makes certain that she and her mother are in Washington for the social season. Both Sewall and O'Hara are great successes in the capital. As the only "Mugwump" Independent in a House evenly divided between Republicans and Democrats, he is often the swing vote. O'Hara, who is taken up by a well-connected friend from her days at Miss Porter's, also enjoys an unexpected popularity. Disdained by Cincinnati society for Irish ancestry and the mercantile origins of her family's wealth, she finds that Washington is not nearly so narrow minded and quickly leaps from social success to social success while pursuing Sewall. The entrance of O'Hara into Washington society prompts extended observations on its essence, and Sewall's political stances get rehearsed in perorations in favor of free trade and in opposition to the corruption of industrial capitalism.

369. Whitehurst, Ben, and Faith Wiley. *Death on Capitol Hill.* New York: Vantage Press, 1970. 161pp.

Although the authors acknowledge in their foreword that the Senate has many honorable members, their focus is on those who use their office for personal gain. At the center of the plot is George Macer, who is found shot. Macer is an administrative assistant to Senator Barton of Delaware, and the senator, insisting the shooting was attempted suicide, makes certain Macer is placed in a government mental hospital where he is denied visitors. Barton's new administrative assistant Ben Whitehurst is suspicious and eventually uncovers the scandals the senator is covering up. The novel includes references to the Vietnam War, Cold War rhetoric, and sexual and other scandals involving senators. Descriptions of Washington buildings, neighborhoods, and social events form a backdrop for this mystery, but most of the details concern the workings of U.S. Senate offices and the Senate itself.

370. Whitlock, Brand. *The Thirteenth District; A Story of a Candidate.* Indianapolis: Bowen-Merrill, [1902]. 490pp.

Jerome Garwood campaigns for Congress in the Thirteenth District of Illinois, while ignoring the needs of his family; he uses all of his money and mortgages his house to obtain more. His wife stands by him, even when his behavior is appalling and even when, deeply in debt, he loses his re-election campaign and they are forced out of the family house she had inherited. Although less than fifty pages, this novel is physically set in Washington; the city dominates the work as the symbol of unhealthy political ambition.

371. Whitten, Les H. *Conflict of Interest.* New York: Doubleday, 1976. 391pp.

When investigative reporter Aubrey Warder pursues a scandalous story about the speaker of the House's drunkenness and acceptance of graft, he uncovers more serious wrongdoing linked to the White House. Skirmishes with FBI agents are the least of his problems as it begins to seem clear that he will not live to tell his story. Written by a well-known investigative reporter, the book captures some of the conflict between newsmen and politicians so characteristic of the time period in which it was written.

372. Willard, Rosseter. *The Senator's Sweetheart.* Illustrated by Felix Mahoney. New York: Grafton Press, 1903. 266pp.

This anecdotal novel is set during the Theodore Roosevelt administration and has no central plot, although the dominant theme is the celebration of American women with careers and those whose career is to support their husbands through efforts at social advancement. The narrator is the niece of Mrs. Cushman, the recent widow of a widely admired senator, and the stories are mostly about Mrs. Cushman and women in her circle, particularly Mrs. Alton. One section of the novel relates the complete biography of Mrs. Cushman, née Chester, one of the daughters of a wealthy Scottish immigrant, including her youth in St. Anthony, Indiana, and courtship by the much older, divorced ex-governor, Allerton Cushman. Allerton had had a bad marriage and developed a drinking problem. The new Mrs. Cushman quickly broke him of that and advanced his career by establishing him socially. When he was elected to the U.S. Senate, she continued her efforts, becoming a famous hostess and aiding the senator, who was eventually regarded as a future presidential candidate. One of Mrs. Cushman's Washington friends, Mrs. Alton, also made a career for herself, but not as a society hostess. She had a very hard youth as the daughter of an innkeeper on the frontier in Platteville, Illinois. Through many trials, which the author describes in minute detail, she established herself as a political reporter and moved to Washington. Willard describes other working women, including government clerks, and refers to businesswomen's luncheons, a national suffragette convention, and meetings of the Daughters of the American Revolution. Other social events described include New Year's receptions (including ones at the White House and the Chinese legation), balls, dinners, and automobile outings to Cabin John Bridge and Arlington Cemetery. In addition, a wide variety of Washington scenes are lovingly described, and there are many lists and glowing descriptions of Washington figures. The introduction is by

Mrs. Anna Agnew Cushman K. Davis who says that the book's characters may be recognized by readers and that the book was written by a Washington society figure.

373. Williams, Anna Vernon (Dorsey). *The Spirit of the House.* New York: D. Appleton, 1924. 328pp.

In 1894, Lewis Lowden, whose father, Philemon, lost his ancestral Georgetown house, Guildford Place, through bad investments, marries Coralie Brett, daughter of ambitious Ohio senator "Spread-Eagle" Brett for the tens of thousands of dollars that will come to him from the union and free him from his family's poverty. Desiring social prestige, Senator Brett had previously purchased Guildford Place and hired Courtney Lowden, the sister of Lewis and a school friend of Coralie, to live with the Brett family and instruct them in "cave dweller" behavior and etiquette. He sees the marriage of Coralie to Lewis, who is his daughter by a woman other than his wife, as a good, if costly, investment.

Within a few years, Coralie, now a young matron with a house in Washington and a young son, realizes that the old status markers of Washington society have changed and people like the Lowdens are no longer consequential. She positions herself in a new social environment that admires wit and money and is focused on Europe. Her social successes make her see Washington society as limited. She yearns to join an international set, and her husband Lewis is irrelevant to this new ambition. Fortunately, his naval service takes him far from home, and she is able to do anything she wishes, including beginning an affair with the secretary of state whose wealthy wife has devoted herself to spiritualism and is above noticing things of this world, including her own health. When she dies and her husband inherits her fortune, Coralie's maneuvering finally convinces Lewis to divorce her. She marries the secretary of state and enters the highest social circles in Washington and abroad, eventually reuniting with her natural brother. Their mother had been an Austrian Jewish music hall performer, and her brother has been raised as a German. As World War I begins, Coralie sees the conflict as a way to enrich herself and, plotting with her brother, allies herself with Germany.

In contrast to Coralie's dizzying social advance, Lewis' sister, Courtney, works as a teacher, supports her parents, and lives with the Bretts, who consider her a daughter. From her perspective, the reader is able to see the changes in Washington social life and the impact of national and international events. Her idealism and intellectualism give her objectivity, even when she is in the midst of emotional scenes, but also prevent her from really connecting with very many people, particularly potential beaus. However, in her early forties, she meets an Englishman, Kenneth Tyrrell, with whom she develops an intellectual and spiritual intimacy. Unlike the Bretts, he is fascinated by the Lowdens' connection to the past since he believes that by understanding the past one can make contact with eternal verities—an idea that Courtney embraces. Before volunteering as a stretcher-bearer, Tyrell pledges to marry Courtney; however, he dies on the battlefield. In the house of her ancestors, Courtney believes she can maintain her contact with Tyrell on a spiritual plane that is more real than the world of Coralie and those like her.

374. Williams, C. R., and Clifton Waller Barrett. *Aristocracy; or, The Holbey Family; a National Tale.* Providence, R.I.: J. Knowles, 1832. 312pp.

In the year 1800 the Augustus Holbey family leaves their comfortable rural life along the Delaware River. Mr. Holbey is the son of a regimental drummer and a camp laundress in Burgoyne's army. His parents had deserted and started a public house. Holbey was sent to college and became a writer of witty satire directed against politicians, particularly men like Thomas Jefferson. Claiming social distinction for himself, he disdains Jefferson's emphasis on the common man. He writes that the French spirit of revolution will soon destroy the United States as the common man begins attacking his social betters. The success of his writing prompts him to move closer to New York City so that he and his wife can enter society.

Their family includes two daughters and a niece, Adelaide Melville. Adelaide is an orphan and has been told that her father's estate, for which Holbey served as executor, was so modest that the Holbeys took her in as a charity case. However, Holbey simply took her father's money. The Holbeys spend money extravagantly in New York and attempt all sorts of deceptions to attain social prominence. Adelaide disdains their behavior and pays attention to her spiritual life. She falls in love with Sidney, the son of a wealthy family who is also a clergyman. However, shortly after they meet, he is forced to travel abroad as a cure for his tuberculosis.

Holbey soon accepts an appointment in the office of a prominent Washington politician who wants to foster increased attacks on Jefferson, and the family moves to the Federal City. In 1807, Adelaide discovers that Holbey is involved in a plot against Jefferson concerning stolen papers. She goes directly to the White House with the papers, not realizing that letters from her Uncle Edward Melville are among the papers that prove he has been paying the Holbeys for her support and providing money for her that she has never received. The President pledges his aid for her to go to her uncle in New Orleans, which has recently become a U.S. territory. Before she goes, she witnesses federal agents forcing the Holbeys out of Washington. She is united with her uncle, eventually marries Sidney, and begins a life of affluence and social prominence in upstate New York.

375. Wilson, Mary Badger. *Borrowed Plumes*. Philadelphia: Penn, 1935. 305pp.

Widowed Amelia Byrne lives with her three daughters, Sally Anne, Julia, and Agnes, in the Southern town of Edgeriver during the Depression. Although from a family with a long and distinguished ancestry, the impoverished Amelia takes in elderly relatives to help cover household expenses. She strives to see her daughters make good marriages, and, when a great aunt gives her the money to pay off her mortgage, she uses it to buy clothes they need to attract men. The girls themselves have goals consistent with their personalities. Sally Anne wants to be a mother and marries her childhood sweetheart, a college-educated department store clerk who makes so little money that after the couple elopes they must live in Amelia's house. Julia, the prettiest and most popular, wants to parlay her assets into a marriage to someone outside Edgeriver with prospects for an important career. Agnes wants to leave Edgeriver as well but is less concerned with marriage than fulfilling her intellectual curiosity by attending college and training for a career. She figures out a way to escape Edgeriver by appealing to a local political boss to influence their congressman for a New Deal secretarial job in Washington which would let her pay her way through college.

When Julia hears Agnes' plan she acts first and is soon off to Washington after jilting her fiancé, promising Agnes that she will send for her. The novel describes Julia's experiences in Roosevelt's newly invigorated Washington, detailing the life of single women. Exercising her Southern charm and employing her beauty, Julia finds a job, despite her lack of skills, and lets the awkward Eliot Clay, a man of lower-class origins working his way through law school, escort her to social events so she can meet more eligible men.

When she meets affluent and politically ambitious Derek Kirby, she finally invites Agnes to Washington in order to rent an apartment and establish the respectable environment Derek looks for in a future wife. As she becomes absent-minded toward Eliot, he becomes increasingly distraught. Agnes, who begins college and studies psychol-

ogy, becomes the confidante of Eliot and other Washingtonians, be-
friending characters who are more likely to frequent Dupont Circle than
Capitol Hill receptions. After a tragedy reveals Julia's self-serving behavior, Agnes, to everyone's surprise, wins the most eligible man in the
novel for her husband. Most of the book's physical description of
Washington centers on apartment living; however, the social description is rich.

376. Wilson, Mary Badger. *New Dreams for Old.* New York: A. L.
Burt, 1931. 284pp.
   Celia Brooke, with all of her possessions in two straw suitcases,
leaves the Maryland village near which she grew up on her father's
farm to experience the excitement and possibilities of Washington. She
works in a lending library and lives in the uncomfortable house of a
relative, longing for the day she can move to a boarding house and
mingle with fashionable people. Eventually, a government clerk, Donald Nesbitt, comes courting, and her life becomes a whirl of drives,
cafeteria dates, and parties with other dating couples. Her interests
shift, however, when she meets Hugh Cornell, secretary to a congressman, who impresses and attracts her with his ambitions. However when
Nesbitt hears of Cornell, he becomes jealous and soon afterward he and
Celia are engaged to be married. A few years later they have an infant
daughter and are living in a depressing Washington suburb in a charm-
less house. Celia's life is filled with frustration over Nesbitt's impru-
dence and lack of ambition. Accepting her brother's offer to buy her
share of the family farm, she opens her own bank account and starts a
lending library and bookstore near Dupont Circle. Taking the advice of
Cornell, who has now been elected to Congress, she expands her business with a lecture series for women's clubs around the country. Within
two years she has the money to move her family to a fashionable
apartment, where each of them have their own bedroom and she employs a maid, cook, and governess. When Cornell tries to persuade her
to divorce and marry him, she refuses. Cornell pulls strings to get
Nesbitt a major promotion, and, for a while, home life is much happier
as he becomes filled with new ambitions. However, when Cornell presents evidence that Nesbitt has been having an affair with his stenogra-
pher while Celia is on her lecture tours, she insists on a separation.
Once Nesbitt is gone, however, Celia's belief in the sanctity of marriage is renewed, and she realizes Nesbitt truly loved her. She also believes that she has had a significant influence on Nesbitt, inspiring him
to become more ambitious and self-determining. Hearing he has resigned his job after finding out that Cornell had gotten it for him, she

tells him she wants them to reconcile and work together in the book-store. The novel contains few physical descriptions of Washington. However, it presents insights into the nature of the city as a place that attracts people with ambitions in realms other than politics or society. These working class people come to improve their lives by finding their place in an economy fueled by the presence of the federal government.

377. Wilson, Mary Badger. *The Painted City: Dry-Points of Washington Life.* New York: Frederick A. Stokes, 1927. 247pp.

In a series of short stories, Wilson portrays social conflicts in Washington and depicts the city as "bloodless," "anemic"—"a city of employees" and with the power of its beauty to inspire. In one story, Ruth Tennant, who came to Washington as a clerk during World War I and was lucky enough to receive a continuing federal appointment after the Armistice, is dismissed and forced to return to her hometown when she unwittingly dates a married man. In another story, a reporter catches influenza just as he is disillusioned by the realization that Washington is merely a "stage setting" with no real substance. Other characters in the stories include an archeologist returned from Egypt to spend a winter in the city with his wife, a female government clerk with a tedious job who sees Washington's cultural offerings as adequate recompense, and a recently pensioned female government clerk who had worked for the government for fifty years. Another government clerk is demoted in a government cutback and must deal with the complications of living on a much smaller salary. Despite the sorrows residents face, the city's beauty has inspirational power, and, in another story, women visiting Washington are so moved by the cherry blossoms that they decide to relocate there, no matter what the sacrifice. In addition to the stories of government clerks and newcomers, Wilson illustrates the tensions between old Washington families and the influx from elsewhere. In one story, a single woman living with her father is forced to rent out rooms in her house and is disgusted when her new neighbors are rich with bootleg money. In the final story, the life of Maria Welbon, a "cave dweller," is recounted. The Washington in which she lives has been taken over by new money, although she tearfully declares that the newcomers cannot usurp the aristocracy of birth.

378. Winchester, Paul. *Around the Throne: Sketches of Washington Society during a Recent Administration.* Baltimore: B. G. Eichelberger, 1902. 187pp.

Descriptions of people and events during a Washington season are detailed with little overarching plot, except for the fact that one of the characters, Mr. Warham, is a journalist writing about the city and has conversations with various people. In this Washington, nouveaux riches with government positions have taken control and wield power over society figures, military officers, and other political appointees through gossip and scandal mongering. Obviously regarded by the author with contempt, one of them gets her comeuppance at the end of the novel. This new society scorns the President for his overt religiosity and the First Lady for her ban on alcohol (presumably the characters are based on the McKinleys). When Warham has lunch in the White House, he seeks the couples' perspective on a Washington society whose conversation is mostly composed of gossip and scandal. The President confesses his longing for the republican simplicity of the Federal period. In addition to the descriptions of food, attire, and social events, social phenomena are noted like contract houses complete with furnishings being sold or rented to government officials.

379. Winslow, Barbara. *Samantha Goes to Georgetown on the C & O Canal.* Richmond, Va.: Westover, 1973. 28pp. juvenile.

During the highpoint of canal travel, Samantha rides on the packet boat "James Rumsey," sailing the C & O Canal from Cumberland, Maryland, to visit her grandmother in Georgetown. On the way she finds out about the operations of a canal boat and the history of the canal.

380. Wise, Thomas A. *A Gentleman from Mississippi.* Based on a play by Frederick R. Toombs and Harrison Rhodes. Illustrated with cast member photographs. New York: J. S. Ogilvie, 1909. 189pp.

"Big Bill" Langdon (230lbs) has been elected senator from Mississippi. He has extensive family lands in the state and a family consisting of a son, Randolph, and two daughters, Carolina and Hope Georgia. Without understanding the true nature of the situation, Langdon is beholden for his office to Senator Stevens and Congressman Charles Norton. Norton wants to marry Carolina, and both politicians want the government to make a naval base at Altacola, Mississippi. They plan to use Langdon—manipulating his naïveté and hiding behind his reputation for honesty. To guarantee his support for the naval base, they secretly convince Randolph and Carolina to invest large sums of money in Altacola land. Langdon, feeling out of depth in Washington, hires reporter Bud Haines as his personal secretary. Haines accepts the job, realizing that he will be able to manipulate the senator for good ends in opposition to the control of the "Boss of the Senate," Senator Peabody.

He will also be able to court Carolina, with whom he was immediately infatuated. With Haines' help, Langdon quickly becomes influential and his daughters are launched in society. Resenting Haines' influence, and wanting to guarantee their investment in Altacola, Carolina and Randolph force Haines out with false accusations. The youngest daughter, Hope Georgia, remains loyal to Haines, convincing Langdon of his innocence. He is eventually rehired and falls in love with her. When Langdon hears about the land deals made in advance of the vote on Altacola, he pledges his opposition to the base. The Altacola faction employs threats, bribes, and a beautiful female lobbyist, but with Haines' aid Langdon defeats his enemies.

381. Woods, Kate Tannatt. *Six Little Rebels*. Boston: D. Lothrop, 1879. 412pp.

   Near the beginning of the Civil War, Dr. Warrington, a widowed, invalid physician, living with his schoolgirl daughter, Dolly, on the heights of Georgetown, receives a letter from a friend and distant cousin, Colonel Gresham of Richmond. Gresham's brother-in-law, Judge Neville, is very ill, and the doctors have advised a trip to Europe which he plans to undertake with his sister, Mrs. Alice Neville, and the judge. Concerned about leaving his sons and nephews in Richmond or sending them to a boarding school, he asks Warrington to take them in. Before the five boys and a very young slave named Lexis descend on the household, reinforcement in the form of an elderly relative, Lucinda Dodge, is successfully recruited. Once the boys arrive, the narrative is dominated by amusing and calculatedly touching stories about the Gresham boys, whose mother died some years ago, and the Neville sons, whose father eventually dies and whose mother goes mad with grief. The tricks Lexis plays on Aunt Axy, the African American maid of all work, and the appearance and behavior of the overweight, Yankee spinster, Lucinda Dodge, and her cat, "General Scott," provide comic relief. The work gives some indication of life in Georgetown during the war. Hostilities develop among residents with conflicting allegiances and animosity toward the "six little rebels" taken in by Warrington, becomes increasingly harsh among the boys' schoolmates. Eventually one of them is seriously injured by a thrown rock. Dolly becomes directly involved in the war effort when she volunteers at Union Hospital. She befriends Union officers and hospital staff members and gets taken to a White House reception.

382. Worthen, J. Henry. *Old Sile Ridleigh; or, the Serio-Comic Adventures of a Down-East Yankee in Washington.* Fruitport, Mich.: John Chapman, c. 1894. 80pp.
No additional information available.

383. Yulee, C. Wickliffe. *The Awakening: A Washington Novel.* Photographic illustrations. Washington, D.C.: Neale, 1905. 379pp.
Montresor, an English nobleman of simple habits and philosophical detachment, travels by ship with other people from England bound for the social season in Washington. He has been sent by his brother to determine if Americans are likely to provide financial support for the aggressive wing of the Irish republican movement. Montresor's own goal for his first trip to Washington is to discover the nature of society in the United States. On ship, he develops a new ambition, when he falls in love with Mrs. Rae, a twenty-five-year-old widow and sister to a congressman. Montresor's exploration of Washington society brings him into contact with legislators, successful businessmen, scientists, writers, and retired military officers. He also meets a priest who wants to found a national Catholic university, members of a land syndicate that is accumulating large tracts for suburban development through shady legislative maneuvers, and a number of people advocating the construction of a bridge over Rock Creek. Through puzzling out the motivations of the people he meets, and assessing his own relationship to several beautiful women, Montresor is "awakened" and returns to England an engaged man of action, rather than the detached, philosophical observer he had been. In addition to the work's verbal descriptions of Washington society, the novel is illustrated with five photographs: downtown Washington near the Post Office, the Washington Monument, the St. Gaudens monument from Rock Creek Cemetery, Cabin John Bridge, and Lafayette Square.

Biographies

Aarons, Edward S[idney] [Ronns, Edward, pseud.] (1916-1975)
   Born in Philadelphia, Aarons was a graduate of Columbia University and served in the Navy during World War II. He sold his first short story when he was eighteen and his first novel when he was nineteen. He wrote two hundred magazine stories and novellas before turning his focus to novel-length work. By the end of his career he had written eighty books. Of these, forty were published by Fawcett Books as part of his *Assignment* series in which fictional Central Intelligence Agency officer Sam Durrell is on assignment, often to some remote or exotic place. Books in the *Assignment* series sold over twenty-three million copies and were known for accurate and intriguing information, often historical, about their settings.
   (*New York Times,* 20 June 1975, 38). *See* entry 1.

Adams, Charles [Templeton, Timothy, pseud.]
   See entry 2.

Adams, Henry (Brooks) (February 16, 1838-March 27, 1918)
   A great-grandson of John Adams, and grandson of John Quincy Adams, Henry Adams was educated at Harvard University and the University of Berlin and is noted for histories, memoirs, and travel writing. He wedded Marian Hooper in 1872 and the couple moved to Washington in 1877. They lived just off Lafayette Square in a house designed for them by Henry Hobson Richardson. Marian committed suicide in the house in 1885. The memorial Adams commissioned from Henry St. Gaudens for her Rock Creek Cemetery grave became an attraction for visitors to Washington and is mentioned in several of the novels included here.
   (*Dictionary of Literary Biography,* vol. 12, s.v. "Adams, Henry [Brooks]"). *See* entry 3.

Adams, Samuel Hopkins (January 26, 1871-November 15, 1958)

Author of more than forty books, including those he wrote under the *nom de plume* Warner Fabian, Hopkins was known for the muckraking journalism of his early career as a newspaper reporter and, in later life, as the author of film scripts and historical novels. Born in Dunkirk, New York, on the Erie Canal, Adams was the son of a Presbyterian minister and a graduate of Hamilton College. His articles for such publications as *Collier's Weekly* on patent medicines were a significant impetus for the enactment of the Federal Pure Food and Drug Laws. In recognition of his contributions, he was made an associate member of the American Medical Association in 1913.

(*New York Times,* 17 November 1958, 31). *See* entries 4, 5, 6.

Adler, Warren (c.1929-?)

Born in Brooklyn and a graduate of New York University, Adler served in the Armed Forces Press Service as Pentagon Washington correspondent during the Korean War. He stayed in Washington, creating a publishing firm and, at one time or another, owned four radio stations, a television station, and an advertising and public relations agency. He did not publish his first novel until he was forty-three. When the book was successful, he began devoting himself to writing. He has written a series of homicide detective novels with a U.S. senator's daughter as the protagonist. The novels are based on the knowledge and life experiences of Judy Roberts, a detective with the D.C. Police Department.

(*New York Times,*1 April 1991, C11). *See* entries 7, 8.

Alexander, Holmes (Moss) (January 29, 1906-December 5, 1985)

Alexander was the descendant of Scottish immigrants who arrived in America in the 1630s and founded Alexandria, Virginia. He was born in Parkersburg, West Virginia, and graduated from Princeton University in 1928 and Trinity College, Cambridge (U.K.), in 1929. He served as a Democratic member in the House of Delegates of the Maryland General Assembly from 1931 to 1935. From 1935 to 1941, he wrote biographies of Martin Van Buren and Aaron Burr. While continuing to write biographies and novels, he afterward began his long career as a magazine contributor and reporter and political columnist with McNaught Syndicate. An author of twenty books, he was a one-time governor of the National Press Club. He was also a member of other clubs headquartered in Washington, such as the Society of the

Cincinnati, 1925 F Street Club, and the Metropolitan Club. (*Contemporary Authors Online*, New York: Gale Group, 2003, accessed, 9 June 2005). *See* entry 9.

Altsheler, Joseph A. (April 29, 1862-June 5, 1919)
    Born in Three Springs, Kentucky, the author attended Liberty College (Glasgow, Ky.) and Vanderbilt University (Nashville, Tenn.). He became a features writer for the *World* (New York City) in 1892, covering the Chicago World's Fair and Hawaii's attempt to reestablish a monarchy. He began writing stories for children after becoming the editor of the *World*'s magazine section since he could not find enough stories appropriate for publication. His books, mostly for a juvenile audience, primarily focus on American history and, particularly, the West. They were praised for the quality of their writing and contrasted favorably with earlier works for children.
    (W. J. Burke and Will D. Howe. *American Authors and Their Books: 1640 to the Present Day*, New York: Crown, 1962, s.v. "Altsheler, Joseph A."). *See* entry 10.

Anderson, Patrick (July 11, 1936-?)
    Anderson came to public attention with a non-fiction work, *The President's Men* (Doubleday, 1968). An outgrowth of working in the White House during the Kennedy and Johnson administrations, the book presents a study of presidential aides since the Franklin Delano Roosevelt administration. He has written other non-fiction and more than seven novels.
    (*Contemporary Authors Online*, New York: Gale Group, 2003, accessed, 9 June 2005). *See* entries 11, 12, 13.

Andrews, Mary Raymond Shipman (April 12, 1860-August 2, 1936)
    Born in Mobile, Alabama, Andrews was the daughter of an Episcopal priest. She grew up in Lexington, Kentucky, and married lawyer William S. Andrews in 1884. Her husband soon entered the judiciary, eventually becoming a judge on the New York State Supreme Court and, later, a judge of the New York State Court of Appeals. In the early 1900s, Andrews wrote numerous works of fiction serialized in magazines. Her most successful creation, *The Perfect Tribute* (Scribner's, 1906), sold over six hundred thousand copies. She lived the last years of her life in Syracuse, New York, with her son Paul Shipman Andrews, dean of the College of Law at Syracuse University.
    (*New York Times*, 3 August 1936, 15). *See* entry 14.

Anonymous
     See entries 15, 16.

Argenteuil, Paul d'
     See entry 17.

Arnold, Elliott (September 13, 1912-May 13, 1980)
     Arnold began his career as a reporter for the *Brooklyn (N.Y.) Daily
Times* at the age of 15 in 1927. He went on to graduate from New York
University in 1934, the same year he published his first novel, *Two
Loves* (Greenberg, 1934). After his college graduation, he wrote feature
articles for *The New York World-Telegram* before joining the Army Air
Corps in 1942. His Army service included tours of duty in the Pacific
and Mediterranean, and he was eventually promoted to captain and
earned the Bronze Star. His 1947 historical fiction, *Blood Brother* (Duell, Sloan, & Pearce, 1947), dramatized the lives of Cochise and Indian
agent Thomas J. Jeffords. A best seller, the work was adapted into a
movie and, later, into a television series for which Arnold wrote epi-
sodes. His book, *A Night of Watching* (New York: Scribner, 1967),
about the Danish underground's successful protection of Jews during
World War II was also a best seller and a Literary Guild Selection. In
the course of his career, Arnold wrote a total of twenty-five fiction and
non-fiction books.
(New York Times, 14 May 1980, B6). *See* entry 18.

Atherton, Gertrude (October 30, 1857-June 14, 1948)
     Born in San Francisco, the novelist, journalist, and social historian
Atherton spent her first thirty years following the traditional role of a
woman of her time. She married George Atherton (who belonged to
one of San Francisco's most prominent families), gave birth to two
children, and participated in society. Having anonymously published
one serialized story in 1883 and suffered ostracism by her family and
San Francisco society as a result, after her husband's death in 1887 she
moved to New York to fulfill her literary ambitions. During the next
sixty years, she supported herself by publishing thirty-four novels and
many short stories and articles. Much of her writing deals with the
American West. Although her work received few favorable comments
from American critics, British writers considered her an important in-
terpreter of American themes for a British audience. Atherton lived
primarily in New York, Paris, London, and San Francisco. She also
lived in Washington for a time to research her book *Senator North* (J.

Lane, 1900) and modeled its protagonist on Senator Hale of Maine. (*Dictionary of Literary Biography*, vol. 186, s.v. "Atherton, Gertrude"). *See* entry 19.

Ayers, Daisy
      See entry 20.

Babcock, Bernie (née Smade) (1868-June 14, 1962)
      Although she was born in Unionville, Ohio, her family moved to Little Rock, Arkansas, when she was a girl. She lived there for the rest of her life, marrying William F. Babcock and raising three children. A staff writer for *The Arkansas Democrat,* she later owned and edited *The Arkansas Sketch Book.* She was greatly interested in history and wrote historical novels, several about Lincoln. In addition to writing about history, she founded the Arkansas Museum of Natural History and Antiquities.
      (*New York Times,* 15 June 1962, 27). *See* entries 21, 22.

Badeau, General Adam (December 29, 1831-March 19, 1895)
      Born and educated in New York City, Badeau worked as a drama critic before the Civil War. He enlisted when the war began, and served as an aide on the staff of Brigadier General Thomas W. Sherman through the Louisiana campaign, during which he was severely wounded. In March 1864, he was appointed military secretary on the staff of General Grant. He remained on Grant's staff throughout the war and until 1869, when he resigned with the rank of brevet brigadier general. A friendship he had developed with Grant continued, and during Grant's presidency he was appointed to diplomatic posts, culminating as consul general to London, a position he held until 1881, taking a leave of absence in 1877-1878 to accompany General Grant on his trip around the world. He ended his diplomatic career as consul general to Cuba, resigning over a disagreement with the State Department. He wrote extensively about Grant and assisted with his autobiography.
      (*New York Times*, 21 March 1895, 9). *See* entry 23.

Bailey, Temple (c.1870-July 6, 1953)
      Known for her romance novels about young love that always ended happily, Bailey lived much of her life in and around Washington, D.C. Born in Petersburg, Virginia, she attended school in Washington and Richmond. From the time she published her first book in 1907 she wrote a profusion of books, short stories, and magazine serials. By the

early 1950s, it was estimated that more than three million copies of her books were in print. She was also reputed to be one of the world's highest-paid writers. During the Depression she was signing contracts for serial rights that were sometimes as high as $325,000. Given the subject matter of her work, it is perhaps ironic that Bailey never married. She was, however, devoted to club life in Washington, particularly as a member of the Arts Club of Washington, the Authors' Club of Boston, the Chevy Chase Club, and the Pen and Brush Club.
(*New York Times*, 8 July 1953, 27). *See* entries 24, 25.

Baldwin, Faith (October 1, 1893-March 18, 1978)
    The author of more than eighty books, Baldwin fed the fantasies of her working-class audience of living the affluent life described in her novels. The daughter of Stephen Baldwin, a well-known New York trial lawyer, she attended private schools, including a finishing school in Briarcliff Manor, and lived in Dresden for several years after graduating. She lived a life of material ease from the time she was born. In 1920, she married Hugh H. Cuthrell, at the time a Navy pilot, who would become the president and chairman of the board of the Brooklyn Union Gas Company. The popularity of her novels was greatest during the Depression, when she earned more than $315,000 in 1936. Four of her books were made into movies, starring the likes of Clark Gable, Henry Fonda, and Jean Harlow.
(*New York Times*, 19 March 1978, 38). *See* entry 26.

Banks, (Laura) Stockton V[oorhees] (1908-June 18, 1980)
    Born in Washington, D.C., Banks was a historical researcher who wrote novels for children, as well as serving at one time as a research assistant to historian Allen Nevins and as editor of the *Review of the American Historical Association*.
(*Contemporary Authors Online*, New York: Gale Group, 2004, accessed, 25 October 2005). *See* entry 27.

Barry, John D[aniel] (1866-November 3, 1942)
    A native Bostonian and Harvard graduate (1888), Barry was the drama critic at *Harper's Weekly* and later at *Collier's Magazine*. His career also included an instructorship at the Academy of Dramatic Arts and lectureships for the New York Board of Education for which he spoke on social and literary questions. In 1910, he became a staff member of the *San Francisco Bulletin* and later worked for *The San Francisco News* as a columnist on such topics as moral character, literature, and art. He was appointed a member of the Ford Peace Party

during World War I and was assigned duties in Germany and Switzerland. In the last year of his life he became the first recipient of the Isidore M. Golden Honor Medal, as the San Franciscan who had been most prominent in the previous year in advancing "the principles of true Americanism and the elimination of prejudice, and tolerance among all the people."
(*New York Times*, 4 November 1942, 23). *See* entry 28.

Bartlett, Nancy, [pseud.], *see* Strong, Charles S[tanley]

Barton, George (1866-1940)
A native of Philadelphia, Barton began working as a reporter when he was seventeen and joined the staff of *The Philadelphia Inquirer* the following year in 1887, the newspaper with which he was to remain for the rest of his career. For over twenty yeas he covered politics and reported on the national political conventions and Presidential inaugurations. He published hundreds of short stories, many mysteries, and more than twenty books.
(*New York Times*, 17 March 1940, 49). *See* entries 29, 30, 31, 32.

Barton, Wilfred M
See entry 33.

Bayer, Oliver Weld [pseud.], *see* Perry, Eleanor

Bayne, Jessica
See entry 34.

Bell, Margaret (1894-?)
See entry 35.

Benjamin, Lewis
See entry 36.

Benson, Mildred Augustine Wirt [Emerson, Alice B., pseud.] (July 10, 1905-May 28, 2002)
Benson grew up on a farm near Ladora, Iowa, and sold her first story when she was fourteen to *St. Nicholas* magazine. She studied journalism at the University of Iowa, becoming the program's first woman graduate in 1927. When she married Asa A. Wirt in 1928, she moved with him first to Cleveland and then Toledo, Ohio. While still in graduate school she began writing for the Edward Stratemeyer Syndi-

cate, initially as a ghostwriter for the Ruth Fielding series. She went on to write twenty-three of the first thirty of the Nancy Drew books published by the syndicate under the author name of Carolyn Keene. She also wrote under four other pseudonyms for the Syndicate. Beginning in 1944, she was a columnist for the *Toledo (Ohio) Blade*. By the end of her writing career she had produced more than one hundred novels in addition to her many news articles and columns, and was officially recognized as the original author for the Nancy Drew books.
(*Major Authors and Illustrators for Children and Young Adults*, 2nd ed., s.v. "Benson, Mildred Augustine Wirt"). *See* entries 37, 38.

Benton, John (1891-?)
    See entry 39.

Bergengren, Anna Farquhar (December 23, 1865-?)
    Although the Farquhars had long connections to Maryland, originally receiving land grants from Lord Baltimore, Bergengren's family lived in Cincinnati, Ohio, and Indianapolis, Indiana, while she was growing up, where her father became a bank president. A lawyer, he was also a state politician and served in the U.S. Congress from 1865 to 1867. As a young woman she studied voice in Boston, but when the harsh climate brought on illnesses and vocal chord damage, she moved to Baltimore and then Washington. However, her voice was ruined, and she began writing as an alternative outlet for her artistic interests. Her first real success was *Her Washington Experiences* (L. C. Page, 1902). Her husband, Ralph Wilhelm Bergengren, was a Boston journalist and essayist.
(Edward Francis Harkins, *Famous Authors [Women]*, Boston: L. C. Page, 1901, s.v. "Farquhar, Anna [Mrs. Berengren]"). *See* entry 40.

Black, Alexander (February 7, 1859-1940)
    Black, a native of Brooklyn, began working for *The Brooklyn Daily Times* as soon as he was of age. A member of the Authors' Club, as a young man, he befriended writers, such as Mark Twain, Frank Stockton, Watson Gilder, and James Russell Lowell at the beginnings of their careers. However, he is best known for making important contributions to the origins of cinema through creating slide shows, and utilizing filmic dissolves between images to create a sense of motion. His first "photoplay," *Miss Jerry,* was produced in 1894. *The New York World* later employed him as a photographic editor, and he was an editor for many years with Randolph Hearst's Newspaper Feature Service.
(*New York Times*, 7 February 1937, 99). *See* entry 41.

Blair, Anne Denton (February 4, 1914-May 20, 1993)

Born in Oakmont, Pennsylvania, Blair attended Bryn Mawr College from 1931 to 1932 before marrying and having children. She worked as a radio commentator on WQQW-Radio (now WGMS-Radio) in Washington, D.C., from 1948 to 1958. She then became director of radio and television for the National Red Cross in Washington, 1959-1962; bureau chief for the Triangle Stations in Washington from 1962-1973; and bureau chief with TelePrompter Cable-TV in Washington 1973-1975. Starting in 1975 she worked in public relations for the Environmental Protection Agency for one year and as Washington correspondent for *Programmer* magazine for many years.
(*Contemporary Authors Online*, New York: Gale Group, 2003, accessed, 23 February 2005). *See* entry 42.

Blair, Clay (1925-1998)

A native of Lexington, Virginia, Blair was educated at Tulane University and Columbia before working as a reporter trainee at *Time* magazine starting in 1949. He spent a significant portion of his life in Washington, first as a correspondent for *Time* and *Life* from 1950 to 1957 and later as the Washington correspondent for *The Saturday Evening Post*. Curtis Publishing Company owned the *Post*, and Blair eventually became editor in chief of the Curtis family of magazines. His campaign against the mismanagement of Curtis' president, chairman, and chief executive, Matthew J. Culligan, was joined by fifteen Curtis editors and employees but ultimately led to the departure of Blair, as well as Culligan. Starting in the 1950s he wrote books about U.S. submarines and their commanders. Other books with military subjects included accounts of the Korean conflict, World War II paratroopers, the development of the hydrogen bomb, and a biography of General Omar Bradley.
(*New York Times*, 20 December 1998, 67). *See* entries 43, 44.

Blatty, William Peter (January 7, 1928-?)

The son of Lebanese immigrants, Blatty had an impoverished childhood in New York City and won a scholarship to Georgetown University, where he completed a bachelor's degree in 1950. He then earned a master's degree from George Washington University in 1954. He worked for most of the 1950s as a public relations director for universities in the Los Angeles area until the sale of *Which Way to Mecca, Jack?* (B. Geiss/Random House, 1960), after which he began writing fiction full-time. He sold the film rights to several of his early novels, but his great success came with *The Exorcist* (Harper & Row, 1971).

The book sold thirteen million copies, and the movie earned $165 million during its first release in 1973.
(*Contemporary Authors Online*, New York: Gale Group, 2004, accessed, 23 February 2005). *See* entry 45.

Blythe, Samuel G[eorge]. (May 19, 1868-July 17, 1947)
    Born the son of newspaperman Samuel H. Blythe of Geneseo, New York, Blythe's career began in his father's print shop. While on the New York staff of *The World,* Joseph Pulitzer appointed him head of that publication's Washington bureau, a position he held from 1900 to 1907, before joining *The Saturday Evening Post* to write a weekly feature, "Who's Who—and Why." Along with diplomats and other correspondents, he was in China in 1915 and was credited with helping avert a war between China and Japan over Manchuria.
(*New York Times*, 19 July 1947, 13). *See* entries 46, 47, 48.

Bogy, Lewis Vital (April 9, 1813-September 20, 1877)
    A Missouri native, Bogy graduated with a law degree from Transylvania University (Lexington, Ky.) in 1835. The St. Louis law practice he founded was highly lucrative, although he lost large amounts of money through bad investments in railroads and iron mines. He entered politics in 1840, serving several terms in the Missouri legislature before the Civil War. A supporter of the Southern cause, Bogy refused to take the oath of loyalty to the United States required of attorneys and abandoned his law practice. After the war, however, he was elected to the Senate and, despite an investigation into campaign irregularities, served his term as an advocate for legislation favorable to the West.
(*Dictionary of American Biography*, s.v. "Bogy, Lewis Vital"). *See* entry 49.

Bonnamy, Francis [pseud.], *see* Walz, Audrey

Bowles, John
    See entry 50.

Branch, Florenz, [pseud.], *see* Stonebraker, Florence

Brossard, Chandler (1922-1993)
    The self-educated Brossard was born in Idaho Falls but grew up in Washington, leaving school at eleven to read the great classics of Western literature under the tutelage of his brother, Vincent. He went on to publish seventeen books of non-fiction and fiction during a career

that also included work as an editor and teacher. He began work as a copy boy at *The Washington Post* at age eighteen, later advancing to reporter, before moving to New York. He worked as an editor and writer at *The New Yorker,* a senior editor at *Time,* assistant managing editor at *Coronet,* and executive editor at *American Mercury.* At *Look* magazine he was senior editor from 1956-1967.
(*New York Times,* 1 September 1993, A20). *See* entry 51.

Brown, George Rothwell
    See entry 52.

Brown, Zenith Jones [Ford, Leslie, pseud.] (December 8, 1898-August 25, 1983)
    Born in Smith River, California, beginning in 1929, Brown wrote over sixty novels under the pen names Leslie Ford and David Frome. She developed four series centered on different detectives: Inspector Bull and Mr. Pinkerton were English, and Colonel Primrose and Sergeant Buck were American. *The Saturday Evening Post* published several of her books in serial form. She was educated at the University of Washington, Seattle and married to Ford Keeler Brown, a college professor.
(*Contemporary Authors Online,* New York: Gale Group, 2003, accessed, 23 February 2005). *See* entries 53, 54, 55.

Bugbee, Emma (1888-October 6, 1981)
    At a time when female reporters were few in number and assigned to the society pages, Bugbee achieved a national readership and worked to increase opportunities for women in journalism. Born in Shippensburg, Pennsylvania, Bugbee graduated from Barnard College and taught briefly at a high school in Methuen, Massachusetts, before getting a job with *The New York Herald Tribune.* Her first major assignment was coverage of a suffragists march from New York to Albany. However, her career's big break came when she was sent to Washington in 1933 to write about new First Lady, Eleanor Roosevelt. When the *Tribune* discovered that Roosevelt had invited Bugbee to lunch, they gave her a standing assignment to cover the Roosevelt White House. She continued to write about Eleanor Roosevelt after the death of Franklin and up until Eleanor's death in 1962. Bugbee's entire fifty-five-year career was spent at the *Tribune;* she retired in 1966 only a few days before the newspaper's last issue.
(*New York Times,* 10 October 1981, 17). *See* entry 56.

Burnett, Frances (Eliza) Hodgson (November 24, 1849-October 29, 1924)

An English immigrant, Burnett, began publishing stories in popular magazines when she was sixteen. She married Dr. Swan Moses Burnett in 1873, and the couple settled in Washington, where he became a widely known specialist in ophthalmic and aural surgery. Her writings soon achieved popularity, and, after the publication of *Little Lord Fauntleroy* (Scribner's, 1886), she had a significant income that enabled her to live apart from Dr. Burnett. Scandal magazine stories about her domestic arrangements led to a formal divorce from Burnett in 1898. Public criticism of her way of living continued but had no impact on her literary output; she eventually saw more than forty titles into print and authored essays and short stories for a wide range of publications.

(*Dictionary of Literary Biography*, vol. 42, s.v. "Burnett, Frances Eliza Hodgson"). *See* entry 57.

Burton, Thomas [pseud.], *see* Longstreet, Stephen

Camera, Cara [pseud.].
    See entry 58.

Carter, John Franklin (April 27, 1897-November 27, 1967)

Carter attended the St. Mark's School and graduated from Yale in 1920. After periods working as a journalist in Rome and New York City, he began working as an economic specialist in the State Department in Washington in 1928, continuing in that position until 1932, when he accepted the post of Washington correspondent for *Liberty* magazine. From 1934 to 1936 he worked in the office of the undersecretary of Agriculture. Carter was a personal friend of President Franklin Delano Roosevelt and wrote a syndicated column in the New Deal period under the pen name Jay Franklin, supporting the President's policies. During World War II he had a special intelligence appointment in the White House. After the war he worked with the New York State Department of Commerce and, later, the New York State Publicity Department. He continued to publish and wrote over thirty books, most of which were about politics or political figures.

(*New York Times*, 29 November 1967, 47). *See* entries 59, 60, 61.

Cater, (Silas) Douglass, (Jr.) (August 24, 1923-September 15, 1995)

Born in Montgomery, Alabama, Cater was educated at Harvard University obtaining his bachelor's degree in 1947 and a master's in

1948. As Washington editor of *The Reporter* magazine from 1950 to 1963 and national affairs editor from 1963 to 1964, he covered events on Capitol Hill. Cater's journalism career in Washington led to government service and political campaign work. President Lyndon B. Johnson appointed him as a special assistant from 1964 to 1968, focusing on educational issues, including the development of federal aid programs for education and the establishment of the Public Broadcasting System. After working on the Hubert Humphrey presidential campaign, he became vice chairperson of the *London Observer* in 1976, a founding fellow and trustee of the Aspen Institute, and, in 1982, president of Washington College until his retirement in 1990. With the exception of one novel, Cater wrote non-fiction books about government and politics.
(*Contemporary Authors Online*, New York: Gale Group, 2003, accessed, 9 June 2005). *See* entry 62.

Chambrun, Mme. De (née Clara Longworth) (1873-June 1, 1954)
    Born in Cincinnati, the Comtesse de Chambrun was the sister of Nicholas Longworth, for many years the speaker of the United States House of Representatives and husband of Alice Roosevelt Longworth, daughter of Theodore Roosevelt. The Comtesse was the wife of General Adelbert de Chambrun, a descendant of the Marquis de Lafayette, and the couple divided their time between the United States and France. The Comtesse received wide attention for an account of her experiences in occupied France during World War II. Recognized as a Shakespeare scholar, she also wrote a biography of her brother, a history of Cincinnati, several volumes of memoirs, and four novels.
(*New York Times*, 2 June 1954, 31). *See* entry 63.

Chatfield-Taylor, Hobart C[hatfield] (March 24, 1865-January 16, 1945).
In addition to novels, Chatfield-Taylor wrote biographies of Moliere and Goldoni. He was born in Chicago, Illinois.
(W. J. Burke and Will D. Howe, *American Authors and Their Books, 1640 to the Present*, New York: Crown, 1962, s.v. "Chatfield-Taylor, Hobart C[hatfield]"). *See* entry 64.

Chatterton, Ruth (December 24, 1893-November 24, 1961)
    Born in New York City, Chatterton first appeared on the professional stage while a schoolgirl in Washington, D.C. However, her first success as a headliner on Broadway was at twenty-one when she appeared in *Daddy Long-Legs*. Many stage successes followed, and in

1928 she began appearing in movies in starring roles. Her first book, *Homeward Borne* (Simon and Schuster, 1950), the story of a child whose life was lived entirely within the confines of a concentration camp, was a bestseller and was followed by three more well-received novels: *The Betrayers* (Houghton Mifflin, 1953), *The Pride of the Peacock* (Doubleday, 1954), and *The Southern Wild* (Doubleday, 1958). (*New York Times*, 25 November 1961, 23). *See* entry 65.

Chidsey, Alan Lake (March 13, 1904-October, 1981)
    Chidsey was a graduate of Union College and Harvard University. He served in the U.S. Army during World War II in the Office of Procurement Service and, later, as supervisor of instruction at the Armed Forces Service and Civilian Schools. A headmaster at the Arizona Desert School and assistant dean of students at the University of Chicago, Chidsey was founding headmaster of the St. John's School in Houston, Texas, in 1946. His books are mostly illustrated works for children that deal with animals and characters from the Bible and the classics.
(St. John's School, Houston, Texas, Official Web Site, http://www.sjs.org, accessed, 10 October 2005). *See* entry 66.

Childs, Marquis W[illiams] (1903-1990)
    Born in Clinton, Iowa, Childs was a graduate of the University of Wisconsin and earned a master's degree at the University of Iowa. He began work at the *St. Louis (Mo.) Post-Dispatch* in 1926 and, with the exception of ten years with the United Features Syndicate (1944-1954), worked for that paper until 1974. Childs was respected for his coverage of Washington politics and was *The Post-Dispatch*'s chief Washington correspondent from 1962-1968. He won a Pulitzer Prize in 1970 while a contributing editor at the newspaper. His interviews with presidents and world leaders were extraordinary for the confidences such men shared with him. Throughout his career he tried to bring attention to the struggles of the poor and advocated for the civil rights of all Americans. He also promoted improved diplomatic relations between the United States and the Soviet Union, decrying the evils of the nuclear arms race. He was a Washington resident for much of his adult life but retired to San Francisco in 1974.
(*New York Times*, 2 July 1990, D10). *See* entry 67.

Clark, Arthur C[harles] (December 16, 1917-?)
    A 1948 graduate of King's College (London, UK) with a bachelor's degree in science, Clarke worked as a civil servant and editor before becoming a freelance writer in 1951. A popularizer of scientific

theory through non-fiction and fiction, Clarke has been surprisingly prolific. His best known work remains the screenplay (with Stanley Kubrick) for *2001: A Space Odyssey* (Metro-Goldwyn-Mayer, 1968). (*Contemporary Authors Online*, New York: Thomson Gale, 2004, accessed, 25 February 2005). *See* entry 68.

Clemens, Samuel L[anghorne] (November 30, 1835-April 21, 1910)
Considered one of America's most important writers, Clemens' life has been extensively documented. Born in Missouri and raised in Hannibal, he began work at twelve as a printer's apprentice and typesetter. By 1857 he was an apprentice riverboat pilot, and, starting in 1859, worked as a pilot until the Civil War temporarily ended travel on the Mississippi. After serving briefly in the Confederate Army, Clemens headed West, working alternately as a miner and reporter in mining camps and in Virginia City, Nevada, and San Francisco and Sacramento, California. In 1870 he married Olivia Langdon, the daughter of a wealthy New Yorker, and began a settled life as a writer, publisher, and father. With the exception of about a year lived in Buffalo, New York, and extended travels in Europe, Clemens resided in a Hartford, Connecticut, mansion he had designed for himself.
(*Contemporary Authors Online*, New York: Thomson Gale, 2004, accessed, 15 December 2004). *See* entry 69.

Cleveland, Cynthia Eloise
See entries 70, 71.

Colby, Merle (1902-January 1, 1969)
A 1924 graduate of Harvard College, Colby's first novel, *All Ye People* (Viking, 1931), dealt with the settlement of the West, as did his second novel, *New Road* (Viking, 1933). Colby was appointed principal editor of the Federal Writers Project in 1935. During World War II he successively worked as chief of the News Writing Division of the Office of War Information, chief of information for the War Manpower Commission, and chief of reports of the office of War Mobilization and Reconversion. He later worked as a staffer in the Truman White House, leaving federal employment in 1948. When his novel *The Big Secret* (Viking, 1949) was panned for being too broadly satirical, he claimed nothing in the novel was as outrageous as real-life Washington bureaucracy. He joined the public relations firm Newmeyer Associates, Inc., becoming a partner in 1957 and vice president in 1959 not long before his retirement.
(*New York Times*, 15 January 1969, 47). *See* entry 72.

Cole, Cyrenus (1863-November 14, 1939)

Cole, a newspaperman and editor, culminated his working life as the Republican House member from the Fifth Iowa District. Born on a farm near Pella in Marion County, Iowa, he graduated from Central College (Pella, Iowa) in 1887, eventually working as a journalist with the *Des Moines (Ia.) Register* from 1888 to 1898, after which he was a part owner of *The Cedar Rapids (Ia.) Republican* and founder of *The Cedar Rapids (Ia.) Evening Times*. He was first elected to the House of Representatives July 19, 1921, to fill a vacancy caused by the resignation of James W. Good and was re-elected five more times, ending his last term in 1932. He continued to live in Washington until his death. In addition to two works of fiction, he wrote a history of Iowa and a biography of Black Hawk.

(U.S. Congress, *Biographical Directory of the United States Congress, 1774 to the Present*, http://bioguide.congress.gov, accessed, 12 November 2005). *See* entry 73.

Colver, Anne [Graff, Polly Anne, pseud.] (June 28, 1908-?)

The author of a number of works of historical fiction for children, Colver was born in Cleveland, the daughter of newspaper editor William Byron Colver. She received her bachelor's degree in 1931 from Whitman College (Walla Walla, Wa.). In addition to her own juvenile fiction, she has co-authored books with her husband, Stewart Graff, a lawyer and businessman. She has also written several mysteries using the pen name Colver Harris.

(*Contemporary Authors Online*, New York: Gale Group, 2001, accessed, 15 December 2004). *See* entry 74.

Copley, Frank Barkley

See entry 75.

Crane, Laura Dent

See entry 76.

Crawford, Theron Clark (c.1823-?)

A journalist, Crawford was born in Crawford, New York.

(W. J. Burke, and Will D. Howe. *American Authors and Their Books: 1640 to the Present Day*, New York: Crown, 1962, s.v. "Crawford, Theron Clark"). *See* entry 77.

Crissey, Forrest (1864-November 5, 1943)

An Illinois journalist, during the course of his career, Crissy was the editor of *The Geneva (Ill.) Patrol,* a reporter for *The Chicago Tribune,* and an editorial writer for *The Saturday Evening Post.* He wrote fiction, as well as poetry and biographies.

(*New York Times,* 6 November 1943, 13). *See* entry 78.

Cruger, Mrs. Julie Grinnell (Storrow) [Gordon, Julien, pseud.] (1850?-July 12, 1920)

Cruger wrote sixteen novels about Washington and New York Society under the pen name Julien Gordon. Her husband, Colonel Stephen Van Rensselaer Cruger (1844-1898), of the famous New York Van Rennsselaer family, distinguished himself in the Civil War and was a successful investment manager. Julie Cruger was known for creating French-style salons at her homes in Manhattan and Oyster Bay. After Colonel Cruger's death in 1898, his estate came to her and she sold her New York house and began spending most of the social season in a large house on the Potomac in Washington. The novels she published as a widow were popular, and she made an extended trip to Italy in the first decade of the twentieth century. Upon her return to Washington, in 1908, she caused a scandal by marrying a much younger man with mysterious origins. They soon separated and both filed for divorce. After a lengthy and public legal struggle, her husband won a decree in 1915. Cruger was the daughter of Thomas Wentworth Storrow of Boston and the grandniece of Washington Irving. She was born in Paris, spent much of her youth there, and returned there after her divorce.

(*New York Times,* 13 July 1920, 10). *See* entry 79.

Cunningham, Chet [Derrick, Lionel, pseud.] (December 9, 1928-?)

Primarily known for writing Western and adventure novels, Cunningham has developed a number of series, some of which he writes under pseudonyms. Two of his series have been described as pornographic. One deals with the adventures of Lee Morgan, a man who lives by the gun in the Old West. The other follows Spur McCoy, a U.S. Secret Service agent.

(*Contemporary Authors Online,* New York: Gale Group, 2001, accessed, 25 February 2005). *See* entry 80.

Curtis, Mrs. Isabel Gordon (April 24, 1863-December 23, 1915)

Curtis was a Scottish immigrant born in Huntly, Aberdeenshire, who had finished cooking school before arriving in Springfield, Massachusetts, in 1886. She worked in the woman's department of the *New*

England Homestead, Hearth, and Home from 1892 to 1896 before marrying Francis Curtis. Later, on the editorial staff of *Good Housekeeping* magazine, she became nationally known when she began an advice column for homemakers. She also published a number of cookbooks while at *Good Housekeeping,* distinguished by their practical design, as well as their tested recipes. Devoted to domestic efficiency and scientific approaches to nutrition and health care, her career also included positions as a woman's editor at *Collier's Weekly,* the *Delineator,* and *Success Magazine.* When she retired from *Success* in 1911, she began writing fiction and published a novel each year until her death in Washington in 1915.

(Michigan State University, *The Historic American Cookbook Project*, http://digital.lib.msu.edu/projects/cookbooks/html, accessed 12 November 2005). *See* entries 81, 82.

Dahlgren, Sarah Madeleine Vinton (1825-1898)

Although she was born in Gallipolis, Ohio, Dahlgren spent most of her formative years in Washington. Her father was Samuel Finley Vinton, a congressman for more than twenty years. After the death of her mother and brother when she was six, Vinton was her father's close companion, becoming the hostess at his Washington house as soon as she was of age. A graduate of Monsieur Picot's boarding school (Philadelphia) and the Visitation Academy (Georgetown), Dahlgren married Ohio lawyer Daniel C. Goddard in 1846. An assistant secretary in the Department of the Interior, Goddard died in 1851. She later married Rear Admiral John Adolphus Dahlgren in 1865 only to be widowed again in 1870. She then constructed an elegant Massachusetts Avenue house and used it as her main residence for the rest of her life, summering at a house named *Dahlgren* on South Mountain in Maryland. Although her writings included translations of French novels, family histories, and essays opposing woman's suffrage, Washington was her main inspiration, and she is notable for conveying an intimate knowledge of social life in the city. Her guide, *Etiquette of Social Life in Washington* (Wineberger, 1873), was widely read. Dahlgren was also an active participant in literary circles in Washington; she was one of the founders of the Washington Literary Society in 1873.

(*American National Biography*, s.v. "Dahlgren, Sarah Madeleine Vinton"). *See* entries 83, 84, 85.

Dall, Caroline Wells (née Healey) (June 22, 1822-December 17, 1912)

Daughter of an affluent Bostonian, Dall's private education was unusual for women of her time. She was publishing items in religious

periodicals by the time she was thirteen, and her education culminated with participation in the "Conversations" of the Transcendentalists led by Elizabeth Palmer Peabody, Margaret Fuller, Ralph Waldo Emerson, and Theodore Parker. When she was twenty, she was forced by her father's continued financial difficulties to earn money teaching at the preparatory school of the Visitation Academy (Georgetown). Two years later, in 1844, she married a Baltimore-based Unitarian minister, Henry Appleton Dall. Her books on women's history and the right of women to get an education and to work received a good deal of attention. By the late 1860s, disillusioned with the women's rights movement, she turned her attention to history, writing about Egypt and the real-life characters that may have inspired her literary works. During this period, she also wrote her three-volume series for children, *Patty Gray's Journey* (Lee and Shepard, 1869-70). In 1878, Dall moved to Washington, D.C., and became a well-known hostess to the capital's political and scientific elites. In this last stage of her life, she published several important records of Boston in the 1840s and 1850s, including reminiscences of the leading figures of the American Renaissance she had known and a transcription of lectures by Margaret Fuller that she had attended.
(*Dictionary of Literary Biography*, vol. 235, s.v. "Dall, Caroline Wells [Healey])." *See* entry 86.

Darling, Mrs. Flora Adams (1840-1910)

Darling, a member of a branch of the Adams family, for many generations prominent in American life, was born in Lancaster, New Hampshire. She married General Irving Darling before the Civil War and moved with him to Louisiana. At the outbreak of war, Darling enlisted with the Confederate army and was later killed in battle. Mrs. Darling, with a son to support, moved to Washington after the war, living at first on her husband's estate. When the money was lost through unprofitable investments, she was able to support herself through her writing, which included several popular titles, including her own letters and reminiscences of the Civil War. She was a founding member of the Daughters of the American Revolution and devoted a great deal of time to the organization's activities. When her son, musical composer Edward Irving Darling, died suddenly, Darling successfully called for a murder investigation, accusing his young widow and the physician she had promptly married. During the final years of her life, Darling resided at 1907 N Street, NW.
(*New York Times*, 7 January 1910, 9). *See* entries 87, 88.

Davey, Jocelyn [pseud.], *see* Raphael, Chaim

Davidov, Len
   See entry 89.

Davies, Acton (1870?-June 12, 1916)
   After completing his secondary school education, Davies moved to New York City in 1887 and worked for the New York Gas Company and was also soon freelancing for newspapers. In 1890, he began working fulltime as a journalist, eventually specializing in writing dramatic criticism and becoming drama critic for *The Evening Sun* in 1893. When the Spanish-American War broke out, the *Sun* dispatched Davies to Cuba and Puerto Rico as a war correspondent. In addition to journalism, Davies wrote novels and short stories and in the final years of his life devoted himself to screenplays.
(*New York Times*, 13 June 1916, 11). *See* entry 90.

Davis, Foxcroft [pseud.], *see* Seawell, Molly Elliott

Davis, Harriet Riddle (1854-June 3, 1938)
   The daughter of Albert Gallatin Riddle (1816-1902), a United States attorney for the District of Columbia and U.S. congressman (1861-1863), Davis was born in Cleveland, Ohio. Her father had been a friend of President Lincoln's, and she met him a number of times as a young girl. Riddle was one of the prosecutors in the conviction of John H. Surratt. Davis was the wife of Henry E. Davis, who, like her father, was a United States attorney for the District. Although she was an associate editor of the *Saturday Evening Post* for a time, she devoted most of her literary efforts to writing novels, producing more than twenty-eight before her death. A resident of Washington for most of her life, her final residence was at 1931 19th Street, NW.
(*The [Washington, D.C.] Evening Star*, 5 June 1938). *See* entry 91.

Davis, Mary Lee (March 21, 1935-?)
   Born in Worthington, Minnesota, and a graduate of the University of Minnesota and Mankato (Minn.) State College, with the exception of the year she spent as a political press aide in Washington, D.C., she lived and worked in Minnesota. She was a staff writer for the *St. Paul (Minn.) Dispatch* from 1958 to 1960, a public relations representative from 1961 to 1971, and has worked as a freelance writer for most of her career. In addition to works for children, she has written books for two

publisher's series: the "Early Career" series by Lerner and the "Women in American Life" series by Denison.
(*Contemporary Authors Online*, New York: Gale Group, 2001, accessed, 25 February 2005). *See* entry 92.

Davis, Gordon [pseud.], *see* Hunt, E[verette] Howard (Jr.)

De Forest, John William (March 31, 1826-July 17, 1906)
    Known as an early literary realist, De Forest is best remembered for his novel *Miss Ravenel's Conversion from Secession to Loyalty* (Harper, 1867). The son of affluent manufacturer John Hancock De Forest, De Forest attended Yale University, traveled extensively in the Near East and Europe, and had completed an important history of Connecticut Indians before he was twenty-five. During the Civil War, he organized a New Haven, Connecticut, company of Union volunteers that served in Louisiana and the Shenandoah Valley. Discharged for health reasons at the end of 1864, De Forest was commissioned a captain in the Veteran Reserve Corps and stationed in Washington, where he finished *Miss Ravenel's Conversion*.
(*Dictionary of Literary Biography*, vol. 12, s.v. "De Forest, John William"). *See* entries 93, 94, 95.

Deiss, Joseph Jay (January 25, 1915-?)
    The son of a Twin Falls, Idaho rancher, Deiss was educated at the University of Texas at Austin and worked in Washington, D.C., from 1936 to 1944 as an editor and writer for the federal government, before moving to New York City in 1944 to work for two years as an editor for *Executive's War Digest*. From 1947 to 1950, he was a freelance writer and then became a partner in the public relations firm, Medical & Pharmaceutical Information Bureau. Since 1954, he has primarily worked as a freelance writer of non-fiction.
(*Contemporary Authors Online*, New York: Gale Group, 2001, accessed, 9 June 2005). *See* entry 96.

Denison, Mary Andrews (1826-October 18, 1911)
    Denison grew up in Cambridge, Massachusetts, and married the Rev. Charles W. Denison. She traveled with him to the West Indies, where he served as consul, and, during the Civil War she was a nurse in the regiment for which he was a chaplain. She was a resident of Washington, D.C., for many years.
(*New York Times*, 18 October 1911, 11). *See* entry 97.

Derrick, Lionel [pseud.], *see* Cunningham, Chet

Derville, Leslie
    See entry 98.

Devries, Julian (also, Julianne) (1904-?)
    Author of a series of books featuring the Campfire Girls.
See entry 99.

Dietrich, Robert [pseud.], *see* Hunt, E[verette] Howard (Jr.)

Dillon, Mary C. (née Johnson) (?)
    The daughter of Herman Merrills Johnson, professor and later
president of Dickinson College in Carlisle, Pennsylvania, Dillon grew
up in Carlisle and wrote the book *In Old Bellaire* (Century, 1906) about
her childhood in the town at the time of the Civil War. In 1908, she
received the first honorary degree awarded to a woman by Dickinson.
(Dickinson College, Carlisle, Penn., Official Web Site, http://www
.dickinson.edu, accessed 11 November 2005). *See* entry. 100.

Dos Passos, John (January 14, 1896-September 28, 1970)
    Although he first wrote poetry in response to his war experiences,
his novel *Three Soldiers* (Doran, 1921), an attack on war in general, received wide attention and critical acclaim, launching his career. In the
1920s, he lived the life of one of America's prominent men of letters, a
friend of Hemingway, Fitzgerald, Edmund Wilson, and Malcolm Cow-
ley. His books earned him a reputation for insightful criticism of the
American capitalist system. After the late 1930s, however, he became
increasingly conservative socially and politically, alienating his earlier
advocates.
(Dictionary of Literary Biography, vol. 9, s.v. "Dos Passos, John"). *See*
entries 101, 102, 103.

Douglas, Amanda Minnie (1831-1916)
    Although Douglas was born in New York City and received her
education at the City Institute, her family moved to Newark, New Jersey, in 1853, where she spent the rest of her life. Before the appearance
of her first book in 1866, she published a number of short stories in the
Saturday Evening Post, New York Ledger, and the *Lady's Friend.* From
In Trust (Lee & Shepard, 1866), her first book, until *Red House Children Growing Up* (Lothrop, Lee, & Shepard, 1916), she published one
or two books annually. *Larry* (Lee & Shepard, 1893) received the

Youth's Companion prize for best young people's fiction. Most of her works were for young adults. She published three extensive series: the Kathie Series, the Little Girl Series, and the Helen Grant Series. Even though her characters sometimes travel, Douglas's works celebrate the virtue of family life and all the traditional virtues with which it is associated.
(*Dictionary of American Biography*, s.v. "Douglas, Amanda Minnie").
See entry 104, 105.

Drake, Alice Hutchins (October 11, 1889-February 6, 1975)
Drake was known for her radio lectures on art and wrote devotional material. She was a Washington, D.C., resident for many years.
(*Contemporary Authors Online*, New York: Gale Group, 2002, accessed, 25 February 2005). *See* entry 106.

Drury, Allen (Stuart) (September 2, 1918-September 2, 1998)
Drury joined United Press International in 1943 to cover the U.S. Senate. He continued to work in Washington for *Pathfinder* magazine and *The (Washington, D.C.) Evening Star* before joining the *New York Times'* Washington bureau in 1954. His novels, typically set in Washington, usually focus upon politicians and high-level bureaucrats confronting crises and potential scandals and are known for the deep knowledge of political life that they demonstrate.
(*Contemporary Authors Online*, New York: Gale Group, 2003, accessed, 25 February 2005). *See* entries 107, 108, 109, 110.

Eaton, Paul Webster (December 27, 1861-June 25, 1943)
Born in Maine, Eaton wrote popular song lyrics and was a freelance sports writer for publications such as *Sporting Life* and *Sporting News*. He lived in Washington and ended his career as a writer for the U.S. State Department.
(Bill Burgess, "Sports Writers Register," http://www.baseballguru.com, accessed 10 October 2005). *See* entry 111.

Eberhart, Mignon Good (July 6, 1899-1996)
Born and educated in Nebraska, Eberhart married Alanson C. Eberhart in 1923, and his career as a civil engineer proved influential in two ways. First, she traveled a great deal to keep her husband company on business trips and she wrote as a distraction. Second, many of her romantic male protagonists are civil engineers. Although she authored several novels and a number of short stories, Eberhart is best known for her mysteries that provide all of the clues needed by the reader to un-

cover the solution. She wrote more than sixty books during her fifty-year career.
(Robin W. Winks, ed., *Mystery and Suspense Writers: The Literature of Crime, Detection, and Espionage*, New York: Charles Scribner's Sons, 1998, s.v. "Eberhart, Mignon Good"). *See* entry 112.

Edwards, James A[lexander].
   See entry 113.

Ehrlichman, John Daniel (March 20, 1925-February 15, 1999)
   Born in Tacoma, Washington, and educated at the University of California at Los Angeles and Stanford University, Ehrlichman was a partner in a Seattle law firm before working on Richard Nixon's unsuccessful 1960 presidential race. He is best known for his posts in the Nixon White House and his conviction as one of the Watergate conspirators.
(*Contemporary Authors Online*, New York: Gale Group, 2000, accessed, 25 February 2005). *See* entry 114.

Eiker, Mathilde [Evermay, Marcia, pseud.] (January 5, 1893-?)
   Eiker was a life-long resident of Washington, D.C., the daughter of John Tripner Eiker, chief clerk of the Rivers and Harbor Division of the Office of Chief of Engineers in the U.S. War Department. She grew up in Northwest and suburban Washington, graduating from Central High School and George Washington University (D.C.) in 1914. She was interested in writing throughout her education and began publishing short stories under the pseudonym Marcia Evermay soon after she graduated from college.
(W. J. Burke and Will D. Howe. *American Authors and Their Books: 1640 to the Present Day*, New York: Crown, 1962, s.v. "Eiker, Mathilde"; *The Washington [D.C.] Post*, 22 November 1941, 16). *See* entries 115, 116, 117, 118.

Emerson, Alice B. [pseud.], *see* Benson, Mildred Augustine Wirt

Erskine, John (October 5, 1879-June 2, 1951)
   A musician, scholar, poet, and teacher as well as a novelist, Erskine was educated through his doctorate at Columbia University, began teaching there in 1906, and was connected with the institution until his death. His first novel, *The Private Life of Helen of Troy* (Bobbs-Merrill, 1925), was both popular and praised by critics. A number of other works of historical fiction, most with more conventional ap-

proaches, followed, including accounts of Galahad, Adam and Eve, Francois Villon, and Patrick Henry as well as Walt Whitman (for which he is included here).
(*Dictionary of Literary Biography*, vol. 9, s.v. "Erskine, John"). *See* entry 119.

Evermay, Marcia [pseud.], *see* Eiker, Mathilde

Eustis, Edith Livingston, (née Morton) (1874-1964)
The daughter of New York banker Levi Morton (1824-1920), from 1889 on, Eustis' childhood included periods of residence in Morton's Washington mansion at 1500 Rhode Island Avenue, NW, (originally constructed for Alexander Graham Bell). Her father served as vice president under Benjamin Harrison (1889-1893). Edith married William Corcoran Eustis, the grandson of Washingtonian William Wilson Corcoran, one of the United States' wealthiest and most influential men before the Civil War.
(National Trust for Historic Preservation, Official Web Site for Oatlands Plantation, http://www.oatlands.org, accessed, 11 November 2005). *See* entry 120.

Fairbank, Janet Ayer (1878-December 28, 1951)
Born in Chicago, Fairbank attended the University of Chicago and, in 1900, married Kellogg Fairbank, an attorney and leader in city politics, who was president of the Chicago Shipbuilding Company during World War I. Most of Fairbank's writings are set in Illinois, particularly Chicago. She was a very active clubwoman (with memberships in more than seven clubs) and involved in several philanthropic and civic organizations. A supporter of women's suffrage, she was active in politics, serving as a member of the executive committee of the Democratic National Committee in 1900 and a member of the Woman's Division of the Illinois Democratic National Committee from 1924 to 1928. Her sister was the novelist Margaret Ayer Barnes.
(*New York Times*, 29 December 1951, 11). *See* entry 121.

Farrar, Larston D[awn] (February 25, 1915-1970)
Farrar was born in Birmingham, Alabama, and studied at Birmingham Southern College, Emory University, and Millsaps College, from which he earned his bachelor's degree in 1940. In addition to novels, he wrote *How to Make $18,000 a Year, Free Lance Writing* (Hawthorn, 1957) and several other non-fiction books, including *Successful Writers*

and *How They Work* (Hawthorn, 1959) and *Whatever Happened to the White Backlash?* (Macfadden, 1965).
(*Dictionary of Literary Biography*, vol. 9, s.v. "Farrar, Larston D.").
See entries 122, 123.

Fergusson, Harvey (1890-1971)
    Primarily known for writing about the American Southwest, Fergusson graduated from Washington and Lee University in 1911 and published his first novel, *The Blood of the Conquerors*, in 1921. Two of his books were made into movies that featured major Hollywood actors and actresses. His regional history, *Rio Grande* (Knopf, 1931), achieved enduring popularity. He published an autobiography, *Home in the West* (Duell, Sloan, and Pearce), in 1944.
(*New York Times*, 29 August 1971, 57). *See* entry 124.

Fitzgerald, Robert
    See entry 125.

Fleming, Thomas (1853-1931)
    A cartoonist for the Capital Cartoon Syndicate, Fleming published several books of caricatures and cartoons, as well as a history of Newark and a guide to Washington and its politicians.
(Peter H. Falk, *Who Was Who in American Art*, Madison, Conn.: Sound View Press, 1985, s.v. "Fleming, Thomas").
See entry 126.

Ford, Leslie [pseud.], *see* Brown, Zenith Jones

Fradin, Morris
    See entry 127.

Frank, Pat (Harry Hart) (May 5, 1907-October 12, 1964)
    Born in Chicago in 1907, Frank took courses in journalism at the University of Florida while working for *The Jacksonville (Fla.) Journal*. He worked for years as a reporter covering murder trials, baseball, and horse racing for *The New York World, The New York Journal*, and *The Washington Times-Herald*. He was named chief of the Washington Bureau of the Overseas News Agency shortly before World War II, but resigned in 1941 to help organize what would become the Office of War Information and the Office of Strategic Services. The publication of *Mr. Adam* (Lippincott, 1946) when he was thirty-nine, a novel about a geologist who remains the only fertile man on earth after an atomic

explosion, changed his life. The book was favorably reviewed and enormously popular (selling more than two million copies), enabling Frank to devote his time to writing novels.
(*New York Times*, 13 October 1964, 43). *See* entry 128.

Futrelle, Jacques (April 9, 1875-April 15, 1912)
    Born in Pike County, Georgia, Futrelle began his writing as a journalist, but later devoted himself to writing genre fiction, including romances, westerns, and detective stories. He introduced the character Professor Augustus S. F. X. Van Dusen in the novel *The Thinking Machine* (Dodd, Mead, 1907) and went on to write several more stories featuring Van Dusen. Their realism, analysis of human nature, and plots focused on less violent crimes have come to be seen as precursors of much later developments in the mystery genre. Futrelle and his wife, writer L. May Peel, were aboard the *Titanic* on its maiden voyage. He was one of the men whose refusal to board a lifeboat in deference to the women on board was recounted in news coverage of the disaster.
(*New York Times*, 19 April 1912, 6; *Contemporary Authors Online*, New York: Gale Group, 2003, accessed, 27 May 2005). *See* entry 129.

Gallagher, Phyllis Moore
    See entry 130.

Galsworthy, John (August 14, 1867-January 31, 1933)
    The product of an affluent youth spent in mansions designed for his businessman-solicitor father and educated at Harrow and Oxford, Galsworthy is best known for a series novels and short stories collectively known as the Forsyte Chronicles in which he depicted the English upper-middle class with characters often modeled upon his own ancestors and family members.
(*Dictionary of Literary Biography*, vol. 34, s.v. "Galsworthy, John").
See entry 131.

Gardener, Helen Hamilton (née Chenoweth) (1858-July 27, 1925)
    The great-great-granddaughter of Lord Baltimore, Gardener became active in the women's suffrage movement in 1888, was closely associated with all of its leaders, and held important posts with the American Woman Suffrage Association and the League of Woman Voters. In 1901, two years after the death of her first husband, she married retired U.S. Army Captain Selden Allen Day and moved to Washington, D.C. When Gardener died, the public was fascinated to learn that she had bequeathed her brain to Cornell University so that a com-

parison could be made between her organ and those of distinguished
men housed at the brain research center there.
(*New York Times*, 4 August 1925, 1; 5 August 1925, 3; 29 September
1927, 1; 7 November 1972, 37). *See* entry 132.

Gardenhire, S[amuel] M[ajor] (1855-1923)
    Gardenhire studied law and was admitted to the bar in Missouri
when he was twenty-one. He practiced in St. Louis and later in Topeka,
Kansas, where he also worked as a newspaper editor. He moved to
New York City in 1895 and continued in legal practice until 1904,
when ill health forced him to retire. He wrote his first novel when he
was fifty and went on to author four more books.
(*New York Times*, 1 March 1923, 15). *See* entries 133, 134.

Gardiner, Mrs. Ruth Kimball (1872-November 23, 1924)
    Born in Carlinville, Illinois, and educated in public schools in
Fargo, North Dakota, Omaha, Nebraska, and St. Paul, Minnesota, Gardiner began working for a newspaper at age eighteen when she became
the first woman telegraphic correspondent as the Washington reporter
for *The St. Paul (Minn.) Globe*. Her husband, Cornelius Gardiner, was
the Washington correspondent for *The Chicago Post*. Gardiner was a
leader of the National Association Opposed to Woman Suffrage in
1917. However, her 1924 obituary lists her as secretary of the National
League of Women Voters.
(*New York Times*, 22 July 1905, BR492; 17 January 1917, 7; 23 November 1924). *See* entry 135.

Garland, Hamlin (September 14, 1860-March 4, 1940)
    Raised on farms in Wisconsin, Iowa, and South Dakota, Garland
embraced the economic theory of Henry George and tried to improve
the lot of farmers, frontier dwellers, and American Indians through
more than fifty works of fiction and non-fiction. Although his idealistic
portrayals were intended to evoke admiration and support for his subjects, his subjects themselves often resented his works.
(*Dictionary of Literary Biography*, vol. 186, s.v. "Garland, Hamlin").
See entry 136.

Garland, Rufus Cummins
    See entry 137.

Garth, David (July 3, 1908-?)

While a student a Williams College, Garth wrote three novels, one of which was published. In the years before he entered Army Intelligence in 1943, he published eight novels and a number of short stories. During World War II, he was a combat historian. He continued to publish novels and magazine fiction after the war and worked as a cultural affairs officer with the U.S. Information Service.

(*Wilson Library Bulletin*, May 1957, 688). *See* entry 138.

Gerould, Gordon Hall (October 4, 1877-1953)

Gerould had a distinguished academic career. A graduate of Dartmouth (1899) and Oxford University (1901), he was among the group of forty-seven men selected to institute Woodrow Wilson's preceptorial method of instruction at the Princeton University. At various times the president of both the Medieval Academy of America and the Modern Language Association, he was an expert on fiction, as well as medieval literature and folklore.

(*New York Times*, 12 April 1953, 88). *See* entry 139.

Gerry, Margarita Spaulding (July 28, 1870-?)

Gerry was born in Washington, D.C.

(W. J. Burke and Will D. Howe, *American Authors and Their Books: 1640 to the Present Day*, New York: Crown, 1962, s.v. "Gerry, Margarita Spaulding"). *See* entry 140.

Glenn, Isa (April, 1874-?)

Glenn was born in Atlanta, Georgia, where her father, Colonel John Thomas Glenn, was a prominent lawyer and, later, the mayor. She was privately schooled and studied painting for a year in Paris with her cousin James McNeil Whistler. She returned to Atlanta and married Brigadier General J. S. Bayard Schindel in 1903. He was stationed at various times in the Philippines, South American, and Washington, D.C. She consistently drew upon her travels as the basis for her novels and short stories. Under her maiden name, she was the author of eight books published between 1926 and 1936.

(W. J. Burke and Will D. Howe. *American Authors and Their Books: 1640 to the Present Day*. New York: Crown, 1962, s.v. "Glenn, Isa"). *See* entry 141.

Godfrey, Hollis (1875-January 17, 1936)

Born in Lynn, Massachusetts, and a graduate of Tufts College, Godfrey held doctorates in law and science earned through study at

Harvard, MIT, and Queen's University in England. His acclaimed book *The Man Who Ended War* (Little, Brown, 1908) led to his appointment, along with Howard Coffin, Elihu Root, and General Leonard Wood, to help create the Council of National Defense of the United States. Godfrey held positions with the council through 1918. He also served as president of Drexel Institute of Art, Science and Industry in Philadelphia from 1913-1921.
(*New York Times*, 19 January 1936, N8). *See* entry 142.

Goldsmith, John Francis
     See entry 143.

Gordon, Julien, [pseud.], *see* Cruger, Mrs. Julie Grinnell (Storrow)

Gould, Elizabeth Lincoln
     See entry 144.

Graff, Polly Anne [pseud.], *see* Colver, Anne

Grant, A. F.
     See entry 145.

Grant, Robert (1852-May 19, 1940)
     Judge Grant served in Suffolk County (Mass.) Probate Court from 1893 to 1923 and was one of the reviewers of the Sacco-Vanzetti case. In his writing, both light essays and novels, Grant often dealt with the subject of marriage and divorce.
(*New York Times*, 25 January 1902, BR10; *New York Times*, 20 May 1940, 21). *See* entry 146.

Green, Anna Katherine (November 11, 1846-April 11, 1935)
     Anna Green was the daughter of prominent New York City defense lawyer James Wilson Green. After being discouraged by Ralph Waldo Emerson from making poetry her career, she turned to fiction, and at the age of thirty-two she became an overnight success with her novel *The Leavenworth Case* (Putnam, 1878). The naturalism of her work, which centers upon police and courtroom procedures and the use of medical and scientific evidence, won her a great deal of admiration, and her reputation continues for publishing a mystery only ten years before the publication of Sir Arthur Conan Doyle's first Sherlock Holmes story. She married a much younger actor, Charles Rohlfs, in 1884, who later would become an internationally famous Mission style

designer. During her career she wrote thirty-three novels. Her work is still admired for masterful plot construction and the introduction of many devices of modern detective stories.
(*Dictionary of Literary Biography*, vol. 221, s.v. "Green, Anna Katherine"). *See* entry 147.

Greene, Talbot
    See entry 148.

Griffith, Patricia Browning (November 9, 1935-?)
    Griffith graduated from Baylor University in 1958 and has worked as a freelance writer and writing teacher since 1962. She has taught at both George Washington University and Goucher College and is a member of the board for the PEN/Faulkner Award for Fiction. She was born in Fort Worth, Texas, and lives in Washington, D.C.
(*Contemporary Authors Online*, New York: Gale Group, 2001, accessed, 15 December 2004). *See* entry 149.

Gunter, Archibald Clavering (1848-1907)
    Born in Liverpool, England, Clavering emigrated with his parents to New York City at the age of six. However, they soon relocated to San Francisco where Clavering was educated in public schools, completing a degree from the School of Mines of the University of California. As a young man, he worked for Central Pacific Railroad as a civil engineer, and later as a chemist with the California Assay Office, and Superintendent of the McKay mines in Utah. He returned to San Francisco to work as a stockbroker for a time before moving to New York City in 1879. His novel *Mr. Burns of New York* was published in 1887 (D. Welch) and sold more than one million copies. Using his royalties, he established the Home Publishing Company. He also wrote successful works for the stage, including *Prince Karl* in 1907, the vehicle that brought Richard Mansfield to prominence as an actor. During the course of his writing career he produced thirty-nine novels and several plays.
(*New York Times*, 26 February 1907, 11). *See* entry 150.

Hackett, Francis (1883-April 24, 1962)
    Born in Ireland, Hackett worked as a journalist in the United States, particularly for *The New Republic*. He met Signe Toskvig, who worked for the same publication, and married her in 1918. In 1937, he moved to Denmark with the Danish-born Toskvig, returning to the United States only after the occupation of Denmark by the Nazis. He

wrote *I Chose Denmark* (Doubleday, 1940) on the basis of which King
Christian X awarded him the Christian X Liberty medal. Hackett and
his wife returned to Denmark after the war.
(*New York Times*, 26 April 1962, 33). *See* entry 151.

Hager, Alice Rogers (August 3, 1894-December 5, 1969)
    A 1915 graduate of Stanford University, Hager began her career as
a journalist in Los Angeles. She developed an interest in aviation, writing freelance articles for *The Washington (D.C.) Star* and *The New
York Times*. Eventually, based in Washington, she became the aviation
correspondent for the North American Newspaper Alliance. During
World War II, she was the Washington editor for *Skyways* and a war
correspondent in the Burma-China-India theater. After the war she
worked as a public relations officer for the federal government in a
number of agencies, including the Department of Labor, Civil Aero-
nautics Board, State Department, and United States Information
Agency. She was a charter member of the Aviation and Space Association and a fellow of the American Geographical Society. During the
course of her life, she traveled more than half a million miles by air.
Most of her books deal with aviation, but she also wrote about Brazil
and authored several novels.
(*Contemporary Authors Online*, New York: Gale Group, 2003, accessed, 2 March 2005). *See* entries 152, 153, 154.

Hall, A[braham] Oakey (1826-1898)
    Hall, the son of an Albany carpenter, moved to New York City to
attend college and later earned a master's degree. He moved to New
Orleans, supporting himself as a reporter, before he was admitted to the
bar and returned to New York City. He was the city's district attorney
by the time he was twenty-nine, enjoying the support of Fernando
Wood. However, he allied himself with Tammany Hall in 1864. During
his time as District Attorney, although he sent twelve thousand people
to jail, he refused to pursue ten thousand indictments. Having earned
William M. Tweed's gratitude, he was elected mayor in 1868 and continued to serve Tammany in that office. Although he was indicted in
1872, he won an acquittal by conducting his own defense. He subsequently was the city editor for *The New York World* (1879-1882) and
then worked as a London correspondent for *The New York Herald*. He
wrote several novels and a play in which he acted.
(*New York Times*, 16 September 1945, SM9). *See* entry 155.

Hansbrough, H[enry] C[lay] (1848-November 16, 1933)

After a significant career as a journalist in California, Hansbrough moved to the Dakota Territory in 1881 where he started newspapers in Grand Forks and later in Devil's Lake. He entered politics as an advocate for statehood for two Dakotas and was in 1889 elected as one of the first congressmen from the newly created state of North Dakota. After the railroad lobby thwarted his election to a second term, he was voted into the U.S. Senate in 1891, where he served for eighteen years. He proved himself an outspoken advocate for farmers, crossing party lines when necessary, and would earn the title "father of irrigation." The bill for which he was best known, however, was the "second free alcohol law," which permitted the tax-free manufacture of alcohol by small distillers and was signed into law by President Theodore Roosevelt in 1907. In addition to a novel, he wrote a book on monetary policy.

(*New York Times*, 17 November 1933, 19). *See* entry 156.

Harrison, Mrs. Burton Constance (née Cary) (1843-November 21, 1920)

Mrs. Harrison was born into a family that traced its ancestry to seventeenth-century Virginia. During most of the Civil War, she worked as a hospital nurse in Richmond. She and her mother lived in Paris for a time after the war, and in 1867 she married Burton Norvell Harrison, a Virginia lawyer who had recently been imprisoned for serving as a personal secretary to Jefferson Davis. The couple began their married life in New York City. The union produced two sons who became men of some note: Francis Burton Harrison, governor general of the Philippines, and Fairfax Harrison, president of the Southern Railway Company. She began writing in the 1870s while living in Manhattan, and became a frequent contributor of short stories and serialized novels to *The Century* magazine. In her best-known work, *Recollections Grave and Gay* (Scribners, 1911), she recounts her life in the Confederate South. Her other best sellers include *The Anglomaniacs* (Cassell, 1880) and *Sweet Bells Out of Tune* (Century, 1893). Her Washington residence was at 1362 18th Street, NW.

(*New York Times*, 24 December 1911, BR852; 22 November 1920, 14). *See* entry 157.

Hart, Frances Noyes (Newbold) (August 10, 1890-October 25, 1943)

Hart, the daughter of Thurston Newbold Noyes, who was the editor and proprietor of the *Washington (D.C.) Star*, had an affluent, sophisticated childhood, even though she grew up on a farm in Silver Spring,

Maryland. During World War I, she was a YMCA canteen worker in France, an experience that inspired her first novel, *My A. E. F.: A Hail and Farewell* (Frederick A. Stokes, 1920). Subsequently a frequent contributor of stories to *Scribner's, The Saturday Evening Post,* and the *Ladies' Home Journal,* Hart also published several mystery novels. The most famous of her mysteries is *The Bellamy Trial* (Pocket Books, 1927). Her mysteries are unusual for having likable, intelligent, self-controlled female murderers.
(*Contemporary Authors Online,* New York: Gale Group, 2003, accessed, 2 March 2005). *See* entry 158.

Hart, Helen [pseud.], *see* Lowe, Samuel E[dward]

Hay, James Jr. (1881-May 7, 1936)
    Born in Harrisonburg, Virginia, Hay was the son of Congressman James Hay, a twenty-year veteran of the House of Representatives. He graduated from the University of Virginia in 1903 and became a reporter at *The Washington Post.* However, within a few years, he gave up journalism to become a full-time fiction writer, developing a career as the author of popular mysteries. His first novel, *The Man Who Forgot* (Grosset & Dunlap), was published in 1915. In addition to mysteries, he wrote about Augustus Saint-Gaudens' Rock Creek Cemetery memorial "Grief" and was at work on a novel about Mary Queen of Scots at the time he died. He had also begun working with the Federal Housing Administration in the public relations office.
(*New York Times,* 7 May 1936, 23). *See* entries 159, 160, 161.

Hayworth, A. D. (?)
    Hayworth was the founder and proprietor of Hayworth Printing Company of Washington, D.C. His son was television actor Vinton Hayworth, whose daughter Rita achieved significant popularity in motion pictures.
(*Washington Post,* 6 February 1970, C7). *See* entry 162.

Higgins, George V. (November 3, 1939-November, 1999)
    Educated at Boston College and Stanford University, Higgins worked as a journalist covering criminal trials for several years before returning to Boston College to get a law degree. Working with units battling organized crime, he became a Massachusetts, then a federal, prosecutor. He had been writing novels since his youth, all unpublished, but sold *Eddie Coyle,* drawn from his experiences as a prosecutor, to Knopf in 1971. The work was immediately successful and was

made into a motion picture. From then on, Higgins devoted himself to writing. In the course of his lifetime he wrote thirty books, twenty-six of them novels. Such writers as David Mamet and Elmore Leonard acclaimed his skill at telling a story through authentic dialogue. (*New York Times*, 8 November 1999, B10). *See* entry 163.

Hill, Grace Livingston (1865-February 23, 1947)
Grace Livingston was born in Wellsville, New York, the daughter of a Presbyterian minister. She was educated at Cincinnati Art School and Elmira College and published her first novel when she was twenty-two. Her aunt, Mrs. G. R. Alden, a popular writer of religious stories under the pen name "Pansy", inspired her early writing. Grace married the Rev. Thomas G. F. Hill, a Presbyterian minister from Pittsburgh, in 1892. The couple had two daughters before his death in 1899. Confronted with supporting her children, Hill turned her writing hobby into an occupation. By the end of her life she had written over one hundred novels, which had sold over four million copies. At the time of her death, she had just signed a contract with Lippincott, her long-time publisher, to continue to submit two novels a year. (*New York Times*, 24 February 1947, 19). *See* entry 164.

Holden, E. Goodman
See entry 165.

Holmes, John
See entry 166.

Holmes, Marjorie (Rose) (September 22, 1910-March 13, 2002)
Born in Storm Lake, Iowa, Holmes graduated from Cornell College. After working in radio in Idaho and Ohio, Holmes published a novel in 1943. This and a subsequent book sold well enough to confirm her interest in writing and she began authoring a bi-weekly column for the *The Washington (D.C.) Star* in 1959 that she would continue until 1973. Entitled "Love and Laughter," the column was domestic themed and earned her great popularity with homemakers. She also wrote many religious-themed books and articles. (*Contemporary Authors Online*, New York: Gale Group, 2004, accessed, 9 June 2005). *See* entries 167, 168, 169.

Hope, Laura Lee [pseud.]
Hope was a pseudonym used to produce "Bobbsey Twins" stories commencing in 1904 by the literary syndicate formed by Edward

Stratemeyer. The Stratemeyer Syndicate, which also produced "Nancy Drew" and "Hardy Boys" series, introduced the Bobbseys to appeal to a younger audience (seven to nine year olds). Eventually seventy books were produced as part of the series. To continue their appeal, the books were updated in the 1950s and in the 1980s.
(*Contemporary Authors Online*, New York: Gale Group, 2001, accessed, 15 December 2004). *See* entry 170.

Hopkins, Pauline Bradford (née Mackie) (July 6, 1873-?)
    A daughter of Reverend Andrew Mackie, Bradford spent most of her life in Ohio, graduating from Toledo High School and working for the *Toledo (Ohio) Blade*. As an author she specialized in works of historical fiction, often drawing upon her own family history, which dated back to the colonial period. She was also known as Mrs. Herbert Müller Hopkins.
(Edward Francis Harkins, *Famous Authors [Women]*, Boston: L. C. Page, 1901, s.v. "Mackie, Pauline Bradford"). *See* entry 171.

Hopkins, William B.
    See entry 172.

Howard, Milford Wrarison (December 18, 1862-December 29, 1937)
    Howard had a successful legal career in Dekalb County, Alabama, before relocating to Washington, D.C., to study drama and oration, hoping to establish a career as a lecturer. He was inspired by living in Washington to write *If Christ Came to Congress* (Author, 1894) and received national attention that helped get him elected to the U.S. Congress in 1895 and 1899. Turning down an offer by a prestigious New York City law firm, he returned to Fort Payne, Alabama, in 1904 to his own successful law practice and began making and, mostly, losing fortunes through real estate, a Mexican mine, a Louisiana oil field, Alaskan gold prospecting, and a salmon cannery. In 1923 he bought one thousand acres of land on Lookout Mountain near Mentone, Alabama, to build a school for poor children to be financed through a housing development on part of the land. The development was unsuccessful, and the land is now part of DeSoto State Park.
(U.S. Congress, *Biographical Directory of the United States Congress, 1774 to the Present*, http://bioguide.congress.gov, accessed, 12 November 2005; Desoto [Ala.] State Park, Official Web Site; http://www.Desoto statepark.com, accessed 13 March 2005). *See* entries 173, 174.

Hubbard, Freeman (Henry) (1894-1991)

Born in Philadelphia, Hubbard was educated at the Pennsylvania Academy of Fine Arts. He worked as a journalist, starting out at the *Philadelphia Evening Bulletin* and later working for the *Philadelphia Inquirer, New York Journal-American,* and *New York Post.* He authored or co-authored nine books, mostly about railroads. His interest in trains led to his editorship of *Railroad Magazine* and authorship of *Encyclopedia of North American Railroading* (McGraw Hill, 1981).

(*Contemporary Authors Online*, New York: Gale Group, 2002, accessed, 9 June 2005). *See* entry 175.

Hughes, Robert
See entry 176.

Hulbert, James
See entry 177.

Hunt, E[verette] Howard (Jr.)[Davis, Gordon; Dietrich, Robert; pseud.] (October 9, 1918-?)

A 1940 graduate of Brown University, Hunt worked as a screenwriter and editor for the motion picture newsreel series *March of Time* from 1942-1943 and as a war correspondent for *Life Magazine* in 1943. He began a twenty-year career with the Central Intelligence Agency in 1949. During his time with the CIA he published numerous works of political intrigue, often under pseudonyms (John Baxter, Gordon Davis, Robert Dietrich, and David St. John). As a consultant to the Nixon White House, Hunt was responsible for organizing the break-ins at the office of Daniel Ellsberg's psychiatrist and the Democratic National Headquarters at the Watergate office complex, for which he served three years in federal prison.

(*Contemporary Authors Online*, New York: Gale Group, 2001 accessed 5 October 2005). *See* entries 178, 179, 180, 181.

Hunt, Una

Daughter of Dr. F. W. Clarke of Washington, D.C. (a founding member of the National Academy of Sciences), Hunt married the vicar of Pickering (England), the Reverend Evelyn Drage.

(Beck Isle Museum of Rural Life, Pickering, North Yorkshire, U.K., Official Web Site, http://www.beckislemuseum.co.uk, accessed, 11 November 2005). *See* entry 182.

James, (Robert) Leigh (July 29, 1918-?)

Known for writing convincing spy thrillers, James served in the U.S. Navy and as a U.S. Foreign Service officer in Cuba, before he went on to a successful career as a banker and attorney for mining and banking companies. He writes best-selling novels under the name Leigh James.

(*Contemporary Authors Online*, New York: Gale Group, 2004, accessed, 2 March 2005). *See* entry 183.

Janeway, Elizabeth (Hall) (October 7, 1913-January 17, 2005)

Known for her feminist writings, Janeway was also the author of a number of novels and works of juvenile fiction. Her insights into the role of women in society were firmly grounded in her own experiences as a wife and mother. Born in Brooklyn, New York, Janeway studied at Swarthmore College and received her bachelors degree from Barnard College in 1935.

(*Contemporary Authors Online*, New York: Gale Group, 2003, accessed, 2 March 2005). *See* entry 184.

Johnson, Ivar [pseud.], *see* Tibbetts, Edgar Alfred

Johnson, William Franklin

Johnson founded the Washington (D.C.) National Building and Loan Association.

(*New York Times*, 27 September 1902, BR10). *See* entry 185.

Jones, John Beauchamp (March 6, 1810-February 4, 1866)

Known for capturing life on the Kentucky and Missouri frontier, reflecting his boyhood experiences, Jones was the husband of Frances Thomas Custis, a descendent of Martha Custis Washington with extensive and prominent family connections, including Robert E. Lee and Virginia Governor Henry Wise. As the owner and editor of newspapers, he tried to defuse the tensions between North and South. During the Civil War, he supported the Southern cause and lived in Richmond. However, he was critical of Southern politicians, and when he published his *A Rebel War Clerk's Diary* (Lippincott, 1866) after the war. Southerners reacted with contempt.

(*Dictionary of Literary Biography*, vol. 202, s.v. "Jones, John Beauchamp"). *See* entry 186.

Just, Ward S[wift] (September 5, 1935-?)

After working as a reporter with *Newsweek* magazine, Just became a correspondent for the *Washington Post* based in Saigon, South Vietnam, from 1965 to 1967. He continued to work for the newspaper from 1968 to 1970, but has since devoted himself to writing fiction. All of his work uses Washington, D.C., as a backdrop, and, although he is interested in the political struggles within official Washington, he convincingly presents the private lives of his characters as well.

(*Contemporary Authors Online*, New York: Gale Group, 2004, accessed, 15 December 2004). *See* entry 187.

Kane, Harnett T. (1910-September 4, 1984)

A New Orleans native, Kane was the author of twenty-six books of fiction and non-fiction dealing with the South. He also wrote book reviews and travel articles for *Saturday Review, Reader's Digest, The New York Times,* and *National Geographic.* He was a native of New Orleans and a 1931 graduate of Tulane University.

(*New York Times*, 14 September 1984, B5). *See* entry 188.

Karig, Walter (1898-September 30, 1956)

After studying art, the serving in World War I, Karig worked as a journalist with *The Newark (N.J.) Evening News* from 1921-1942. He was employed as both a writer and artist and was sent to Washington to head the newspaper's bureau there in 1933, a position in which he remained until becoming a lieutenant commander in the U.S. Naval Reserve in 1942. During the war, he performed convoy duty in the Mediterranean, served with the commander in chief of the Pacific Fleet, and was press aide to Fleet Admiral Chester Nimitz after the war. He retired from the service in 1948 and went on to co-author a multi-volume history of the U.S. Navy in World War II and serve as technical director for the television series *Victory at Sea,* based on his work and produced by the National Broadcasting Company. He was also the author of a wide range of fiction.

(*New York Times*, 1 October 1956, 27). *See* entry 189.

Karp, David (May 5, 1922-September 1, 1999)

A graduate of City College (now part of the City University of New York), Karp served in the U.S. Army during World War II in the Pacific theater. Beginning in 1950, he worked as a television and film producer and produced award-winning scripts for television series. He also wrote fourteen novels.

(*New York Times*, 20 September 1999, A15). *See* entry 190.

Keats, Charles B. (July 21, 1905-February 1978)

Keats held positions in Connecticut state government, including secretary of state (1953-1955), as well as being the author of six novels published between 1955 and 1973.

(*Contemporary Authors Online,* New York: Gale Group, 2001, accessed, 4 March 2005). *See* entry 191.

Keenan, Henry Francis (1850-1928)

Born in Rochester, New York, Keenan wrote several novels. However, he is best known for *The Money-Makers* (D. Appleton, 1885), a work he published anonymously as an attack on corporate business.

(Vincent Benet, *Reader's Encyclopedia of American Literature,* New York: Harper-Collins, 1991, s.v. "Keenan, Henry Francis"). *See* entry 192.

Kennelly, Ardyth. (1892-January 19, 2005)

See entry 193.

Keyes, Frances Parkinson (1885-July 3, 1970)

Keyes' girlhood was spent on Beacon Street during the winter social season and during the rest of the year at a family house in Newbury, Vermont, and traveling in the United States and abroad. She was educated in fashionable private schools and completed her education with studies in Geneva and Berlin. In 1903, at age eighteen, she married Henry Wilder Keyes, a man from her social circle, who became governor of New Hampshire and served in the U.S. Senate from 1919 to 1937. Keyes was a great social success in Washington during the 1920s and 1930s, and she wrote about her experiences in *Letters from a Senator's Wife* (D. Appleton, 1924) and *Capital Kaleidoscope* (Harper, 1937). She published her first novel, *The Old Gray Homestead* (Houghton Mifflin), in 1919 and in 1923 became a contributing editor for *Good Housekeeping Magazine,* eventually authoring a monthly column describing her travels. She continued to publish books until a few years before her death, completing more than fifty in her lifetime, among them several titles that sold over a million copies.

(*New York Times,* 4 July 1970, 21). *See* entries 194, 195, 196, 197.

Knebel, Fletcher (1912-1993)

Knebel had a long and successful career as a journalist before writing his first novel. Educated at Miami University of Ohio, he worked for newspapers in Pennsylvania, Tennessee, and Ohio before moving to Washington in 1936 as a correspondent to *The Cleveland Plain Dealer.*

He served in the U.S. Navy during World War II, returning to journalism after the war. The daily column "Potomac Fever" that he began in 1951 for Cowles Communications was nationally syndicated and appeared for the next thirteen years. In 1962, a book he co-authored with Charles W. Bailey, II, *Seven Days in May,* was published by Harper and Row. A great success, the novel was released as a movie in 1964 (Warner Brothers), starring Kirk Douglas, Burt Lancaster, and Fredric March. He afterward wrote thirteen more books and had lifetime sales figures of over six million copies. An advocate of the legalization of marijuana, he was also a member of the Hemlock Society. Suffering from a heart condition and lung cancer, he took his own life in 1993. (*New York Times,* 28 February 1993). *See* entries 198, 199, 200.

Knowland, Helen (née Herrick) (c. 1907-1981)
The author married her grade-school sweetheart, William Fife Knowland (1908-1974), the son of a wealthy California politician, businessman, and owner of the *Oakland (CA) Tribune.* During the course of their marriage each had long-standing affairs (in addition to three children), and the plot for Knowland's book was drawn from her real-life experience.
(Gayle B. Montgomery and James W. Johnson. *One Step from the White House: The Rise and Fall of Senator William F. Knowland.* Berkeley: University of California Press, 1998). *See* entry 201.

Lasalle, Mrs. E. L.
See entry 202.

Laselle, Mrs. Nancy Polk
See entries 203, 204.

Leighton, Frances Spatz (c.1930-?)
Leighton was a nationally known journalist before she began writing books. An Ohioan who attended Ohio State University, she began covering Washington in 1950 as a feature writer for the Metro Group Syndicate. She is best known, however, as a ghostwriter, particularly for White House insiders. Her first book, *White House Chef* (Putnam, 1957), detailed the experiences of François Rysavy, chef to the Eisenhowers. Perhaps her most successful work was *My Thirty Years Backstairs at the White House* (Prentice-Hall, 1978), the story of Lillian Rogers Parks, a maid and seamstress.
(*Contemporary Authors Online,* New York: Gale Group, 2001, accessed, 8 March 2005). *See* entries 205, 206.

Levy, Lewis [Stonewall, Cutter, pseud.]
    See entry 207.

Lewis, Alfred Henry (January 20, 1857-December 24, 1914)
    At various times an attorney and itinerant cowboy, Lewis' writing
career took off after his brother, who was city editor of the *Kansas City
Times,* allowed him to publish an imaginary interview with an old cat-
tleman. The story was widely reprinted, and Lewis began working for
the *Kansas City (Mo.) Star* and was soon hired as Washington correspondent of the *Chicago Times.* In 1894, he became head of William
Randolph Hearst's Washington bureau. Lewis' position in the Hearst
organization was soon considerable, since he attained a well-earned
reputation for yellow journalism and character assassination during
political campaigns. In 1898, he moved to New York City and became
a full-time freelance writer of book-length fiction and collections of
short stories, as well as articles for newspapers and magazines. By the
end of his life, he had published eighteen books.
(New York Times, 24 December 1914, 9). *See* entries 208, 209.

Lincoln, Jeanie (Thomas) Gould (February 13, 1846-August 8, 1921)
    Lincoln was born in Troy, New York, and was the author of poems
and novels. She was the wife of Dr. Nathan S. Lincoln, White House
physician during the Garfield administration and mother of Natalie
Sumner Lincoln.
(New York Times, 1 September 1935, 18). *See* entries 210, 211, 212.

Lincoln, Natalie Sumner (October 4, 1881-August 31, 1935)
    Born in Washington, Lincoln was the daughter of Dr. Nathan S.
Lincoln, a Union Civil War officer and a White House physician during
the Garfield administration. Her mother was Jeanie Gould Lincoln, and
her brother, G. Gould Lincoln, was a journalist for *The Washington
(D.C.) Star.* Lincoln was the author of twenty-two mystery and detective novels. She also served as the editor of the *The Daughters of the
American Revolution Magazine* for over twenty years. She lived at
3104 Hawthorne Street, NW.
(New York Times, 1 September 1935, 18). *See* entries 213, 214, 215,
216, 217, 218, 219, 220, 221, 222.

Lipton, Lew (1893-1961)
    See entry 223.

Litchfield, Grace Denio (November 19, 1849-December 4, 1944)
    A prolific writer of poetry and novels, Litchfield was born in Brooklyn. The daughter of a successful attorney, she was privately tutored at home and in Europe, spending much of her early life abroad, between seasonal trips to the United States. After her father's death in 1882, she lived continuously in Europe until 1888. Although she began writing at an early age, her first novel, *Only an Incident* (Putnam's), was not published until 1883. From approximately 1894 until her death fifty years later she was a resident of Washington, D.C., and summered at her house on Lake Minnewaska (New York).
    (*New York Times*, 5 December 1944, 23). *See* entry 224.

Lockling, Lydia Waldo
    See entry 225.

Longstreet, Stephen [Burton, Thomas, pseud.] (April 18, 1907-February 20, 2002)
    The prolific author of more than one hundred novels, plays, screenplays, and works of non-fiction, Longstreet was also a painter and art critic. While studying painting in Berlin, London, Paris, and Rome as a young man, he became acquainted with Picasso, Gertrude Stein, James Joyce, and Ernest Hemingway. In addition to his career as an artist, he wrote for the radio shows of Bob Hope and Rudy Vallee and authored screenplays, most notably *The Jolson Story* (Columbia, 1949) and *The Greatest Show on Earth* (Paramount, 1952) for which he received an Oscar nomination.
    (*Contemporary Authors Online*, New York: Gale Group, 2004, accessed, 8 March 2005). *See* entry 226.

Loring, Emilie Baker (1864?-March 13, 1951)
    Loring was descended from a literary, Boston family. *The American Eagle,* predecessor of the *The Boston Herald,* was founded by her grandfather, George Melville Baker. She published her first stories under the name "Josephine Story" and went on to write a total of thirty romance novels.
    (*New York Times*, 15 March 1951, 29). *See* entries 227, 228.

Low, Alfred Maurice, Sir (1860-June 17, 1929)
    Low was born in London and educated at King's College, Oxford. He subsequently studied in Austria and completed a master's degree at Dartmouth College. He worked as a journalist, beginning his career with *The Boston Globe,* for which he served as a war correspondent

during the Spanish-American War. He was later the Washington correspondent for *The London Daily Chronicle* and then worked for many years as the chief American correspondent for *The London Morning Post*. The United States Department of Labor hired him to investigate some aspects of British labor legislation in 1900, and he later investigated English trade unions. In addition to the many articles he wrote, he published books on the United States and Britain. He was knighted in Great Britain, Belgium (the Order of Leopold), Japan (Imperial Order of the Rising Sun), and Greece (Order of the Redeemer).
(*New York Times*, 18 June 1929, 28). *See* entry 229.

Lowe, Samuel E[dward] [Hart, Helen, pseud.] (1884-?)
    See entry 230.

Ludlow, Louis (Leon) (June 24, 1873-November 28, 1950)
    Born and educated in Indiana, Ludlow became a reporter after graduating from high school, eventually specializing in political coverage in Indianapolis. He moved to Washington as a correspondent for Indiana and Ohio newspapers and was a member of the Congressional Press Galleries from 1901 to 1929. In 1929 he was elected to the U.S. Congress as representative from Indiana and was re-elected to serve until 1949 when he did not stand for re-election. Returning to journalism, he continued to live in Washington until his death.
(U.S. Congress, *Biographical Directory of the United States Congress, 1774 to the Present*, http://bioguide.congress.gov, accessed, 6 October 2005). *See* entry 231.

MacGrath, Harold (September 4, 1871-October 30, 1932)
    MacGrath was born in Syracuse, New York, and spent much of his life there. Educated in public schools in the city, he began working as a reporter with *The Syracuse Herald,* and later as a columnist for *The Chicago Evening Mail*. However, the success of his novels *Arms and the Woman* (Doubleday & McClure, 1899), *The Puppet Crown* (Bowen-Merrill, 1901), and *The Man on the Box* (Bobbs-Merrill, 1904) meant he could devote himself full time to writing popular fiction, a career that he found very lucrative. In addition to time at his residence in Syracuse, MacGrath spent part of each year in a villa he owned on Lake Como and enjoyed extensive foreign travel.
(*New York Times*, 30 October 1932, 37). *See* entry 232.

Mackie, Pauline Bradford, *see* Hopkins, Pauline Bradford (Mackie)

Magruder, Julia (1854-1907)

A niece of Confederate General John Bankhead Magruder, the author's family moved to Washington in 1857, and she maintained a residence there during the rest of her life. Although she received a very traditional Southern upbringing and embraced its ideals, she took an interest in writing at an early age and successfully pursued this career. Several of her novels received a great deal of attention. Much of her magazine writing consisted of short stories, but she also wrote articles on the social position of women and child labor issues. All of her writing is directed at a female audience, dealing most often with romantic themes. Shortly before her death, she was awarded the *Order of the Palm* by the French Academy.

(*Dictionary of American Biography*, s.v. "Magruder, Julia"). *See* entry 233.

Malloy, John Edward
See entry 234.

Maltz, Albert (October 28, 1908-April 26, 1985)

Maltz, educated at Columbia University and Yale's School of Drama, is known as a writer of proletarian literature, focusing on the victims of the Depression, the plight of the working poor, and the effects of racial discrimination. He achieved early recognition for his short fiction, novels, and screenplays and won two Academy Awards in the 1940s. His outspoken political views and long membership in the Communist Party brought him before the House Committee on Un-American Activities as one of the Hollywood Ten. Cited for contempt of Congress in 1947, he was sentenced to one year in federal prison. After serving his sentence, he immediately moved to Cuernavaca, Mexico, where he continued to write. He returned to the United States in 1962 and received wide attention for his screenplay for *Two Mules for Sister Sara* (Universal, 1970) and published well-received novels and short stories.

(*Dictionary of Literary Biography*, vol. 102, s.v. "Maltz, Albert"). *See* entry 235.

Malvern, Gladys (?-1962)

The author of more than forty-six books for children published between 1931 and 1969, Malvern was also an actress and advertising manager.

(*Contemporary Authors Online*, New York: Gale Group, 2002, accessed, 9 March 2005). *See* entry 236.

Mazor, Julian (1929-?)
A native of Baltimore and Washington, D.C., and graduate of
Yale, Mazor's stories have appeared in the *New Yorker* and *Shenan-
doah.*
See entry 237.

McAdoo, Eleanor Randolph Wilson (1890-April 5, 1967)
The second daughter of Woodrow Wilson, McAdoo was known
for her life-long dedication to his philosophies of liberalism and inter-
nationalism. She was the focus of national attention when she married
William Gibbs McAdoo in a White House wedding in 1914. At the
time, McAdoo, fifty-years-old, a grandfather and widower, was the
secretary of the Treasury. She divorced McAdoo, then a senator, in
1934, charging mental cruelty, and lived most of the rest of her life in
Los Angeles. Although she stayed out of the public eye as much as
possible, she sometimes permitted interviews and wrote magazine articles. Two books, *The Woodrow Wilsons* (MacMillan, 1937) and *The
Priceless Gift: The Love Letters of Woodrow Wilson and Ellen Axson
Wilson* (MacGraw-Hill, 1962), were attempts to preserve the memory
of her father.
(*New York Times*, 7 April 1967, 37). *See* entry 238.

McCutcheon, John T. (May 6, 1870-June 10, 1949)
Born and educated in Indiana at Purdue University (Lafayette,
Ind.) he began his career as a political cartoonist in 1889 at the *Chicago
Record* and continued working for its successor *The Record Herald.*
His cartoons first received national attention during the 1896 presidential race. He was a foreign correspondent during the Spanish-American
War, Philippine Rebellion, and Boer War. When he returned to the
United States in 1903, he joined the staff of *The Chicago Tribune* for
whom he traveled in Crimea, the Caucasus, Persia, Russia, and Turke-
stan. He later traveled with Theodore Roosevelt's African safari, covered the early parts of World War I from the trenches with the Belgian
and German armies, and reported from the Gobi Desert in the 1920s. In
1931, one of McCutcheon's cartoons won the Pulitzer Prize. In addition
to political subjects, he drew popular cartoons capturing Hoosier common sense and humor.
(*New York Times*, 10 June 1949, 17). *See* entry 239.

McGerr, Patricia (December 26, 1917-May 11, 1985)
McGerr developed a reputation for creating innovative mysteries
with unexpected focuses, such as searching for the victim, rather than

the murderer. In addition to novels, she frequently contributed book reviews and short stories to *This Week* and *Ellery Queen's Mystery Magazine*. Born in Falls City, Nebraska, she was educated at Trinity College (Washington, D.C.), the University of Nebraska, and Columbia University, where she received a master's degree in 1937. In addition to writing, she worked as an editor and beginning in 1960 and for many years afterward was a consultant and lecturer at the Georgetown University Writers' Conference.
(*Contemporary Authors Online*, New York: Gale Group, 2003, accessed, 9 March 2005). *See* entry 240.

McLaughlin, Nathan Monroe
    See entry 241.

McLaws, (Emily) Lafayette
    Lafayette was born in Augusta, Georgia, the daughter of A. H. McLaws (1823-1901) and the niece of Confederate General Lafayette McLaws (1821-1907).
(Stanley Kunitz and Howard Haycraft, eds., *Twentieth Century Authors, a Biographical Dictionary of Modern Literature*, New York: H. W. Wilson, 1942, s.v. "McLaws, Emily"). *See* entry 242.
Medora, Marie
    See entry 243.

Mellett, Berthe K[natvold] (?-1936)
    Born in Tacoma, Washington, Mellett spent her childhood on the Alaskan frontier during the gold rush. She met and married Lowell Mellett in 1914, while he was editor of the *Seattle Sun*. The couple lived in Washington, D.C., for many years, and Lowell became editor of the *Washington (D.C.) Daily News*. They resided at 3308 N Street, NW.
(*Washington Post*, 2 June 1936, 4). *See* entries 244, 245.

Mertz, Barbara (Gross) [Michaels, Barbara, pseud.] (September 29, 1927-?)
    Mertz has written more than fifty novels of mystery and suspense under the pseudonyms Barbara Michaels and Elizabeth Peters. Born in Canton, Illinois, she obtained her entire education at the University of Chicago, culminating with a doctorate in 1952. Like one of her characters, she is an Egyptologist and a member of such organizations as the Egypt Exploration Society and the society for the Study of Egyptian

Antiquities and serves on the Board of Governors of the American Research Center in Egypt.
(*Contemporary Authors Online*, New York: Thomson Gale, 2005, accessed, 9 June 2005). *See* entry 246.

Merwin, Samuel (1874-October 17, 1936)
	Born in Evanston, Illinois, and a graduate of Northwestern University, Merwin edited magazines, operated a playhouse, and wrote plays before he began attracting attention for his short stories and serialized fiction just before World War I. Initially, he used his work to advocate social upheaval to overturn the conservatism of Americans. He also was an outspoken proponent of women's suffrage, influenced, perhaps, by his aunt, Frances E. Willard. In the 1920s he reversed himself and was openly critical of an American society that had abandoned traditions and used the suffering of World War I as an excuse for embracing licentiousness. He railed, in particular, against flappers, whom he identified as the trivial product of the promising women's rights movement.
(*New York Times,* 18 October 1935, N8). *See* entry 247.

Michaels, Barbara, *see* Mertz, Barbara (Gross)

Miller, Merle (May 17, 1919-June 10, 1986)
	Although he wrote novels and screenplays, Miller was a journalist and worked as an editor with *Time* (1945), *Harper's* (1947-1949), and, during World War II, *Yank* (1941-1945). His historical works on Harry S. Truman, Lyndon Johnson, and Dwight D. Eisenhower received a great deal of attention for their evocative power stemming from personal interviews and anecdotes, although they were sometimes criticized by critics who believed his personalized approach resulted in shortcomings. Miller was educated at the University of Iowa (1935-1938; 1939-1940) and the London School of Economics and Political Science (1938-1939).
(*Contemporary Authors Online*, New York: Gale Group, 2003, accessed, 9 March 2005). *See* entry 248.

Miller, Mrs. Alexander McVeigh
	See entries 249, 250.

Mixon, Ada (c.1860-1946)
	See entry 251.

Moore, Olga (January 1900-January 9, 1981)
    Moore grew up in frontier Wyoming, the daughter of a man active
in state politics. A graduate of the University of Wyoming, she published a number of short stories before World War II and was a journalist during the war. A public relations specialist for food-related
industries, she also worked for almost twenty years with the U.S. Information Agency in Washington, D.C.
(*Contemporary Authors Online*, New York: Gale Group, 2003, accessed, 10 October 2005). *See* entry 252.

Morris, Charles
    See entry 253.

Morris, Willie (November 29, 1934-August 2, 1999)
    Author of more than nineteen books, Morris grew up in Jackson,
Mississippi. He received his bachelor's degree from the University of
Texas at Austin (1956), completed a Rhodes scholarship at Oxford
University (1956-1959), and lived in New York City for many years.
One of his first books, *North Toward Home* (Houghton, 1967), was a
well-received autobiography, published the year that he was appointed
the youngest editor in chief in the history of *Harper's*, the nation's oldest continuously published magazine. Both his fiction and documentary
writing focuses on the American South, and his non-fiction works often
deal with racism in the United States.
(*Contemporary Authors Online*, New York: Gale Group, 2001, accessed, 9 June 2005). *See* entry 254.

Morrow, Honoré Willsie (1880-1940)
    Morrow grew up in Ottumwa, Iowa, and was educated at the Uni-
versity of Wisconsin. After her graduation she went to live in Arizona,
gathering material for her writing. She published her first novel, *The
Heart of the Desert* (Frederick A. Stokes), in 1913. Other early novels
dealt with forest conservation, land reclamation, frontier settlement,
and the American Indian. She moved to New York City after two years
in Arizona, selling stories to magazines on themes similar to her novels,
but also writing about current social problems such as immigration and
divorce. In the 1920's she became increasingly critical of American
culture, calling her fellow citizens to re-dedicate themselves to the religious faith and pioneer ideals of their ancestors. In 1922 she divorced
her husband, Henry Elmer Willsie and in 1923 married the publisher
William Morrow. The work for which she is still known is her trilogy
of novels on Abraham Lincoln, though she also wrote biographies of

Bronson Alcott, Mary Todd Lincoln, John Gough, and Adoniram Judson.
(*New York Times,* 13 April 1940, 22). *See* entries 255, 256, 257, 258.

Murray, Charles Theodore (1843-?)
    Murray was a journalist and a novelist. Born in Goshen, Indiana, he was one of the founders of the Gridiron Club in 1885.
(Stanley Kunitz and Howard Haycraft, eds., *Twentieth Century Authors, a Biographical Dictionary of Modern Literature,* New York: H. W. Wilson, 1942, s.v. "Murray, Charles Theodore"). *See* entry 259.

Neill, Esther W[aggaman] (1873-?)
    Neill was born in Washington, D.C., into the Waggaman family, which had a long history in the city. She had relatives who were congressmen and Waggaman family businesses included realty operations with significant landholdings. She married Charles P. Neill (1865-1942) in 1901. He was a professor of economics at The Catholic University (Washington, D.C.) and received important presidential appointments, including an investigation of the meat-packing industry that inspired Upton Sinclair to write *The Jungle.*
(Finding Aid for the Charles Patrick Neill Papers. The Catholic University of America. American Catholic History Research Center and University Archives). *See* entry 260.

Nichols, Laura D.
    See entry 261.

Nirdlinger, Charles Frederick (c.1863-May 13, 1940)
    Born in Fort Wayne, Indiana, and an 1883 graduate of Harvard College, Nirdlinger wrote several successful plays, including *Madame Pompadour, The World and His Wife,* and *The First Lady.* He worked as a drama critic for the *New York Herald* and was an editor of *The Illustrated American Magazine.*
(*New York Times,* 14 May 1940, 30). *See* entry 90.

Noble, Hollister (1900-1954)
    Much of Noble's career was spent in New York City as a journalist and publicist. Born in Auburn, New York, he began studying at the United States Naval Academy and served in the Marine Corps in World War I and in the Office of War Information in World War II. In New York, he worked as the editor of *Musical America* magazine and for Columbia Broadcasting. After World War II he worked in Hollywood

as a screenwriter. He was the author of several novels, receiving most attention for *Woman with a Sword* (Doubleday, 1948), a recreation of the life of Anne Ella Carroll. Depressed after the death of close friend Alexander Marx, a motion picture actor, he committed suicide by methods paralleling a scene from his last novel, *One Way to Eldorado* (Doubleday, 1954).
(*New York Times*, 21 July 1954, 15). *See* entry 262.

Parker, Maude, *see* Pavenstedt, Mrs. Edmund Maude

Pavenstedt, Mrs. Edmund Maude (née Parker) [Parker, Maud, pseud.] (?-November 13, 1959)
    After a childhood spent in Galveston, Texas, Pavenstedt studied at the University of Wisconsin. She began writing at an early age and was first published in H. L. Mencken's *The Smart Set*. She married Richard Washburn Child, who was later Ambassador to Italy. She used her experiences as a witness to the rise of Mussolini to publish a series of articles in *The Saturday Evening Post* in 1930. Most of her ten books, however, were mystery novels, published under her maiden name, Maude Parker. She divorced Child in 1931 and subsequently married New York lawyer Edmund W. Pavenstedt.
(*New York Times*, 13 November 1959, 29). *See* entry 263.

Paynter, John H. (1862-1947)
    After serving in the US Navy, Paynter worked as a Treasury Department clerk and a land developer. He was chairman of the board of the directors of the Universal Development Land Company, the firm that created Suburban Gardens amusement park in the Washington suburb of Deanwood. At the time of his death, he resided at 701 51st Street, NE.
(Marya Annette McQuirter, "Claiming the City: African Americans, Urbanization and Leisure in Washington, D.C., 1902-1954," Ph.D. dissertation, University of Michigan, 2000, 136-137). *See* entry 264.

Pearson, Drew (December 13, 1897-September 1, 1969)
    Pearson commanded a national audience for thirty-six years through his syndicated newspaper column, "Washington Merry-Go-Round." He joined the staff of *The Baltimore Sun* in 1929, later heading its Washington bureau. While he was in Washington he married Countess Felicia Gizcka, daughter of Cissy Patterson, publisher of *The Washington Post*, though the marriage ended in divorce and Pearson remarried. His column, originally co-authored with Robert S. Allen

(chief of *The Christian Science Monitor* Washington bureau), got
started after the two anonymously published a book entitled *Washington Merry-Go-Round*, which contained material about the Hoover administration that neither man would be able to get his own newspaper
to publish. When they published another volume their identities were
disclosed and each was fired by his newspaper. They then began the
column, which Pearson later authored by himself and still later was
joined by Jack Anderson.
(*New York Times*, 2 September 1969, 1). *See* entry 265.

Pendleton, Don (1928-1995)
   Pendleton had no formal education. Born in Little Rock, Arkansas,
he enlisted in the Navy when he was fourteen years old. In 1957, he
enrolled in a mail order writing course and published a book before he
completed the program. Although he began writing full time when he
was forty, producing a few mysteries and science fiction books each
year, his breakthrough came when he wrote the first book featuring
Mack Boland, "The Executioner," who battled the Mafia. With the
book and the thirty-seven that followed, he has been credited with creating the action-adventure genre.
(*New York Times,* 28 October 1995, 50). *See* entry 266.

Perry, Eleanor [Bayer, Oliver Weld, pseud.] (1925-1981)
   Perry achieved great success as a screenwriter, both on her own
and with scripts she co-authored with her second husband Frank Perry.
She was known as one of the first feminist voices in the movie industry, as well as for her knowledgeable portrayals of the mentally ill.
Born Eleanor Rosenfield in Cleveland, Ohio, she received a master's
degree in psychiatric social work from Western Reserve University
before embarking on her writing career. With her first husband, Leo
Bayer, she wrote several plays, as well as thrillers. The couple published the latter under the name Oliver Weld Bayer.
(*New York Times*, 17 March 1981, B14). *See* entry 267.

Peterson, Bettina (June 19, 1910-July 2, 1994)
   Peterson worked as an editor at Ives Washburn, Inc., a firm that
specialized in children's books. Between 1959 and 1962 she authored
or co-authored four books, mostly focused on holidays, for Washburn.
(*New York Times*, 1 February 1968, 34). *See* entry 268.

Philips, Melville
   See entry 269.

Philips, Page
See entry 270.

Phillips, David Graham (October 31, 1867-1911)
An 1887 graduate of Princeton University, Phillips began his career as a newspaperman in Cincinnati and, in 1890, while quite young, was hired by Charles A. Dana to work on the staff of the *New York Sun*. Through his work at the *Sun*, opinion pieces for magazines, and his later work for the *New York World* he exposed corruption of all kinds and crusaded against poverty and disease. After the 1901 success of his pseudonymous novel *The Great God Success* (published under the name John Graham by Stokes), he resigned from the *World* in 1902 to devote himself to fiction as a more effective way of advocating his reform agenda. His exposé *The Treason of the Senate,* published as a series in *Cosmopolitan* in 1906, earned him Theodore Roosevelt's epithet "Man with the Muck-Rake." Eventually publishing more than twenty-five novels with average sales of one hundred thousand copies each, Phillips assailed the evils of great wealth and the political influence it bought, as well as calling for the enfranchisement of women. Phillips was mortally wounded when Fitzhugh Coyle Goldsmith, a Washingtonian who had become obsessed by the idea that the Goldsmith family had been maligned in Phillip's novels, shot him.
(*Dictionary of Literary Biography*, vol. 303, s.v. "Phillips, David Graham"). *See* entries 271, 272, 273, 274, 275.

Pierce, Gilbert A[shville] (January 11, 1839-February 15, 1901)
Born in Cattaraugus County, New York, Pierce moved with his family to the Indiana frontier in 1854. He attended the University of Chicago Law School for two years before enlisting with the Ninth Indiana Regiment at the beginning of the Civil War. After he was mustered out with the rank of colonel, he read law, was admitted to the bar, and began practice in Valparaiso in 1865. He was elected to the Indiana House of Representatives in 1869 and served as assistant financial clerk of the United States Senate from 1869 to 1871. From 1871 to 1883, he was managing editor of *The Chicago (Ill.) Inter Ocean,* leaving the newspaper to become the Territorial governor of Dakota, a post he filled from 1884 to 1886. He continued to work as a journalist on the editorial staff of *The Chicago(Ill.) News.* He served one term as U.S. senator from North Dakota (1889 to 1891). When he was not reelected, he purchased the *Minneapolis (Minn.) Tribune* and became editor in chief in 1891. He briefly served as Minister to Portugal, start-

ing in 1893, but was forced to resign due to ill health and lived the rest of his life in retirement. In addition to novels, he wrote several plays. (*New York Times*, 16 February 1901, 7). *See* entry 276.

Pierson, Eleanor
  See entry 277.

Plum, Mary
  See entry 278, 279.

Popham, William Lee (April 14, 1885-?)
  Born in Hardin County, Kentucky, Popham won early fame when he began appearing on the lecture circuit as a seventeen year old. The "boy lecturer" soon began publishing poetry, as well. He eventually wrote eight books of poetry and two novels. Toward the end of the first decade of the twentieth century he became a real estate promoter on St. George Island off the coast of Florida and built successful businesses, including a hotel, restaurant, and oyster-processing firm.
(Maude Miller Ester, *Love Poems and the Boyhood of Kentucky's Poet*, Louisville, Ky., s.n., 1910). *See* entry 280.

Porter, Duval [Slick, Sam, Jr., pseud.] (1844-?)
  Born in Appomattox County, Virginia, Porter began writing at an early age and started supplying stories to local newspapers when he was fourteen. His devotion to the antebellum South is indicated by the fact that one of his volumes of poetry is entitled *Lyrics of the Lost Cause* (J. T. Townes, 1914).
(Poetry and Music of the War Between the States, Official Web Site, http://civilwarpoetry .org, accessed, 11 November 2005). *See* entry 281.

Price, William
  See entry 282.

Ragan, Emily Lee Sherwood (1839-?)
  See entry 283.

Raphael, Chaim [Davey, Jocelyn, pseud.] (1908-1994)
  Raphael's career included work as a lecturer at Oxford in the 1930s, writing detective novels published under the name Jocelyn Davey, and holding senior posts in the British government. He was born in Middlesbrough, northern England, and was educated at Oxford. He did not begin writing detective fiction until the mid-1950s when he

first introduced the character of Ambrose Usher, an Oxford don, who is utilized by the British Foreign Office for undercover assignments. He ended his working life as the chief information officer at the British Treasury from 1957 to 1968. In 1951 he was awarded the Order of the British Empire and in 1965 was made a Commander of the Order of the British Empire.
(*New York Times*, 13 October 1994, B15). *See* entry 284.

Reed, Sarah Ann (March 16, 1838-April 21, 1934)
    See entry 285.

Rennert, Maggie (February 11, 1922-?)
    Born in New York City, while living in Washington Rennert studied political science and journalism and worked as a reporter for a Washington news service. For many years she was a book reviewer and poet, publishing in the *Boston Globe, Washington Post, Saturday Review,* and poetry magazines. After she was widowed, she emigrated to Israel, writing about her experiences in *Shelanu: An Israel Journal* (Prentice-Hall), published in 1979.
(*Contemporary Authors Online*, New York: Gale Group, 2001, accessed, 9 March 2005). *See* entry 286.

Revell, Louisa [pseud.], *see* Smith, Ellen Hart

Riddle, Albert Gallatin (May 28, 1816-May 16, 1902)
    Riddle grew up in Ohio Western Reserve, completing all of his studies locally, and was admitted to the bar in 1840. He served as prosecuting attorney of Geauga County from 1840 to 1846 and was elected to the Ohio House of Representatives for one term (1848-1850), after which he moved to Cleveland, Ohio, in 1856. He later served one term in the U.S. House of Representatives, (March 4, 1861-March 3, 1863) and was consul to Matanzas, Cuba, from 1863 to 1864. He returned to Washington where he practiced law and was one of the federal prosecutors in the John H. Surratt trial. From 1877 to 1889 he was a law officer of the District of Columbia, where he continued to live until his death.
(U.S. Congress, *Biographical Directory of the United States Congress, 1774 to the Present,* http://bioguide.congress.gov, accessed, 12 November 2005). *See* entry 287.

Rinehart, Mary Roberts (August 12, 1876-September 23, 1958)

A highly prolific author, Rinehart produced a book per year for more than forty years. Although she wrote plays, short stories, and humorous essays, she was best known for her mystery novels, which helped to establish the genre. Two of her most successful crime stories were published as serials in *Munsey's Magazine*. Released as books, *The Circular Staircase* (Review of Reviews, 1908) and *The Man in Lower Ten* (Bobbs-Merrill, 1909) remained in print for the next forty years. After her husband's death in 1922, she moved to Washington and lived there for ten years, until 1932, when she moved to New York City, where her two oldest sons had formed the publishing firm Farrar & Rinehart. Rinehart, in addition to being the firm's most productive author, was on the board of directors.

(*New York Times*, 23 September 1958, 1). *See* entry 288.

Rohlfs, Anna Katherine Green, *see* Green, Anna Katherine

Rollins, Montgomery (1867-April 19, 1918)

A native of Concord, New Hampshire, in his youth Rollins began working as a clerk in the banking firm E. H. Rollins & Company founded by his father, Edward Henry Rollins, who served in the U.S. Congress from 1861 to 1867 and in the Senate from 1877 to 1883 and was a secretary and treasurer of the Union Pacific Railroad. Rollins, the son, directed a Boston incarnation of the firm E. H. Rollins & Sons from 1890 to 1899, before founding his own banking house, Montgomery Rollins & Company. Rollins authored several books on bonds, stocks, and other forms of investments. Late in his life, however, he wrote one novel, *The Village Pest* (Lothrop, Lee & Shepard, 1917), which is a fictionalized account of his youth.

(*New York Times*, 19 April 1918, 13). *See* entry 289.

Roosevelt, Alice (1906-1975)

See entry 290.

Roosevelt, Eleanor (October 11, 1884-November 7, 1962)

The wife of Franklin Delano Roosevelt and First Lady from 1933 until 1945, Roosevelt was one of America's most respected women and an outspoken advocate of human rights.

(The White House, Official Web Site, http://www.whitehouse.gov, s.v. "Roosevelt, Anna Eleanor"). *See* entry 291.

Roudybush, Alexandra (Brown) (March 14, 1911-?)

The daughter of Constantine, a journalist, and Ethel (Wheeler) Brown, Roudybush was born in Hyeres, Cote d'Azur. She was educated at the London School of Economics and Political Science where she earned a bachelor's degree in 1929. In 1941, she married Franklin Roudybush, an American diplomat, and lived with him during postings to Dublin, Pakistan, Paris, Saarland, and Strasbourg. She has worked as a journalist or administrative assistant with *London Evening Standard, Time,* Columbia Broadcasting System, Mutual Broadcasting System, and the National Academy of Science.

(*Contemporary Authors Online*, New York: Gale Group, 2002, accessed, 9 March 2005). *See* entry 292.

Runbeck, Margaret Lee (1905-1956)
See entry 293.

Schindel, Isa Urquhart Glenn, *see* Glenn, Isa

Sanborn, Mary Farley (1853-?)
See entry 294.

Schneider, Martha Lemon (1856-1938?)

Martha Lemon, who was born and raised in Washington, married Charles W. Schneider of New York. When she was widowed at age forty-five, she began a twenty-year career at the New York Public Library.

(Finding Aid. Lemon Family Papers. Historical Society Washington, D.C.). *See* entry 295.

Scott, John Reed (September 8, 1869-?)
See entries 296, 297, 298.

Seawell, Molly Elliot (1860-1919) [Davis, Foxcroft, pseud.]

Seawell was born and raised on a plantation in Gloucester County, Virginia. Her mother was a Baltimore native, and her lawyer father was a nephew of President Tyler. Most of her writing was inspired by her childhood in the Tidewater region of the Chesapeake Bay and by stories she heard from a seafaring uncle who lived with her family. She was educated at home and schooled in the running of a plantation household. After the death of her father in the 1880s, however, she and her mother moved to town, living first in Norfolk and then Washington, where Seawell would spend the remainder of her life. Her house became a meeting place for artists and writers. In addition to writing novels and biographies, she contributed essays, political commentary, and stories to magazines and newspapers. Her opposition to woman's suffrage was a frequent subject of her political writings.

(*Dictionary of American Biography*, s.v. "Seawell, Molly Elliott"). *See* entries 299, 300, 301.

Seifert, Shirley (1888-1971)
    Known for the careful research on which her historical fiction was based, Seifert often chose to dramatize important figures, such as Ulysses S. Grant, Jefferson Davis, and George Rogers Clark. However, she also told the stories of now-forgotten Americans, focusing in all of her work on Kentucky and Missouri. She was born in St. Peters, Missouri, and graduated from Washington University in St. Louis with majors in classical and modern languages. After working for a time as a teacher, she took courses in journalism and began writing. She published her first short story in 1919.
(*New York Times*, 4 September 1971, 24). *See* entries 302, 303.

Seton, Anya (January 23, 1906-November 8, 1990)
    Seton was the daughter of Grace Gallatin—a well-known English artist, naturalist, and author of travel accounts—and author Ernest Thompson Seton. She was born in Manhattan and raised on the Cos Cob estate of her family. Primarily schooled by tutors, she was awarded a diploma by the Spence School. Her first book, *My Theodosia* (Houghton Mifflin Company, 1941), about Theodosia Burr, received critical praise and a warm public response for the qualities that characterized the rest of her books: careful research, evocative power, and accurate portrayals of language and ways of life. Several of her other novels were made into movies, notably *Dragonwyck* about an 1840s Hudson River manor, starring Vincent Price (20th Century Fox, 1946), and *Foxfire* about an Arizona ghost town, starring Jane Russell (Universal, 1955). In her later work she returned to writing biographical novels about women.
(*New York Times*, 10 November 1990, 29). *See* entry 304.

Shackelford, Harvey King [pseud.], *see* Standish, Hal

Slick, Sam, Jr. [pseud.], *see* Porter, Duval

Smith, Ellen Hart [Revell, Louisa, pseud.]
    See entry 305.

Smith, Margaret Bayard (1778-1844)

Smith married her second cousin, Samuel Harrison Smith, who became Thomas Jefferson's political editor soon after the marriage. Her husband's position put her at the center of Washington society. She was well adapted to the role, becoming noted for her charm as a hostess and for her intelligent conversation. Perhaps surprisingly for a woman of privilege, she raised her own four children, baked bread, and churned butter. Her reputation as an author was established in her lifetime by her contributions to the most prestigious publications of the day and her several novels. Her letters were collected posthumously in *The First Forty Years of Washington Society* (edited by Gaillard Hunt, Scribner, 1906). Historians value this work, along with her Washington-based fiction, as social history.

(*American National Biography*, s.v. "Smith, Margaret Bayard"). *See* entry 306.

Smith, William Russell (?)

See entry 307.

Southworth, Mrs. E[mma] D[orothy] E[liza] N[evitte] (December 26, 1810-June 30, 1899)

Born in Washington, Emma Dorothy Eliza Nevitte Southworth, or "E.D.E.N" as she came to call herself, wrote more than sixty novels. Her father was Captain Charles Le Compte Nevitte, a middle-aged, moderately successful Alexandria businessman, and her mother was Susanna Wailes, who at the time of her marriage was fifteen years old. Nevitte died when Southworth was four years old, and, despite the elegant surroundings in which they lived, her family began to endure the financial hardship that would last throughout Emma's childhood. Immediately upon graduating from school at the age of sixteen, she began teaching in the Washington public school system. She married Frederick Hamilton Southworth in 1840 and moved with him to Prarie du Chien, Wisconsin. In 1844, she returned to Washington, pregnant and with a son, Richmond, but no husband. Identifying herself as a widow, she began teaching again and took up writing to supplement her income, submitting short stories to newspapers. Harper's published her first novel under the title *Retribution* in 1849. She received a generous contract from *The New York Ledger* in 1856 for exclusive rights to her novels, which were published in the newspaper in serial form. Some of her works were first printed in this form in *The Saturday Evening Post* and *The New York Ledger* before publication in book form. Her books consistently portrayed Southern life and customs and highlighted the

implications of the economic and legal subordination of women to men. With the exception of a few years during which she lived in Yonkers, she lived most of her life overlooking the Potomac, in her later years occupying Prospect Cottage in Georgetown.
(*Dictionary of Literary Biography*, vol. 239, s.v. "Southworth, E.D.E.N."). *See* entry 308.

Spofford, Harriet Prescott (April 3, 1835-August 14, 1921)
Born into a distinguished, but financially troubled family, in Calais, Maine, Spofford knew many hardships and began writing as a way of helping her family. By 1856, she was supporting her invalid parents and three sisters by publishing in Boston story papers. In 1859 she began publishing work in *The Atlantic Monthly*, which later collected and published her stories in book form (*The Amber Gods and Other Stories*, Ticknor & Fields, 1863). A sixty-year career followed, during which Spofford published thirty-two books. Wife of Richard S. Spofford, Jr., a Newburyport, Massachusetts, lawyer whose practice eventually flourished, the couple divided their time between Newburyport and Washington, D.C. Her *Old Washington* (Little, Brown, 1906) is based upon her first hand observations of Washington as it changed after the Civil War. By 1868, Spofford had become a frequent contributor to *Harper's Bazaar* and had developed a public which embraced her celebration of domesticity that in real life centered on her house on Deer Island, Massachusetts. After the death of her husband in 1888, Spofford became increasingly dependent upon a circle of Boston writers for social life and emotional support including Sarah Orne Jewett, Alice Brown, and Annie Adams Fields.
(*Dictionary of Literary Biography*, vol. 221, s.v. "Spofford, Harriet Prescott"). *See* entry 309.

Stacton, David (Derek) (April 25, 1925-January 19, 1968)
Born near Minden, Nevada, Stacton was educated at Stanford, the University of California, and the Stanford Radio and Television Institute. An author of twenty-six books during his brief life, Stacton focused on historical and biographical subjects, writing about characters and events that were unfamiliar to him. His focus on the individuality of his subjects, often eccentric or even insane, constituted a new approach in historical fiction.
(*Contemporary Authors Online*, New York: Gale Group, 2002, accessed, 15 December 2004). *See* entry 310.

Standish, Hal [Shackelford, Harvey King, pseud.]
See entry 311, 312.

Stanley, Caroline Abbot (1849-1919)
Widowed four years into her marriage and with her parents having died, Missouri native Stanley was left to raise her infant son on her own. She became a school teacher, working at that profession for eighteen years until her son graduated from college, when she turned to her real life's interest, writing.
(*New York Times*, 27 February 1904, BR144). *See* entry 313.

Starnes, Richard (July 4, 1922-?)
Born in Washington, D.C., Starnes had a long career as a journalist before writing fiction. Starting out in 1938 as a copy boy for Scripps-Howard Newspapers' *Washington Daily News*, he was promoted to reporter, and eventually managing editor. His career also included the position of managing editor for the *New York World-Telegram and Sun*, Washington correspondent for the Scripps-Howard chain, and writer of a syndicated column. After publishing several mystery novels, Starnes turned his focus to spy novels, developing the character Max Speed, a fictional journalist.
(*Contemporary Authors Online*, New York: Gale Group, 2003, accessed, 11 March 2005). *See* entries 314, 315, 316.

Stead, Christina (July 17, 1902-March 31, 1983)
An author of short stories, editor, and contributor to periodicals, Stead wrote more than fourteen books, mostly between 1930 and 1960. Although her life began and ended in Australia, she lived as an expatriate from 1928 to 1974, and her best known fiction explores American capitalist culture and post-war European (particularly English) culture. She was the wife of Wilhelm Blech (later anglicized to William Blake), an investment banker and Marxist whose views Stead embraced and through whom she met literary and intellectual leftists in Britain, Europe, and the United States, where the couple lived from 1937 to 1946. The couple experienced firsthand the dramatic shift of the United States' political climate and as the era of McCarthyism approached were subjected to FBI surveillance and harassment. Stead's reputation suffered and did not revive until the republication in 1965 of her novel *The Man Who Loved Children* (Angus & Robertson, 1978), which was championed by Randall Jarrell.
(*Dictionary of Literary Biography*, vol. 260, s.v. "Stead, Christina").
See entry 317.

Stoddard, William Osborn. [Jr.] (March 5, 1873-?)

Born in New York City, Stoddard was the son of William Osborn Stoddard (1835-1925), who was assistant private secretary to President Abraham Lincoln and a prolific author. In addition to several novels, Stoddard edited the memoirs of his father, which were published in 1955.

(Stanley Kunitz and Howard Haycraft, eds., *Twentieth Century Authors, a Biographical Dictionary of Modern Literature*, New York: H. W. Wilson, 1942, s.v. "Stoddard, William O., Jr."). *See* entry 318.

Stone, Grace Zaring (January 9, 1891-September 29, 1991)

Stone was the great-great-granddaughter of Englishman Robert Owen, founder of New Harmony, Indiana, a utopian community established as an expression of his theories focusing on reform and socialism. She got to know many of Owen's other descendants well because she was orphaned at birth and lived with relatives in serial fashion. She later attributed her interest in writing to the reflective, diary-keeping Owens. The wife of naval officer Ellis Stone, she lived with her husband for periods of time in Washington, D.C. She is, perhaps, best known for three of her books, all made into movies: *The Heaven and Earth of Doña Elena* (Bobbs-Merrill, 1929), *The Bitter Tea of General Yen* (Bobbs-Merrill, 1930), and *The Almond Tree* (Bobbs-Merrill, 1931). She began using the pen name Ethel Vance when she wrote *Escape* (Editor's Press Service, 1939), a novel of political espionage attacking the Nazis, because she and her husband were living in Paris at the time, where he was the United States naval attaché and her daughter Eleanor Perenyi had married a Czechoslovakian nobleman and was living in occupied Europe. Retiring to Stonington, Connecticut, she lived to be a centenarian.

(*New York Times,* 1 October 1991, D23). *See* entry 319.

Stone, Irving (July 14, 1903-1989)

Stone's many biographical novels were hailed for the documentary research behind them, even if historians sometimes disagreed with his interpretation of the lives about which he wrote.

(*New York Times,* 28 August 1989, B6). *See* entries 320, 321, 322, 323.

Stone, Thomas [pseud.], *see* Stonebraker, Florence

Stonebraker, Florence [Branch, Florenz; Stone, Thomas; pseuds.] (1896-?)

See entries 324, 325, 326.

Stonewall, Cutter, [pseud.], *see* Levy, Lewis

Strizzi, Michele Cristofora (1878-1948)
See entry 327.

Strong, Armour
See entry 328.

Strong, Charles S[tanley] [Bartlett, Nancy, pseud.] (1906-?)
Strong authored numerous books under more than eight pseudonyms.
See entry 329.

Sutton, Henry Sidney
See entry 330.

Tate, Allen (November 19, 1899-1979)
Tate was born in Kentucky in a family with long connections to the state, and his subject matter was drawn from his knowledge of the region and its inhabitants. He received a bachelor's degree from Vanderbilt University in 1923, spent most of his life as a college teacher, and published thirteen books of poetry and one novel.
(George Hemphill and Allen Tate, *American Writers*, vol. 4, New York: Scribner's Sons, 1974, 120-143). *See* entry 331.

Taylor, Mary Imlay (1878-August 28, 1938)
A long time resident of Washington, D.C., Taylor published her first book, *The Rebellion of the Princess* (McClure, Phillips, and Company), in 1903. She continued to write novels and short stories, mostly with romantic themes, up until 1927.
(*New York Times*, 29 August 1938, 13). *See* entry 332, 333.

Templeton, Timothy, [pseud.], *see* Adams, Charles.

Thomas, Katherine Elwes (1857-December 7, 1950)
Thomas grew up in Washington and lived there most of her adult life, working as a newspaper reporter for more than fifty years. She was the daughter of General George Comyns Thomas, who was commanding general of troops stationed in the District of Columbia throughout the Civil War. Her family had rich social connections and she was a personal acquaintance of every United States President from Ulysses S. Grant to Theodore Roosevelt. Her newspaper career was built on her

work for Washington-based publications, but she was also a correspondent for *The New York Times* and wrote the "Cholly Knickerbocker" column for *The New York American*. For the latter paper, she covered the social season in Newport, Rhode Island. In addition to books on diplomatic and official etiquette, she wrote an academic study of Mother Goose rhymes, *The Real Personages of Mother Goose* (Lothrop, Lee, Shepard, 1930), analyzing the political origins of the rhymes, and the Washington novel *Not All the King's Horses* (Cassell, 1896).
(New York Times, 9 December 1950, 15). *See* entry 334.

Thomas, Ross (Elmore) (February 19, 1926-December 18, 1995)
A native of Oklahoma, Thomas served in the Philippines during World War II and later graduated from the University of Oklahoma. He worked for a number of years in public relations, eventually founding his own firm. In addition, he was a federal political consultant from 1964 to 1966 before becoming a full-time freelance writer. Known for critically acclaimed works of political espionage, he wrote twenty-five novels and several screenplays.
(New York Times, 19 December 1995, B14). *See* entry 335.

Tibbetts, Edgar Alfred [Johnson, Ivar, pseud.] (1848-1908)
A clerk in the U.S. surgeon general's office, Tibbetts was fluent in ten languages and could translate ten additional languages into English. He was killed when his bicycle collided with a horse-drawn wagon while he was riding home from work.
(New York Times, 31 December 1997, C21). *See* entry 336.

Tilden, Freeman
See entry 337.

Toombs, Alfred Gerald (1912-1968)
Although he was born in Dallas, Texas, Toombs moved to Washington as a child. He earned his way through the University of Maryland as a copy boy at the *Washington (D.C.) Times Herald* and later worked for the *Daily News* and *The Evening Star*. He served in the OSS in Europe during World War II and after the war was chief of political intelligence for the U.S. Army in Berlin. His first novel, *Raising a Riot* (Thomas Y. Crowell, 1949), was made into a motion picture in England. Several other humorous books followed, including *Good as Gold* (Thomas Y. Crowell, 1955), which was acclaimed for the accuracy with which it captured Washington politics and social functions. The

novel later enjoyed some success as a play. Toombs received national attention as the editor of *The Enterprise*, a weekly newspaper published in Lexington Park, Maryland, and owned by J. Sheridan Fahnestock. The newspaper was singled out by *Time* magazine as one of the nation's top ten weeklies for being a small town newspaper that published investigative journalism. The paper's stories about the local Democratic organization headed by Circuit Judge Philip H. Dorsey, Jr., provoked legal action that received national coverage and ended in an acquittal for Toombs and his publisher. Toombs lived for many years at Colton's Point, Maryland and an apartment at 2501 Calvert Street, NW, in Washington.
(*The Washington Post*, 30 December 1968, C8). *See* entry 338.

Toomer, Jean (Nathan Eugene) (December 26, 1894-March 30, 1967)
    Born in Washington, D.C., Toomer was raised by his mother, who was from a wealthy and politically powerful Louisiana family. Her father was Pickney B. S. Pinchback, the first African American to serve as acting governor of Louisiana. Toomer's light skin and powerful family meant that he was shielded from racism in the affluent areas of Washington and New Orleans where he grew up. He studied agriculture at the University of Wisconsin and the Massachusetts College of Agriculture and physical training at the American College of Physical Training in Chicago. Toomer's book *Cane* (New York: Boni and Liveright, 1923) dealt with the black experience and immediately earned him national recognition.
(*Dictionary of Literary Biography*, vol. 51, s.v. "Toomer, Jean"). *See* entry 339.

Tourgée, Albion Winegar (May 2, 1838-May 21, 1905)
    Tourgée was born in Ohio and educated at the University of Rochester. During the Civil War, he fought with the Union army in the battles of Cold Harbor, Murfreesboro, Tullahoma, Chickamauga, Lookout Mountain, and Missionary Ridge. After his war service, he studied law and was admitted to the bar in Ohio in May 1864. He moved to Guilford County, near Greensboro, North Carolina, to start a nursery business in 1865. His acceptance of blacks as equals in his business socially outraged his white neighbors, and he quickly found himself involved in politics. In 1868, he was a delegate to the North Carolina constitutional convention and was appointed to develop a new legal code and procedures for the state. He was also elected a state superior court judge, although he failed to win re-election in 1874. He began writing fictionalized versions of his experiences in the Reconstruction South, and his

third novel, *A Fool's Errand: By One of the Fools* (Fords, Howard &
Hulbert, 1879), was immediately popular. That book, and his following
novel, *Bricks without Straw* (Fords, Howard & Hulbert, 1880), earned
him a national reputation and made him briefly wealthy. He continued
writing novels, newspaper articles, and magazine fiction while advocating on behalf of black civil rights. One of the organizers of the National
Citizens Rights Association in 1891 with the goal of organizing Southern blacks in their own behalf, he represented Homer Adolph Plessy in
Plessy v. Ferguson as a means of testing Jim Crow laws. He spent the
final years of his life, from 1897 to 1905, as consul to Bordeaux,
France.
(*Dictionary of Literary Biography*, vol. 79, s.v. "Tourgée, Albion W.").
See entry 340.

Trumbo, Dalton (December 9, 1906-September 10, 1976)
    Famed as an author and screenwriter in the 1930s, Trumbo was
one of the highest paid screenwriters in Hollywood in the 1940s. He
joined the American Communist Party in 1944 and spent several years
involved in labor activism in Hollywood. Imprisoned and blacklisted
for thirteen years after refusing to cooperate with the House Un-American Activities Committee in 1947, he moved to Mexico and continued
to sell screenplays under pseudonyms, one of which won an Academy
Award for best screenplay. After he could once again work legitimately
in Hollywood, he achieved several triumphs, including the opportunity
in 1971 to direct a screenplay for World Entertainments of his own
early novel, *Johnny Got His Gun* (Lippincott, 1939), considered an
important anti-war novel by critics. The film won the *Prix Special du
Jury* at the Cannes Film Festival in 1971.
(*Dictionary of Literary Biography*, vol. 26, s.v. "Trumbo, Dalton"). *See*
entry 341.

Tuel, John E. (c. 1830-1880)
    A newspaper correspondent and editor, Tuel wrote serious histori-
cal works as well as novels. He lived in Washington for approximately
thirty years, roughly between 1850 and 1878. His historical works
mostly focused on the Mexican War.
(Albert Johannsen, "The House of Beadle and Adams and Its Dime and
Nickel Novels," Northern Illinois University Libraries Dime Novels
Project, Official Web Site, http://niulib.niu.edu/badndp, accessed
11/15/05). *See* entry 342.

Tully, Andrew F., Jr. (October 24, 1914-September 27, 1993)
Tully was a professional writer for sixty of his seventy-six years and produced sixteen books of fiction and non-fiction, as well as writing a nationally syndicated newspaper column. Born in Southbridge, Massachusetts, he worked as a sports reporter for his hometown paper while still in high school and bought the paper with loans from his friends when he was twenty-one. For the two years before selling *The Southbridge (Mass.) Press*, he was the youngest newspaper publisher in the United States. He went on to work for *The Worcester (Mass.) Gazette*, before leaving for Europe to as a World War II correspondent for *The Boston (Mass.) Traveler*. In 1961, he began writing a syndicated column, eventually titled "Capital Fare," which for some years was carried by 150 newspapers around the country. He lived in the Washington, D.C., metropolitan area up until the time of his death.
(*New York Times*, 9 September 1993, B9). *See* entries 343, 344.

Tweed, Thomas Frederic (1890-April 30, 1940)
Born in Liverpool, England, and educated at the Liverpool Institute and Liverpool University, Tweed was a famous Liberal Party political organizer in England and an adviser to Lloyd George from 1926 until his death. In addition to his political career, he worked as an underwriter with Lloyd's of London. His first book, written anonymously, was entitled *Gabriel Over the White House* (Farrar & Rinehart, 1933) and was made into a motion picture in the year of publication (MGM, starring Walter Huston). The work was said to foresee some aspects of the New Deal. He also wrote *Destiny's Man* (Farrar & Rinehart, 1935) about an imaginary European state.
(*New York Times*, 1 May 1940, 29). *See* entry 345.

Tybout, Ella Middleton (January 4, 1871-1952)
Tybout was born on an estate named "Stockton" near New Castle, Delaware, created by her grandfather, George Z. Tybout, an agriculturalist with significant land holdings. Tybout published her first short story in 1901 and became a frequent contributor to popular magazines of her time, particularly *Lippincott's*. Her work tended to be in the genres of romance and humor and often had a basis in the people and places she had known in childhood. She lived in Washington during part of her adult life but moved to Warren, Pennsylvania, during her final years.
(Delaware, Official State Web Site, "Historical Markers Program, NC 119," accessed 12 May 2005). *See* entry 346.

Tyson, J. Aubrey (1870-1930)
  See entry 347.

Vanderbilt, Cornelius Jr. (April 30, 1898-July 8, 1974)
  Vanderbilt, the son of Cornelius and Grace Graham Wilson Vanderbilt chose to become a newspaperman rather than following the pursuits more typical in his family. Although he worked for several publications, including *The New York Times*, on an extended assignment in Washington, for most of his career he freelanced and wrote books about society figures and royalty. He was a staunch campaigner for Franklin Delano Roosevelt and during World War II was a major in U.S. Army Intelligence. After the war he published mostly travel columns for Affiliated News Features, and *The New York Post*.
  (*New York Times*, 8 July 1974, 32). *See* entry 348.

Vidal, Gore (October 3, 1925-?)
  Vidal has been a prolific author and public figure ever since the publication of his first book in 1946. The grandson of Oklahoma senator Thomas P. Gore, Vidal has written novels, essays, histories, historical novels, and plays that often take American politics and political figures as their theme. He has been a candidate for the House of Representatives (1960) and the Senate (1982), a talk show host on radio and television, and a frequent political commentator.
  (*Contemporary Authors Online*, New York: Thomson Gale, 2004, accessed, 29 March 2005). *See* entries 349, 350, 351.

Vingut, Mrs. Gertrude (Fairfield) (1830-?)
  Born in Philadelphia, Vingut was a daughter of Sumner Lincoln Fairfield (1803-1844), a poet and founder of *North American Magazine*. Gertrude's mother, Jane (Frazee) Fairfield, involved herself in Sumner's career and wrote an autobiography after his death that presented a full account of his life (*The Autobiography of Jane Fairfield, Embracing a Few Select Poems by Sumner Lincoln Fairfield*, Bazin & Ellsworth, 1860). Vingut's sister, Genevieve Genevra, published short stories and painted despite mental health problems that eventually led to her commitment at St. Elizabeth's Insane Asylum (Washington, D.C.); a brother, Eugene, was also institutionalized. Vingut married Francesco Xavier Vingut, a Cuban immigrant who was a Spanish professor at New York University.
  (James Wilson, James Grand, and John Fiske, ed. *Appleton's Cyclopædia of American Biography*. New York: D. Appleton, 1887-1900). *See* entry 352.

Vrooman, Julia Scott
   See entry 353.

Walker, Mannix (1904-1957)
   Walker was a Foreign Service officer who, after his retirement, ran
a school in Georgetown (D.C.) to prepare young men to take the Foreign Service Examination.
(*Washington Post and Times Herald*, 1 July 1957, B2). *See* entry 354.

Wallace, Irving (March 19, 1916-June 29, 1990)
   Author of sixteen novels and seventeen non-fiction books, almost
every title Wallace published, after his first unsuccessful book, was a
bestseller.
(*New York Times*, 30 June 1990, 29). *See* entry 355.

Walworth, Mansfield Tracy (1830-June 3, 1873)
   Walworth was the son of New York State Chancellor Reuben
Hyde Walworth and nephew of Supreme Court Justice Philip Barbour.
A graduate of Union College (1849), he produced his first novel, *The
Mission of Death* (D. J. Sadlier), in 1853. Encouraged by the book's
reception (it went through twelve editions) he went on to publish seven
more novels. Walworth married Nelly Hardin, daughter of Colonel
John J. Hardin of Illinois, a lawyer and politician, who first became
famous through his political rivalry with Senator Stephen A. Douglas
and later for his heroism during the Mexican War. At the battle of
Buena Vista Hardin suffered a mortal wound. Hardin's widow later
married Walworth's widowed father and soon afterward, Walworth
married Hardin's daughter. During the marriage Walworth abused
Nelly mentally and physically, and, although the couple had a son and
two daughters, Nelly left Walworth with the support of Walworth's
own father, who gave her a property in Saratoga Springs on which she
established a school for girls. From his residence in New York, Walworth made trips to Saratoga and continued to harass Nelly with threatening correspondence. Finally, his son, Frank Hardin Walworth,
traveled to New York to persuade Walworth to end his harassment and
ended up fatally shooting him.
(*New York Times*, 4 June 1873, 8). *See* entry 356.

Walz, Audrey Boyers [Bonnamy, Francis, pseud.] (1907-February 14,
1983)
   A native of Mobile, Alabama, Walz received her bachelor's degree
Phi Beta Kappa from the University of Chicago. She wrote twelve mys-

teries under the name Francis Bonnamy. She also wrote several histori-
cal novels with her husband, former *New York Times* correspondent Jay
Walz.
(*New York Times*, 17 February 1983). *See* entries 357, 358, 359.

Ware, Richard D[arwin] (1869-1931)
See entry 360.

Warren, Stanley Sevier
See entry 361.

Wartofsky, [William] Victor (June 15, 1931-?)
    The author of a short story collection and two novels, Wartofsky
worked as a Washington reporter for United Press International from
1954 to 1960 and a publicist and writer for B'nai B'rith in Washington,
before beginning a career as a writer at the National Institute of Health
in Bethesda, Maryland. He was educated at George Washington University and American University.
(*Contemporary Authors Online*, New York: Gale Group, 2002, accessed, 9 June 2005). *See* entries 362, 363.

Watterson, George (1783-1854)
    The son of a Scottish master builder, Watterson arrived in the Fed-
eral City at the age of eight when his father arrived to help build the
city. Watterson read law and eventually went into partnership with
Thomas Law in Washington. He published his first novel in 1808 and
in the next several years published a comedy, another novel, and two
poems. He was named editor of the *Washington City Gazette* in 1813
and fought in the battle of Bladensburg in 1814. The following year,
Watterson was made Librarian of Congress after Thomas Jefferson's
6,500-volume collection was acquired to replace the books destroyed
by the British. Although he only had one assistant, he acquired 15,000
volumes by the time he was displaced by a political appointee in 1829.
Throughout his career, Watterson wrote novels, guidebooks (several for
Washington), statistical compilations, textbooks, lectures, and biographical sketches and served as editor on various newspapers. He
founded the Washington National Monument Society in 1833 and remained its secretary until his death in 1854, by which time the monument had risen to a height of 150 feet.
(*American National Biography*, s.v. "Watterson, George"). *See* entry
364.

Weaver, John D[owning] (February 4 1912-December 4, 2002)

The son of Henry Byrne who worked as the official reporter for the House of Representatives, Weaver grew up in Washington, attended Georgetown University from 1928 to 1929 (although he completed his undergraduate education at the College of William and Mary in 1932), and received a master's degree from George Washington University in 1933. Before turning to writing full time, Weaver worked for several government agencies, including the National Recovery Administration from 1933 to 1935. Although his first two books were novels and he wrote a number of short stories, Weaver spent most of his career writing non-fiction. He is, perhaps, best-known for his book *The Brownsville Raid: The Story of America's "Black Dreyfus" Affair* (Norton, 1970) that vindicated 167 black men who had been members of the First Battalion of the 25th Infantry and were falsely accused of disorderly conduct that led to their dishonorable discharge from the military. (*Contemporary Authors Online*, New York: Gale Group, 2003, accessed, 29 March 2005). *See* entry 365.

Weidman, Jerome (4 April 1913-)

The author of more than twenty-seven books, Weidman grew up in New York City and was educated at City College (now City College of the City University New York), Washington Square College and New York University Law School. He has been a freelance writer since the publication of his first novel in 1937. In addition to novels, Weidman was the author of several successful plays and screenplays. (*Contemporary Authors Online*, New York: Gale Group, 2003, accessed 10 October 2005). *See* entry 366.

Wheeler, Mrs. William Lamont (?)

Hester Grace Lawrence was the daughter of William Beach Lawrence of New York City. She married William Lamont Wheeler, a physician who had been commissioned by President Lincoln as assistant Naval surgeon. The couple married after Wheeler's retirement from the Navy and settled in Newport where Wheeler established a practice. Mrs. Wheeler was considered a leader of society, and she had artistic as well as literary interests. She and her husband's annual social circuit included Boston, New York City, Newport, and Washington. Dr. Wheeler fell while climbing in Switzerland, and after a long period of suffering committed suicide in 1887. After Mrs. Wheeler's brother, General Lawrence, died at almost the same time, she lived in seclusion. (*New York Times*, 17 October 1887; 28 February 1893). *See* entry 367.

Wheelwright, John Tyler (February 26, 1856-December 23, 1925)
    Born in Roxbury, Massachuetts, Wheelwright was a prominent
Boston attorney. He graduated from Harvard College and was a founder of *Harvard Lampoon*. His brother, Edmund M. Wheelwright, an
architect, designed the Lampoon building. Wheelwright primarily
wrote children's books.
(Stanley Kunitz and Howard Haycraft, eds., *Twentieth Century Authors, a Biographical Dictionary of Modern Literature*, New York: H.
W. Wilson, 1942, s.v. "Wheelwright, John Tyler"). *See* entry 368.

Whitehurst, Ben (November 6, 1897-September 21, 1990)
    Born in a Western mining camp, Whitehurst earned a bachelor's
degree from Peniel University (now Southern Nazarene University,
Oklahoma City) and studied in 1919 at the Massachusetts Institute of
Technology. In World War I, he was an instructor at the ground school
at M.I.T. and a pilot; he later worked as a government clerk and an oil
prospector and traveled extensively in Mexico and South and Central
America. He was chief of correspondence for the FERA and WPA
from 1933 to 1935, an editorial writer for *Liberty Magazine* from 1936
to 1938, and later held several public relations positions with the National Republican Committee. He served in the U.S. Senate from 1950
to 1954. In addition to publishing books, Whitehurst was a contributor
to national magazines and a feature writer for the *Saturday Evening
Post*.
(*Who's Who in the East*. 6th ed, Boston: Larkin, Roosevelt, & Larkin,
1957). *See* entry 369.

Whitlock, Brand (4 March 1869-24 May 1934)
    Born in Ohio, Whitlock worked as journalist before his admission
to the bar of the state of Ohio. After working as a lawyer in Toledo,
Ohio from 1897 to 1905, he served as a reform mayor of that town
from 1904 to 1913. From 1913 to 1919 he served as U.S. minister to
Belgium and from 1919 to 1922 as ambassador to Belgium. His efforts
to relieve wartime suffering and its aftermath earned him numerous
honors from Belgium and other countries. He wrote more than seventeen books of fiction and non-fiction.
(*Contemporary Authors Online,* New York: Gale Group, 2003, accessed 10 October 2005). *See* entry 370.

Whitten, Les[lie] H[unter] (February 21, 1928-?)
Raised in Jacksonville, Florida, Whitten served in the United States
Army from 1946 to 1948 and graduated magna cum laude from Lehigh

University in 1950. He began working as a journalist, first with Radio Free Europe in Munich and New York City, then as International News Service desk editor in Washington, D.C. He was a reporter with the *Washington Post* from 1958 to 1962, and, starting in 1963, he worked as a Washington reporter for Hearst Newspapers, becoming assistant bureau chief in 1966 and columnist with Jack Anderson from 1969 to 1992.
(*Contemporary Authors Online*, New York: Gale Group, 2001, accessed, 9 June 2005). *See* entry 371.

Wiley, Faith
    See entry 369

Willard, (Alice) Rosseter (1860-?)
    See entry 372.

Williams, Anna Vernon (Dorsey)
    See entry 373.

Williams, C[atherine] R[ead] (1790-1872)
    See entry 374.

Wilson, Mary Badger (?-June 6, 1953)
    The daughter of Ellen Hale and Peter Mitchell Wilson, the author was a descendant of George E. Badger of Raleigh, North Carolina, a superior court judge, secretary of the Navy, and U.S. senator (1844-1855). She was a long-time resident of Washington, D.C., and resided at 1763 Columbia Road, NW.
(*Washington Post*, 9 June, 1953, 20). *See* entries 375, 376, 377.

Winchester, Paul (1851-1932)
    See entry 378.

Winslow, Barbara
    See entry 379.

Wise, Thomas A. (1865-1928)
    See entry 380.

Woods, Kate Tannatt (1840-July 12, 1910)
    Woods' husband, Colonel George Henry Woods, was a Union officer throughout the Civil War, and she served with him as an army

nurse. Although born in Peekskill, New York, she spent most of her married life in Boston where she was known for her devotion as a clubwoman, founding both the General Federation of Women's Clubs and the Massachusetts State Federation of Women's Clubs. Her writing career included the publication of twenty books of fiction. She was also a frequent contributor to magazines and newspapers and served on the editorial departments of several of them.
(*New York Times*, 13 July 1910, 7). *See* entry 381.

Worthen, J. Henry
    See entry 382.

Yulee, C. Wickliffe (1849-1921)
    Yulee was a son of David Levy Yulee, Florida territorial delegate and later U.S. senator from Florida, and Nannie C. (Wickliffe) Yulee, the daughter of Governor Charles Wickliffe of Kentucky. David Levy Yulee was an advocate of Florida statehood, a fighter for the expansion of the number of slave states and territories in the Union, and the founder of the Florida Railroad Company. He was acknowledged as the first Jewish person to serve in the Senate. After selling the Florida Railroad, he retired to Washington, D.C., where members of the Wickliffe family lived.
(U.S. Congress, *Biographical Directory of the United States Congress, 1774 to the Present*, http://bioguide.congress.gov, accessed, 12 November 2005). *See* entry 383.

Appendix A
Works First Published after 1976

Abercrombie, Neil, and Richard Hoyt. *Blood of Patriots*. New York: Forge, 1997. 317pp.

Ackerman, Karl. *Dear Will*. New York: Scribner, 2000. 246pp.

———. *The Patron Saint of Unmarried Women*. New York: St. Martin's, 1994. 246pp.

Adams, Anna. *The Bride Ran Away*. Harlequin Super Romance 1,168. New York: Harlequin, 2003. 299pp.

Adler, Warren. *American Quartet: A Novel*. New York: Arbor House, 1981. 287pp.

———. *American Sextet*. New York: Arbor House, 1983. 256pp.

———. *Immaculate Deception: A Novel*. New York: Donald I. Fine, 1991. 241pp.

———. *Senator Love: A Novel*. New York: Donald I. Fine, 1991. 263pp.

———. *The Ties That Bind: A Fiona Fitzgerald Mystery*. New York: Donald I. Fine, 1994. 263pp.

———. *The Witch of Watergate: A Novel*. New York: Donald I. Fine, 1992. 256pp.

Aguilar, Rebeca, and Asa Zatz. *Cristina's Secret*. New York: Kensington, 1999. 171pp.

Alderson, T. A. *Subversion: A Romantic Suspense Story.* New York: Broadway Books, 2001. 277pp.

Alers, Rochelle. *No Compromise.* Washington D.C.: BET, 2002. 379pp.

Allbeury, Ted. *Aid and Comfort.* London, U.K.: Hodder & Stoughton, 1997. 320pp.

Amos, Robyn. *Promise Me.* New York: Kensington, 1997. 252pp.

Anderson, Patrick. *Busybodies: A Novel.* New York: Simon & Schuster, 1989. 256pp.

Andrews, Donna. *Access Denied.* New York: Berkley Prime Crime, 2004. 251pp.

———. *Click Here for Murder.* New York: Berkley Prime Crime, 2003. 295pp.

———. *You've Got Murder.* New York: Berkley Prime Crime, 2002. 298pp.

Andrews, Robert. *Death in a Promised Land.* New York: Pocket Books, 1993. 305pp.

———. *A Murder of Honor.* New York: Putnam's Sons, 2001. 284pp.

———. *A Murder of Justice.* New York: G. P. Putnam's Sons, 2004. 319pp.

———. *A Murder of Promise.* New York: Putnam's, 2002. 317pp.

Andrews, Virginia. *Rain.* New York: Pocket Books, 2001. 440pp.

Austin, Raymond. *The Eagle Heist: A Beauford Sloan Mystery.* Indian Wells, Calif.: McKenna, 2002. 203pp.

Avila, Vernon L. *Smokescreen: A Novel of Medical Intrigue.* Granite Bay, Calif.: Penmarin Books, 2000. 330pp.

Bagni, Gwen, Paul Dubov, and Lillian Rogers Parks. *Backstairs at the White House: A Novel.* Englewood Cliffs, N.J.: Prentice-Hall, 1978. 469pp.

Bailey, Daniel. *Execute the Office.* Johnson City, Tenn.: Silver Dagger Mysteries, 2004. 202pp.

Bain, Donald. *A Vote for Murder: A Murder, She Wrote Mystery.* New York: New American Library, 2004. 277pp.

Baker, Nicholson. *Checkpoint.* New York: Alfred A. Knopf, 2004. 115pp.

Baldacci, David. *Saving Faith.* New York: Warner Books, 1999. 451pp.

————. *The Simple Truth.* New York: Warner Books, 1998. 470pp.

Banks, Carolyn. *The Girls on the Row.* New York: Fawcett Crest, 1984. 249pp.

Bardi, Abby. *The Book of Fred.* New York: Washington Square Press, 2002. 304pp.

Bartolomeo, Christina. *Cupid and Diana.* New York: Scribner, 1998. 222pp.

————. *The Side of the Angels: A Novel.* New York: Scribner, 2002. 304pp.

Baxter, Mary Lynn. *Southern Fires.* New York: Warner Books, 1996. 359pp.

Bayard, Louis. *Fool's Errand.* Los Angeles: Alyson Books, 1999. 486pp.

Bell, James Scott. *Deadlock.* Grand Rapids, Mich.: Zondervan, 2002. 319pp.

Bencastro, Mario, and Susan Giersbach Rascón. *Odyssey to the North.* Houston, Tex.: Arte Público Press, 1998. 192pp.

Bennet, Rick. *The Lost Brother*. New York: Arcade, 1996. 210pp.

Benson, Chris. *Special Interest: A Novel*. Chicago: Third World Press, 2001. 279pp.

Bergstrom, Kay. *Fear Was My Father*. New York: Berkley Books, 1993. 250pp.

Berne, Suzanne. *A Crime in the Neighborhood: A Novel*. Chapel Hill, N.C.: Algonquin Books of Chapel Hill, 1997. 285pp.

Berry, Venise T. *So Good*. New York: Dutton, 1996. 280pp.

Blackwood, Gary L. *Second Sight*. New York: Dutton Children's Books, 2005. 288pp. juvenile.

Blair, Cynthia. *The Pink Lemonade Charade*. New York: Fawcett Juniper, 1988. 119pp.

Blair, Margaret Whitman. *House of Spies: Danger in Civil War Washington*. Shippensburg, Pa.: White Mane Kids, 1999. 169pp. juvenile.

Blatty, William Peter. *Legion: A Novel*. New York: Simon & Schuster, 1983. 269pp.

Bowen, Michael. *Collateral Damage*. New York: St. Martin's, 1999. 211pp.

———. *Corruptly Procured*. New York: St. Martin's, 1994. 279pp.

———. *Faithfully Executed*. New York: St. Martin's, 1992. 230pp.

———. *Worst Case Scenario: A Washington, D.C. Mystery*. New York: Crown, 1996, 254pp.

Bradley, John Ed. *Love & Obits*. New York: Henry Holt, 1992. 276pp.

Brady, Esther Wood. *The Toad on Capitol Hill*. New York: Crown, 1978. 139pp.

———. *A Wish on Capitol Hill*. New York: Crown, 1989. 139pp.

Bram, Christopher. *Gossip*. New York: Dutton, 1997. 337pp.

Brandon, Jay. *Executive Privilege*. New York: Forge, 2001. 414pp.

Briscoe, Connie. *Big Girls Don't Cry*. New York: HarperCollins, 1996. 406pp.

———. *Sisters & Lovers*. New York: HarperCollins, 1994. 339pp.

Brophy, Beth. *My Ex-Best Friend: A Novel of Suburbia*. New York: Pocket Books, 2004. 307pp.

Brown, Joan Winmill. *If Love Be Ours*. Rhapsody Romances 7. Eugene, Ore.: Harvest House, 1984. 192pp.

Brown, Richard E., and Beverly A. Brown. *The Rose Engagement*. Kent, Ohio: Kent Information Services, 1996. 201pp.

Brown, Sandra. *Exclusive*. New York: Warner Books, 1996. 457pp.

———. *Tomorrow's Promise*. Harlequin American Romance 1. New York: Harlequin, 1983. 253pp.

Bruns, Don. *Barbados Heat*. New York: St. Martin's / Minotaur, 2003. 302pp.

Buckley, Christopher. *Little Green Men*. New York: HarperPerennial, 2000. 300pp.

———. *The White House Mess*. 1986, New York: Alfred A. Knopf, 1986. 224pp.

Bunn, T. Davis. *The Ultimatum: A Novel*. Nashville, Tenn.: Thomas Nelson, 1999. 312pp.

Bunn, T. Davis, and Isabelle Bunn. *The Solitary Envoy*. Heirs of Acadia 1. Minneapolis: Bethany House, 2004, 319pp.

Burnes, Caroline. *Familiar Lullaby*. Harlequin Intrigue 614. New York: Harlequin, 2001. 249pp.

Burnham, Sophy. *The Dogwalker*. New York: Frederick Warne, 1979. 151pp.

Burston, Betty, and Bruce Brown. *24/7*. Los Angeles: Holloway House, 1994. 255pp.

Byerrum, Ellen. *Designer Knockoff: A Crime of Fashion Mystery*. New York: Signet, 2004. 325pp.

————. *Hostile Makeover: A Crime of Fashion Mystery*. New York: Signet, 2005. 278pp.

————. *Killer Hair: A Crime of Fashion Mystery*. New York: Signet, 2003. 276pp.

Cabot, Meg. *All-American Girl*. New York: HarperCollins, 2002. 247pp.

Callahan, David. *State of the Union: A Novel*. Boston: Little, Brown, 1997. 371pp.

Camacho, Austin S. *The Troubleshooter*. Woodmere, N.Y.: Intrigue Books, 2004. 236pp.

Carr, Josephine. *My Very Own Murder*. New York: New American Library, 2005. 258pp.

Carrington, Tori. *License to Thrill*. Harlequin Temptation 740. New York: Harlequin, 1999. 218pp.

Case, John. *The Eighth Day: A Thriller*. New York: Ballantine Books, 2002. 404pp.

————. *The Genesis Code: A Novel*. New York: Ballantine Books, 2005. 435pp.

Chambers, Christopher. *Sympathy for the Devil: An Angela Bivens Thriller*. New York: Crown, 2001. 306pp.

Charrette, Robert N. *Just Compensation, Shadowrun*. New York: ROC, 1996. 280pp.

Chase, Jack. *Fatal Analysis*. New York: Signet, 1996. 364pp.

Cheney, Lynne V. *Executive Privilege: A Washington Novel*. New York: Simon & Schuster, 1979. 288pp.

Chesley, Donald. *Black Vendetta*. Los Angeles: Holloway House, 1988. 211pp.

Christie, Amanda. *Learning the Ropes*. New York: Random House, 2001. 131pp.

Clark, Mary Higgins. *Stillwatch*. New York: Simon & Schuster, 1984. 302pp.

Clarke, Breena. *River, Cross My Heart*. Boston: Little, Brown, 1999. 245pp.

Clute, Sylvia. *Destiny*. Fairfield, Iowa: Sunstar, 1997. 275pp.

Cohen, Richard. *The Seduction of Joe Tynan*. New York: Dell, 1979. 320pp.

Cohen, William S. *Murder in the Senate*. New York: Nan A. Talese, 1993. 306pp.

Collins, Max Allan. *Majic Man: A Nathan Heller Novel*. New York: Dutton, 1999. 293pp.

Collins, Robert J. *Ambassador Strikes*. Indian Wells, Calif.: McKenna, 2003. 256pp.

Colson, Charles W., and Ellen Santilli Vaughn. *Gideon's Torch*. Dallas, Tex.: Word, 1995. 553pp.

Compton, David. *Impaired Judgment*. New York: Dutton, 2000. 322pp.

Coner, Kenyetta. *The Mockingbirds: A Maxine Michaels Mystery*. Washington, D.C.: 52 Weeks, 1998. 242pp.

Conroy, Richard Timothy. *The India Exhibition: A Mystery at the Smithsonian*. New York: St. Martin's, 1992. 227pp

————. *Mr. Smithson's Bones: A Mystery at the Smithsonian.* New York: St. Martin's Press, 1993. 194pp.

————. *Old Ways in the New World: A Mystery at the Smithsonian.* New York: St. Martin's, 1994. 302pp.

Conroy, Sarah Booth. *Refinements of Love: A Novel about Clover and Henry Adams.* New York: Pantheon Books, 1993. 301pp.

Coonts, Stephen. *America: A Jake Grafton Novel.* New York: St. Martin's, 2001. 390pp.

————. *Liars & Thieves.* New York: St. Martin's, 2004 383pp.

————. *Liberty.* New York: St. Martin's, 2003. 420pp.

————. *The Minotaur.* New York: Doubleday, 1989. 436pp.

————. *Under Siege.* New York: Pocket Books, 1990. 408pp.

Corn, David. *Deep Background.* New York: St. Martin's Press, 1999. 370pp.

Cote, Lyn. *Chloe: A Novel.* The Women of Ivy Manor Book 1. New York: Warner Faith, 2005. 296pp.

Coughlan, William D. *Legacy or Love.* Columbia, Md.: Coughlan & Associates, 2000. 227pp.

Coulter, Catherine. *Hemlock Bay.* New York: G. P. Putnam's Sons, 2001. 375pp.

Cox, Ana Marie. *Dog Days: A Novel.* New York: Riverhead Books, 2006. 288pp.

Crittenden, Danielle. *Amanda.Bright@Home.* New York: Warner Books, 2003. 322pp.

Crosland, Susan. *Dangerous Games.* London, U.K.: Weidenfeld & Nicolson, 1991. 298pp.

Cullen, Robert. *Heirs of the Fire.* New York: Fawcett / Columbine, 1997. 325pp.

Cummings, Priscilla. *Saving Grace.* New York: Dutton Children's Books, 2003. 240pp. young adult.

Cutler, Jessica. *The Washingtonienne.* New York: Hyperion, 2005. 291pp.

Dailey, Janet. *A Capital Holiday.* New York: Zebra, 2001. 350pp.

Daish, Elizabeth. *Emma's Journey.* Sutton, U.K.: Severn House, 1999. 214pp.

Dalton, James. *City of Shadows.* New York: Forge, 2000. 381pp.

David, Peter. *One Knight Only.* New York: Ace Books, 2004. 373pp.

Davis, Calvin. *Love in Opposing Colors: Unsanctioned Romance.* Clarksville, Md.: T. Z. Leether, 1993. 160pp.

Davis, Patrick A. *The General.* New York: G. P. Putnam's Sons, 1998. 376pp.

————. *The Passenger.* New York: G. P. Putnam's Sons, 1999. 370pp.

Dawson, Saranne. *Exposé.* Harlequin Intrigue 356. New York: Harlequin, 1996. 248pp.

Dean, Maureen. *Capitol Secrets.* New York: Putnam, 1992. 284pp.

————. *Washington Wives: A Novel.* New York: Arbor House, 1987. 315pp.

Deaver, Jeffery. *The Devil's Teardrop: A Novel of the Last Night of the Century.* New York: Simon & Schuster, 1999. 396pp.

Delton, Judy, and S. D. Schindler. *Next Stop, the White House!* Lottery Luck 6. New York: Hyperion Paperbacks for Children, 1995. 92pp. juvenile.

Deutermann, Peter T. *The Firefly.* New York: St. Martin's, 2003. 387pp.

———. *Hunting Season: A Novel.* New York: St. Martin's, 2001. 402pp.

———. *Official Privilege.* New York: St. Martin's, 1995. 392pp.

Dezenhall, Eric. *Money Wanders.* New York: Thomas Dunne Books, 2002. 338pp.

Dinallo, Gregory S. *Red Ink.* New York: Pocket Books, 1994. 341pp.

Dixon, Collen. *Behind Closed Doors: In My Father's House: A Novel. Simon Says Trilogy.* Mitchellville, Md.: FIN Group, 2002. 248pp.

———. *Every Shut Eye.* New York: Strivers Row, 2005. 352pp.

———. *Simon Says: Life's a Game—Are You Ready to Play? A Novel.* Mitchellville, Md.: FIN Group, 2001. 304pp.

———. *Simon Says: A Novel of Intrigue, Betrayal—and Murder.* New York: Villard, 2003. 320pp.

Douglas, Carole Nelson. *White House Pet Detectives: Tales of Crime and Mystery at the White House from a Pet's-Eye View.* Nashville, Tenn.: Cumberland House, 2002. 243pp.

Drucker, Jacki Lippman, and Chris Krupinski. *Silly Sights Washington, D.C.* Arlington, Va.: Peeking Duck Books, 1995. unpaged. juvenile.

Drury, Allen. *Anna Hastings: The Story of a Washington Newspaperperson! A Novel.* New York: Morrow, 1977. 300pp.

———. *Decision.* Garden City, N.Y.: Doubleday, 1983. 502pp

———. *Mark Coffin, U.S.S.: A Novel of Capitol Hill.* Garden City, N.Y.: Doubleday, 1979. 343pp.

Duarte, Stella Pope. *Let Their Spirits Dance.* New York: Rayo, 2002. 312pp.

Duey, Kathleen. *Francesca Vigilucci, Washington, D.C., 1913.* American Diaries 17. New York: Aladdin Paperbacks, 1999. 128pp. juvenile.

Duhon, Jean. *The Pygmalion Venture*. Mobile, Ala.: Magnolia Mansions Press, 2004. 391pp.

DuPree, Kia. *Robbing Peter*. Hampton, Va.: Prism Pages, 2004. 209pp.

Earley, Pete. *Lethal Secrets*. New York: Forge, 2005. 334pp.

Elam, Patricia. *Breathing Room*. New York: Washington Square Press, 2002. 335pp.

Ellis, Robert. *Access to Power*. New York: Kensington, 2001. 380pp.

Emerson, Sally. *Heat*. London: Little, Brown, 1998. 334pp.

Emmer, E. R. *Me, Minerva, and the Flying Car*. New York: Four Corners, 2000. 121pp. juvenile.

————. *Me, Minerva, and the Flying Flora*. New York: Four Corners, 2003. 133pp. juvenile.

English, Brenda. *Corruption of Faith*. New York: Berkley Prime Crime, 1997. 260pp.

Epps, Garrett. *The Floating Island: A Tale of Washington*. Boston: Houghton Mifflin, 1985. 286pp.

Everett, Percival. *Erasure: A Novel*. Hanover, N.H.: University Press of New England, 2001. 320pp.

Farris, John. *The Fury and the Terror*. New York: Tom Doherty Associates, 2001. 384pp.

Faulks, Sebastian. *On Green Dolphin Street: A Novel*. New York: Random House, 2001. 351pp

Ferrarella, Marie. *Choices, Harper Monogram*. New York: Harper-Paperbacks, 1993. 327pp.

Fitzgerald, Sara. *Rumors*. New York: Warner Books, 1992. 358pp.

Fleming, Barbara. *Hot Stones, Cold Death: A Matthew Alexander Mystery*. Yellow Springs, Ohio: Silver Maple, 2001. 293pp.

————. *Murder on the Gold Coast: A Matthew Alexander Mystery.* Yellow Springs, Ohio: Silver Maple, 2005. 361pp.

Flynn, Vince. *Separation of Power.* New York: Pocket Books, 2001. 356pp.

————. *Term Limits.* New York: Pocket Books, 1997. 403pp.

————. *The Third Option.* New York: Pocket Books, 2000. 358pp.

Flynn, Vince. *Transfer of Power.* New York: Pocket Books, 1999. 395pp.

Ford, Susan, and Laura Hayden. *Double Exposure: A First Daughter Mystery.* New York: Thomas Dunne Books, 2002. 213pp.

Forrest, Katherine V. *Liberty Square.* New York: Berkley Prime Crime, 1996. 242pp.

Frank, Jeffrey. *The Columnist: A Novel.* New York: Simon & Schuster, 2001. 237pp.

Frederick, Heather Vogel, and Sally Wern Comport. *The Black Paw. Spy Mice.* New York: Simon & Schuster Books for Young Readers, 2005. 231pp. juvenile.

Freemantle, Brian. *Triple Cross.* New York: Thomas Dunne Books, 2004. 323pp.

Frey, Stephen W. *The Inner Sanctum.* New York: Dutton, 1997. 308pp.

————. *Trust Fund.* New York: Ballantine Books, 2001, 341pp.

Friedlander, Mark P., and Robert W. Kenny. *The Shakespeare Transcripts.* Woodbridge, Conn.: Ox Bow Press, 1993. 275pp.

Fullilove, Eric James. *Blowback.* New York: Amistad Press, 2001. 295pp.

Gavin, William F. *The Ernesto "Che" Guevara School for Wayward Girls: A Novel.* New York: Thomas Dunne Books, 2006. 304pp.

Giff, Patricia Reilly, and Blanche Sims. *Look Out, Washington, D.C.!* New York.: Bantam Doubleday Dell Books for Young Readers, 1995. 122pp. juvenile.

Gifford, Thomas. *Gomorrha: Roman.* N.p.: Bastei Lubbe, 1998. 516pp.

———. *Saints Rest: A Novel.* New York: Bantam Books, 1996. 406pp.

Gilmore, Monique. *Hearts Afire.* New York: Pinnacle, 1995. 254pp.

Golden, Marita. *The Edge of Heaven.* New York: Doubleday, 1998. 242pp.

Golden, Marita. *Long Distance Life.* New York: Doubleday, 1989. 321pp.

Goodrum, Charles A. *The Best Cellar.* New York: St. Martin's, 1987. 218pp.

———. *Dewey Decimated.* New York: Crown, 190pp.

———. *A Slip of the Tong.* New York: St. Martin's, 1992. 180pp.

Goodwin, Stephen. *Breaking Her Fall.* Orlando, Fla.: Harcourt, 2003. 408pp.

Gordon, Guanetta. *The Aurora Tree: A Novel of Early Washington, D.C.* Rancho Palos Verdes, Calif.: Dennart, 1998. 633pp.

Gore, Kristin. *Sammy's Hill: A Novel.* New York: Miramax Books, 2004. 387pp.

Gorman, Edward. *The First Lady.* New York: Forge, 1995. 319pp.

Gough, William J. *Miss Conchita Gray Paws: A Tale for Cat Lovers of All Ages.* London, U.K.: Minerva, 1998. 67pp.

Grady, James. *Thunder.* New York: Warner Books, 1994. 380pp.

———. *White Flame: A Novel.* Beverly Hills, Calif.: Dove Books, 1996. 294pp.

Greeley, Andrew M. *The Bishop in the West Wing: A Blackie Ryan Story*. New York: Forge, 2002. 255pp.

Green, Tim. *The First 48*. New York: Warner Books, 2004. 318pp.

Greenberg, Martin Harry, and Edward Gorman. *Danger in D.C.: Cat Crimes in the Nation's Capital*. New York: Donald I. Fine, 1993. 262pp.

Griffiths, John. *The Presidential Archive*. New York: Carroll & Graf, 1996. 378pp.

Grisham, John. *The King of Torts*. New York: Doubleday, 2003. 376pp.

Grisham, John. *The Pelican Brief*. New York: Doubleday, 1992. 371pp.

———. *The Street Lawyer*. New York: Doubleday, 1998. 348pp.

Gross, Martin L. *Man of Destiny*. New York: Avon Books, 1997. 374pp.

Grossman, Richard. *The Alphabet Man*. Boulder, Colo.: Fiction Collective Two, 1993. 443pp.

Haig, Brian. *The Kingmaker*. New York: Warner Books, 2003. 391pp.

———. *The President's Assassin*. New York: Warner Books, 2005. 404pp.

———. *Private Sector*. New York: Warner Books, 2003. 439pp.

Hall, James O. *Will We Save Ourselves? A Novel*. Arlington, Mass.: Dallin, 2000. 277pp.

Hand, Elizabeth. *Waking the Moon*. New York: HarperPrism, 1995. 390pp.

Hare, Neil. *An Animal Cries*. Washington, D.C.: Castle Pacific, 1998. 192pp.

Hart, Neesa. *A Kiss to Dream On*. New York: Avon Books, 1999. 372pp.

Haynes, David. *The Full Matilda: A Novel*. New York: Harlem Moon, 2004. 370pp.

Haywood, Gar Anthony. *Bad News Travels Fast*. New York: G. P. Putnam's, 1995. 244pp.

Heggan, Christiane. *Moment of Truth*. Don Mills, Ontario, Can.: Mira, 2002. 400pp.

Heller, Joseph. *Good as Gold*. New York: Simon & Schuster, 1979. 447pp.

Herron, Carolivia. *Thereafter Johnnie*. New York: Random House, 1991. 243pp.

Hill, Donna. *A Scandalous Affair*. Washington, D.C.: BET Books, 2000. 349pp.

Holt, A. J. *Catch Me*. New York: St. Martin's, 1999. 327pp.

Hoopes, Roy. *Our Man in Washington*. New York: Forge, 2000. 380pp.

———. *A Watergate Tape*. New York: Forge, 2002. 282pp.

Horn, Stephen. *In Her Defense*. New York: HarperCollins, 2000. 376pp.

Horrock, Henry. *Potomac Fever: A Novel*. Boston: Little, Brown, 1999. 292pp.

Huddle, David. *Tenorman: A Novella*. San Francisco: Chronicle Books, 1995. 121pp.

Huggins, James Byron. *The Scam*. New Kensington, Penn.: Whitaker House, 2005. 302pp.

Humphrey, David M. *Dark Things*. Chicago: Moody, 2005. 299pp.

Hunt, E. Howard. *Guilty Knowledge*. New York: Forge, 1999. 320pp.

———. *Murder in State*. New York: St. Martin's, 1990. 296pp.

Hunter, Fred. *Capital Queers*. New York: St. Martin's, 2000. 214pp.

Hynd, Noel. *The Enemy Within*. New York: Forge, 2006. 432pp.

Ignatius, David. *A Firing Offense*. New York: Random House, 1997. 333pp.

———. *The Sun King: A Novel*. New York: Random House, 1999. 320pp.

Ingram, Kristen Johnson. *Angel in the Senate*. Sisters, Ore.: Palisades, 1998. 261pp.

Insel, Deborah. *Clouded Dreams*. Harrison, N.Y.: Delphinium Books, 1995. 273pp.

Jasper, Kenji. *Seeking Salamanca Mitchell: A Novel*. New York: Broadway Books, 2004. 355pp.

Jensen, Kathryn. *Mail-Order Prince in Her Bed*. Silhouette Desire 1,498. New York: Silhouette Books, 2003. 187pp.

Johnson, Keith Lee. *Pretenses*. Bowie, Md.: Strebor Books International: New York, 2004. 244pp.

Jones, Edward P., *Lost in the City: Stories*. Photographs by Amos Chan. New York: Morrow, 1992. 250pp.

Junkin, Tim. *Good Counsel: A Novel*. Chapel Hill, N.C.: Algonquin Books of Chapel Hill, 2001. 291pp.

Just, Ward S. *In the City of Fear*. New York: Viking, 1982.

Kafka-Gibbons, Paul. *Dupont Circle: A Novel*. Boston: Houghton Mifflin, 2001. 248pp.

Kaiser, Janice. *The Yanqui Prince*. Harlequin Super Romance 597. New York: Harlequin, 1994. 299pp.

Kauffman, Donna. *The Cinderella Rules*. New York: Bantam Books, 2004. 398pp.

Kava, Alex. *The Soul Catcher*. Don Mills, Ontario, Can.: Mira, 2002. 400pp.

Kelly, Katy. *Lucy Rose: Big on Plans*. Illustrated by Adam Rex. New York: Delacorte, 2005. 163pp. juvenile.

————. *Lucy Rose: Busy Like You Can't Believe*. Illustrated by Adam Rex. New York: Delacorte, 2006. juvenile.

————. *Lucy Rose, Here's the Thing about Me*. Illustrated by Adam Rex. New York: Delacorte, 2004. 137pp. juvenile.

Kenner, Laura. *Hero for Hire*. Harlequin Intrigue 405. New York: Harlequin, 1997. 248pp.

Kent, Andrea, and Bette McNicholas. *An Obsession with Honor*. New York: Warner Books, 1987. 375pp.

Killham, Nina. *How to Cook a Tart: A Novel*. New York: Bloomsbury, 2002. 250pp.

————. *Mounting Desire*, New York: Bloomsbury, 2005. 259pp.

Knudson, R. Rozanne. *Rinehart Shouts*. New York: Farrar, Straus, Giroux, 1987. 115pp.

Krist, Gary. *Chaos Theory*. New York: Random House, 2000. 347pp.

LaMarr, Tom. *October Revolution: A Novel*. Niwot, Colo.: University Press of Colorado, 1998. 201pp.

Langan, Ruth Ryan. *Banning's Woman*. Silhouette Intimate Moments 1,135. New York: Silhouette Books, 2002. 250pp.

————. *By Honor Bound*. Silhouette Intimate Moments 1,111. New York: Silhouette Books, 2001. 248pp.

————. *His Father's Son*. Silhouette Intimate Moments 1,147. New York: Silhouette Books, 2002. 251pp.

Lasky, Kathryn. *A Time for Courage: The Suffragette Diary of Kathleen Bowen*. New York: Scholastic, 2002. 217pp. juvenile.

Law, Janice. *Backfire*. New York: St. Martin's, 1994. 200pp.

Lawson, Michael. *The Inside Ring*. New York: Doubleday, 2005. 264pp.

Leavy, Jane. *Squeeze Play*. New York: Perennial, 2003. 384pp.

Lebherz, Richard. *Pilgrims into Light*. Baltimore: PublishAmerica, 2003. 195pp.

Lefcourt, Peter. *The Woody: A Novel*. New York: Simon & Schuster, 1998. 316pp.

Lehmann-Haupt, Christopher. *A Crooked Man: A Novel*. New York: Simon & Schuster, 1995. 351pp.

Lehrer, James. *Blue Hearts: A Novel*. New York: Random House, 1993. 214pp.

———. *Purple Dots: A Novel*. New York: Random House, 1998. 268pp.

Lerner, Preston. *Fools on the Hill*. New York: Pocket Books, 1995. 342pp.

Leuci, Bob. *Double Edge*. New York: Dutton, 1991. 272pp.

———. *Sweet Baby James*. Wakefield, R.I.: Moyer Bell, 2001. 272pp.

Levine, Paul. *9 Scorpions*. New York: Pocket Books, 1998. 373pp.

Lewis, Philip. *Life of Death*. Boulder, Colo.: Fiction Collective Two, 1993. 253pp.

Lewis, Shelby. *Simply Marvelous*. Washington, D.C.: BET, 2002. 250pp.

Lind, Michael. *Powertown*. New York: HarperCollins, 1996. 264pp.

Lindbergh, Anne. *The People in Pineapple Place*. San Diego, Calif.: Harcourt Brace Jovanovich, 1982. 147pp.

Lindbergh, Anne, and Julie Brinckloe. *The Hunky-Dory Dairy*. San Diego, Calif.: Harcourt Brace Jovanovich, 1986. 147pp.

Linsley, Clyde. *Death Spiral*. New York: Avalon Books, 2000. 215pp.

Lowell, Heather. *When the Storm Breaks*. New York: HarperTorch, 2003. 452pp.

Lucas, Daryl. *The Smithsonian Connection*. Choice Adventures 2. Wheaton, Ill.: Tyndale House, 1991. 151pp. juvenile.

Luckett, Jonathan. *How Ya Livin': A Novel*. Bowie, Md.: Strebor Books International, 2004. 651pp.

Lustbader, Eric. *Robert Ludlum's Jason Bourne in the Bourne Legacy: A Novel*. New York: St. Martin's, 2004. 453pp.

Lynds, Gayle. *Mesmerized*. New York: Pocket Books, 2001. 454pp.

MacKinnon, Douglas. *First Victim*. New York: M. Evans, 1997. 239pp.

Maddox, Muriel. *Myra's Daughters: A Novel*. Santa Fe, N.Mex: Sunstone Press, 2001. 254pp

Madsen, David. *Vodoun: A Novel*. New York: Morrow, 1994. 349pp.

Mallon, Thomas. *Two Moons: A Novel*. New York: Pantheon Books, 303pp.

Mann, Catherine. *Capitol Hill*. New York: Dell, 1992. 458pp.

Markun, Patricia Maloney. *The Congressman's Daughter*. St. Petersburg, Fla.: Willowisp Press, 1994. 143pp. juvenile.

Marlowe, Stephen. *Drum Beat: The Chester Drum Casebook*. Waterville, Maine: Five Star, 2003. 263pp.

Marshall, Leslie. *A Girl Could Stand Up: A Novel*. New York: Grove Press, 2003. 374pp.

Massey, Sujata. *The Bride's Kimono*. New York: HarperCollins, 2001. 310pp.

———. *The Pearl Diver.* New York: HarperCollins, 2004. 335pp.

———. *The Typhoon Lover / Sujata Massey.* New York: Harper-Collins, 2005. 320pp.

Mathews, Francine. *Blown.* New York: Bantam Books, 2005. 325pp.

Maul, Brian M. *God Is Dead.* Berkeley, Calif.: Creative Arts, 2002. 191pp.

Mayhew, Dianne. *Playing with Fire.* Washington D.C.: BET, 2000. 304pp.

McCann, Richard. *Mother of Sorrows.* New York: Pantheon Books, 2005. 196pp.

McConnell, Melissa. *Evidence of Love.* Orlando: Harcourt, 2005. 307pp.

McCourt, James. *Delancey's Way.* New York: Alfred A. Knopf, 2000. 369pp.

McGrath, James P. *The President's Cat.* Washington, D.C.: Feline Press, 1996. 203pp.

McGrory, Brian. *The Incumbent.* New York: Pocket Books, 2000.

McLaughlin, Ann L. *The House on Q Street: A Novel.* Santa Barbara, Calif.: John Daniel, 2002. 287pp.

McMullan, Kate, and Mavis Smith. *Fluffy Goes to Washington.* New York: Scholastic, 2002. unpaged. juvenile.

McMurtry, Larry. *Cadillac Jack: A Novel.* New York: Simon & Schuster, 1982. 395pp.

Means, Howard B. *C.S.A—Confederate States of America: A Novel.* New York: Morrow, 1998. 369pp.

Meltzer, Brad. *The First Counsel.* New York: Warner Books, 2001. 479pp.

——. *The Tenth Justice.* New York: Rob Weisbach Books, 1997. 389pp.

——. *The Zero Game.* New York: Warner Books, 2004. 460pp.

Merlis, Mark. *American Studies.* Boston: Houghton Mifflin, 1994. 275pp.

——. *Man About Town.* New York: Fourth Estate, 2003. 360pp.

Michael, J. J. *Life Is Never as It Seems.* Columbus, Miss.: Genesis Press, 2005. 269pp.

Michaels, Fern. *Free Spirit.* New York: Ballantine Books, 1983. 215pp.

——. *The Real Deal.* New York: Pocket Books, 2004. 440pp.

——. *Weekend Warriors.* New York: Zebra Books, 2004. 304pp.

Michaels, Kasey. *This Must Be Love.* New York: Zebra Books, 2003. 319pp.

Mickelbury, Penny. *Keeping Secrets: A Gianna Maglione Mystery.* Tallahassee, Fla.: Naiad Press, 1994. 189pp.

——. *Night Songs: A Gianna Maglione Mystery.* Tallahassee, Fla.: Naiad Press, 1995. 217pp.

——. *One Must Wait.* New York: Simon & Schuster, 1998. 252pp.

——. *Where to Choose.* New York: Simon & Schuster, 1998. 255pp.

Mikulski, Barbara, and Marylouise Oates. *Capitol Offense.* New York: Dutton, 1996. 312pp.

——. *Capitol Venture: A Novel.* New York: Dutton, 1997. 299pp.

Miller, Linda Lael. *Just Kate.* Don Mills, Ontario, Can.: Mira Books, 1989. 253pp.

Mills, Charles. *Stranger in the Shadows.* Shadow Creek Ranch Series 11. Hagerstown, Md.: Review and Herald, 1998. 151pp.

Mitchell, Michele. *The Latest Bombshell: A Novel.* New York: Henry Holt, 2003. 277pp.

———. *Our Girl in Washington: A Kate Boothe Novel.* New York: Plume, 2006. 288pp.

Molay, Mollie. *Commander's Little Surprise.* Harlequin American Romance 954. New York: Harlequin, 2003. 248pp.

Monfredo, Miriam Grace. *Sisters of Cain.* New York: Berkley Prime Crime, 2000. 368pp.

Moore, Marshall. *The Concrete Sky.* New York: Harrington Park Press, 2003. 273pp.

Morris, Judy K. *The Crazies & Sam: A Novel.* New York: Viking, 1983. 136pp.

Mrazek, Robert J. *Unholy Fire: A Novel of the Civil War.* New York: Thomas Dunne Books, 2003. 299pp.

Myers, Anna. *Assassin.* New York: Walker, 2005. 212pp.

Myers, John L. *Holy Family: A Mystery.* Boston: Alyson, 1992. 231pp.

Nance, John J. *Medusa's Child.* New York: Doubleday, 1997. 451pp.

Nesbit, Jeffrey Asher. *The Insider: A Novel.* Grand Rapids, Mich.: Zondervan, 1996. 325pp.

Nessen, Ron, and Johanna Neuman. *Death with Honors: A Knight & Day Mystery.* New York: Forge, 1998. 286pp.

———. *Knight & Day.* New York: Forge, 1995. 256pp.

———. *Press Corpse: A Knight & Day Mystery.* New York: Forge, 1996. 256pp.

North, Oliver, and Joe Musser. *Mission Compromised: A Novel.* Nashville, Tenn.: Broadman & Holman, 2002. 605pp.

Nye, Joseph S. *The Power Game: A Washington Novel.* New York: Public Affairs, 2004. 247pp.

O'Brien, Patricia. *The Ladies' Lunch: A Novel.* New York: Simon & Schuster, 1994. 284pp.

O'Reilly, Victor. *The Devil's Footprint.* New York: G. P. Putnam's Sons, 1996. 375pp.

Oestreicher, Mark. *The Monumental Discovery.* Choice Adventures 6. Wheaton, Ill.: Tyndale House, 1992. 121pp. juvenile.

Olshaker, Mark. *The Edge.* New York: Crown, 1994. 335pp.

Osborne, Denise. *Evil Intentions: A Feng Shui Mystery.* McKinleyville, Calif.: John Daniel, 2005. 186pp.

Osborne, Mary Pope. *After the Rain.* New York: Scholastic, 2002. 108pp. juvenile.

Pade, Victoria. *From Boss to Bridegroom.* New York: Silhouette Books, 2001. 248pp.

Patterson, James. *Along Came a Spider: A Novel.* Boston: Little, Brown, 1993. 435pp.

———. *The Big Bad Wolf.* New York: Warner Books, 2004. 390pp.

———. *Cat & Mouse: A Novel.* Boston: Little, Brown, 1997. 399pp.

———. *Four Blind Mice: A Novel.* Boston: Little, Brown, 2002. 387pp.

Patterson, James. *Jack and Jill: A Novel.* Boston: Little, Brown, 1996. 432pp.

———. *Kiss the Girls: A Novel.* Boston: Little, Brown, 1995. 451pp.

———. *The Lake House: A Novel.* Boston: Little, Brown, 2003. 376pp.

———. *London Bridges: A Novel.* New York: Little, Brown, 2004. 391pp.

———. *Mary Mary*. Boston: Little, Brown, 2005. 400pp.

———. *Pop Goes the Weasel: A Novel*. Boston: Little, Brown, 1999. 423pp.

———. *Roses Are Red: A Novel*. Boston: Little, Brown, 2000. 400pp.

———. *Violets Are Blue: A Novel*. Boston: Little, Brown, 2001. 393pp.

Patterson, Richard North. *Balance of Power*. New York: Ballantine Books, 2003. 611pp.

———. *The Lasko Tangent*. New York: Ballantine Books, 1980. 534pp.

Patterson, T. D. *The Vote*. Waterville, Maine: Five Star, 2004. 376pp.

Pease, William D. *The Monkey's Fist*. New York: Viking, 1996. 358pp.

Pelecanos, George P. *The Big Blowdown*. New York: St. Martin's, 1996. 313pp.

———. *Down by the River Where the Dead Men Go*. New York: St. Martin's, 1995. 234pp.

———. *Drama City: A Novel*. Boston: Little, Brown, 2005. 295pp.

———. *A Firing Offense*. New York: St. Martin's, 1992. 216pp.

———. *Hard Revolution: A Novel*. Boston: Little, Brown, 2004. 376pp.

———. *Hell to Pay: A Novel*. Boston: Little, Brown, 2002. 344pp.

Pelecanos, George P. *King Suckerman: A Novel*. Boston: Little, Brown, 1997. 264pp.

———. *Nick's Trip*. New York: St. Martin's, 1999. 276pp.

———. *Right as Rain: A Novel*. Boston: Little, Brown, 2001. 332pp.

————. *Shame the Devil: A Novel*. Boston: Little, Brown, 2000. 299pp.

————. *Shoedog*. New York: St. Martin's, 1994. 200pp.

————. *Soul Circus: A Novel*. Boston: Little, Brown, 2003. 341pp.

————. *The Sweet Forever: A Novel*. Boston: Little, Brown, 1998. 298pp.

Peters, Ralph. *The Perfect Soldier*. New York: Pocket Books, 1995. 303pp.

————. *Traitor: A Novel*. New York: Avon Books, 1999. 305pp.

————. *Twilight of Heroes*. New York: Avon Books, 1997. 451pp.

Pierce, Margret. *Most Wanted*. New York: St. Martin's Paperbacks, 1996. 274pp.

————. *Wild Justice*. New York: St. Martin's, 1995. 200pp.

Pita, Maria Isabel. *The Fabric of Love: An Erotic Romance*. New Milford, Conn.: Magic Carpet Books, 2004. 254pp.

Pottinger, Stanley. *The Fourth Procedure*. New York: Ballantine Books, 1995. 550pp.

Powell, J. Mark, and L. D. Meagher. *The Curse of Cain*. New York: Forge Books, 2005. 316pp.

Poyer, David. *Tomahawk*. New York: St. Martin's, 1998. 371pp.

Pyatt, Sue, and Keith A. Gaston. *Call Me Madame President*. Arlington, Va.: Imagination Station Press, 2003. 31pp. juvenile.

Quattlebaum, Mary, and Cat Bowman Smith. *Underground Train*. New York: Bantam Doubleday Dell Books for Young Readers, 1999. (unpaged). juvenile.

Quinn, Sally. *Happy Endings*. New York: Simon & Schuster, 1991. 566pp.

———. *Regrets Only*. New York: Simon & Schuster, 1986. 556pp.

Racina, Thom. *Hidden Agenda*. New York: Dutton, 1997. 358pp.

Rada, James R. *Between Rail and River*. Cumberland, Md.: Legacy Press, 2003. 296pp.

———. *Canawlers*. Cumberland, Md.: Legacy Press, 2001. 295pp.

Ransom, Candice F., and Shelly O. Haas. *Jimmy Crack Corn*. Minneapolis: Carolrhoda Books, 1994. 72pp.

Rawlings, Ellen. *The Murder Lover*. New York: Fawcett Gold Medal, 1997. 246pp.

Reiss, Bob. *The Last Spy*. New York: Simon & Schuster, 1993. 300pp.

Richards, Emilie. *Prospect Street*. Don Mills, Ontario, Can.: Mira, 2002. 461pp.

Richman, Phyllis C. *The Butter Did It: A Gastronomic Tale of Love and Murder*. New York: HarperCollins, 1997. 311pp.

———. *Murder on the Gravy Train*. New York: HarperCollins, 1999. 243pp.

———. *Who's Afraid of Virginia Ham?* New York: HarperCollins, 2001. 243pp.

Ricks, Thomas E. *A Soldier's Duty: A Novel*. New York: Random House, 2001. 250pp.

Rinaldi, Ann. *An Acquaintance with Darkness*. San Diego, Calif.: Harcourt Brace, 1997. 294pp.

———. *Girl in Blue*. New York: Scholastic, 2001. 310pp.

Ripley, Ann. *The Christmas Garden Affair: A Gardening Mystery*. New York: Kensington Books, 2002. 293pp.

———. *Death at the Spring Plant Sale*. New York: Kensington Books, 2003. 314pp.

————. *Death of a Garden Pest*. New York: St. Martins, 1996. 241pp.

————. *Death of a Political Plant*. New York: Bantam Books, 1998. 308pp.

————. *Harvest of Murder: A Gardening Mystery*. New York: Kensington Books, 2001. 290pp.

————. *Mulch: A Novel*. New York: St. Martin's, 1994. 163pp.

————. *Summer Garden Murder: A Gardening Mystery*. New York: Kensington Books, 2005. 293pp.

Rivers, Caryl. *Camelot*. Cambridge, Mass.: Zoland Books, 1998. 372pp.

————. *Girls Forever Brave and True*. New York: St. Martin's, 1986. 371pp.

Robbins, Arthur D. *Greenfield for President*. New York: Acropolis Books, 2001. 212pp.

Roberts, Carey. *Pray God to Die*. New York: Scribner, 1993. 354 pp.

Roberts, Nora. *The Baby Exchange*. Richmond, Va.: Silhouette, 1997. 251pp.

————. *Brazen Virtue*. New York: Bantam Books, 2001. 261pp.

————. *Honest Illusions*. New York: Putnam, 1992. 383pp.

————. *Sacred Sins*. New York: Bantam Books, 2000. 293pp.

Robinet, Harriette. *Washington City Is Burning*. New York: Atheneum Books for Young Readers, 1996. 149pp. juvenile.

Robinson, C. Kelly. *Between Brothers: A Novel*. New York: Villard, 1999. 373pp.

Robinson, Kim Stanley. *Fifty Degrees Below*. New York: Bantam Books, 2005. 416pp.

——. *Forty Signs of Rain*. New York: Bantam Books, 2004. 358pp.

Roosevelt, Elliott. *Elliott Roosevelt's Murder in the Lincoln Bedroom: An Eleanor Roosevelt Mystery*. New York: St. Martin's Paperbacks, 2002.

——. *Murder and the First Lady*. New York: St. Martin's, 1984. 227pp.

——. *Murder at Midnight: An Eleanor Roosevelt Mystery*. New York: St. Martin's, 1997. 216pp.

——. *Murder in Georgetown: An Eleanor Roosevelt Mystery*. New York: St. Martin's, 1999. 230pp.

——. *Murder in the Blue Room*. New York: St. Martin's, 1990. 215pp.

——. *Murder in the East Room*. New York: St. Martin's, 1993. 201pp.

——. *Murder in the Executive Mansion*. New York: St. Martin's, 1995. 197pp.

——. *Murder in the Lincoln Bedroom: An Eleanor Roosevelt Mystery*. New York: Thomas Dunne Books, 2000. 228pp.

——. *Murder in the Map Room: An Eleanor Roosevelt Mystery*. New York: St. Martin's, 1998. 251pp.

——. *Murder in the Oval Office*. New York: St. Martin's, 1989. 247pp.

——. *Murder in the Red Room*. New York: St. Martin's, 1992. 249pp.

——. *Murder in the Rose Garden*. New York: St. Martin's, 1989. 232pp.

——. *Murder in the West Wing: An Eleanor Roosevelt Mystery*. New York: St. Martin's, 1992. 247pp.

Roosevelt, Elliott. *New Deal for Death: A "Blackjack" Endicott Novel.* New York: St. Martin's, 1993. 251pp.

———. *The White House Pantry Murder: An Eleanor Roosevelt Mystery.* New York: St. Martin's, 1987. 231pp.

Roper, Robert. *Victory to the Moth.* New York: Context Books, 2002. 288pp.

Rosemoor, Patricia. *After the Dark, Seven Sin.* Silhouette Intrigue. Richmond, Va.: Silhouette, 1998. 248pp.

Roy, Ron, and Timothy Bush. *The Skeleton in the Smithsonian.* Capital Mysteries 3. New York: Random House, 2003. 86pp. juvenile.

———. *Who Broke Lincoln's Thumb?* Capital Mysteries 5. New York: Random House, 2005. juvenile.

Russell, Pamela Redford. *The Woman Who Loved John Wilkes Booth.* New York: Putnam, 1978. 379pp.

Ryan, Mary. *Hope.* London, U.K.: Headline, 2001. 470pp.

Salamanca, J. R. *That Summer's Trance: A Novel.* New York: Welcome Rain, 2000. 424pp.

Sanchez, Patrick. *The Way It Is.* New York: Kensington Books, 2003. 335pp.

Sandlin, Tim. *Honey Don't.* New York: G. P. Putnam's Sons, 2003. 352pp.

Sappey, Maureen Stack. *Letters from Vinnie.* Asheville, N.C.: Front Street, 1999. 248pp. juvenile.

Schamess, Lisa. *Borrowed Light: A Novel.* Dallas, Tex.: Southern Methodist University Press, 2002. 174pp.

Schutz, Benjamin M. *All the Old Bargains.* New York: Bluejay Books, 1985. 162pp.

———. *A Fistful of Empty.* New York: Viking, 1991. 192pp.

Schutz, Benjamin M. *Mexico Is Forever*. New York: St. Martin's, 1994. 230pp.

Schwartz, Karen. *Clearing the Aisle*. New York: Downtown Press, 2004. 350pp.

Seidel, Kathleen Gilles. *A Most Uncommon Degree of Popularity*. New York: St. Martin's, 2006.

Service, Pamela F. *Stinker's Return*. New York: Scribner 1993. 87pp. juvenile.

Shelby, Philip. *Days of Drums: A Novel*. New York: Simon & Schuster, 1996. 318pp.

———. *Last Rights: A Novel*. New York: Simon & Schuster, 1997. 333pp.

Sheldon, Sydney. *The Sky Is Falling*. New York: Morrow, 2000. 317pp.

Shreve, Susan Richards. *Children of Power*. New York: Macmillan, 1979. 294pp.

———. *Plum and Jaggers*. New York: Farrar Straus Giroux, 2001. 192pp.

———. *The Train Home*. New York: Nan A. Talese, 1993. 262pp.

Siman, Ken. *Pizza Face, or The Hero of Suburbia*. New York: Grove Weidenfeld, 1991, 179pp.

Slavin, Julia. *Carnivore Diet*. New York: W.W. Norton, 2005. 299pp.

Smith, Mary-Ann Tirone. *An American Killing: A Novel*. New York: Henry Holt, 1998. 360pp.

———. *Love Her Madly*. New York: Henry Holt, 2002. 307pp.

Smolonsky, Marc. *Dirty Laundry*. New York: Walker, 1991. 246pp.

Spencer, Scott. *Secret Anniversaries*. New York: Alfred A. Knopf, 1990. 257pp.

Spencer-Strachan, Louise. *The Train Ride*. New York: Spenchan Press, 1997. 200pp.

Spruill, Steven G. *Daughter of Darkness*. New York: Doubleday, 1997. 307pp.

————. *Rulers of Darkness*. New York: St. Martin's, 1995. 357pp.

Statham, Frances Patton. *The Roswell Legacy*. New York: Fawcett / Columbine, 1988. 379pp.

Steel, Danielle. *Journey*. New York: Delacorte, 2000. 323pp.

Sterling, Bruce. *The Zenith Angle*. New York: Del Rey, 2004. 306pp.

Stern, Mark. *Inadmissible*. New York: Carroll & Graf, 1994. 215pp.

Steven, Daniel. *Final Remedy*. New York: HarperPaperbacks, 1996. 376pp.

Stevens, Gordon. *Kennedy's Ghost*. New York: HarperPaperbacks, 1996. 424pp.

Steward-Hedrick, Paula. *Innocent Involvement*. Baltimore: Publish-America, 2004. 249pp.

Stone, Eric. *In a Heartbeat*. Novato, Calif.: Lyford Books, 1996. 313pp.

Stone, Katherine. *Rainbows*. New York: Kensington, 1992. 381pp.

Sullivan, Eugene. *The Majority Rules*. New York: Forge, 2005. 398pp.

Swann, S. Andrew. *Zimmerman's Algorithm*. DAW Book Collectors 1,142. New York: DAW Books, 2000. 387pp.

Tarloff, Erik. *Face-Time*. New York: Crown, 1998. 249pp.

Taylor, Janelle. *Night Moves*. New York: Zebra Books, 2002. 352pp.

Terry, Michael. *So Shine before Men: A Novel*. Santa Fe, N.Mex.: Sunstone Press, 2002. 376pp.

Thomas, Ross. *The Money Harvest*. New York: Warner Books, 1993. 247pp.

———. *No Questions Asked*. New York: Harper & Row, 1984. 188pp.

———. *Twilight at Mac's Place*. New York: Mysterious Press, 1990. 343pp.

Thor, Brad. *State of the Union: A Thriller*. New York: Atria Books, 2004. 340pp.

Tiede, Tom. *Welcome to Washington, Mr. Witherspoon: A Novel*. New York: Morrow, 1979. 324pp.

Tillis, Tracey. *Final Act*. New York: Onyx, 1998. 298pp.

Truman, Margaret. *Murder at Ford's Theatre: A Capital Crimes Novel*. New York: Ballantine Books, 326pp

———. *Murder at the FBI: A Novel*. New York: Arbor House, 1985. 256pp.

———. *Murder at the Kennedy Center*. New York: Random House, 1989. 310pp.

———. *Murder at the Library of Congress*. New York: Random House, 1999. 322pp.

———. *Murder at the National Cathedral*. New York: Random House, 1990. 293pp.

———. *Murder at the National Gallery*. New York: Random House, 1996. 340pp.

———. *Murder at the Pentagon*. New York: Random House, 1992. 291pp.

———. *Murder at the Washington Tribune. A Capital Crimes Novel;* New York: Ballantine Books, 2006. 366pp.

———. *Murder at the Watergate: A Novel.* New York: Random House, 1998. 333pp.

Truman, Margaret. *Murder at Union Station: A Capital Crimes Novel.* New York: Ballantine Books, 2004. 327pp.

———. *Murder in Foggy Bottom.* New York: Random House, 2000. 314pp.

———. *Murder in Georgetown.* New York: Arbor House, 1986. 267pp.

———. *Murder in the CIA.* New York: Random House, 1987. 371pp.

———. *Murder in the House.* New York: Random House, 1997. 322pp.

———. *Murder in the Smithsonian: A Novel.* New York: Arbor House, 1983. 298pp.

———. *Murder in the Supreme Court: A Novel.* New York: Arbor House, 1982. 284pp.

———. *Murder in the White House: A Novel.* New York: Arbor House, 1980. 235pp.

———. *Murder on Capitol Hill: A Novel.* New York: Arbor House, 1981. 255pp.

———. *Murder on Embassy Row: A Novel.* New York: Arbor House, 1984. 316pp.

———. *Murder on the Potomac.* New York: Random House, 1994. 230pp.

Vasile, Nick. *A Member of the Family.* New York: TOR, 1993. 320pp.

Vaughn, Ellen Santilli. *The Strand: A Novel.* Dallas, Tex.: Word, 1997. 323pp.

Vidal, Gore. *Empire.* New York: Random House, 1987. 486pp.

Villemur, Michéle. *The Adventures of Clappety Clop in Washington, D.C.* Washington, D.C.: Capital Children's Museum, 1996. 20pp. juvenile.

Viorst, Judith. *Murdering Mr. Monti: A Merry Little Tale of Sex and Violence.* New York: Simon & Schuster, 1994. 254pp.

Vitola, Denise. *The Winter Man.* New York: Berkeley Books, 1995. 331pp.

Wakling, Christopher. *The Immortal Part.* New York: Riverhead Books, 2003. 305pp.

Walker, Robert W. *Absolute Instinct.* New York: Berkley Books, 2004. 377pp.

Walker, Trish. *Blue Holes to Terror.* Nederland, Tex.: Quest Books, 2001. 217pp.

Warner, Gertrude Chandler, and Charles Tang. *The Mystery in Washington, D.C., The Boxcar Children Mysteries.* Morton Grove, Ill.: A. Whitman, 1994. 110pp. juvenile.

Webb, Debra. *Her Hidden Truth.* Harlequin Intrigue 697. New York: Harlequin, 2003. 248pp.

Weber, Janice. *Hot Ticket.* New York: Warner Books, 1998. 337pp.

Weinberger, Caspar W., and Peter Schweizer. *Chain of Command.* New York: Atria Books, 2005. 360pp.

Weiss, Ellen, and Betina Ogden. *Voting Rights Days.* Hitty's Travels 3. New York: Aladdin Paperbacks, 2002. 75pp. juvenile.

Weitzman, Jacqueline Preiss, and Robin Preiss-Glasser. *You Can't Take a Balloon into the National Gallery.* New York: Dial Books for Young Readers, 2000. 36pp. juvenile.

West, Chassie. *Killing Kin.* New York: Avon Books, 2000. 329pp.

White, Ann Howard. *The Mother of His Child.* Silhouette Special Edition 948. New York: Silhouette Books, 1995. 248pp.

Whitfield, Van. *Dad Interrupted: A Novel*. New York: Harlem Moon, 2004. 271pp.

———. *Something's Wrong with Your Scale! A Romantic Comedy*. New York: Doubleday, 1999. 293pp.

Wickert, Gary L. *Dark Redemption*. Greensboro, N.C.: Tudor Publishers, 1999. 475pp.

Wiggs, Susan. *Halfway to Heaven*. Don Mills, Ontario, Can.: Mira Books, 2001. 401pp.

Williams, Edward Christopher, Adam McKible, and Emily Bernard. *When Washington Was in Vogue: A Lost Novel of the Harlem Renaissance*. New York: Amistad, 2005. 285pp.

Wilson, F. Paul. *Deep as the Marrow*. New York: Forge, 1997. 352pp.

———. *Implant*. New York: Forge, 1995. 348pp.

Wilson, Josef. *The Fourth Branch*. Martinsburg, W.Va: Quiet Storm, 1999. 391pp.

Winters, Angela. *A Capitol Affair*. Washington D.C.: BET, 2005. 315pp.

Witham, Larry. *Dark Blossom: A Novel of East & West*. Burtonsville, Md.: Meridian Books, 1997. 261pp.

Woodbury, Derrik F. *Deception*. Plainville, Conn.: Woodstock Books, 1998. 276pp.

Woods, Sherryl. *Wages of Sin*. New York: Warner Books, 1994. 250pp.

Woods, Stuart. *Capital Crimes*. New York: G. P. Putnam's Sons, 2003. 292pp.

———. *Grass Roots: A Novel*. New York: Simon & Schuster, 1989. 459pp.

Wouk, Herman. *A Hole in Texas: A Novel*. Boston: Little, Brown, 2004. 278pp.

Appendix B
Annotated Works Listed
Chronologically

1822-1850

364. Watterson, George. *The L... Family at Washington; or, A Winter in the Metropolis.* Washington, D.C.: Davis & Force, 1822. 159pp.

306. Smith, Margaret Bayard. *A Winter in Washington: or, Memoirs of the Seymour Family.* New York: E. Bliss & E. White, 1824.

374. Williams, C. R., and Clifton Waller Barrett. *Aristocracy; or, The Holbey Family; a National Tale.* Providence, R.I.: J. Knowles, 1832. 312pp.

282. Price, William. *Clement Falconer; or The Memoirs of a Young Whig.* 2 vols. Baltimore: N. Hickman, 1838. 229pp. 192pp.

342. Tuel, John E. *St. Clair, or The Protégé: A Tale of the Federal City.* New York: W. Taylor & Company, 1846. 142pp.

16. Anonymous. *Scenes at Washington: A Story of the Last Generation; By a Citizen of Baltimore.* New York: Harper & Brothers, 1848. 197pp.

1851-1875

203. Lasselle, Mrs. Nancy Polk. *Annie Grayson: or, Life in Washington.* Washington, D.C.: H. Laselle, 1853. 345pp.

352. Vingut, Mrs. Gertrude (Fairfield). *Irene: or, the Autobiography of an Artist's Daughter and Other Tales.* Boston: Damrell & Moore, 1853. 383pp.

2. Adams, Charles [Templeton, Timothy, pseud.]. *The Adventures of My Cousin Smooth.* New York: Miller, Orton, and Mulligan, 1856. 236pp.

202. Lasalle, Mrs. E. L. *Magdalen, the Enchantress: Founded on Fact.* Philadelphia: J. B. Lippincott, 1858. 302pp.

204. Lasselle, Mrs. Nancy Polk. *Hope Marshall; or, Government and Its Offices.* Washington, D.C.: H. Laselle. 1859. 396pp.

148. Greene, Talbot. *American Nights' Entertainments; Compiled from Pencilings of a United States Senator; Entitled a Winter in the Federal City.* Jonesborough, Tenn.: William A. Sparks, 1860. 266pp.

307. Smith, William Russell. *As It Is....* Albany, N.Y.: Munsell & Rowland, 1860. 260pp.

15. Anonymous. *Brisée.* Philadelphia: J. B. Lippincott, 1862. 255pp.

356. Walworth, Mansfield Tracy. *Lulu: A Tale of the National Hotel Poisoning.* New York: Carleton, 1863. 367pp.

86. Dall, Caroline. *Patty Gray's Journey: From Baltimore to Washington.* Boston: Lee & Shepherd, 1870. 283pp. young adult.

155. Hall, A. Oakey. *The Congressman's Christmas Dream; and the Lobby Member's Happy New Year.* New York: Scribner, Welford, 1870. 64pp.

69. Clemens, Samuel L., and Charles Dudley Warner. *The Gilded Age: A Tale of Today.* Hartford, Conn.: American Publishing, 1874. 574pp.

93. De Forest, John William. *Honest John Vane.* New Haven, Conn.: Richmond & Patten, 1875. 259pp.

95. De Forest, John William. *Playing the Mischief.* Illustrated by John Hyde. New York: Harper, 1875. 185pp.

287. Riddle, A. G. *Alice Brand: A Romance of the Capitol.* New York: D. Appleton, 1875. 384pp.

1876-1900

94. De Forest, John William. *Justine's Lovers.* Library of American Fiction 2. New York: Harper's & Brothers, 1878. 135pp.

186. Jones, John Beauchamp. *The Rival Belles; or, Life in Washington.* Peterson's Dollar Series. Philadelphia: T. B. Peterson Brothers, 1878. 270pp.

381. Woods, Kate Tannatt. *Six Little Rebels.* Boston: D. Lothrop, 1879. 412pp.

3. Adams, Henry. *Democracy; an American Novel.* Leisure-Hour Series 112. New York: Henry Holt, 1880. 374pp.

165. Holden, E. Goodman. *A Famous Victory.* Chicago: Jansen, McClurg, 1880. 368pp.

276. Pierce, Gilbert A. *Zachariah, The Congressman; A Tale of American Society.* Chicago: Donnelly, Gassette, & Lloyd, 1880. 440pp.

57. Burnett, Frances Hodgson. *Through One Administration.* Boston: J. R. Osgood, 1883. 564pp.

84. Dahlgren, Madeleine Vinton. *A Washington Winter.* Boston: James R. Osgood and Company, 1883. 247pp.

145. Grant, A. F. *The War Detective; or, The Plotters at Washington, a Tale of Booth's Conspiracy.* New York: War Library / Novelist Publishing, 1883. 96pp.

250. Miller, Mrs. Alexander McVeigh. *The Senator's Favorite.* New York: Street & Smith, 1883. 215pp.

259. Murray, Charles Theodore. *Sub Rosa: A Novel.* New York: G. W. Carleton, 1883. 419pp.

192. Keenan, Henry Francis. *The Money-Makers.* Boston: D. Appleton, 1884. 337pp.

212. Lincoln, Jeanie Gould. *Her Washington Season.* Boston: James R. Osgood, 1884. 207pp.

23. Badeau, Adam. *Conspiracy: A Cuban Romance.* New York: R. Worthington, 1885. 324pp.

233. Magruder, Julia. *Across the Chasm.* New York: Scribner's, 1885. 310pp.

261. Nichols, Laura D. *Nelly Marlow in Washington.* Boston: Lothrop, c. 1886. 296pp. young adult.

71. Cleveland, Cynthia Eloise. *See-Saw; or, Civil Service in the Departments by One Of'm.* Detroit, Mich.: F. B. Dickerson, 1887. 226pp.

249. Miller, Mrs. Alexander McVeigh. *The Senator's Bride.* New York: Street & Smith, 1887. 211pp.

368. Wheelwright, John Tyler. *A Child of the Century.* New York: Charles Scribner's Sons, 1887. 346pp.

36. Benjamin, Lewis. *Why Was It?* Chicago: Belford, Clarke, 1888. 257pp.

58. Camera, Cara [pseud.]. *Society Rapids: High Life in Washington, Saratoga and Bar Harbor; by "One in the Swim."* Philadelphia: T. B. Peterson, 1888. 250pp.

70. Cleveland, Cynthia Eloise. *His Honor; or, Fate's Mysteries: A Thrilling Realistic Story of the United States Army.* New York: American News, 1889. 258pp.

87. Darling, Mrs. Flora Adams. *A Social Diplomat.* New York: National Book, 1889. 186pp.

88. Darling, Flora Adams. *A Winning, Wayward Woman: Chapters in the Heart-History of Amélie Warden.* Judge's Novels 4. New York: Judge, 1889. 158pp.

283. Ragan, Emily Lee Sherwood. *Willis Peyton's Inheritance: The Story of a Claim.* Boston: Universalist Publishing House, 1889. 237pp.

340. Tourgée, Albion Winegar. *Pactolus Prime.* New York: Cassell, c. 1890. 359pp.

49. Bogy, Lewis Vital. *In Office: A Story of Washington Life and Society.* Chicago: F. J. Schulte, c. 1891. 202pp.

253. Morris, Charles. *The Stolen Letter; or, Frank Sharp, the Washington Detective.* Patrol Detective Series. Chicago: Continental, 1891. 199pp.

83. Dahlgren, Madeleine Vinton. *Chim: His Washington Winter.* New York: C. L. Webster, 1892. 334pp.

136. Garland, Hamlin. *A Spoil of Office: A Story of the Modern West.* Boston: Arena, 1892. 385pp.

367. Wheeler, Mrs. William Lamont. *A Washington Symphony.* New York: G. P. Putnam's Sons, 1893. 194pp.

77. Crawford, Theron Clark. *A Man and His Soul.* New York: Charles B. Reed, 1894. 255pp.

173. Howard, Milford Wrarison. *If Christ Came to Congress.* Washington, D.C.: Author, 1894. 364pp.

382. Worthen, J. Henry. *Old Sile Ridleigh; or, the Serio-Comic Adventures of a Down-East Yankee in Washington.* Fruitport, Mich.: John Chapman, c. 1894. 80pp.

113. Edwards, James A. *In the Court Circle: A Tale of Washington Life.* Washington, D.C.: Columbian, 1895. 167pp.

91. Davis, Harriet Riddle. *In Sight of the Goddess: A Tale of Washington Life.* Philadelphia: J. B. Lippincott, 1896. 228pp.

150. Gunter, Archibald Clavering. *Her Senator; A Novel.* New York: Hurst, 1896. 261 pages.

210. Lincoln, Jeanie Gould. *A Genuine Girl.* Boston: Houghton Mifflin / Riverside Press, 1896. 264pp.

334. Thomas, Katherine Elwes. *Not All the King's Horses.* New York: Cassell, 1896. 210pp.

41. Black, Alexander. *A Capital Courtship.* New York: Scribner's Sons, 1897. 104pp.

64. Chatfield-Taylor, Hobart C. *The Vice of Fools.* Illustrated by Raymond M. Crosby. Chicago: Herbert S. Stone, 1897. 310pp.

162. Hayworth, A. D. *Uncle Hank and Aunt Nancy in Washington.* Washington, D.C.: Hayworth, 1897. 165pp.

166. Holmes, John. *Magdalen: A Novel of the Social Crusade.* Washington, D.C.: Columbia, 1897. 128pp.

174. Howard, Milford Wrarison. *What Christ Saw: Sequel to "If Christ Came to Congress."* Washington, D.C.: The Author, 1897. 96pp.

224. Litchfield, Grace Denio. *In the Crucible.* New York: G. P. Putnam's Sons, 1897. 344pp.

10. Altsheler, Joseph A. *A Herald of the West: An American Story of 1811-1815.* New York: D. Appleton, 1898. 359pp.

132. Gardener, Helen Hamilton. *An Unofficial Patriot.* New York. R. F. Fenno, 1898. 351pp.

269. Philips, Melville. *The Senator's Wife: Being a Tale of Washington Life.* New York: F. Tennyson Neely, c. 1898. 240pp.

17. Argenteuil, Paul d'. *The Trembling of Borealis.* New York: F. Tennyson Neely, 1899. 316pp.

85. Dahlgren, Madeleine Vinton. *The Woodley Lane Ghost.* Philadelphia: D. Biddle, 1899. 474pp.

207. Levy, Lewis [Stonewall, Cutter, pseud.]. *Senator Cashdollar of Washington.* Chicago: E. A. Weeks, 1899. 246pp.

312. Standish, Hal [Shackelford, Harvey King, pseud.]. *Frank Fair in Congress; or, A Boy among Our Law Makers; a Thrilling Story of Washington.* New York: F. Tousey, 1899. juvenile.

336. Tibbetts, Edgar Alfred [Johnson, Ivar, pseud.]. *The Department Clerk; A Story of Civil Service Reform.* New York: F. Tennyson Neely, 1899. 216pp.

19. Atherton, Gertrude. *Senator North.* New York: John Lane, 1900. 367pp.

50. Bowles, John. *The Masked Prophet; a Psychological Romance.* New York: Alliance, 1900. 190pp.

105. Douglas, Amanda Minnie. *A Little Girl in Old Washington.* New York: Dodd, Mead, 1900. 319pp.

137. Garland, Rufus Cummins. *Zaléa: A Psychological Episode and Tale of Love.* Washington, D.C.: Neale, 1900. 146pp.

146. Grant, Robert. *Unleavened Bread.* New York: Charles Scribner's Sons, 1900. 431pp.

241. McLaughlin, Nathan Monroe. *The Last Man.* Washington, D.C.: Neale, 1900. 221pp.

1901-1925

79. Cruger, Mrs. Julie Grinnell [Gordon, Julien, pseud.]. *The Wage of Character.* New York: D. Appleton, 1901. 272pp.

229. Low, Alfred Maurice, Sir. *The Supreme Surrender.* New York: Harper & Brothers, 1901. 329pp.

328. Strong, Armour. *Dear Days: A Story of Washington School Life.* Philadelphia: Henry T. Coates, 1901. 316pp. young adult.

40. Bergengren, Anna Faquhar. *Her Washington Experiences: As Related by a Cabinet Minister's Wife in a Series of Letters to Her Sister.* Illustrated by T. de Thulstrup. Boston: L. C. Page, 1902. 222pp.

120. Eustis, Edith. *Marion Manning*. New York and London: Harper & Brothers, 1902. 338pp.

126. Fleming, Thomas. *Around the Capital with Uncle Hank*. New York: Nutshell, 1902. 346pp.

171. Hopkins, Pauline Bradford Mackie. *The Washingtonians*. Boston: L. C. Page, 1902. 357pp.

185. Johnson, William Franklin. *Poco a Poco*. Illustrated by W. H. Fry. Akron, Ohio: Saalfield, 1902. 307pp.

275. Phillips, David Graham. *A Woman Ventures*. New York: Stokes, 1902. 331pp.

330. Sutton, Henry Sidney. *Rhoda Roland: A Woman from the West in Washington*. New York: Abbey Press: 1902. 300pp.

370. Whitlock, Brand. *The Thirteenth District; A Story of a Candidate*. Indianapolis: Bowen-Merrill, [1902]. 490pp.

378. Winchester, Paul. *Around the Throne: Sketches of Washington Society during a Recent Administration*. Baltimore: B. G. Eichelberger, 1902. 187pp.

28. Barry, John D. *The Congressman's Wife: A Story of American Politics*. Illustrated by Rollin G. Kirby. New York: Smart Set, 1903. 359pp.

147. Green, Anna Katherine. *The Filigree Ball: Being a Full and True Account of the Solution of the Mystery Concerning the Jeffrey-Moore Affair*. Illustrated by C. M. Relyea. Indianapolis: Bobbs-Merrill, 1903. 418pp.

172. Hopkins, William B. *Milliner to a Mouse: A Capital Chat*. New York: Knickerbocker, 1903. 119pp.

208. Lewis, Alfred Henry. *Peggy O'Neal*. Illustrated by Henry Hutt. Philadelphia: D. Biddle, 1903. 494pp.

299. Seawell, Molly Elliott. *Despotism and Democracy*. New York: McClure, Phillips, 1903. 311pp.

372. Willard, Rosseter. *The Senator's Sweetheart*. Illustrated by Felix Mahoney. New York: Grafton Press, 1903. 266pp.

78. Crissey, Forrest. *Tattlings of a Retired Politician*. Illustrated by John T. McCutcheon. Chicago: Clarkson & Cooper, 1904. 487pp.

98. Derville, Leslie. *The Other Side of the Story: A Novel*. New York: G. W. Dillingham, 1904. 318pp.

104. Douglas, Amanda Minnie. *Honor Sherburne*. New York: Dodd, Mead, 1904. 340pp.

209. Lewis, Alfred Henry. *The President*. New York: A. S. Barnes, 1904. 514pp.

232. MacGrath, Harold. *The Man on the Box*. Illustrated by Harrison Fisher. Indianapolis: Bobbs-Merrill, 1904. 361pp.

271. Phillips, David Graham. *The Cost*. Indianapolis: Bobbs-Merrill, 1904. 402pp.

281. Porter, Duval [Slick, Sam, Jr., pseud]. *Adventures of an Office Seeker*. Richmond, Va.: Everett Waddey, 1904. 159pp.

308. Southworth, E.D.E.N. *Ishmael; or In the Depths*. The Companion Series. New York: R. F. Fenno, [1904]. 549pp.

311. Standish, Hal. *Fred Fearnot and His Dog; or, The Boy Who Ran for Congress*. Work and Win Series 278. New York: F. Tousey, 1904. 28pp. juvenile.

318. Stoddard, William Osborn. *Long Bridge Boys: A Story of '61*. Illustrated by I. B. Hazelton. Boston: Lothrop, 1904. 344pp.

361. Warren, Stanley Sevier. *In Defense of His Excellency*. New York: Broadway, 1904. 118pp.

97. Denison, Mary Andrews. *That Husband of Mine*. Library of Popular Fiction 36. New York: American News, 1905. 227pp.

211. Lincoln, Jeanie Gould. *A Javelin of Fate*. Boston: Houghton Mifflin / Riverside Press, 1905. 295pp.

273. Phillips, David Graham. *The Plum Tree.* Indianapolis: Bobbs-Merrill, 1905. 389pp.

274. Phillips, David Graham. *The Social Secretary.* Illustrated by Clarence F. Underwood. Indianapolis: Bobbs-Merrill, 1905. 197pp.

285. Reed, Sarah A. *A Romance of Arlington House.* N.p., 1905. 116pp.

294. Sanborn, Mary Farley. *Lynette and the Congressman.* Boston: Little, Brown, 1905. 396pp.

295. Schneider, Martha Lemon. *A Government Countess: A Novel of Departmental Life in Washington.* Washington, D.C.: Neale, 1905. 221pp.

300. Seawell, Molly Elliott [Davis, Foxcroft, pseud.]. *Mrs. Darrell.* Illustrations by William Sherman Potts. New York: MacMillan, 1905. 391pp.

346. Tybout, Ella Middleton. *The Wife of the Secretary of State.* Philadelphia: J. B. Lippincott, 1905. 359pp.

383. Yulee, C. Wickliffe. *The Awakening: A Washington Novel.* Photographic illustrations. Washington, D.C.: Neale, 1905. 379pp.

14. Andrews, Mary Raymond Shipman. *The Perfect Tribute.* New York: C. Scribner's Sons, 1906. 47pp.

133. Gardenhire, S. M. *The Long Arm.* New York: Harper & Brothers, 1906. 345pp.

309. Spofford, Harriet Prescott. *Old Washington.* Boston: Little, Brown, 1906. 279pp.

313. Stanley, Caroline Abbot. *Modern Madonna.* New York: Century, 1906. 401pp.

332. Taylor, Mary Imlay. *The Impersonator.* Illustrated by C. Grunwald. Boston: Little, Brown, 1906. 392pp.

20. Ayers, Daisy. *The Conquest.* New York: Neale, 1907. 344pp.

135. Gardiner, Ruth Kimball. *The World and the Woman.* New York: A. S. Barnes, 1907. 292pp.

239. McCutcheon, John T. *Congressman Pumphrey the People's Friend.* Indianapolis: Bobbs-Merrill, 1907. 126pp.

242. McLaws, [Emily] Lafayette. *The Welding.* Boston: Little, Brown, 1907. 360pp.

134. Gardenhire, S. M. *Purple and Homespun.* New York: Harper & Brothers, 1908. 371pp.

140. Gerry, Margarita Spalding. *The Toy Shop: A Romantic Story of Lincoln the Man.* New York: Harper & Brothers, 1908. 50pp.

142. Godfrey, Hollis. *The Man Who Ended War.* Boston: Little, Brown, 1908. 301pp.

157. Harrison, Mrs. Burton. *The Count and the Congressman.* Illustrated by Alex O. Levy. New York: Cupples & Leon, 1908. 300pp.

333. Taylor, Mary Imlay. *The Reaping.* Boston: Little, Brown, 1908. 334pp.

100. Dillon, Mary C. *The Patience of John Morland.* Illustrated by C. M. Relyea. New York: Doubleday, Page, 1909. 406pp.

111. Eaton, Paul Webster. *The Treasure.* New York: R. F. Fenno, 1909. 410pp.

125. Fitzgerald, Robert. *The Statesmen Snowbound.* Illustrated by Wad-el-Ward. Washington, D.C.: Neale, 1909. 217pp.

129. Futrelle, Jacques. *Elusive Isabel.* Illustrated by Alonzo Kimball. New York: A. L. Burt, 1909. 273pp.

272. Phillips, David Graham. *The Fashionable Adventures of Joshua Craig.* New York: D. Appleton, 1909. 365pp.

288. Rinehart, Mary Roberts. *The Man in Lower Ten.* Illustrated by Howard Chandler Christy. New York: Review of Reviews, 1909. 282pp.

301. Seawell, Molly Elliot [Davis, Foxcroft, pseud.]. *The Whirl: A Romance of Washington Society.* New York: Dodd, Mead, 1909. 306pp.

380. Wise, Thomas A. *A Gentleman from Mississippi.* Based on a play by Frederick R. Toombs and Harrison Rhodes. Illustrated with cast member photographs. New York: J. S. Ogilvie, 1909. 189pp.

156. Hansbrough, H. C. *The Second Amendment.* Minneapolis: Hudson, 1911. 359pp.

280. Popham, William Lee. *Washington Monument Romance.* Seven Wonders of the World Series (American) 7. Louisville, Ky.: World Supply, 1911. 109pp.

30. Barton, George. *Barry Wynn; or, The Adventures of a Page Boy in the United States Congress.* Illustrated by John Huybers. Boston: Small, Maynard, 1912. 348pp. young adult.

82. Curtis, Isabel Gordon. *The Woman from Wolverton: A Story of Washington Life.* New York: Century, 1912. 342pp.

90. Davies, Acton, and Charles Nirdlinger. *The First Lady in the Land; or, When Dolly Todd Took Boarders.* Illustrated by Howard Giles. New York: H. K. Fly, 1912. 309pp.

222. Lincoln, Natalie Sumner. *The Trevor Case.* Illustrated by Edmund Frederick. New York: D. Appleton, 1912. 332pp.

225. Lockling, Lydia Waldo. *The Adventures of Polly and Gilbert in Washington, D.C.* New York: Cosmopolitan Press, 1912. 130pp. young adult.

247. Merwin, Samuel. *The Citadel: A Romance of Unrest.* New York: Century, 1912. 409pp.

47. Blythe, Samuel G. *The Price of Place.* New York: George H. Doran, c. 1913. 359pp.

75. Copley, Frank Barkley. *The Impeachment of President Israels.* New York: Macmillan, 1913. 124pp.

76. Crane, Laura Dent. *The Automobile Girls at Washington; or, Checkmating the Plots of Foreign Spies.* Philadelphia: Henry Altemus, 1913. 253pp. young adult.

144. Gould, Elizabeth Lincoln. *Polly Prentiss Goes A-Visiting.* Philadelphia: Penn, 1913. 200pp. young adult.

216. Lincoln, Natalie Sumner. *The Lost Despatch.* New York: D. Appleton, 1913. 309pp.

46. Blythe, Samuel G. *The Fakers.* New York: George H. Doran, 1914. 388pp.

81. Curtis, Isabel Gordon. *The Congresswoman.* Chicago: Browne & Howell, 1914. 505pp.

217. Lincoln, Natalie Sumner. *The Man Inside.* New York: D. Appleton, 1914. 303pp.

270. Philips, Page. *At Bay.* Based on the drama by George Scarborough. Illustrated with photographs from the production. New York: Macaulay, 1914. 253pp.

298. Scott, John Reed. *The Red Emerald.* Philadelphia: J. B. Lippincott, 1914. 352pp.

63. Chambrun, Mme. De. *Pieces of the Game.* New York: G. P. Putnam's Sons, 1915. 259pp.

220. Lincoln, Natalie Sumner. *The Official Chaperon.* New York: D. Appleton, 1915. 331pp.

48. Blythe, Samuel G. *A Western Warwick.* New York: George H. Doran, 1916. 345pp.

296. Scott, John Reed. *The Cab of the Sleeping Horse.* New York: G. P. Putnam's Sons, 1916. 361pp.

52. Brown, George Rothwell. *My Country: A Story of Today.* Illustrated by Chase Emerson. Boston: Small, Maynard, 1917. 359pp.

289. Rollins, Montgomery. *The Village Pest: A Story of David.* Illustrated by J. Henry. Boston: Lothrop, Lee & Shepard, 1917. 360pp.

297. Scott, John Reed. *The Man in Evening Clothes.* New York: G. P. Putnam's Sons, 1917. 387pp.

32. Barton, George. *The Strange Adventures of Bromley Barnes.* Illustrated by Charles E. Meister. Boston: L. C. Page, 1918. 345pp.

22. Babcock, Bernie. *The Soul of Abe Lincoln.* New York: Grosset & Dunlap, 1919. 328pp.

29. Barton, George. *The Ambassador's Trunk.* Illustrated by Charles E. Meister. Boston: Page, 1919. 310pp.

33. Barton, Wilfred M. *The Road to Washington.* Boston: Richard C. Badger / Gorham Press, 1919. 197pp.

170. Hope, Laura Lee [pseud.]. *The Bobbsey Twins in Washington.* New York: Grosset & Dunlap, 1919. 250pp. juvenile.

176. Hughes, Robert. *The Cup of Fury: A Novel of Cities and Shipyards.* Illustrated by Henry Raleigh. New York: Harper & Brothers, 1919. 350pp.

360. Ware, Richard D. *Rollo's Journey to Washington.* Boston: L. C. Page, 1919. 170pp. young adult.

31. Barton, George. *The Pembroke Mason Affair.* Illustrated by Charles E. Meister. Boston: L. C. Page, 1920. 331pp.

37. Benson, Mildred Wirt [Emerson, Alice B., pseud.]. *Betty Gordon in Washington, or Strange Adventures in a Great City.* New York: Cupples & Leon, 1920. 210pp. young adult.

73. Cole, Cyrenus. *From Four Corners to Washington: A Little Story of Home, Love, War, and Politics.* Cedar Rapids, Iowa: Torch Press, 1920. 80pp.

159. Hay, James Jr. *The Melwood Mystery.* New York: Dodd, Mead, 1920. 323pp

160. Hay, James Jr. *The Unlighted House.* New York: Dodd, Mead, 1921. 281pp.

347. Tyson, J. Aubrey. *The Scarlet Tanager.* New York: Macmillan, 1922. 340pp.

24. Bailey, Temple. *Dim Lantern.* Illustrated by Coles Phillips. Philadelphia: Penn, 1923. 344pp.

124. Fergusson, Harvey. *Capitol Hill: A Novel of Washington Life.* New York: Alfred A. Knopf, 1923. 309pp.

339. Toomer, Jean. *Cane.* Foreword by Waldo Frank. New York: Boni & Liveright, 1923. 239pp.

353. Vrooman, Julia Scott. *The High Road to Honor.* New York: Minton, Balch & Company, 1924. 299 pp.

373. Williams, Anna Vernon (Dorsey). *The Spirit of the House.* New York: D. Appleton, 1924. 328pp.

117. Eiker, Mathilde. *Mrs. Mason's Daughters.* New York: Macmillan, 1925. 367pp.

139. Gerould, Gordon Hall. *A Midsummer Mystery.* New York: D. Appleton, 1925. 256pp.

1926-1950

6. Adams, Samuel Hopkins. *Revelry.* New York: Boni & Liveright, 1926. 318pp.

161. Hay, James Jr. *That Washington Affair.* New York: Dodd, Mead, 1926. 254pp.

214. Lincoln, Natalie Sumner. *The Blue Car Mystery.* New York: D. Appleton, 1926. 314pp.

25. Bailey, Temple. *Wallflowers.* Philadelphia: Penn, 1927. 350pp.

35. Bell, Margaret. *Hubble-Bubble.* New York: Dodd, Mead, 1927. 337pp.

182. Hunt, Una. *Young in the "Nineties."* New York: Charles Scribner's Sons, 1927. 313pp.

215. Lincoln, Natalie Sumner. *The Dancing Silhouette.* New York: D. Appleton, 1927. 277pp.

221. Lincoln, Natalie Sumner. *P.P.C.* New York: D. Appleton, 1927. 259pp.

231. Ludlow, Louis. *Senator Solomon Spiffledink.* Illustrated by Ray Evans. Washington, D.C.: Pioneer, 1927. 430pp.

256. Morrow, Honoré Willsie. *Forever Free: A Novel of Abraham Lincoln.* New York: William Morrow, 1927. 405pp.

377. Wilson, Mary Badger. *The Painted City: Dry-Points of Washington Life.* New York: Frederick A. Stokes, 1927. 247pp.

38. Benson, Mildred Wirt [Emerson, Alice B., pseud.]. *Betty Gordon on the Campus; or The Secret of the Trunk Room.* New York: Cupples & Leon, 1928. 208pp. young adult.

116. Eiker, Mathilde. *The Lady of Stainless Raiment.* Garden City, N.Y.: Doubleday, Doran, 1928. 340pp.

131. Galsworthy, John. *Two Forsyte Interludes: A Silent Wooing, Passers By.* New York: Charles Scribner's Sons, 1928. 60pp.

244. Mellett, Berthe K. *The Ellington Brat.* New York: Dodd, Mead, 1928. 340pp.

258. Morrow, Honoré Willsie. *With Malice toward None.* New York: William Morrow, 1928. 342pp.

21. Babcock, Bernie. *Lincoln's Mary and the Babies.* Philadelphia: J. B. Lippincott, 1929. 316pp.

293. Runbeck, Margaret Lee. *People Will Talk.* Chicago: Reilly & Lee, 1929. 334pp.

60. Carter, John Franklin. *Murder in the Embassy.* New York: Jonathan Cape & Harrison Smith, 1930. 250pp.

61. Carter, John Franklin. *Murder in the State Department.* New York: Jonathan Cape & Harrison Smith, 1930. 253pp.

121. Fairbank, Janet Ayer. *The Lion's Den.* Indianapolis: Bobbs-Merrill, 1930. 374pp.

196. Keyes, Frances Parkinson. *Queen Anne's Lace.* New York: Horace Liveright, 1930. 288pp.

218. Lincoln, Natalie Sumner. *Marked "Cancelled."* New York: D. Appleton, 1930. 285pp.

230. Lowe, Samuel E. [Hart, Helen, pseud.]. *Mary Lee at Washington.* Racine, Wis.: Whitman, 1930. 124pp. young adult.

257. Morrow, Honoré Willsie. *The Last Full Measure.* New York: William Morrow, 1930. 340pp.

263. Parker, Maude. *Secret Envoy.* Indianapolis: Bobbs-Merrill, 1930. 303pp.

264. Paynter, John H. *Fugitives of the Pearl.* Washington, D.C.: Associated Publishers, 1930. 209pp.

255. Morrow, Honoré Willsie. *Black Daniel: The Love Story of a Great Man.* New York: William Morrow, 1931. 370pp.

260. Neill, Esther W. *The Tragic City: A Story of Washington in the Eighties.* Notre Dame, Ind.: Ave Maria, 1931. 290pp.

319. Stone, Grace Zaring. *The Almond Tree.* Indianapolis: Bobbs-Merrill, 1931. 350pp.

376. Wilson, Mary Badger. *New Dreams for Old.* New York: A. L. Burt, 1931. 284pp.

59. Carter, John Franklin. *Corpse on the White House Lawn.* New York: Covici-Friede, 1932. 274pp.

118. Eiker, Mathilde. *The Senator's Lady: A Novel.* Garden City, N.Y.: Doubleday, Doran, 1932. 306pp.

213. Lincoln, Natalie Sumner. *13 Thirteenth Street.* New York: D. Appleton, 1932. 293pp.

245. Mellett, Berthe K. *Wife to Caesar.* New York: Brewer, Warren, & Putnam, 1932. 312pp.

197. Keyes, Frances Parkinson. *Senator Marlowe's Daughter.* New York: Julian Messner, 1933. 465pp.

345. Tweed, Thomas Frederic. *Gabriel Over the White House: A Novel of the Presidency.* New York: Farrar & Rinehart, 1933. 309pp.

4. Adams, Samuel Hopkins. *The Gorgeous Hussy.* Boston: Houghton Mifflin, 1934. 549pp.

158. Hart, Frances Noyes. *The Crooked Lane Mystery.* Garden City, N.Y.: Doubleday, Doran, 1934. 310pp.

219. Lincoln, Natalie Sumner. *The Meredith Mystery.* New York: D. Appleton-Century, 1934. 279pp.

290. Roosevelt, Alice. *Scamper, the Bunny Who Went to the White House.* Illustrated by Marjorie Flack. New York: Macmillan, 1934. 72pp. juvenile.

99. DeVries, Julian. *The Campfire Girls at the White House.* Cleveland, Ohio: World Syndicate, 1935. 250pp.

141. Glenn, Isa. *The Little Candle's Beam.* Garden City, N.Y.: Doubleday, Doran, 1935. 307pp.

143. Goldsmith, John Francis. *President Randolph as I Knew Him: An Account of the Historic Events of the 1950s and 1960s Written from the Personal Experiences of the President.* Philadelphia: Dorrance, 1935. 448pp

291. Roosevelt, Eleanor. *A Trip to Washington with Bobby and Betty.* [New York]: Dodge Publishing Company, 1935. 91pp. juvenile.

375. Wilson, Mary Badger. *Borrowed Plumes.* Philadelphia: Penn, 1935. 305pp.

195. Keyes, Frances Parkinson. *Honor Bright.* New York: Julian Messner, 1936. 583pp.

243. Medora, Marie. *Patty McGill, Investigator.* Philadelphia: Penn, 1936. 206pp. young adult.

337. Tilden, Freeman. *Square Yards of Roofing.* Albuquerque, N.Mex.: Laugh O' the Month Book, 1936. 24pp.

341. Trumbo, Dalton. *Washington Jitters.* New York: Alfred A. Knopf, 1936. 287pp.

56. Bugbee, Emma. *Peggy Covers Washington.* New York: Dodd, Mead, 1937. 297pp.

67. Childs, Marquis W. *Washington Calling!* New York: William Morrow, 1937. 280pp.

115. Eiker, Mathilde. *Key Next Door.* Garden City, N.Y.: Doubleday, 1937. 354pp.

223. Lipton, Lew. *Ideas.* New York: Chatham, 1937. 344pp.

325. Stonebraker, Florence. [Branch, Florenz, pseud.]. *Pay for Your Pleasure.* New York: Phoenix, 1937. 251pp.

348. Vanderbilt, Cornelius Jr. *A Woman of Washington.* New York: E. P. Dutton, 1937. 282pp.

119. Erskine, John. *The Start of the Road.* New York: Frederick A. Stokes, 1938. 344pp.

164. Hill, Grace Livingston. *Marigold.* New York: Grosset & Dunlap, 1938. 299pp. young adult.

329. Strong, Charles S. [Bartlett, Nancy, pseud.]. *Embassy Ball.* New York: Gramercy, 1938. 252pp.

331. Tate, Allen. *The Fathers.* New York: G. P. Putnam's Sons, 1938. 306pp.

54. Brown, Zenith Jones [Ford, Leslie, pseud.]. *False to Any Man.* New York: Scribner, 1939. 254pp.

227. Loring, Emilie Baker. *Across the Years.* Boston: Little, Brown, 1939. 298pp.

39. Benton, John. *Faith, Hope and a Horse.* New York: D. Appleton-Century, 1940. 249pp.

226. Longstreet, Stephen [Burton, Thomas, pseud.]. *And So Dedicated.* New York: Harrison-Hilton, 1940. 416pp.

194. Keyes, Frances Parkinson. *All That Glitters.* New York: Julian Messner, 1941. 820pp.

304. Seton, Anya. *My Theodosia.* Boston: Houghton Mifflin, 1941. 422pp.

26. Baldwin, Faith. *Washington, U.S.A.* New York: Farrar & Rinehart, 1942. 364pp.

251. Mixon, Ada. *Washington Shadows.* Philadelphia: Dorrance, 1942. 284pp.

277. Pierson, Eleanor. *The Defense Rests.* New York: Howell, Soskin, 1942. 229pp.

326. Stonebraker, Florence [Stone, Thomas, pseud.]. *The Playboy's Girl.* New York: Phoenix Press, 1942. 250pp.

74. Colver, Anne [Graff, Polly Anne, pseud.]. *Mr. Lincoln's Wife.* New York: Farrar & Rinehart, 1943. 406pp.

103. Dos Passos, John. *Number One.* Boston: Houghton Mifflin, 1943. 303pp.

112. Eberhart, Mignon Good. *The Man Next Door.* New York: Random House, 1943. 281pp.

151. Hackett, Francis. *The Senator's Last Night.* Garden City, N.Y.: Doubleday, Doran, 1943. 272pp.

324. Stonebraker, Florence. [Branch, Florenz, pseud.]. *Passion on the Potomac.* New York: Phoenix, 1943. 256pp.

357. Walz, Audrey [Bonnamy, Francis, pseud.]. *Dead Reckoning.* New York: Duell, Sloan, & Pearce, [1943]. 248pp.

53. Brown, Zenith Jones [Ford, Leslie, pseud.]. *All for the Love of a Lady.* New York: Charles Scribner, 1944. 261pp.

66. Chidsey, Alan Lake. *Heintz.* Illustrated by F. Moylan Fitts. Kingsport, Tenn.: Southern Publishers, 1945. 155pp.

278. Plum, Mary. *State Department Cat.* Garden City, N.Y.: Crime Club / Doubleday, Doran, 1945. 208pp.

354. Walker, Mannix. *Everything Rustles.* Illustrated by Helen E. Hoskinson. New York: Dodd, Mead, 1945. 242pp.

358. Walz, Audrey. *The King Is Dead on Queen Street.* New York: Duell, Sloan, & Pearce, 1945. 198pp.

106. Drake, Alice. *Miss Hutchinson Steps Out.* New York: House of Field / Doubleday, 1946. 77pp. juvenile.

188. Kane, Harnett T. *New Orleans Woman: A Biographical Novel of Myra Clark Gaines.* Garden City, N.Y.: Doubleday, 1946. 344pp.

238. McAdoo, Eleanor Randolph Wilson. *Julia and the White House.* New York: Dodd, Mead, 1946. 187pp. young adult.

138. Garth, David. *Gray Canaan.* New York: G. P. Putnam's Sons, 1947. 280pp.

240. McGerr, Patricia. *Pick Your Victim.* Garden City, N.Y.: Crime Club / Doubleday, 1947. 222pp.

267. Perry, Eleanor [Bayer, Oliver Weld, pseud.]. *Brutal Question.* Garden City, N.Y.: Crime Club / Doubleday, 1947. 190pp.

359. Walz, Audrey. *Murder as a Fine Art.* New York: New American Library, 1949. 160pp. First published as *Portrait of the Artist as a Dead Man* in 1947 by Signet / Duell, Soan & Pearce.

366. Weidman, Jerome. *The Captain's Tiger.* New York: Reynal & Hitchcock, 1947. 230pp.

5. Adams, Samuel Hopkins. *Plunder.* New York: Random House, 1948. 348pp.

18. Arnold, Elliott. *Everybody Slept Here.* New York: Duell, Sloan & Pearce, 1948. 345pp.

128. Frank, Pat. *An Affair of State.* Philadelphia: Lippincott, 1948. 256pp.

153. Hager, Alice. *Janice, Air Line Hostess.* New York: Julian Messner, 1948. 190pp. young adult.

262. Noble, Hollister. *Woman with a Sword: The Biographical Novel of Anna Ella Carroll of Maryland.* Garden City, N.Y.: Doubleday, 1948. 395pp.

365. Weaver, John D. *Another Such Victory.* New York: Viking Press, 1948. 250pp.

72. Colby, Merle. *The Big Secret.* New York: Viking Press, 1949. 373pp.

102. Dos Passos, John. *The Grand Design.* Boston: Houghton Mifflin, 1949. 440pp.

175. Hubbard, Freeman. *Vinnie Ream and Mr. Lincoln.* New York: Whittlesey House, 1949. 271pp.

184. Janeway, Elizabeth (Hall). *The Question of Gregory.* Garden City, N.Y.: Doubleday, 1949. 309pp.

201. Knowland, Helen. *Madame Baltimore: A Novel of Suspense.* New York: Dodd, Mead, 1949. 210pp.

228. Loring, Emilie Baker. *Love Came Laughing By*. New York: Grosset, Dunlap, 1949. 274pp.

248. Miller, Merle. *The Sure Thing*. New York: William Sloane Associates, 1949. 341pp.

327. Strizzi, Michele Cristofora. *All Came by the Sea*. Philadelphia: Dorrance, 1949. 414pp.

1. Aarons, Edward S. [Ronns, Edward, pseud.]. *State Department Murders*. New York: Fawcett, 1950. 171pp.

27. Banks, Stockton V. *Washington Adventure*. Illustrated by Henry C. Pitz. New York: Whittlesey House / McGraw-Hill, 1950. 191pp. young adult.

96. Deiss, Joseph Jay. *A Washington Story*. New York: Duell, Sloan & Pearce, 1950. 313pp.

252. Moore, Olga. *I'll Meet You in the Lobby*. Philadelphia: J. B. Lippincott, 1950. 250pp.

314. Starnes, Richard. *Another Mug for the Bier*. Philadelphia: J. B. Lippincott, 1950. 248pp.

316. Starnes, Richard. *And When She Was Bad She Was Murdered*. Philadelphia: Lippincott, [1950]. 224pp.

1951-1976

189. Karig, Walter. *Caroline Hicks*. New York: Rinehart, 1951. 438pp.

193. Kennelly, Ardyth. *The Spur*. New York: Julian Messner, 1951. 304pp.

315. Starnes, Richard. *The Other Body in Grant's Tomb*. Philadelphia: Lippincott, [1951]. 249pp.

322. Stone, Irving. *The President's Lady: A Novel about Rachel and Andrew Jackson*. Garden City, N.Y.: Doubleday, 1951. 338pp.

101. Dos Passos, John. *District of Columbia*. Boston: Houghton Mifflin, 1952. 446pp.

279. Plum, Mary. *Murder of a Red-Haired Man*. New York: Arcadia, [1952]. 220pp.

303. Seifert, Shirley. *Three Lives of Elizabeth*. Philadelphia: Lippincott, 1952. 287pp.

51. Brossard, Chandler. *The Bold Saboteurs*. New York: Farrar, Straus & Young, 1953. 303pp.

55. Brown, Zenith Jones [Ford, Leslie, pseud.]. *Washington Whispers Murder*. New York: Charles Scribner, 1953. 194pp.

65. Chatterton, Ruth. *The Betrayers*. Boston: Houghton Mifflin / Riverside Press, 1953. 310pp.

234. Malloy, John Edward. *Potomac Poppies*. New York: Pageant Press, 1953. 198pp.

321. Stone, Irving. *Love Is Eternal: A Novel about Mary Todd and Abraham Lincoln*. Garden City, N.Y.: Doubleday, 1954. 462pp.

236. Malvern, Gladys. *Mamzell: A Romance for Teen-Age Girls Set in the Days of Dolly Madison*. Philadelphia: Macrae Smith, 1955. 208pp. young adult.

305. Smith, Ellen Hart [Revell, Louisa, pseud.]. *The Men with Three Eyes*. New York: MacMillan, 1955. 188pp.

338. Toombs, Alfred. *Good as Gold*. New York: Thomas Y. Crowell, 1955. 281pp.

284. Raphael, Chaim [Davey, Jocelyn, pseud.]. *A Capitol Offense: An Entertainment*. New York: Knopf, 1956. 252pp.

180. Hunt, E. Howard [Dietrich, Robert, pseud.]. *Murder on the Rocks*. New York: Dell, 1957. 192pp.

235. Maltz, Albert. *A Long Day in a Short Life*. New York: International, 1957. 350pp.

123. Farrar, Larston D. *The Sins of Sandra Shaw.* New York: New American Library, 1958. 126pp.

154. Hager, Alice Rogers. *Washington Secretary.* New York: Julian Messner, 1958. 192 pp.

320. Stone, Irving. *Immortal Wife: The Biographical Novel of Jessie Benton Fremont.* Garden City, N.Y.: Doubleday, 1958. 456pp.

107. Drury, Allen. *Advise and Consent.* Garden City, N.Y.: Doubleday, 1959. 616pp.

179. Hunt, E. Howard [Dietrich, Robert, pseud.]. *The House on Q Street.* New York: Dell, 1959. 160pp.

167. Holmes, Marjorie. *Cherry Blossom Princess.* Philadelphia: Westminster Press, 1960. 188pp. young adult.

168. Holmes, Marjorie. *Follow Your Dream.* Philadelphia: Westminster Press, 1961. 188pp. young adult.

181. Hunt, E. Howard [Davis, Gordon, pseud.]. *House Dick.* Greenwich, Conn.: Fawcett, 1961. 144pp. Later published as, *Washington Pay-Off* (New York: Pinnacle, 1975).

310. Stacton, David. *The Judges of the Secret Court.* New York: Pantheon, 1961. 255pp.

9. Alexander, Holmes. *West of Washington.* New York: Fleet, 1962. 254pp.

130. Gallagher, Phyllis Moore. *All Is Not Quiet on the Potomac.* Baltimore: Reid, Alton, 1962. 374pp.

177. Hulbert, James. *Noon on the Third Day.* New York: Holt, Rinehart & Winston, 1962. 366pp.

169. Holmes, Marjorie. *Senior Trip.* Philadelphia: Westminster, 1962. 191pp. young adult.

199. Knebel, Fletcher. *Seven Days in May.* New York: Harper & Row, 1962. 341pp.

268. Peterson, Bettina. *Washington Is for You.* New York: Washburn, 1962. 63pp. juvenile.

343. Tully, Andrew. *Capitol Hill.* New York: Simon & Schuster, 1962. 412pp.

344. Tully, Andrew. *Supreme Court: A Novel.* New York: Simon & Schuster, 1963. 409pp.

34. Bayne, Jessica. *When Love Must Hide.* New York: Lancer Books, 1964. 142pp.

206. Leighton, Frances Spatz. *Patty Goes to Washington.* New York: Ace Books, 1964. 142pp. young adult.

205. Leighton, Frances Spatz. *The Memoirs of Senator Brown, a Capitol Cat.* New York: Fleet, 1965. 164pp.

317. Stead, Christina. *The Man Who Loved Children.* New York: Holt, Rhinehart & Winston, 1965. 527pp.

323. Stone, Irving. *Those Who Love: A Biographical Novel of Abigail and John Adams.* Garden City, N.Y.: Doubleday, 1965. 650pp.

152. Hager, Alice. *Cathy Whitney, President's Daughter.* New York: Messner, 1966. 192pp. young adult.

92. Davis, Mary Lee. *Polly and the President.* Illustrated by Jan Jackson. Minneapolis, Minn: Lerner, 1967. 32pp. juvenile.

190. Karp, David. *The Brotherhood of Velvet.* New York: Banner, 1967. 159pp.

302. Seifert, Shirley. *The Senator's Lady.* Philadelphia: Lippincott, 1967. 377pp.

109. Drury, Allen. *Preserve and Protect.* Garden City, N.Y.: Doubleday, 1968. 405pp.

183. James, Leigh. *The Capitol Hill Affair.* New York: Weybright & Talley, 1968. 213pp.

200. Knebel, Fletcher. *Vanished.* Garden City, N.Y.: Doubleday, 1968. 407pp.

237. Mazor, Julian. *Washington and Baltimore.* New York: Alfred A. Knopf, 1968. 212pp.

246. Mertz, Barbara [Michaels, Barbara, pseud.]. *Ammie, Come Home.* New York: Meredith Press, 1968. 252pp.

265. Pearson, Drew. *The Senator.* Garden City, N.Y.: Doubleday, 1968. 447pp.

286. Rennert, Maggie. *A Moment in Camelot.* New York: Grove Press / Bernard Geis, 1968. 713pp.

43. Blair, Clay. *The Board Room: A Novel.* New York: Dutton, 1969. 352pp.

292. Roudybush, Alexandra. *A Capital Crime.* Garden City, N.Y.: Doubleday, 1969. 192 pp.

12. Anderson, Patrick. *The Approach to Kings.* Garden City, N.Y.: Doubleday, 1970. 373pp.

62. Cater, Douglass. *Dana, The Irrelevant Man.* New York: McGraw-Hill, [1970]. 275pp.

122. Farrar, Larston D. *Conflict of Interest: A Novel.* New York: Bartholomew House, 1970. 275pp.

149. Griffith, Patricia Browning. *The Future Is Not What It Used to Be.* New York: Simon & Schuster, 1970. 224pp.

369. Whitehurst, Ben, and Faith Wiley. *Death on Capitol Hill.* New York: Vantage Press, 1970. 161pp.

44. Blair, Clay. *Pentagon Country.* New York: McGraw-Hill, 1971. 318pp.

45. Blatty, William Peter. *The Exorcist.* New York: Harper & Row, 1971. 340pp.

Index

The numbers refer to entries, not pages.

Crittenden, John, (1781-1863), 303

Depression. *See* historical periods; social life and customs

description and travel, 33, 37, 50, 70, 86, 90, 95, 99, 111, 117, 120, 124, 126, 136, 144, 162, 164, 167, 169, 170, 176, 188, 206, 212, 225, 255, 259, 260, 261, 268, 280, 288, 290, 291, 306, 328, 364, 372, 377, 378, 383

diplomatic intrigue, 23, 29, 32, 35, 60, 61, 112, 128, 133, 161, 232, 278, 284, 296

diplomatic life, 63

District of Columbia Committee, 47, 82, 289

domestic fiction, 9, 44, 47, 82, 96, 97, 115, 117, 118, 128, 141, 158, 182, 194, 293, 306, 317, 319, 327, 331, 333, 373

Douglas, Stephen A., (1813-1861), 302

dueling, 15, 249, 250, 342

Eaton, Peggy (Margaret O'Neale), (1799-1879), 4, 100, 191, 208

epistolary fiction, 2, 40, 212, 285

espionage, 10, 29, 52, 76, 129, 138, 145, 159, 160, 176, 178, 183, 200, 211, 216, 217, 227, 228, 250, 256, 262, 263, 284, 329, 346, 347, 354, 374

ethnic groups, 89, 139, 148, 170, 213, 243, 305: Irish, 2, 51, 89, 151, 186, 368, 383; Italian, 20, 89, 129, 139, 157, 305; Russian, 29, 139, 209, 232, 263, 277, 325, 346

federal employees: Census Bureau, 98; Civilian Conservation Corps, 337; Central Intelligence Agency, 200; Commerce Department, 34; Federal Bureau of Investigation, 200; Pension

Office, 24; Pentagon, 18, 44, 66; State Department, 59, 60, 61, 128, 167, 248, 329; Treasury Department, 71, 259, 295

Federal era. *See* historical periods; social life and customs

First Lady, role of, 196

Frémont, Jessie Benton, (1824-1902), 320

Frémont, John, (1813-1890), 320

future fiction, 17, 68, 143, 156, 345, 347

Gaines, Myra Clark, (1805-1885), 188

Gallatin, Albert, (1761-1849), 10

gay men, 1, 51, 179, 180, 190

globalization, 143

Graham, Katherine, (1917-2001), 7

Greeley Horace, (1811-1872), 171

Hale, Eugene, (1836-1918), 19

historical periods (for books that deal substantially with social life and customs, *see* social life and customs): Federal era, 10, 27, 90, 100, 105, 323, 327; Civil War, 14, 22, 74, 119, 132, 138, 145, 171, 193, 216, 241, 242, 256, 257, 258, 262, 318, 331, 381; 1870-1900, 259; World War I, 29, 73, 124, 176, 197, 230, 251, 360; 1920s, 35, 117; Depression and 1930s, 102, 141, 158; World War II, 5, 18, 26, 53, 66, 112, 151, 184, 189, 252, 324, 326, 366; Cold War and 1950s, 65, 96, 123; Vietnam War and 1960s, 11, 12, 149, 198, 292; 1970s, 7

hotels: Arlington, 77; Hamilton, 196; Jefferson, 139; Lee, 72; Madison, 335; Mayflower, 18, 59, 153, 277, 326, 357; Montrose, 137; National, 2,

About the Author

James A. Kaser is associate professor and archivist at the College of Staten Island/CUNY. He has worked as an archivist and special collections librarian for more than fifteen years, including six years at the George Washington University where he developed an interest in the subject of this book. During his time there, he curated the exhibition "City of Magnificent Illusions, the Washington, D.C., of Fiction" (The Gelman Library, 14 March-10 July, 1998). Kaser is a magna cum laude, Phi Beta Kappa, graduate of Kenyon College and earned a master's degree in library science from Kent State University and a master's degree and doctorate from Bowling Green State University in American culture studies.